Flyfisher's Guide to™ the
FLORIDA KEYS

Captain Ben Taylor

**Wilderness
Adventures
Press, Inc.™**

Belgrade, Montana

This book was made with an easy opening, lay flat binding.

© 2001 Captain Ben Taylor

Cover photograph © 2001 Sam Talarico, "Lefty Kreh, Bill Bishop, and Flip Pallot trying to land a nice Florida tarpon."

Photographs contained herein © 2001 Ben Taylor or as noted

Gamefish Illustrations © 2001 Duane Raver

Information for illustrations and charts provided by Maptech:
        Maptech
        888-839-5551
        Website: www.maptech.com
        E-mail: marinesales@maptech.com

Maps, book design and cover design © 2001 Wilderness Adventures Press, Inc.
Flyfisher's Guide to™

Published by Wilderness Adventures Press, Inc.
45 Buckskin Road
Belgrade, MT 59714
800-925-3339
Website: www.wildadv.com
email: books@wildadv.com

Printed in the United States of America

Library of Congress Cataloging-in-Publication Data
Taylor, Ben, 1949-.
  Flyfisher's guide to the Florida Keys and the Everglades / by Ben Taylor.
    p. cm.
  Includes index.
  ISBN 1-885106-74-2 (pbk. : alk. paper))
  1. Fly fishing—Florida—Florida Keys —Guidebooks. 2. Fly fishing—Florida — Everglades —Guidebooks. 3. Florida — Guidebooks. I. Title.

SH483 .T28 2001
799.1'24'0975941—dc21
                                    2001005267

Flyfisher's Guide to™ the
FLORIDA KEYS

Titles Available in This Series

Table of Contents

One of my favorite fishing buddies, Bill Wilson.

Acknowledgments

This book is dedicated to those that share the dream of capturing giant fish on frail tackle in peaceful surroundings that still offer the comforts of home. I thank those who helped me form a foundation of knowledge that has enabled me to find and fool fish regularly, those who encouraged me to write, and those who remained my friends and supporters as I fought to maintain our fishing heritage during a prolonged 15-year activist period.

Many names of contributors to my career come to mind. Some are included in my introduction. Many are not. I have to thank some such as Dave Whitney who cranked me up and supported me, right or wrong, when I wrote for him while he owned and ran the *Keys Free Press* newspaper. I was well supported by the Wickstrom family-former owners and now publishers of *Florida Sportsman* magazine. Former editorial staff members Biff Lampton, Glenn Law, and Doug Kelly, along with the current crew of Jeff Weakley, Mike Conner, and Frank Bolin, have all shone lights for me at appropriate moments.

I was blessed with great tournament anglers during my short competitive years, and they carried me along. I won tournaments with Angie Lucas, Scott Deal, and Tom Siska. I placed somewhere with Allan Finkelman, Ken Meeks, and Randy Moret. Their dedication touched me, but perhaps not as much as my sorely missed and beloved tournament partner, Louis Leeds. I think of him every time I fish a spot we shared. I've had a myriad of wonderful fishing partners too numerous to mention, some with whom I only spent a day or two. With others, I've shared days or weeks on the water for years, and I consider them friends, not customers.

This is a book for my readers, those who have trusted me most over the years to openly share my knowledge. Fishing in the Keys goes beyond "X marks the spot."

I finally dedicate this book to those who want to know why more than where. The perfect spots change, knowing why they change provides a lifetime of fishing success.

Florida Bay.

Introduction

I was a young Boy Scout in 1959 when Ted Williams fished with Captain Jimmy Albright in front of the camera on today's still famous Buchanan Bank in the Upper Florida Keys backcountry. I saw their film of wildly gyrating giant silver fish later in the year. Their images haunted me for over two decades before I made the pilgrimage to hallowed Keys fishing grounds in 1984. I met Williams, Albright, and many others credited with developing today's fabled Keys light tackle fishery. Several befriended me and stick in my mind. Stu Apte out-fished most and shared what he knew with everyone. Guides George Wood and Vic Gaspenny, along with Bud N' Mary's marina owner Richard Stanczyk, taught me how to deal with a variety of crazy weather situations and why fish did or did not eat flies. I found others willing to share a clue or two.

The Florida Keys are one of the world's premier light tackle fishing destinations, providing unrivaled shots at world-class catches of many species much of the year. Keys fishing today is much like fishing at many of our favored destinations. They've been discovered, but you can still hide and find a "secret" spot. However, trophy fish often take up residence within shouting distance of world-class resorts or fine restaurants.

At any given time, almost ten percent of all light tackle saltwater world-record fish come from the Keys. Key West's Captain Ralph Delph was the first professional anywhere to lead his anglers to 100 IGFA recognized world records. Captain Bob Trosset, fishing from the same Oceanside Marina, closely followed him. You'll find great fishing help from one end of the island chain to the other. The place is addictive, and you may climb into a boat with a former NBA player, Major Leaguer, or bank president like me.

We all share a love for gorgeous sunrises and willing fish. The Keys don't look like much on a highway map, appearing as little more than a road slash in an atlas. There's not much land here, but there are 122 miles of road between the northern reaches of Key Largo and Key West. The boundaries of the Florida Keys National Marine Sanctuary encompass 2600 square miles of water. Florida Bay, the Gulf of Mexico estuary between the Upper Keys and the south Florida coast, hides anglers within an 1100 square mile fish-filled boundary.

Some keys offer a totally suburban atmosphere while others feel remote. One might hide in the darkness and watch the stars in complete serenity at night on one key, go to the movies and eat gourmet-class food on another. Fish swim by and around all the islands and some of the best fishing in the world is within sight of the narrow ribbon of road connecting them. It's the options that separate the Keys from other great fishing destinations. You'll have access to great tackle shops for flies, lures, bait, line, or a replacement rod. Sharing a fishing vacation with the family is easy when non-fishing family members feel at home. It's easy to feel at home here, but the sidewalk, in most cases, rolls up early. We're going fishing in the morning!

We set world records almost every day. In a three-day bonefish tournament in

1999, anglers caught 15-pound fish breaking tippet-class records on consecutive days. Neither record-setting angler caught enough big fish to win the tournament, but one did get the big fish trophy! While fishing does not seem to match "the good old days," record scores were set in 1995 and broken in 1996 for our most recognized fly tarpon tournament. I guided an angler to an all-time single day bonefish tournament scoring record in the spring of 1996, shattering 30 years of history. We saw our record broken in a similar event the same year. Humans do have selective memory and over time we tend to forget the famine between feasts, and we still have fishing feasts in the Keys.

Guiding since 1985, I can honestly say that I never quite get past the thrill of seeing a school of tarpon moving down an edge, bonefish digging for crabs, or tuna boiling in a live pilchard chum line. Once fishing as much as 330 days a year, I've literally seen it a million times. My knees still shake when it's my turn to toss a fly, bait, or lure. I'm typical of the professional help you can find in the Keys. Hundreds like me live to help you catch fish, by either taking you out on the water or providing hints from behind a tackle-shop counter. We're proud of our water and the fishing opportunities. We want visitors to have a great time and come back. We do hedge our bets a lot, though. In a Rocky Mountain fly shop you often find a posted schedule suggesting when a hatch might occur, what rock to stand on, and what fly to throw. Such information for Keys shallow water species is generally worthless from year to year, month to month, or even day to day. Unnoticeable wind shifts move fish miles away from yesterday's hot spot. Today's hot fly may frighten tomorrow's fish for miles around. We face the same challenges offshore as current and wind changes move bait concentrations or weather from the north and west impacts migration patterns.

Nothing cheers me more than helping someone who has never seen a bonefish or tarpon before, catch one. I couldn't afford professional help when I first moved here and well remember struggling mightily to learn enough to start fishing here. I've enjoyed a certain amount of success, placing somewhere in a third of the tournaments I guided in during the decade of the '90s. Still, I learn every day and find new fishing opportunities are endless in the Keys. The fish continue to confound me. What I knew, or thought I knew, ten years ago about locations is mostly worthless to me today.

I find, too, that plenty of people know things I don't know. I'm still impressed by the knowledge and enthusiasm of my peers in the shallows and the depths. I'll share as much as I can in this book about how to find fish, but I'm not the final word, and you'll do best if you're always willing to learn. If I can help you learn why a spot works I'm helping you more than I would if I blindly sent you to a spot that may well be dead before I finish writing this.

I still remember my first jumped tarpon. I pulled the fly out of her mouth on four consecutive casts before letting her swallow it on the fifth try. She darted a few feet when I pricked her with the hook, then shot into the air and shook violently. I'll never forget the thunderous roar of her rattling gill plates, the grace of her jump, or how easily my tippet broke as I held on for dear life. It's a memory I'd like to help you form.

Taking The Heat

I am sure that I am going to take flak for writing this book. Some will feel I'm telling secrets they think belong to them. I apologize to those in the guide ranks who feel a book like this makes it easy for amateurs to catch fish without them. I don't think reading this book is instantly going to make anyone an expert, though it should provide enough basics to lead to some entertaining days.

I strongly believe any guide feeling threatened by the sharing of this knowledge is selling him or herself very short. It is impossible to write a book encompassing everything one needs to know to find fish in every condition, every day. It's impossible for guides with thousands of days of experience to find fish every day even when it is all they think about and do.

It's offensive to anglers when we feel we are the only ones with rights to knowledge. I remember long ago publishing a piece that caused quite a stir among friends and foes. The tarpon spot disclosed was nearly impossible for any but the most talented polers to fish. It's best when the current shoves along at three to five knots, demanding perfect technique and serious determination to move the boat along with a push pole. In such a situation, many are washed back in the current. It's not an easy place to see fish, either. Anglers beware, you're entering the toughest shallow water fishery in the world, but the rewards are worth the effort.

There's an advantage to all participants in our sport, amateur or professional, when someone like me writes about it. I'm an old pro, and I can and will talk about the ethics of properly running from spot to spot without disturbing fish. I can explain how to find a place in line when fish are traveling without ruining the fishing for everyone involved. I'm going to tell the truth, too, not oversell the fishing or suggest that just anyone can catch fish here.

I don't talk as much about spots because I don't believe in spots, getting up early to get to a spot, or arguing about a spot someone is already fishing. Anyone fishing the bonefish tournaments I fished knows I left the dock with just enough time to get somewhere to fish, yet my bonefish tournament record is enviable. There are always hundreds of ways to get in front of fish, though conditions sometimes limit choices.

I fished over 1,600 days my first five years in the Keys. The experience provided me only a fraction of all there is to know about fish habits. Few spots I learned then are worth fishing today. My favorite tarpon resting spot is dead. My favorite migration spot once had fish whenever the tide moved, whether it rose or fell. It's good for an hour or two on one tide now. I made a living for a while bonefishing one stretch of beach and one nearby backcountry corner. Neither holds enough fish today to justify stopping.

This book is intended as a launching pad of discovery for those anglers serious about the never-ending learning process involved in chasing Keys game fish, rather than a detailed list of secret spots that may be worthless tomorrow in different conditions.

The Florida Keys

By Region

1 **Northern Fringe Keys**
2 **Key Largo**
3 **Islamorada**
4 **Everglades**
5 **Middle Keys**
6 **Lower Keys**
7 **Key West**

TO NAPLES

Tamiami Trail

Gulf of Mexico

Northwest Cape

Gulf of Mexico

Florida Ba

4 **EVERGLADES**

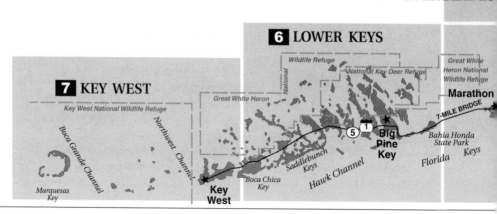

6 **LOWER KEYS**

Wildlife Refuge

Great White Heron National Wildlife Refuge

National Key Deer Refuge

Marathon

National

7 **KEY WEST**

Great White Heron

Key West National Wildlife Refuge

7-MILE BRIDGE

Northwest Channel

5 1 **Big Pine Key**

Bahia Honda State Park

Boca Grande Channel

Saddlebunch Keys

Boca Chica Key

Hawk Channel

Florida Keys

Marquesas Key

Key West

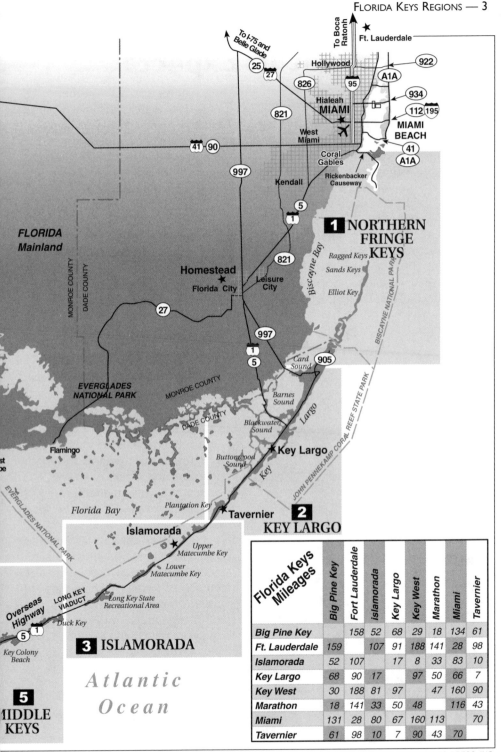

To I-75 and Belle Glade

To Boca Ratonh
Ft. Lauderdale

25
27

922

Hollywood

826

A1A

95

934

Hialeah
MIAMI

821

112 195

West Miami

MIAMI BEACH

Coral Gables

41

A1A

997

Rickenbacker Causeway

Kendall

5
1

1 NORTHERN FRINGE KEYS

FLORIDA Mainland

821

Ragged Keys

Sands Keys

Homestead
Florida City

Leisure City

Elliot Key

MONROE COUNTY

DADE COUNTY

27

997

1
5

Card Sound

905

BISCAYNE NATIONAL PARK

Biscayne Bay

EVERGLADES NATIONAL PARK

MONROE COUNTY

Barnes Sound

Largo

DADE COUNTY

Blackwater Sound

Key Largo

JOHN PENNEKAMP CORAL REEF STATE PARK

Flamingo

Buttonwood Sound

Key

EVERGLADES NATIONAL PARK

Florida Bay

Plantation Key

Tavernier

2 KEY LARGO

Islamorada

Upper Matecumbe Key

Lower Matecumbe Key

Overseas Highway

LONG KEY VIADUCT

Long Key State Recreational Area

Duck Key

5
1

3 ISLAMORADA

Key Colony Beach

Atlantic Ocean

5 MIDDLE KEYS

Florida Keys Mileages	Big Pine Key	Fort Lauderdale	Islamorada	Key Largo	Key West	Marathon	Miami	Tavernier
Big Pine Key		158	52	68	29	18	134	61
Ft. Lauderdale	159		107	91	188	141	28	98
Islamorada	52	107		17	8	33	83	10
Key Largo	68	90	17		97	50	66	7
Key West	30	188	81	97		47	160	90
Marathon	18	141	33	50	48		116	43
Miami	131	28	80	67	160	113		70
Tavernier	61	98	10	7	90	43	70	

What To Expect

The Florida Keys are a slice of earth attracting visitors from all over the world, seeking a variety of escapes. Visitors come to dive the reefs, watch the birds, escape a winter chill, or see what inspired Hemingway, Grey, or Williams. Fishermen are outnumbered. The Keys are home to over 80,000 permanent residents and another 50,000 part-time residents. Those who fish may be surprised by this, as they expect a more remote fishing experience. Don't worry, you can find some of the best fishing for shallow water species while still enjoying a wealth of comfort if you seek it. After a short boat ride, thousands of square miles of water easily insulate us from the sights and sounds of society.

While the Keys offer rather delightful year-round weather, flats anglers are usually best served if they plan trips spring through fall if they prefer tarpon, bonefish, and permit. If you just want to bend a rod, you can come in the winter and catch a variety of lesser inshore species. Winter is preferable for many offshore species, and early spring and late fall fishing in the depths is usually pretty good, too.

THE KEYS BY REGION

The Keys logically break down into several regions. Fishing for some species is much the same wherever you go, but there are important differences. Civilization in each area has its own flavor, ranging from modern suburban convenience to remote charm. The waters are very different, too. For our purposes, we'll cut the Keys into five regions.

The Keys don't start when you reach Key Largo from the mainland. The Northern Fringe Keys, the stretch of islands reaching toward Miami from the northeastern end of Key Largo, and the water between them and Florida's coast is surprisingly remote. Much of the

Visitors come to fish the waters, dive reefs, watch birds, escape a winter chill, or to see what inspired Hemingway, Grey, or Williams.

area's shoreline is national park or state areas of critical concern forever protected. While access is a bit tough, long boat rides are worthwhile, and you can fish the area from the mainland if you're stuck in the city or from Key Largo.

What is considered the Upper Keys begins with Key Largo and ends at the southwestern end of Long Key. You may feel you're in the suburbs on land, but you have quick access to the remote reaches of Florida Bay and the Oceanside is littered with flats. The concentration of bridges in the middle of the region provides a good exchange of water from the bay to the ocean. Channel edges provide some easy first-trip prospecting. Florida Bay chills quickly during wintertime cold fronts, though, and its flush of water chases fish far from those same edges. They are easily found on the Key Largo Oceanside shoreline or in Biscayne Bay waters. If you fish near civilization, the area is often crowded with non-fishing tourists or shoreline residents generating lots of random boat traffic.

The Middle Keys run from Conch Key to the western end of the Seven Mile Bridge. You'll find a broad range of civilization, yet there is still predominately a suburban rather than urban feel. The wide expanse of the neighboring Gulf, deeper than Florida Bay waters bordering the Upper Keys, maintains warmer winter water temperatures. The area's hard current flows attract more permit. First time boating visitors are comfortable here since there are fewer obstacles, although the obstacles are cement hard!

The Lower Keys end at Boca Chica. While things are a bit hectic on Big Pine Key, the rest of the area seems rather remote. It is well settled, but there is less commercial development and likely always will be for a number of environmental reasons. Navigation is tricky, especially on the Gulfside, and the bottom is hard almost everywhere. The area is loaded with shallows and channels moving lots of water, making it easy to hide and find fish.

Key West claims it is a world all its own and perhaps it is. On land, it's crowded and congested, but it's always interesting. You would never guess at the quality of the fishing in the surrounding water. While flats fishing is good here with excellent permit and tarpon opportunities, the offshore and intermediate-depth action is phenomenal.

While often overlooked, the "lay of the land" throughout the Keys is an important consideration. The Keys don't run in a straight line, instead facing the ocean in a gentle arch. They appear almost as a dam defending the Gulf. And they were once—the inner reef was shoreline and Florida Bay an isolated swamp.

They added "west" to Key West's name for a reason. The Lower Keys run far more east to west than they do north to south. The Upper Keys run pretty much northeast to southwest. Winds affect each area differently and the sun's seasonal shifts are a consideration if you sight fish.

Paying attention to the regional differences will increase your chances of success. You'll find plenty of enjoyable fishing opportunities throughout the Keys if you visit with an open mind, pursuing the species of the moment. Where you head should depend on the season, your goals, and how you'd like to entertain non-fishing travel companions.

Florida State

Using This Book

I'll cover each species of game fish that is most commonly sought after in the Keys, and offer several chapters related to trip planning, necessary gear, and other things to know before you hit the water. Next, every aspect of fishing will be discussed, from recognizing likely fish hangouts to hooking and landing fish. As this is primarily a flyfishing guidebook, I'll concentrate on the "glamour" species of the flats, but the tremendous offshore fishing around the Keys will also be included in some detail. Finally, I'll run through the Keys from top to bottom to cover the fishing in each area. Travel information related to each area will be provided in the appropriate section. Finding accommodations (and other facilities) is rarely a problem as they are plentiful throughout most regions in the Keys, although planning ahead is always recommended no matter what the season.

I recommend you start exploring slowly if you choose to fish without professional help. If you do seek professional help, I've provided quite a few tips on what to look for throughout the text. As there are currently over 650 registered charter boat captains and guides operating in the Keys, a listing for each and every one is prohibitive. I've provided a brief list of definitions below explaining unique word usage that appears throughout the book. You might want to peruse the definitions before delving into the following chapters on finding and catching fish and fishing throughout the Keys.

Ladyfish are a riot on light tackle of any kind.

DEFINITIONS

Backcountry—Used a couple of ways. Backcountry fishing often means generic fishing for trout, jacks, ladyfish and the occasional snook, redfish, snappers, and maybe tarpon in the Upper Keys. You may not find the snook or ladyfish in the Lower Keys, but snappers are thrown into the mix. It also refers to Gulfside water holding tarpon, bonefish, and permit, typically out of sight of the road. Backcountry fish of the glamour species are said to feed better and they often do!

Bait-type trip—A fun day on the water seeking whatever species grabs the hook.

Fish—The fish sought on a specific day are fish. If you're fishing for tarpon, other species are identified individually. If you're fishing for bonefish, they are fish, but tarpon are tarpon, barracudas are barracudas. Fish are the species you're actively searching for at a given moment, unless you're fishing for whatever will bite on a bait-type trip.

Lake or basin—Flats are underwater ridges and not only extend for miles, but also typically connect to other flats and surround deep areas. We call the deep areas they surround lakes or basins.

Patch reef—Sudden change in the configuration of the bottom often marked by coral heads rising steeply from the bottom. The best patches are typically marked with obvious signs of life like corals of varying colors and living sponges.

Push—An obvious migration of fish whether seasonal or temporary generally used to describe a day's activity. Also, the specific movement of a single fish or a school toward casting range marked by a bit of a wake.

Run out—Small, typically dead end ditches draining or filling a flat depending on the direction of the tide.

Second tier Banks— Banks located farther offshore of the Keys.

Shock leader—Also called a bite tippet. Monofilament heavier than your main line or class tippet used to defend against the raspy teeth of many species and sharp gill plates of others. IGFA rules limiting the length of the shock for fly anglers make it only useful for tooth and gill plate protection. The longer leaders allowed with conventional gear also protect against line fraying when it's across the back or tail of a fish or pulled through bottom cover.

Shot—A reasonable opportunity for presenting some sort of food to fish within decent casting range. Also, an attempt by a fish to eat a bait, lure, or fly.

Spring tide—Typically stronger and higher tides around the full and new moon.

Wakers—Fish showing a wake as they move. They might be high in the water and moving slow or moving fast enough to disturb the surface even if they're deep.

White bait—generic for less than palm-sized silver slab-sided baits including herrings and pilchards. Great for live chum lines and individual baits for a wide variety of Keys fish.

X Does Not Mark The Spot

I'm torn between telling you where fish were yesterday or before the last hurricane and providing instruction on how to find fish on your own. I believe teaching you how to find fish on your own is more helpful and makes the book timeless rather than only briefly useful. A trip I took just before starting this book illustrates why I will not put Xs on the map for you. I joined Grassy Key's Captain Buddy LaPointe to research and photograph a story about catching flats species from a non-traditional vessel in the summer of 1999. We set up to chum for bonefish on a shallow white bar along the Oceanside of Duck Key. Before Hurricane George's attack on the Keys in 1998, the bar was a deep trough used by migrating tarpon and a favorite June destination for many guides. Now, tarpon don't fit there anymore. A later storm may scoop the area out again in the future and the tarpon may return.

In the fall of 1999, Hurricane Irene covered some flats with silt and scrubbed others of everything, including food. I haven't been back to see if it opened up the favored tarpon trough in front of Duck Key. While the storm diminished fishing in some areas, it provided bonuses elsewhere. In other words, current knowledge and the ability to recognize a likely spot is often worth more than a diary containing 15 years of fishing history. Many spots I considered day-savers in the late 1980s hold few fish today, though some are still useful.

I will point out some geography, however, tell why it works, and how to find similar spots on your own. Please realize that sight fishing is not typically a social sport so I can't send the world to a handful of spots three minutes from the dock. The fish won't stand for it.

Reading the Maps and Charts

You will notice a variety of maps and charts placed throughout the book. We can break these down into two types:

Overview Maps—Maps intended to show a broad geographical overview of highways, (note that Highway 1 and the Overseas Highway are the same road) towns, boat ramps, landmasses, parks, areas of special interest, etc.

Fishing Charts—Based on information from nautical charts but clarified to show the geography and structure of the water suitable for fishing. They are generally smaller and more detailed than the overview maps, and in some cases, especially productive situations are highlighted.

Our maps and charts are not intended to be used for navigational purposes!

If you intend to fish the Keys please purchase the appropriate charts for navigation from Maptech or another reputable chart dealer. (See page 325.)

Now, let's take a look at what you need to know about gamefish and fishing to have success in the Florida Keys.

Gamefish

Gamefish regulations change two or three times a year in the Keys, and you should not leave the dock without a current list of rules in your pocket if you intend to keep a fish. Unless you are a Florida resident fishing from shore, or fishing with a licensed charter operator or from a licensed dock, you have to buy a fishing license. Your pro will keep you out of trouble if you are using one, and if you are fishing on your own, pick up a copy of the rules when you buy your license.

While you can fly fish for just about any species native to Keys waters, we don't often bother with some. Most are fun on a fly rod and willing to eat, but it's a matter of perception I suppose. Surrounded by thousands of square miles of clean, clear water, we are not often prospectors, preferring to concentrate on fish you can readily see and deal with using floating or intermediate lines. You might sit in a channel and bump the bottom for snappers and groupers with weighted flies and sinking lines and do quite well. It's hard to justify when the bordering flat is covered with bonefish, redfish, or sharks. Much of the Keys experience revolves around the fish of a lifetime. A single large tarpon or a bonefish on a fly, caught in a week's fishing, is often quite an accomplishment, and you can brag about a permit catch forever.

We do some "blind casting." Mullet muds offer fun fishing for trout, jacks, and ladyfish. Some may also cough up Spanish mackerel or even a bluefish. Shorelines holding redfish and snook are good targets, too. Flies worked through chum lines inshore and off, fool a wide range of species. Any fish willing to eat a jig or a swimming plug will eat a fly worked at the proper depth.

The fish descriptions provided here offer some basic guidance for rigging and food. It's very basic as a variety of factors influence tackle choice. For instance, you need a stout size 5/0 hook to suspend a pinfish or small mullet on the end of a 25- or 30-pound rig when targeting tarpon. If you're using 18-inch mullet you might want a 10/0. If you're throwing crabs at them with a 12- to 15-pound rig, a lighter 4/0 makes better sense, and you might drop down to a 2/0 if the fish are all less than 30 pounds. You couldn't set the bigger hook with the lighter rod and it overwhelms the bait. Many pros swear by circle hooks and won't use anything else for them.

There's disagreement in the bonefish ranks with some preferring short-shanked size 1/0 or 2/0 bait holder type hooks. They usually head hook the shrimp under the horn or lightly in the tail. I prefer a 4/0 Kahle-style hook and Texas worm rig the shrimp on my hook. We all catch fish.

Nervous offshore snappers like yellowtails and mangroves often demand a small size 1 or 1/0 short-shanked bronze hook. In a dusty Gulfside flow, a 3x long-shanked 3/0 is preferred by some. It's easier to recover them from fish and sometimes the fish are mixed with toothy critters. The longer shank gives you a shot at them without using wire.

The use of shock leaders or wire is optional for some species and necessary for others. Some fish under certain conditions will not eat baits tied to either. You can't lose a fish until it eats so you have to balance your concerns.

There are times you when you don't want to touch fish. In this shot, a small gaff is planted in the bend of the hook. Lifting on the gaff while pulling down on the line will flip the fish off the hook.

What tackle you use depends on your skill level. Some anglers tame sea monsters in the right situations on 12- or 15-pound gear, but 50- and 80-pound gear has a place onboard when chasing a few species.

Don't handle a fish if you don't know what it is or don't know how. Cut it off instead. Some species will amaze you with their ability to inflict damage. The bad teeth of a barracuda are not the obvious canines used to latch onto their prey. It's the hidden inner rows that match like shears and resemble well-honed serrated knife blades. They're shared by the mackerel family. Sharks twist and turn, constantly seeking an advantage. Gaff them in the mouth if you must handle them, from the inside out. Do the same with tarpon. Only gaff a fish if you intend to keep it or need control it for some reason. Few fish survive a body shot so the mouth is the right place to grab one. A large shark is easier to hold onto if you grab them in a pectoral fin since they spin and thrash violently, but you leave them a lot of opportunity to reach around for you with their mouth. Never handle a shark by the tail. They can bite their tail since they have no bones. Their skeleton is totally flexible cartilage. If you're new to this fishing, nothing has prepared you for the strength of many saltwater species.

You can net some fish, particularly the obvious catch-and-release species like bonefish, redfish, permit, and trout. You don't need a net for some species as losing them at the boat is not an issue, or they may easily swing into the boat on the end of your string. Some species demand a gaff. Don't mess with untangling a toothy critter from a net. You put yourself at risk. Lip gaff them or cut them off.

They don't call snappers that for nothing and most have some interesting canines. Cuberas, the largest family member, require wire leaders. Many other species, such as grouper, have excessively raspy lips and gill rakers, or razor sharp gill plates. Fins are another concern. Some species prick you and leave toxins buried beneath the skin. You can guess about the fins on a pinfish. Those of a catfish or scorpionfish are much worse. A few fish have pop-up belly spines.

Use gloves or a towel to handle fish you're unsure of, or don't handle them at all. You can make a simple hook remover using a length of wire from a coat hanger. Form a U shaped hook on one end and a handle on the other. Grab the bend of the hook with the U and lift it while pulling down on the line. It should reverse the angle of the hook and release the fish. You can also do this with a small gaff. I don't recommend many products, although I bought a stainless steel Baker Hookout about 16 years ago and it still functions as new. It beats long-nosed pliers by a wide margin (See photo on page 11).

Discussing every species you might catch around the Keys is beyond the scope of this book. We're not going to deep drop for snowy grouper or tilefish in a thousand feet of water. There are a plenty of reasonable targets and the prime species provide more diversions than many of us will ever find time to fully appreciate.

THE SHALLOWS GANG

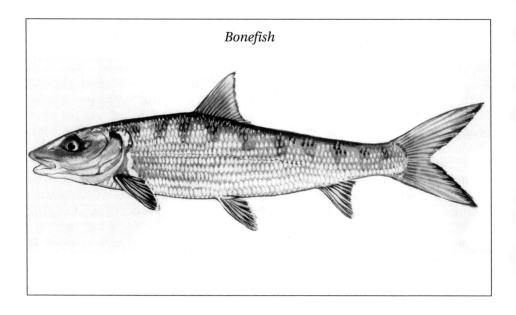

Bonefish

Bonefish

Bonefish can be caught year round, but late spring through fall offers the easiest fishing, if it ever gets easy. Their range extends throughout the Keys, though they are somewhat spotty in the immediate Key West area. Recommended tackle ranges from 8- to 12- pound rigs depending on conditions and food offerings. An 8-weight fly rod is on the light end of the scale. Favored foods include worms, shrimp, crabs, and very small baitfish. Bones are predominately bottom feeders, but hone in on baitfish during late summer and fall. Sometimes they dig hard for burrowing fish and appear unwilling to eat anything else, confounding anglers not willing to bounce the bottom with jigs and flies. They respond well to chum. The best presentation is in their face with something attacking the bottom aggressively (something with enough weight). Double line is useful on rods used with bait and jigs. While bonefish feed over a variety of bottoms, the best fishing usually occurs on the grass flats. The biggest fish like a lot of current.

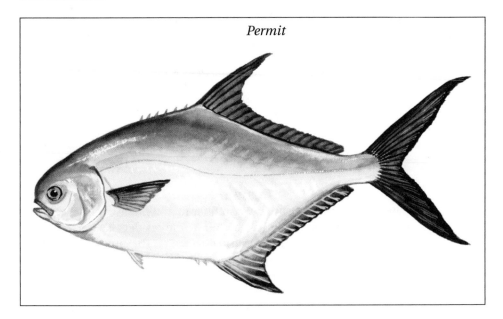

Permit

Permit

Prime permit seasons are the same as bonefish, but they also use wrecks year round and the reef in late spring to spawn. Their range includes the entire Keys, though the Lower Keys through the Marquesas are considered prime territory. As the population improves after the net ban there are enough fish to justify a trip elsewhere. Crabs are their number one food, and they will readily eat a shrimp. Permit eat throughout the water column on rough days, but they prefer food attacking the bottom. A bit of space is required on the cast when the weather is calm. Bonefish gear is a bit light since the fish often exceed 20 pounds. A 12-pound rig or a 10-weight fly rod is minimal tackle if you're targeting them, and a 20-pound rig is often more use-ful if you have a choice. Their tough mouths demand a sharp hook. They are some-times confused with pompano, but pompano don't have the black splotch common under the pectoral fins of permit. Ideal permit country is hard to define. You'll often find them on grass flats and poking around coral heads. They usually prefer rushing current along channel edges, but do sun in minimal flows.

Tarpon

Tarpon

May and June are the core season, but fish filter in and out as early as February and many smaller fish remain as late as October. Some resident fish are available year round, although not enough to justify a trip on a whim. They migrate flats edges, rest and feed in major channels, and sometimes in corners or along edges of major basins when held by current. Tarpon eat crabs, shrimp, and small fish with equal abandon. They hone in on a worm hatch that is dependent on the weather and tide conditions in May or June. They will accept a wide variety of artificials ranging from jerk baits or swimming minnows when resting in basins, to jigs when in channels. Their rough mouths require a shock leader. You might use only 20-pound mono for 5-pound fish, but the big guys can even work through 100-pound. For still fishing with bait you should use at least a fish length shock leader attached to a rod length or longer double line. You can drop to a couple of feet of shock leader for sight fish-ing and blind casting. You can play with small fish on 7- to 9-weight fly rods, but fish over 50 pounds deserve more respect. Many anglers risk the health, and even the lives, of fish by insisting on using inadequate tackle. Use tackle you can handle fish with, like a 12-weight you find just a little hard to cast. Tarpon require a tag for pos-session, but there is no good reason to keep a non-record fish.

Red Drum (Redfish)

Redfish are perhaps the poster fish for conservation efforts by Florida anglers. Scarce in the late '80s, they are now abundant. Redfish are great quarry for beginners as they are tolerant of multiple presentations. They are available year round in the Upper Keys backcountry with an improving population in some parts of the Middle and Lower Keys. They share food preferences with bonefish and the same tackle choices make sense. Double line offers minimum protection against a raspy mouth and a shock leader of at least 25 pounds is better. Fish often tail alone but work edges in large schools. They also frequent channels draining flats and moats around islands, offering blind casting and bait fishing opportunities. Reds are tenacious, if not spectacular, fighters. They are a great fly target on the flats and edges, better on jigs and bait in the channels. They provide moderate table fare.

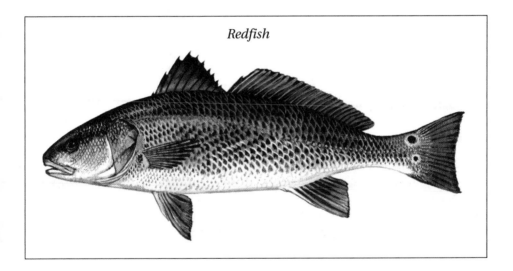

Redfish

Snook

Snook are most easily encountered along the Florida coastline and in the ditches draining from it into Florida Bay and around nearby islands. Their range includes many Everglades National Park islands and edges along the entire Keys shoreline during some parts of the year. Some fish are present around Upper and Middle Keys bridges from fall through spring. They work flats edges and sun in potholes in much of their Florida Bay range, providing good flyfishing opportunities. Small fish tend to remind you of freshwater bass, but larger specimens fight with legendary determination and power. Mostly fish eaters, snook also favor shrimp and crabs. Shock leaders are essential and slightly heavier permit-type tackle is better for them than bonefish stuff. They are excellent on the table, often making conservation efforts more difficult. Jigs, jerk baits, and plugs fool fish, as do similar flies. A tag is required for possession. Watch the gill plate. Look for fish in drainages concentrating food, around bridges, under the mangroves, and sunning in flats edge potholes.

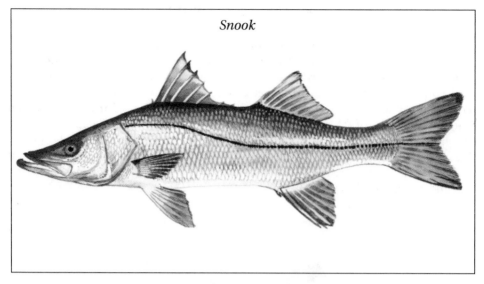

Snook

Spotted Seatrout

There is a rapidly improving fishery for seatrout almost year round, though fall through spring is typically the best time to target them. Fish range from the Florida mainland coast to just beyond the Seven Mile Bridge on the Gulfside. They are easiest to find in mullet muds and ditches draining flats. They are also scattered in wide ranging potholes and island-edge moats. Seatrout eat much like snook. They can be inconsistent fighters depending on their size, but large numbers of fish lead to enjoyable fishing for anglers of all skill levels. They are easily defeated with the lightest range of acceptable all-around Keys tackle. Seatrout have soft mouths so swinging them into the boat on a string is not encouraged if you want to keep the fish.

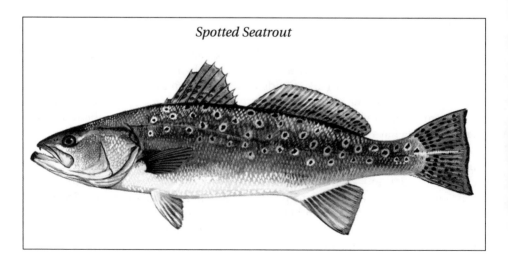

Spotted Seatrout

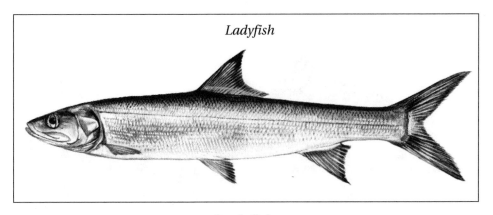

Ladyfish

Ladyfish

Often called the poor man's tarpon, these compact fighters share many trout waters and the same gear is adequate for them. They jump incessantly when hooked and will pursue offerings until they are hooked. While having no real food value, they are fun to pursue and serve as excellent baits or chum for a variety of greater species. They are messy, though, and are best unhooked outside the perimeter of the boat. It's worth your time to stick a ladyfish for bait on a 20-pound rig whether you're drifting or fishing from a fixed position. Something will find it. They are found in typical trout haunts and may travel with them, though you will find both species alone at times.

Jack Crevalle

Jacks are frequent traveling companions of trout and ladyfish. They range from palm-sized in muds and run-outs to true bruisers when hounding rays throughout the Keys or when pushing edges hunting bait. They tail on occasion within Florida Bay and even hound concentrations of bonefish, sometimes beating them to the punch. They have no particular food value, but sharks like them. They'll eat anything if they can get a handle on it.

Jack Crevalle

Black Drum

Black Drum

Black drum are found in a small quadrant of northwest Florida Bay. They are a frequent wintertime catch in channels and run outs while bait fishing or bumping the bottom with jigs. They also use edges favored by redfish and push, sun, and mud much like them, as well. Bait is usually best, but they will eat jigs, spoons, and flies. Flies puffing mud seem to work best. My favorite is an all-silver flashabou 1/0. I give it a tail and a wing and tie oversized bead chain eyes on the shank opposite the point of the hook. Black drum possess some table value, but they are a bit coarse for most folks. A light shock leader is helpful.

Sharks

Common inshore sharks worthy of attention, and available most of the year, include lemons, bonnetheads, and blacktips. You'll also find a scattering of hammerheads and bull sharks, and their numbers increase around the tarpon migration. The uninitiated confuse lemons with blacktips because lemons do have a black-edged fin, but appear almost flaccid when compared to the highly athletic football-shaped bodies of blacktips. Both species have something to offer, though. They are year-round visitors to the shallows, and both will eat a wide range of food we can easily offer. If your bait does not smell you need to swim plastic or flies right on their eyeball so they can get a handle on it. In a chum line sharks often eat offerings drifted along freely like the chum. Sharks have mixed table value but are slow growers, late spawners, and bear few live young. We don't keep them often. They are most easily found along bonefish and redfish flats, and they frequent channels as well as the reef, wrecks, and the depths. Sharks require a wire leader and many anglers prefer braided material for sight fishing work. For bait fishing, a wire leader long enough to provide protection from the tail is helpful when fishing for giants.

THE DEPTH CHALLENGED

This group of fish is not sure where they want to live. You find them on flats edges, in ditches draining flats, scattered in the Gulf, on patch reefs and the reef. Some of the movement is seasonal in response to water temperatures, bait migrations, or spawning urges. Some species are routinely scattered by size, smaller fish in the shallows, and bigger ones in the depths. You might find outsized specimens of any species in surprisingly shallow water.

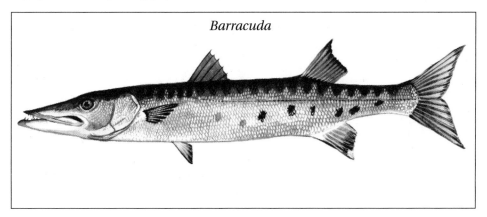

Barracuda

Barracuda

Barracuda are often ignored as a prime species, yet they can be a day saver for many anglers on the flats, the patches, and just off the reef. Barracuda respond to a wide variety of angling techniques and put up a fight ranging from spectacular to worthy depending on your choice of tackle. They are a good entry-level species as you can defeat one on rather light tackle while enjoying a sense of accomplishment. The easiest fly for them is a simple four- to six-inch streamer, preferably of fish hair or another man-made material, consolidated by braiding or with glue on a short-shank 1 or 1/0 hook. You toss it in their face and wiggle it until they show interest, then see if you can take it away from them. Spin anglers have long relied on tube lures, but swimming minnows without the lip let you tease them a bit better on cold mornings. A simple rubber worm works fine while letting you cast a bit closer to them. They are a good trolling target and eat any reasonable hand-sized baitfish suspended from a float. They are of questionable table value—said to be tasty but toxic as they mature in many cases. Wire leaders are a must.

Spanish Mackerel

A mainstay species for many in the Upper and Middle Keys during the winter. They haunt the open Gulf between the eastern Gulf boundary of Florida Bay edges, and the western boundary from Big Pine Key. They frequent potholes, ditches through the strip banks, and the banks themselves. As populations improve, they are increasingly available around the bridges directing flows to the Atlantic from the same reaches as well as on some nearby patch reefs. They love a chum line and feast on responding baits. Catch them on short streamers, nylon jigs, shrimp, and small bait fish. Yellow dots identify them and identification is important as number and length limits vary between them and other family members. Considered by some to be quite tasty broiled or smoked. It is necessary to use wire, as they have nasty teeth. They also have a bad habit of hitting anything on the line raising a bubble trail as they try to steal from siblings, so forego swivels and weights, if possible.

Spanish Mackerel

Cero Mackerel

Ceros are most often encountered on the patch reefs and respond well to chum lines. They share traits with Spanish mackerel, but they also take swimming minnows up to about 4½ inches. Yellow spots give way to dashes.

The Snappers

There are better than two dozen varieties of snappers available in the Keys waters and you may encounter any of them anywhere, although less than a handful are everyday captures and even fewer provide meaningful opportunities for shallow water anglers. The most readily available species are mangroves and yellowtails.

Inshore, between the flats and the patches, mangroves are by far the most numerous species you might catch in meaningful sizes throughout the Keys. You'll find them under mangroves, hovering over shallow wrecks, sometimes following rays, and on the patch reefs. The largest specimens prefer the depths, but fish ranging to four pounds are found everywhere at times. They'll eat a larger bonefish fly, a sweetened jig, and a variety of baits or bait chunks. In the Lower Keys they will sometimes rise for a surface bait. They won't always tolerate a shock leader, but they bite best when the light is low and a shock leader does help. They make excellent table fare.

You'll catch plenty of yellowtails in the shallows, but most are too small to consider keeping. The biggest fish prefer the steep drop-offs on the Oceanside of the outer reef. They are easy to capture when you master the technique of naturally drifting a bait or fly in a chum line. During the day, they seldom tolerate any sort of leader or a double line. Although they fight well, they are rather delicate and demand gentle cooking methods.

Mutton snappers are one of the bullies of the clan. The biggest fish are most often encountered along the reef drop-off or over wrecks, but plenty of good-sized fish haunt the patch reefs and some bridge channels. They also hitchhike rides on the backs of rays in the shallows. Several fly rod world record mutton snappers were Key Largo hitchhikers, and the fishery claims some fame in the Lower Keys. They are excellent eating.

The Groupers

This is another clan populating Keys waters with several dozen subspecies. You won't find them on the flats very often, but they do hang out in many snapper spots in a variety of sizes. Some of the largest members crawl into surprising shallow water. Many jewfish world records were pothole fish encountered while sight fishing for other species. I've found 300-pounders waiting in ambush for laid-up tarpon in backcountry corners, and they are frequent visitors to channels draining the coast and many flats.

They are not really a fly target, although they will eat a fly if you find them in the right location. They prefer meat or a jig carrying some meat, but they will also rise far from the bottom to attack a swimming plug. They are determined fighters and well versed on burying their heads in the sand or the coral in the Keys. They demand stout gear and athletic responses to a bite.

It's important that you can recognize a jewfish, as they are currently the poster subspecies of the grouper clan and protected from all harvest. Their banding is far more brilliant than that of lesser subspecies, and their heads are marked by numerous dark spots. They grow the largest and signify our commitment to maintain the species.

As a whole, the grouper family is highly exploited by both the commercial and recreational fishing groups. They are highly rated on the table but of considerable value as living creatures in the water.

Cobia

This shark look-alike fires the imagination of many anglers. You find them pushing Gulfside flats edges, hovering over shallow wrecks, and hounding rays or sharks seeking a free meal. They pour out of the Gulf and around the Keys into the Atlantic. They are most often fished for at sight fishing depths but are also encountered offshore. Sight fishing depth for this species may be 20 feet or so when they are on rays in Hawks Channel, the water bounded by the Keys and the reef. You might find them cruising on top in 300- to 500-foot depths, too. They willingly eat flies, and a cuda fly or a bucktail works well when they are on rays. Jigs, spoons, top-water baits, and live

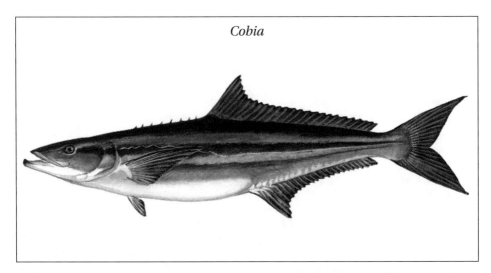

Cobia

baits all find use. They are determined fighters and a prize on the table. Do not handle one if you don't know what you are doing. They might act exhausted boatside, but they can surprise you with their wildly thrashing energy in the boat. Do not net one. Handle them with a gaff.

Sharks

As you move into deeper water you add a new shark species or two and a few more hammerheads and bulls. You might see a tiger in your chum line or a sandbar shark. Bulls are downright aggressive, built with broad shoulders as the name suggests. They will, surprisingly, eat a fly, but the best bait for them according to some anglers is a 100-pound tarpon or a blacktip shark.

Several years ago Ralph Delph told me about a bull trying desperately to crawl over his transom to bite its antagonist. They slipped it off the boat by gunning the throttle. While eating dinner at a tournament function one night, I told the story but was interrupted. A tablemate, Chuck Brodski, completed the tale. He was the angler. It made Ralph quit shark fishing in a flats skiff; he moved to a larger boat! Hammerheads aren't too shy, either. While most species flare from the boat when attacking chum, hammers run right to it. I've also seen them swim under a boat to eat hooked tarpon that anglers tried to protect but couldn't break off.

DWELLERS OF THE DEEP

The warm depths of the Keys attract a wide range of migratory fish seeking comfort or following hordes of bait doing the same. We enjoy seasonal inflows of fish shifting both ways between the Gulf and Atlantic, along with dramatic population shifts during the winter. Some species spend months in local waters, while others simply drive by. There are also specific migrations of the same species leading to very different fishing opportunities.

For instance, sailfish wintering along the lower Florida coast drive into the Keys when cold fronts shove bait our way. This begins as early as October and often reoccurs through April. It is mostly an Upper Keys event. The Lower Keys experience a migration of fish moving to the Gulf to spawn in April and May. The fish must pass the Upper Keys but seemingly do so at depths ignored by anglers. The same fish return in the fall, again offering a separate fishery. Both pushes of fish offer opportunities for Middle Keys anglers.

Not all depth-dwellers offer reasonable flyfishing chances, though you can catch anything on a fly with a bit of luck and lots of preparation. Anything you can attract to a chum line will eat a fly, and there are some teasing techniques that help. A few species are outstanding fly targets.

Dolphin

Dolphin

Late spring through early fall is by far the best time for dolphin. They can actually be a sight-fishing target in thousand foot depths as they chase bait to the surface and migrate high in the water. Dolphin may be located by watching birds, seeking weed lines, or snooping around floating debris. They respond some to chum, usually used to hold them around the boat. They will hit a variety of trolled lures and rigged baits, as well as food tossed to them when a school is located. Fly anglers often enlist the aid of a companion willing to toss them some cut bait and tease them within casting range. A fishy looking bucktail works well. You might get by with an 8-weight for the smallest fish but a 10- or even 12-weight is useful. Many small fish are present through early summer, but 70- pounders are also around. Dolphins make excellent table fare, but fish grow fast so you should keep no more than you can eat right away and let the rest grow. A spring 4- pounder might easily weigh 20 pounds in the fall. Shock leaders help. They can be very energetic in the boat.

Tunas

We generally look at four tuna subspecies in the Keys: blackfins, skipjacks, yellowfins, and bonito. Others are encountered. Yellowfins are highly seasonal, only migrating around the Keys and seldom available for long during the spring and fall. The rest are here late fall through early summer, depending on the weather and bait concentrations.

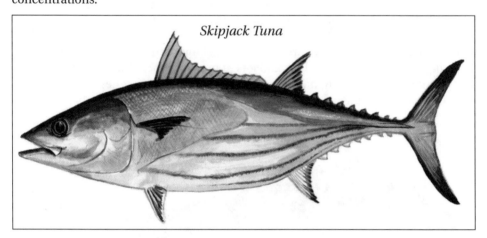

Skipjack Tuna

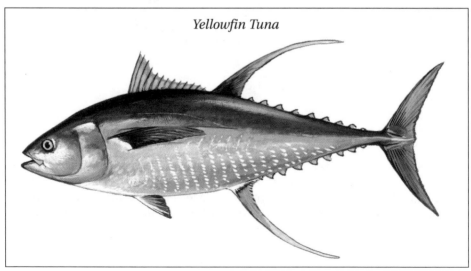

Yellowfin Tuna

Bonito

You can chum for all with live baitfish. They hang over deeper wrecks at times and in up-welling currents of the Gulf Stream. Once on top, they respond well to fishy looking bucktails. You need a 10-weight for bonito and are far better off using a 12-weight for the rest of the crew. These are stubborn fighters. You can certainly catch them on a variety of lures when you have them in a chum line. Trollers do well chasing schools they find watching for fleeing bait. They do not like boats so dropping a trolling bait 100 yards or so from the transom leads to more bites. Yellowfin and blackfin are excellent on the table. Small bonito are often skipped as bait or deep dropped on wrecks for bottom dwellers, and they make good strip baits.

Sailfish

Sailfish are a migratory species responding to a wide variety of fishing methods. They are not often a target of fly anglers in the Keys, but a fly catch is possible with helpers willing to tease fish within casting range with a live bait. They are most often a target of those anglers trolling live bait or rigged dead baits. Sails also offer some sight fishing opportunities as they chase baits to the surface early and late in the day during winter or while they surf when migrating. Concentrations of fleeing bait are aptly called "showers" and are easily spotted a quarter-mile or more from the boat. The fish are often slightly behind the shower, feasting on baits stunned by their bills. Live ballyhoo are often the best bait in the Keys, but sailfish eat anything at times, including some plastics. Shock leaders are essential. Twelve- to twenty-pound gear is most appropriate. Sailfish are seldom killed and are very fast growing.

King Mackerel

Kings are typically a late fall through mid-spring visitor, often responding more to bait migrations than to weather. They are speedy and determined fighters. Fly anglers can try them in a chum line or under a kite-suspended bait. They respond to many live baits. Kings have a bad habit of chopping baits off at the tail when they are trolled or drifted in the current. The use of a multiple tail and head hooked rig is helpful for smaller fish. They require wire as they have very bad teeth. Medium and

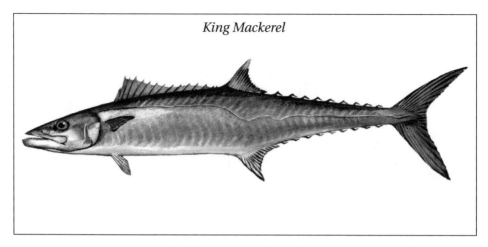

King Mackerel

large species are best chased with 12-weight fly rods or at least 20-pound spin and conventional tackle. These fish frequent surprisingly shallow water at times, crawling up on the reef or around shallow structure just off Key West. Their table value depends on the cooking method. Smoking is usually the best, and they are excellent on the grill.

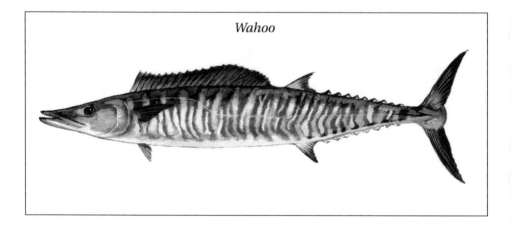

Wahoo

Wahoo

Wahoo, the largest member of the mackerel family, filters in and out of the Keys almost on a whim, but there are notable spring and fall migrations. They often hang below schools of smaller dolphin and the debris attracting them. There is also a notable wahoo migration along the reef line in 100 or so feet of water if lots of bait is present. They are a tough and rare fly catch as they prefer highly charged baits. Their awful teeth requires wire. They are excellent on the table.

The Groupers

The fish get bigger on the outer reef drop-offs and over the deeper wrecks. They are not really fly fish targets, but they may rise into a chum line at times or reward anglers plumbing the depths with Hi-D shooting heads. They will hit a jig, or a jig sporting a whole baitfish bounced along the bottom, or a swimming plug trolled just over their head. Some species really hug the terrain and only the stoutest gear might move them from shelter before they dive for cover. You need a shock leader to deal with the tough mouth of the fish and the rough bottom they prefer.

The Snappers

Like grouper, you'll find the biggest specimens in the depths. You can fly fish for some of them with reasonable expectations, though. Yellowtails often swarm to the surface at the transom in a chum line and sometimes are joined by mangroves. Muttons, too, come to the top on occasion and often suspend off the bottom instead of hugging it. Ten-weight rods and 12-pound gear is usually enough for these excellent eating fish.

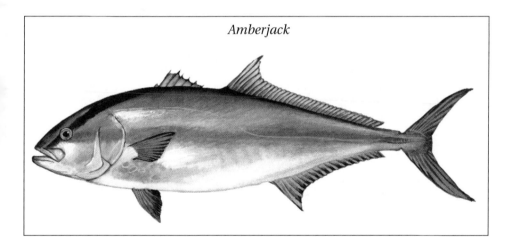

Amberjack

Amberjack

This largest member of the jack family is a sometime visitor to shallow wrecks and the reef, but it really prefers the depths. Amberjacks are readily raised to the surface with live chum and teasers. They'll eat just about anything. Oddly, we seldom see fish much under about 20 pounds. They are out there somewhere, but the average size of readily available fish means you need a 12-weight fly rod or at least 15- to 20-pound spinning and conventional rigs. Even with heavier tackle you may be sorry you bothered to feed these fish. They are bulldogs. While they are edible if you peel off minor slabs of quality flesh, they are best released.

More Sharks

Most types of shark make their way offshore at times to join other family members. Many are only rare visitors to Keys waters but add some spice to a trip. You might raise any to the surface with a good chum line, but here you typically see sharks when they attack a hooked fish. Occasional winter visitors, such as a mako, a rare great white, or a huge tiger, will often only eat the remainders of a fish they killed as you fought it to the boat. Experienced hands carry outsized tackle they can quickly bait with remaining fish chunks.

Blue Marlin

Blue marlin are a somewhat erratic Keys visitor, but enough fish are around to justify a couple of tournaments every year. Some years they seem almost common. They are usually targeted around Keys sea mounts and steep rises in the Gulf Stream by high speed trollers with plastics or rigged whole baits. They may be randomly encountered anytime dolphin populations are high and may hit baits meant for dolphin. Marlin often attack schools of smaller dolphin and those prepared to pitch a live dolphin hooked on appropriate 30- to 50-pound gear return to the dock with a tale to tell. Marlin are also fond of small tuna.

Baitfish

Knowing how to gather bait adds to many Keys fishing experiences even if you intend to fish with flies or lures. You can raise static fish, those resting in channels, hiding in corners, or suspended over structure, with frozen ground chum. They will light up some, but most respond far better for free live baits, or livies as we call them. Response to frozen chum is dependent on how much bait it attracts. Your own school of bait stashed in the live well eliminates your dependence on parking for some time to raise bait, as you can toss livies at a passing school of predators whenever you need to.

There are baits of preference. Big kingfish favor blue runners and cigar minnows are maybe a better second choice. They will eat "white baits" or a pinfish if it's all you have. Sometimes mullet seem like the only right bait for tarpon, yet being on the water at dawn with some pinfish, crabs, or even grunts, might be a better idea than showing up two hours later with mullet.

In other words, you don't want to get too carried away with this, but some effort to gather live bait to use as food or chum often makes the difference between a good or bad day. For some species, you are at a serious disadvantage if you don't make an effort to load your live well with some reasonable baits.

You can use a wide variety of forage for most species. You're ahead of the game if you can throw a cast net just because it's a bit quicker than catching bait with hook and line. You can't net some baits though and pros feel a few baits are better caught with hooks than in a net. Some are fragile and easily damaged or somewhat weakened in net.

Relatively simple baits, those most easily found and captured, work well enough for a fun day on the water. Unless you feel like things are life and death, there is little

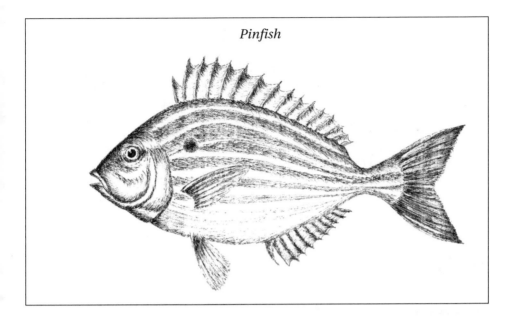

Pinfish

reason to stay up all night trying to catch a few goggle-eyes even if they do sometimes sell for $75 to $125 a dozen during a Palm Beach sailfish tournament. We're going to talk about the simple baits.

We tend to generically lump a handful of small slab-shaped species together as "white baits." These include menhaden, or bunker as they are commonly called, sardines or pilchards, and herring. Depending on size, all are readily eaten and are the best live chum. Pilchards are the most frequent near shore visitor, often marked early in the morning by diving birds somewhat outside of main flows of channel currents. Cast netting is best, but you might chum them up with frozen chum or oats and catch some on a string of gold hooks. Herring lean toward structure and slightly deeper water. You can net them, but they respond well to a Sabiki rig, a string of quill dressed hooks you jig through a school. Two-inchers make great snapper baits while larger specimens are useful for anything from tarpon to sailfish. You can hook them anywhere, but a ridge above the nose works well.

Ballyhoo are most frequently sought on the patch reefs and also gang up on many Gulfside strip banks in main channel flows. They respond well to chum and if you don't throw a net, you can catch them by baiting long-shanked size 12 or 14 hooks with small bits of peeled shrimp drifted with the current on a 6- or 8-pound rig. We call those small hooks "hair hooks." A few years ago, Marathon Captain Danny Strub showed me how to catch them under a bobber if the wind keeps you from tossing the bait away from the boat. They are usually hooked through the lower lip and wired to the hook by their bill.

You can find blue runners around channel markers, and they also frequent the patches. I like to use a crappie jig as an anchor on the end of the line below a couple of hair hooks. This rig also attracts cigar minnows and speedos, little mackerel look-alikes attractive to almost any fish living or hunting beyond the reef. Hook them through the back in front of the dorsal fin.

Pinfish are maybe the easiest hook and line caught species. They usually hang just off the edges of flats, slightly out of the main flow of water and also at channel ends as they begin to broaden. The same hook and crappie jig rig works well for them and they are often joined by runners, little jacks, and another interesting slab-sided species, a generically named skipjack, along with some grunts. They are hooked anywhere in the back, usually in front of the dorsal or through the lips. They naturally dig to the bottom and like to tangle your line.

Mullet are pretty much a cast-net-only species. There are a variety of subspecies and all are useful. In prime time, fall through late spring, you find them pushing the Oceanside shoreline and behind the bridges in muds. Everything capable of eating one will eat one. They are usually hooked through the upper lip, hook point up.

Ballyhoo are great baits for everything living in Keys waters. You can fish them live, cut them into chunks, or troll them when they are dead.

Preparation Leads to Success

The angler's jaw sagged almost to his belt as the great fish opened its mouth and inhaled his carefully crafted streamer. The force of the take against a frozen arm was enough to set the hook. A lifelong dream almost fulfilled ended quickly as the angler, feeling more like an observer than a participant, finally responded just as the perilously fragile tippet parted. Our visibly shaken hero sank to the deck muttering, "So that's what this is all about."

The fish available to fly anglers on the flats of the Florida Keys elicit similar reactions every day from pursuers of all experience levels. If you're planning a first trip to the area the anticipation can be almost as overwhelming as the fishing itself. While the fish deserve their legendary status, catching them is not nearly as mysterious as newcomers often believe.

The single most important aspect of planning a great trip for Keys tarpon or bonefish is likely the choice of competent and friendly help. Most guides are proud to provide gear for your use and usually own the best stuff money can buy. They will carry meticulously assembled flies and leaders appropriate for the spots they usually fish. Trying their tackle may save you from a poor choice, as some of today's gear is not quite capable of delivering tarpon-level performance. Bonefishing is far less demanding on tackle and quality steelhead or salmon gear is often adequate.

Many anglers like to tie their own flies. If you want to use your flies it's wise to ask your guide for recommendations. Guides are fairly persnickety about patterns, hating to waste any of your good casts on less than edible food. Don't take it personally if your flies aren't fawned over. Many guides have watched virtually thousands of fish eat and have a firm idea of what works in a given situation. It is this level of experience that you are paying for, so take advantage of it.

Once you have selected a guide and have some idea of flies to tie as you while away the winter hours, your preparations are still far from over. Casting will be different from what you're used to. There is plenty of talk about the incredible distances you have to cast to trick fish. The truth is that most tarpon and bonefish eat within 60 feet of the boat, a distance most anglers can learn to reach after practicing a couple days a week for a few months.

Casting challenges on the flats are the wind and the short window of opportunity when the fish and the boat line up just right. Typically, you stand on the front of the boat with 12 to 15 feet of fly line and the leader hanging off the rod tip. You should be able to deliver a fly at 60 feet with three false casts, but two is much better.

Mastering the quick delivery required to take advantage of fish spotted at the last moment, or during the perfect moment, leads to the next phase of preparation. Start practicing with the wind hitting you from uncomfortable directions. A steeple cast, something you've likely learned on a local stream, will keep fly lines and flies overhead. Heavier saltwater gear requires a firmer wrist and an exaggerated lifting motion only comfortable after determined repetition. When you can cast your 60 feet with the wind on your wrong shoulder without flinching, you're ready.

You'll seldom intentionally be called on to cast into the wind or with the wind on the wrong side of the boat. Guides will make every effort to ensure fish show up perfectly positioned in the wind. There are days, though, when fish act as if they know more than guides and conspire to make life difficult. Any advantage you have in dealing with rogues increases your chances for success. Of course if you're comfortable with the tough shots, the prime shots become a piece of cake.

The Keys don't lack for facilities. Depending on who you talk to, we cater to anywhere from 2.5 to 4 million visitors each year. You'll find a wide variety of lodging ranging from Islamorada's comfortable Key Lantern offering rooms for $45 a night, to super exclusive digs at Little Palm Island for $800 per night. Prices vary wildly for rooms depending on the time of year. Expect to spend more during the winter even though flats fishing is better in the summer, or "off" season. Winter and holidays are tourist season here.

Free boat ramps are ridiculously few and far between in the Keys considering the area's dependence on fishing. Many motels offer onsite launching for guests. I suggest you seek lodging with ramp access or at least a place capable of suggesting good nearby launching facilities if you are trailering your own boat.

Many eateries change hands often, but there are long-owned standards throughout the Keys or eateries so ingrained in tradition new owners take possession only hoping to maintain and enhance hard-won reputations. You won't find 24-hour service for much of anything in the Keys. Depending on the season, even 24-hour convenience stores can't maintain sufficient staff to stay open all night.

We have pretty good medical help, and the Keys have established 911 emergency service dialing. Vehicle service is a bit scattered. A full-service gas station is not an obvious best use of high-priced land. Those in the business are rather dedicated and tend to treat folks fairly.

If you are going to drag a boat to the Keys, make sure it is in good working order. We are rich with willing and competent mechanics, but they are overloaded when the world descends on us. As in any other business, their steady customers get precedence, and you might wait a few days for simple fixes during the winter. Things even out from late spring through early fall.

We are loaded with tackle shops (see Hub City Information at the conclusion of each region's discussion). It's easy to accept the lure of some big footprint operations in fancy digs, but don't overlook the unassuming shops barely filling a narrow storefront from the road. By and large, Keys tackle shops are owned and staffed by folks who truly care about fishing, all possessing a wealth of knowledge gathered through years of experience. There are treasures hidden behind the least likely looking doors. Not all cater to fly fishers, but most will have a good handle on the fish most of the time.

Getting to the Keys and getting around is not too tough. If you're driving, you work toward South Florida's turnpike. Along the East Coast you might enjoy the trip more if you get on the turnpike at Ft. Pierce. I-95 is pretty crowded along the Gold Coast. We have a couple of airports, but they offer little in the way of direct flights

NOAA Photo

Healthy stand of seagrass with jack crevalle.

from any departure points outside of Florida. It's hard to know from month to month if anyone is flying into Marathon. Flying into Key West may be worthwhile if the price is right and you are staying on that end of the Keys. Costs and time delays seldom justify a commercial trip into Marathon unless you are coming in direct from somewhere in Florida.

We are a relatively short skip and jump on the road from either Miami or Ft. Lauderdale. It's 20 to 30 minutes farther from Ft. Lauderdale than from Miami to the Keys, but it is often cheaper to fly into Lauderdale and the airport is less congested and somehow feels more comfortable.

Once you get into the Keys, you find only one main road. Many businesses refer to a series of mile markers along the highway as reference points for finding them and further identify themselves as being on the bayside or Oceanside. The markers do not exist everywhere but provide a general idea of where you are. The bay is on your right as you head from the mainland toward Key West.

Over time, the best source of information, beyond a friend's recommendation, is often the local Chamber of Commerce. The membership is constantly refreshed as businesses come and go. They want to take good care of you to help build future business.

I hesitate to talk about camping in the Keys. We do have a couple of state parks. At Long Key you'll find tent sites right next to the highway. Bahia Honda is a bit better. I camped in a RV once in the Keys during 1984. I found the KOA on Sugarloaf Key quite comfortable, but when I left I was not happy with my alternatives. In many instances, because land use is very restrictive, many camping sites are crowded and used more as low-cost housing enclaves. Some are so crowded that site-renters are shoved onto roadside buffers.

The following list of Chambers of Commerce might prove helpful in trip-planning in addition to the facilities listed in the individual hub cities included in each region discussed in the book.

The Florida Keys and Key West:	800-FLA-Keys
Key Largo Chamber of Commerce:	305-451-1414
Islamorada Chamber of Commerce:	305-664-4503
Marathon Chamber of Commerce:	305-743-5417
Lower Keys Chamber of Commerce:	305-872-2411
Key West Chamber of Commerce:	305-294-2587

If you are stuck on the mainland, yet have a choice of where you stay on your way to the Keys, I suggest you head south. You can escape most of the clutter of the city just 25 minutes from the airport in the Homestead/Florida City area. This is suburbia, but it beats the congested confines of Miami. Reach the Chamber of Commerce at 888-FL-CITY-1. For a complete listing of the services provided for each specific region, refer to the Hub City Information at the end of the Region Chapters.

Travel Hub City Information
Fort Lauderdale

HOTELS AND MOTELS (At Fort Lauderdale/Hollywood International Airport all hotels and motels have restaurants and are within 3 miles of the airport.)

Hilton, 1870 Griffin Rd., Dania Beach / 954-920-3300
Sheraton, 1825 Griffin Rd., Dania Beach / 954-920-3500
Best Western Marina Inn, 2150 SE 17 St. Causeway / 800-528-1234
Ramada Inn, 2275 State Rd. 84 / 954-4000 / 800-Hol-iday

FT. LAUDERDALE PROPER
Bahia Cabana Resort, 3001 Harbor dr. / 954-524-1555
Doubletree–Oceanfront, 440 Seabreeze Blvd. 954-8733
Holiday Inn, 999 Ft. Lauderdale Beach Blvd. / 305-563-5961
Clarion, 4660 N Ocean Dr. / 954-776-5660

RESTAURANTS
California Cafe Bar & Grill, 2301 SE 17th St. / 954-728-3500 / Views of the Intracoastal Waterway and yacht harbor / Award-winning wine list, full bar
Margarita Café, 221 South Atlantic Blvd. / 954-463-6872 / Fine Mexican dining
Oasis Cafe, 600 Seabreeze Blvd. / 954-463-3130
Pastabilities on the Beach, 201 S. Atlantic Blvd. / 954-463-7209 / Excellent Italian cuisine as well as brick oven pizzas
Sloppy Joe's, 17 S. Fort Lauderdale Beach Blvd. / 954-522-7553 / Popular nightspot with American bar menu
Sloop John B. Raw Bar & Saloon, 239 South Atlantic Blvd. / 954-463-3633 / Excellent local seafood menu
Bahia Mar at the Radisson Hotel, 801 Seabreeze Blvd. / 954-764-2233
Bistro Mezzaluna, 741 SE 17th St. / 954-522-6620
15th Street Fisheries, 1900 SE 15th St. / 954-763-2777 / High-end fantastic seafood restaurant
La Marina @ the Marriott, 1881 SE 17th St. / 954-463-4000 / Fine Florida-style Caribbean fare
Shirttail Charlie's, 400 SW 3rd Ave. / 954-463-3474 / 954-463-9800

FLYSHOPS/BAIT AND TACKLE/MARINE SUPPLIES
Bill Boyd's Tackle Shop, 508 N Andrews Ave / 954-462-8366
Bass Pro Shops Outdoor World, 200 Gulfstream Way, Dania Beach / 954-929-7710
Carl's Bait & Tackle Shop, 2510 Davie Blvd. / 954-581-8890
Competition Tackle & Marine Inc, 4620 Griffin Road / 954-581-4476
Kingsbury & Sons Tackle, 1801 South Federal Hwy. / 954-467-3474
Lauderdale Marina Inc., 1900 Southeast 15th St. / 954-523-8507
Les Wills Bait Tackle & Gun Shop, 217 Southwest 27th Ave. / 954-583-7302
LMR Fly Shop, 1495-F, SE 17th / 954-525-0728
Lou's Tackle & Marina, 3463 Griffin Road / 954-989-9219

T & R Tackle Shop, 228 Commercial Blvd. / 954-776-1055
The Fly Shop of Ft. Lauderdale, 5130 N. Federal Way / 654-772-5822
The Sports Authority
    1901 N. Federal Way / 954-735-1701
    3383 North State Rd 7 / 954-735-1738
    12801 West Sunrise Blvd. / 954-846-9365
West Marine
    1201 North Federal Highway / 654-564-6767
    2300 South Federal Highway /954-527-5540

HOSPITALS
Holy Cross Hospital, 2400 E Commercial Blvd. # 420 / 954-492-5753
North Broward Hospital District, 303 SE 17th Ave. / 954-355-4400
Plantation General Hospital, 401 NW 42nd Ave. / 954-797-6470
Westside Regional Medical Center, 8201 W Broward Blvd. /954-473-6600

AIRPORTS
Fort Lauderdale Executive Airport,1401 W Commercial Blvd. /954-938-4966
Hollywood International Airport, 954-359-6100

TRAINS
Amtrak, 800-USA-RAIL
    Station: 200 SW 21st Terrace
    Silver Service serves stations throughout Florida

Miami

HOTELS & MOTELS (At Miami International Airport all hotels and motels have restaurants and are within 3 miles of the airport.)
Marriott, Courtyard 1201 NW 42nd Ave. / 305-642-8200
Days Inn, 7250 NW 11st St. / 305-261-4230
Hilton, 5500 Blue Lagoon Dr. / 305-261-3335
Comfort Inn & Suites, 5301 NW 36th St., Miami Springs / 305-871-6000

MIAMI PROPER (within 15 minutes of Miami International Airport)
Travelodge Royalton, 131 SE First St. / 305-374-7451
Hyatt Regency Miami, 400 SE 2nd Ave. / 305-358-1234
Holiday Inn Downtown, 200 SE 2nd Ave. / 305-374-3000
Ramada Inn, 300 Biscayne Blvd. Way / 305-531-5771

RESTAURANTS
MIAMI (DOWNTOWN & AIRPORT AREA)
Bayview Grille @ the Biscayne Hotel, 1633 North Bayshore Drive/Miami/
    305-536-6414 / Specializing in seafood
Blue Water Café @ Inter-Continental Hotel, 100 Chopin Plaza/ 305-577-1000 /
    Great gourmet pizzas at moderate prices with view of Biscayne Bay.
Cheescake Factory, 7497 Dadeland Mall / 305-665-5400

Capital Grille, 444 Brickell Ave. / Downtown Miami / 305-374-4500 / One of the best steakhouses in town / Cigar lockers available

Garcia's Seafood Grille, 398 NW North River Dr. /305-375-0765 / A casual, friendly, family-run eatery with a great atmosphere / In and outdoor dining

Tobacco Road, 626 S. Miami Ave. / 305-374-1198 / A casual bar atmosphere, popular with locals – hamburgers & bar menu

FLY SHOPS/BAIT & TACKLE

Atlantic Bait & Tackle, 1690 SW 27th Ave. / 305-444-7101

A Fisherman's Paradise, 3800 Northwest 27th Ave. / 305-634-1578

A Fisherman's Paradise, 17730 South Dixie Hwy. / 305-232-6000

Biscayne Bay Fly Shop, 8243 South Dixie Hwy. / 305-669-5851

Boaters World Discount Marine Centers, 13617 South Dixie Hwy. / 305-278-9878

Capt. Harry's Fishing Supply, 100 NE 11th St. / 305-374-4661

Charlie Richter's Fly Shop, 472 NE 125th St. / 305-893-6663

Complete Angler Fishing, Inc., 6827 SW 40th St. 305-266-2028

Crook & Crook Fishing, 2795 SW 27th Ave. / 305-854-0005

El Capitan International, 1590 NW 27th Ave. / 305-635-7500

Fishing Tackle Unlimited, 10786 SW 188th St. / 305-234-3410

Jet's Florida Outdoors, 9696 SW 40th St. / 305-221-1371

Haulover Marine Center, 15000 Collins Ave. / 305-945-3934

Kendall Bait and Tackle, 9402 S. Dixie Hwy./ 305-665-0215

Marlin's Bait & Tackle, 6911 Collins Ave., Miami Beach / 305-861-9959

Oshman's, 11521 NW 12th St. / 305-716-0229

Reef Bait & Tackle, 760 NE 79th St. / 305-757-4373

River Marine Supply, 260 SW 6th St./ 305-856-0080

Scott's Bait & Tackle, 8241 SW 124th St. / 305-278-7007

The Fishing Line Bait and Tackle, 9379 SW 56th St. / 305-598-2444

The Sports Authority

    8390 South Dixie Hwy / 305-667-2280

    180 Northwest 183rd St. / 305-651-9866

    10688 Northwest 12th St. / 305-591-0622

    12010 SW 88th St. / 305-270-9762

    18499 Biscayne Blvd. /305-682-0717

West Marine

    16215 Biscayne Blvd. / 305-947-6333

    3635 South Dixie Hwy. / 305-444-5520

    8657 Coral Way / 305-263-7465

    19407 South Dixie Hwy. / 305-232-0811

Wolff Fishing Products, 7286 Bird Rd. / 305-2667-4400

CAR RENTALS

Alamo, 1-800-327-9633 / www.alamo.com

Avis, 1-800-311-1212 / 800-452-1494 / www.avis.com

Budget, 1-800-527-0700
Dollar, 1-800-800-4000
Enterprise, 1-800-325-8007
Hertz, 1-800-654-3131 / www.hertz.com
Thrifty, 1-800-367-2277
National, 1-800-227-7368

RV RENTALS

Tour America RV's, 5021 NW 79 Ave. / 305-639-1919
Moturis LTD., 3901 NW 16th St. / Lauderhill / 800-287-2275
Rent a Caravan, Miami / 305-613-0769
Camp USA, Miami / www.onfreewheels.com / 888-647-6665

CAMPGROUNDS & RV PARKS

KOA Kampground (cabins), 20675 SW 162nd Ave./ 305-233-5300
Larry & Penny Thompson RV Park & Campground, 12451 SW 184th St. /
    305-223-1049
Camp Owaissa Bauer (cabins)W 264th St. / 305-247-6016
KOA Kampground, 14075 Biscayne Blvd. / 305-940-4141
Gator RV Park, 13800 SW 8th St. / 305-559-2255

HOSPITALS

Mercy Hospital, 3661 S Miami Ave. / 305-854-4400
South Miami Hospital, 6200 SW 73rd St. / 305-661-4611
Mt Sinai Medical Center, 305-674-2121

AIRPORTS

Miami International Airport, 4300 NW 21st St, Miami / 305 876-7000

TRAINS

Amtrak, 800-USA-RAIL
    Station: 8303 NW 37th Ave.
    Silver Service serving the Southern regions and all of Florida

Key Biscayne

HOTELS & MOTELS

Sonesta Hotel, 350 Ocean Dr.

RESTAURANTS

Bayside Seafood Restaurant, 3501 Rickenbacker Causeway / 305-361-0808 / Very
    casual local's favorite seafood restaurant
Purple Dolphin, 350 Ocean Dr. /305-361-2021 / American continental cuisine
La Piazetta, 260 Crandon Blvd. / 305-361-8916 / Italian cuisine in a quaint setting

Professional Help

While this book offers plenty of clues that should help you catch fish on your own, it's hard to beat experienced help. If you intend to fish only a few days in the Keys or only a few days a year, the cost of good help is far less than gathering gear and learning your own way around. Pros will teach you things very quickly that you might never learn on your own.

Many of my customers, and other anglers I talk to on a regular basis, suggest that picking the right professional help when they started fishing in the Keys was the toughest chore they faced. Guides and captains don't slip well into a one-size-fits-all mold. There are lots of names you'll never hear, and many cater to casual anglers on short vacations that are going to fish once in their lives in the Keys or maybe a few days each year. These pros seldom become famous, but catching fish for someone who has never seen one is a routine task for them.

It might seem the perfect job, but guiding or running a charter boat is a business, and guides face the same daily headaches you do. It's up to you to pick one with a mind-set similar to your own. There's nothing wrong with randomly picking a few names out of the classi-fieds and interviewing them a bit. Many gladly cough up references, and you should ask for some if you're not totally comfort-able making a decision without them.

Mutton snappers are a real taste treat as well as a tough foe.

The best source of names is often a friend or local shop in your area catering to traveling anglers. All pros won't suit you. Some are very results oriented and potentially grating on your nerves. Some are so polite they will never help you improve. A demanding guide may well talk you through every shot. If you can take the heat, you'll learn quickly.

On tough days, you might think a long-time boat team hates each other in must-catch situations like tournaments. When it's windy and hard to see, there is little time for formalities. Guides and anglers are often screaming at each other so no one is guessing about where the fish are or what needs to happen to the boat for a successful shot. Shot windows are open for scant seconds and slam shut with guillotine finality.

I have had some fun with customers on days with great visibility while we were staked out on migration spots. I like to tap them on the shoulder and point out fish swimming toward the boat yet still several minutes away. I ask if they wouldn't mind throwing to them when they are finally in range. Indeed, we sometimes have such luxury, but it is rare.

Few people stay in the business long if they don't love fishing, and in many ways you are their surrogate when they get you in front of fish or get you hooked up. Their excitement is sometimes misinterpreted. Many times things happen so quickly there is no time for polite discussion. By the way, you owe it to your pro to let them know if you don't understand what they are saying. The toughest situation is in sight fishing, of course. A guide needs to know if you see the fish so they can position the boat for a shot. They can't read your mind.

Obviously, a lot of potential charter-operators fish off docks or have ongoing relationships with tackle shops. Those operations are businesses, too, and want to encourage repeat business and build reputations. They are also a good source of referrals if you grill them. No one can fulfill your expectations if you don't voice them. For instance, anglers looking for snook probably shouldn't hire me as I would guess I rank in the bottom one percent of Upper Keys snook guides. You're better off hiring someone else for the job.

Your pro should not take you fishing for something you won't catch because they aren't there, and you shouldn't insist they do. Tarpon fishing in 65-degree water is usually a waste of time as is bonefishing with water temperatures in the 50s.

Some guides do guarantee hookups, but no one can promise them when there are no fish. There is a fine line between taking someone fishing and taking someone fishing for money. You should have a long discussion with a potential guide about your expectations. If you expect too much, like a laid-up fly-caught tarpon in December or tailing bonefish when the wind howls 30 knots, you're doomed to fail most of the time. Your guide can probably find you a shark or barracuda, though, if you are smart enough to take what the day offers.

What the seasons offer depends much on your ability. Some anglers are quite adept at catching bonefish in three to five feet of water with a fly or putting a streamer in front of a rolling tarpon while its upper lip is still out of the water. No matter how hard your guide jumps up and down around fish, they cannot put your fly in the water in the right place, only you can. You may hear of a bonanza elsewhere and never see it if your guide feels you can't deal with the fishing. If fish you can see hundreds of yards from the boat consistently run over you before you can get the fly in the water, you need to practice your casting. At the very least, if fish are moving, a guide owes you a fair shot at them. I suggest you never book flyfishing days outside the April through October high-production window for glamour flats species without understanding that the fishing is very random the rest of the year. On the other hand, much of the best of offshore fly angling happens in the winter and you can still hit a hot day on the flats.

You can catch a bonefish about 330 days a year, though, if you are skilled enough to see a shadow about the size of a Bic lighter in four feet of water and can dump a fly 60 feet from the boat with one false cast. A guide deserves your fee if you tie them up with a reservation. Make a smart choice and come when fishing is good unless you fully understand you might need to fish for something else.

There are endless off-season and marginal day opportunities available. We have wonderful fishing for many overlooked species if you come with an open mind during fringe periods. You can fish for redfish or snook in the Upper Keys backcountry many days when you can't fish for bones or tarpon.

Plenty of the shallow water pros in the Upper and Middle Keys can put you into the Gulfside cero mackerel fishery during the winter. Many can find you great grab bag fishing in muds for trout, ladyfish, and jacks. Maybe chumming over a wreck is not what you envisioned if you planned to catch a tarpon, but around Key West and in the Lower Keys you might catch three varieties of mackerel, a cobia, or a huge jack. Barracuda fishing is often best when there is nothing else to do, and they are a riot.

Give your offshore hire the run of the day and your rod will bend. The Keys are not really a sailfish-on-fly destination but offer solid bait fishing for them. You might want to catch a big mutton snapper yet a big grouper should make your day if you're interested in bottom fishing. Dolphin and tunas offer their own special brand of excitement and both are great fly and light-tackle targets.

The best hire is the one that gives you a good day on the water when they can and kicks you off the dock when they can't, while providing a level of entertainment and motivation that suits you. It's a team sport, the boat against the fish. Your pro is your coach, typically only interested in helping you.

Oh yeah, and your pro is only renting you a spot for the day, not selling it to you. Yes, they might know lots of spots, but their next party may have fished the spot with them for years and have fond memories of it or may only be capable of catching fish there under similar conditions. If you hire someone with the intent of learning places to fish on your own, you owe it to them to tell them. If you're honest, they might show you some spots where you won't bother them later. If not, they'll probably never show you anything again and you might gain a bad reputation.

There are a number of ways to start on the wrong foot, too. You may take some of your hire's ammo away from them if you are late to the dock in the morning. Many know plenty of places to fish, but maybe only one is right for you at a given time. Most don't want to hear where so-and-so took you, either. Why? Many find spot knowledge a very personal thing and may not show you a spot or two if they think you're going to blab.

Over time, relationships between anglers and pros become like many other employer/ employee relationships and in many cases develop into serious friendships. You end up trusting each other explicitly and share a wealth of experiences.

Pros often think you can and should catch most fish you see. We have a selective memory, like all humans, remembering when we last threw at a tough-angle fish and made it eat. One of my customers counsels his friends to silence overly excited guides during tarpon season by making the guide fish. Guides get shaky knees and still make bad casts just like other anglers, no matter how many fish they see. You never outgrow the fever caused by fast moving fish at close range. Your guide might adjust the boat a bit for you or talk in slightly more hushed tones after a few miscues of his or her own!

By the way, if you're fishing with a guide or captain, please provide them your hotel phone number. It's a bit unreasonable to expect them to call you back long distance on your cell phone when you are staying only two miles away.

For a listing of some of the Florida Keys guides and outfitters, please refer to page 326.

Yup, it's a big, fat bait rod, but the fish is still lots of fun.

Thoughts On Fishing Tackle

The right equipment can make or break a dream fishing vacation. I'm not exactly a gear fanatic, though, so I won't cheer for the latest and greatest too much. I use what I like and what makes sense to me. I don't always find useful form following the function of price. I don't have anything to sell myself so I'm going to recommend stuff that does the job at a reasonable price. There are some bare minimum gear demands, but you don't need a $1,000 fly rig or a $400 spinning rig to catch a bonefish. If you are fishing with a pro, they like providing tackle they know and trust so you don't have to worry about it.

Do pay attention to minimum recommendations you'll read from time to time as you plan your fishing. I once had an experience while bonefishing with a professed expert that I couldn't believe at the time but now find amusing. On a bad weather day we sat and chummed for bonefish. A big single I still estimate as weighing well over 15 pounds crawled within range and "garbaged" my angler's fly. I was shocked when the fish popped the leader in less than a second. My angler had no backing on his reel! You need 250 to 300 yards of string for most flashy Keys species.

I've been around a while and my personal choice of gear is not exactly cutting edge. Of course, I might spring for newer stuff if it really worked better. I do get to play with lots of new stuff from time to time. I own a pile of almost two-decade-old Sage RP II rods. These rods were casting nightmares for lots of folks, but you could learn to cast them. While I find some newer rods cast a bit easier, few seem to fight fish with similar authority.

Around 1990, we saw an explosion of stiff tip, soft butt rods, designed for easy casting. Some anglers do fight fish well with soft rods, but they learned their style over decades with captures numbering in the hundreds. Few of us can point a rod basically straight at a fish and fight them only with the reel. The rod as a lever is too ingrained in most us, and we need the cushion of a bent rod and find some reassurance in a powerful curve. If I had to buy a top of the line tarpon rod today, I would lean toward one advertised as a 12/13-weight rather than an 11/12. I have recently used a St. Croix 12-weight that performs well at a fair price. It's good enough for me and fits in with my "reasonable" equipment theme. Rods that bend all the way into the grip are a bit soft for most of us. You can feel it when you shake them.

I'd bet the major discount houses sell workable rods for casual anglers under house brands that are almost identical to the St. Croix or the old Sage, but costing only around $200. If you're going to fish a lot, though, I do believe you should spring for the best gear money can buy. It provides a feeling of security and confidence and one of pride. Many of the new rods are a joy to cast and fight fish well if you lean toward the heavy end. I must add that a lot folks don't want to fight tarpon till they roll over at the boat anymore. After the bite and the first few jumps, it's not much fun wrestling with one!

There are few available compromises for tarpon quality fly reels. If you keep a machined aluminum reel in a proper sock and maintain it with lubricants as suggested, it will increase in value for generations. Big cork drags and one-piece spools provide lots of insurance when you're finally tied to a fish. Large arbors are worth the extra price and are fast becoming the standard. Besides providing much quicker line retrieval, they eliminate some of the problems of geometrically increasing drag pressure as fish suck line off the reel. The more consistent drag is a big plus.

The best reel you can afford is helpful on the bonefish flats too, although I do think you could buy one reel for both tarpon and bonefish and just change lines as seasons progress. I am not a fan of 20-pound backing and the extra weight of a tarpon reel is not so aggravating. You don't really need jeweler quality reels for bonefish. Reels classed as size three for tarpon are reasonable year-round tools you can quickly adapt for a range of fish and line weights.

I caught my first bonefish and my largest ever permit on what was an Orvis Madison 9-weight in the 80s. It's much like today's Pflueger 1495½. My reel was not counterbalanced, and I mashed a big split shot into a ventilation slot opposite the reel handle to calm vibrations. Similar reels today are counterbalanced and some have exposed spool rims. I'd opt for them if you have a choice. There are lots of useful reels in this price range and you can use them for larger freshwater species. Martin offers some very interesting reels with pretty good drags for the price.

I don't like reels with drags resembling vehicle disc brakes for any major flats species unless you are comfortable using a light mechanical drag and applying lots of hand pressure on the spool or finger pressure on the line. Most of those reels are well made and reasonably priced, however, even though the drags aren't much to sing about. I am also not a fan of anti-reverse reels; direct drive reels do a lot of your work. While the spinning reel handle may well bust your fingers if you get them in the way when a fish is running— you'll only do it once.

The right or left hand cranking debate is often heated and confuses many anglers. I've never quite understood it, but I grew up when all plug reels cranked from the right and all spinning reels cranked from the left. We never thought about it and just used the stuff. I like my rod in my strong hand for big fish if I have a choice and feel you should do what feels natural.

Fly lines are a prickly topic for me. We suffered a major design change in the 1980s creating nothing but havoc for anglers. We could once buy a nice fat 82-foot line which laid in the boat just fine while the wind blew 15 to 20 knots. Suddenly, everything on the market for saltwater was a one piece, skinny running line and shooting head combination that was 105 feet long. The skinny running lines are continuously tangled in modest winds, and in the hands of most adrenaline-pumped casters the chubby shooting heads dump flies unceremoniously around fish.

You are stuck with tarpon-taper lines if you use a 12-weight rod, but most flats anglers are better off buying a bass bug or weight forward line for the rest of their flats fishing. Line and leader dumping often occurs if you try to hold too much line in the air before you make your final presentation with the new line designs, although you can overcome it.

Dolphin willingly eat a variety of offerings and put on quite a show on medium-weight tackle.

Learning to shoot much, if not most, of your cast works much better. Many of us have the bad habit of measuring our cast, a hangover from freshwater fishing days where fish lie in ambush. Besides the dumping complication, we end up casting too far as the fish are moving at us continuously. It's a hard habit to break. If you're fishing with a guide who is constantly and gently suggesting you put the fly in the water, you have this problem.

You also might have to dye your line. Many flats fish will not tolerate whites and brights tossed toward them at anything approaching a right angle. Your fishing hero may use a white line all the time, but he never fails to make a good head-on cast, or simply makes enough great casts that it does not matter. The rest of us are always late and deserve better. Some so-called lesser lines come in usable colors. I'm partial to one available in olive. I'm lucky, though, as I own a stockpile of gray and coral lines from the '80s that I still use. Tarpon swim up to a white line, then stop and swim around it.

I'm not in love with multiple ball bearing spinning reels. They are somewhat smoother-feeling in operation, but dump one overboard and the price of replacing a bunch of bearings is frightening. They last for only seconds in a saltwater bath. The most important thing about a spinning reel is an always-functioning bail spring and a smooth drag. I lean toward budget-priced Shimano products, but I intend to see if the current generation of Shakespeare Sigma models are as good as those I bought in the '80s. Both Penn and Daiwa make highly regarded, reasonably priced reels that I have experience with, but I will bet you can also find functional reels from other manufacturers.

I prefer Ugly Stik spin and plug rods. I can still buy them for roughly $30 in 2000. My all-around play and bonefish rods are seven footers rated for 8- to 15-pound line. They toss shrimp well and fight many average flats species better than well enough.

I pine a bit for the new generation of machined bait casting reels, but as I have to maintain about 50 various rigs, price is an object. I am still using some 1980-some-thing Shimano Bantams on my light rigs along with some old Daiwa level wind reels on heavier rods. Some similar freshwater bass quality gear is okay for a random Keys visit. I use the light reels mostly for jigging with 8- to 10-pound lines in muds or back-country ditches. I do bait fish for tarpon and toss plugs at sharks using the old Daiwa reels loaded with 15-pound line, mounted on what some might call freshwater bass pitching or flipping sticks rated for 12- to 25-pound test line.

It's hard to beat the current generation of light bodied space-age material lever drag reels for tasks like live bait tarpon fishing, bottom fishing, or chasing sharks. Little goes wrong with them, and they seem to last forever.

I am sold on the best reasonably-priced line manufacturer's offer. If you're going to deep jig, you might benefit from no stretch space age braided lines testing 30-pound breaking strength at 10-pound diameters. They also fish well when jigging muds and ditches in the shallows on windy days as they telegraph gentle takes. Ultra invisible leader material makes sense for highly nervous species, too. On the other hand, if you properly place a fly for a head-on shot at flats species, they never see the leader, but tuna on a bright day often bite best on invisible line.

I throw the line away every day after a bonefish catch so I appreciate a good product I can afford, like Stren, Silver Thread, or the store cofilament offerings from the major mail-order houses. Single filament lines from Ande and Berkely also deserve support as they function well and both are good companies.

There are myriad touted discoveries in the hook industry, but it's really tough to beat known manufacturers like Eagle Claw and Mustad. I led an angler to a multi-decade old bonefish tournament record a few years ago, and the day we set the record we lost half a dozen fish to a bent hook out of a box costing more per half dozen hooks than a hundred fully functional hooks from the blue collar world. Maybe the hook stuck a bit better without a touch up from a file, but it sure cost us.

Sharpening hooks deserves some discussion. Many hooks are nearly useful right out of the box, depending on the target species and gear, but most need a little bit of work. Smaller species on light tackle stick best with long sharp points. If you're fish-ing for species appropriate for less than 10-weight fly rods, or 12-pound and under spinning or plug gear, you don't need to get crazy with point formation. Just a few strokes of a file should do the job.

Sharpness is relative. The point must dig right into a thumbnail when you test it there. If it slides it won't grab a fish. The fish you seek on bigger gear demand more dangerous hook points. As usual, I recommend against the grain. It's typically suggested you sharpen a hook from the point toward the bend to avoid cutting down the point. I work toward the point, fully intending to cut it. A long point often bends, and I also intend to build a set of cutting edges. I like a diamond shaped point with edges sharp enough to cut a class tippet for hard-mouthed species.

You can spend all kinds of money on hook sharpening tools, but a hardware store mill bastard file appropriate for the hook sizes you use is hard to beat. They won't last long around the salt, but you can prolong their life with regular lubricant baths.

You can really go nuts with tackle. You have to decide the value for yourself. I buy jigs for inshore bottom bumping in 25 unit lots designed for freshwater fish for the same price as three advertised "superior" saltwater offerings. Many of my favorite plugs are designed for bass but work fine in the salt if you change the hooks to stronger, corrosion resistant offerings. If you're on a one-time trip, the bass hooks are okay if you rinse them off and don't try to lift fish into the boat by the string. Lighter hooks demand you net fish or release them in the water. If you want to lift fish with the hook, spring for the heavy-duty jobs. Often the lighter ones are easier to stick, though.

Some products do make a difference. General saltwater jigs designed for bait use sold generically serve a purpose and Captain Hank Brown's Hook Up Lures are favorites of the snook fishing clan and many of his specialty offerings seem superior for other species. It's hard to beat the DOA family of lures for inshore species. There are a lot of great products on the market, but don't feel any obligation to buy them thinking they offer the only hope to catch a fish. They are just tools. Lots of plastics have a place in the salt. Tarpon will eat rubber worms and so will bonefish and redfish. Jerk baits work for many species, too, as do some molded lifelike offerings.

Don't lose your mind because the fish are a little bigger in the salt. You can fish for bonefish as though they were catfish, and tarpon or snook like they were bass. They are different, but not out of reach of much of the tackle you already own. A pitching or flipping bass rod rated for 12- to 25-pound line with a decent star drag reel holding 250 yards of 15-pound cofilament line can deal with 100-pound tarpon.

With fly rods, nine-footers are generally the standard. You can catch a bonefish on a 5-weight, but you're pushing your luck. Some lean to the light end, preferring a 7- or 8-weight rod. They're fine for lightly weighted flies and relatively calm days. I typically load my rod racks with 10-weights. I like heavy flies and don't want to argue with the wind or the fish. A 9 or 10 is a good all-around rod for bones, redfish, snook, permit, and baby tarpon inshore. They are a bit light for most offshore work, except for the smallest members of most species. If you anticipate dolphin much over 20 pounds, kings of the same size, and double-digit tuna, you'll enjoy the muscle of a 12-weight. I recently bought a Pflueger Medalist 9-foot 10-weight at a 6 for 1 kind of price and it makes a pretty good all around inshore/light offshore rod.

Again, if you're hiring a pro, use their gear. Most pros prefer it anyway, and you may not end up liking the sport if you are new to it. I wouldn't buy anything you can't use at home until you know you're going to fish enough to justify the expense. Don't let "gear envy" keep you off the flats or out of the depths in the Keys. Simple tackle provides a lot of fun.

Inshore, we fish with floating lines most of the time. While an intermediate line sinks too fast for tailing species it does have a use for fish in basins and channels. Tarpon on migration routes may not eat flies bouncing too much in rough water created where a lot of wind blows into a stiff current, calling for an intermediate again. You can substitute an intermediate tip line for a full intermediate. They are a bit easier to deal with and work well for mudding bonefish or redfish.

You can use a floater offshore too, but the intermediate comes in handy for a stiff chop and other faster sinking lines have a place on days when chumming for fish that refuse to come to the surface. Sinking lines are not necessarily used to plumb the bottom. They do provide some control from a rocking boat.

She's about to land a nice fish on a light rod.

Recommended Tackle Chart

Species	Fly Rod Weight	Line Type	Bite, Tippet/pound/size
Large Tarpon	12	F, I, S	60-100 mono
Medium Tarpon	10-12	F, I, S	50-80 mono
Small Tarpon	7-9	F, I, S	30-40 mono
Bonefish	8-10	F	----
Permit	9-10	F, I	----
Redfish	8-10	F	30 mono
Trout, Ladyfish,	7-9	F, I	30 mono
Jacks/Snook	8-10	F, I	30 mono
Small Sharks	7-9	F	40 multi-strand wire
Large Sharks	12-13	F	60 multi-strand wire
Barracuda	8-10	F	#4-6 single wire
Spanish/Cero Mackerel	7-9	F, I	#4-6 single wire
King Mackerel	10-12	F, I, S	#4-6 single wire
Small Dolphin/Tuna	8-10	F, I	30 mono
Large Dolphin/Tuna	12	F, I, S	50 mono
Amberjack/Cobia	10-12	F, I, S	50 mono
Snapper inshore	7-9	F, I, S	----
Snapper offshore	9-10	F, I, S	30 mono

LEGEND Line type F=Floating, I=Intermediate, S=Sinking

Other Gear

People often come to the Keys without enough clothes. Even in June you might find a reason to don a fleece-lined jacket, and it is always a good bet to bring one from fall through spring. A rain suit is useful whether it rains or not. It will keep you warm, and some days you're going to get wet without one when running across a stiff chop.

Cotton makes the most comfortable flats fishing raiment on most days. Synthetics are good when it's chilly or a bit wet since they dry quickly, but they can be far too hot on a summer day. Hats provide some shade for the eyes, helping you to see and shading your face so you don't burn. I'm a fan of side shields on sunglasses while staring into the water looking for fish, but I don't use them often as I worry about my peripheral vision while running the boat. Polarized sunglasses are a must, though.

It should go without saying you need sunscreen on the water, but it's often over-looked. Even on a cloudy day you will burn no matter how well you think you've tanned. Sunscreen is most effective when applied as part of your get-ready routine in the morning. It's less useful after you hit the water. "Greasing up" later risks adding unwanted scent to flies or lures and leaves hands a bit slippery, too.

It's become increasingly popular during the last few years to carry something to hold fly line you might ordinarily throw on the deck. The Fly Line Tamer from AlumaPole or weighted, small trashcans are found in many boats. They work well for first shots if you don't let fly line control get in the way of your fishing. Too many people worry about getting the line back into box instead of working the fish they just threw to. A stripping basket provides a more natural and less obtrusive line-gathering function. Most days you don't need them, but sometimes the assistance is invaluable. The trash can or Tamer offers the versatility of simply stuffing the rod in their recesses and taking off for your next destination without reeling up. This can save meaningful fishing time if you're moving a lot.

You must have something to cut line and pull tag ends with as you build leaders and attach flies, lures, and hooks. Pliers have moved into the designer ranks, but function is far more important than form when you choose this critical tool. You can cut string with a pair of fingernail clippers, so pliers that won't positively grasp the tag end of a 100-pound shock leader are worthless. Many won't, including some hundred dollar offerings.

Whether you prefer side cutting or inline pliers, both sets of jaws should mate perfectly. Few side cutters do, and we can't check them anymore since they now come in bubble packs. Check Point and Sport Tools offer reasonably priced inline pliers that do the job if you're searching for a brand name. A good pair of stainless needle nose pliers might suit your needs, and if you buy them at Sears you can replace them whenever they quit working.

You can stay on the good side of your guide or captain if you avoid soft black-soled shoes for boat use. They leave awful marks in the boat that only some nasty abrasive can remove. Many pros just cringe when their boats are soiled for no good reason. You might think it is just a boat, but it is your pro's baby. Someone once asked me why guides were so finicky about their boats. It's their office and second home. I wondered how he might like me slamming a one-pound fly reel down on the $15,000 walnut desk in his office. It's about the same price for a bare-bones flats hull these days.

You might want a stretcher for tarpon fly leaders. The traditional wooden box is an item of pride but a simple canvas valise with an aluminum framed stretcher built in works just fine and costs far less. Almost anything you use with a zipper around salt water requires some extra care. Zippers are failure prone if you don't lubricate them often. Some day everything will come with zippers using plastic pulls–I hope.

The most important things you need in the Keys, besides the obvious fishing gear and personal comfort items like appropriate clothes and sunscreen, are charts of the watery terrain and tides. You can find relatively inexpensive paper charts to use for a few days on the water along with free tide charts. I do recommend you spend the money for the relatively indestructible charts available, and tide charts or books showing the range of the tide are helpful.

The best terrain charts are available from Waterproof Charts at 800-423-9026 and MapTech at 888-839-5551. Both offer marvelous computer mapping programs that help you pinpoint tides almost anywhere, show some fishing spots, and tie into GPS units.

You can order long-life charts concentrating on fishing locations from *Florida Sportsman* magazine, along with a handy tide book by calling toll free: 866-300-1745. They also offer a great guide to the gamefish and baitfish on both sides of the Keys along with the bible for putting gear together: Vic Dunaway's *Bait, Rigs, and Tackle.*

You really need to pick up current fishing and boating regulations locally when you get here. They change so often, you'll end up on the wrong side of a rule if you don't check the day of a trip.

Travel Gear Checklist

TACKLE

_____Rods

_____Reels

_____Spare lines

_____Leader material

_____Flies/lures

_____Hooks/lead

_____Hook remover

_____Pliers with cutter

_____Wire

_____Net/gaff

_____File

_____Line cleaner

_____Tape measure

CLOTHING

_____Shorts

_____Long pants

_____Shirts

_____Hat

_____Rainsuit

_____Jacket

_____Extra insulation fall through spring

_____Polarized sunglasses

MISCELLANEOUS

_____Camera and film

_____Pocket or fillet knife

_____Cutting board

_____Sunscreen

_____Cotton towels for glasses and hands

_____Gloves for handling fish

_____Your itinerary/important contacts

_____Tide charts

_____Cell phone and charger

_____VHF if boating on your own

_____Portable GPS

_____Super glue

_____Bug repellent

_____*Flyfishers Guide to the Florida Keys*

_____Current fishing regulations

_____Fishing license

Flies Are Only Food

You can definitely go overboard on flies. It's one thing to do so in freshwater where a pattern costs maybe a buck but at $5 to $10 a whack for saltwater patterns, you need to use your head. I won't become popular saying so, but you need to use some restraint when stocking a flats fly box. You might find cause to throw maybe a dozen different flies for tarpon or half a dozen for bonefish, but I can hardly imagine needing more if you even need so many. In the shallows of the Keys, the fish eat shrimp, crabs, small fish, worms, and an occasional eel. This food is easily duplicated with a handful of flies and some flies do multiple duty.

TARPON

The standard Apte II, Apte tarpon fly, and Cockroach offer a pretty good starting point for tarpon. A variety of colors for the Apte II, plus rabbit strip fly in rust, purple, black, and electric blue might round out a collection. You could use these in rather fragile sizes in clear water, and oversized bulky flies cover many stained water needs.

You'll find tarpon flies useful in all colors of the rainbow at times, but natural looking choices are the most productive day in and day out. Mottled mixes, like cree or grizzly and bucktail or brown with pale blue, make good crab simulators. Olive and yellow patterns, along with mostly white or the palest green, might suggest baitfish.

Mottled tarpon flies often work best, but sometimes you will want something dark and solid in discolored water or under low light conditions.

When it is dark you can throw something all black for tarpon. In some areas it works on the brightest and calmest days, even in very clear water. Many anglers like to dredge–blind fish in the depths or dark water–with a Big Hurt, a huge (by Keys standards) black fly made with very webby feathers. Big dark rabbit strip flies also work pretty well in dirty water. Yellow and orange, all yellow, and sometimes blue or purple have plenty of uses in discolored water.

There are a couple of things to consider when you buy or tie tarpon flies. The tail, whether a split wing or something simply splaying off the end of the hook, must hang far enough off the back of the hook to avoid wrapping in the bend when you cast it. This usually necessitates an attachment just behind where the shank forms the bend. Almost anything farther up the shank will foul in the wind.

I prefer a fly designed to float somewhat above the fish when throwing at tarpon. The fly can sink, but I like fish to rise to eat the fly so they turn away when they do. It offers a better shot at a hookup. Tarpon eat flies right in their face just fine, but they are awfully hard to hook. I prefer hair heads or collars over palmered hackle most of the time. Palmered hackle is wrapped to flair around the shank of a hook in front of the tail. Spun hair heads barely sink, are very attractive to the fish, lead to spectacular bites, and offer typically firm hookups.

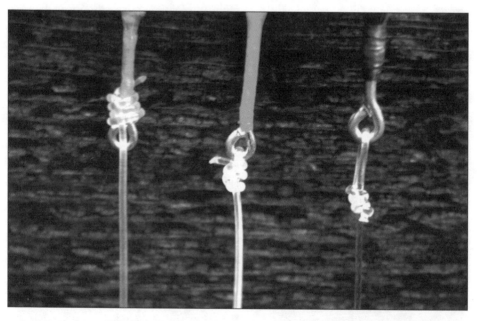

Some anglers snell tarpon flies to leaders while others use a simple three-turn clinch knot. Others like loops. It seems like you get better hookups with a fixed fly. The snell fishes more consistently than the clinch knot, as flies occasionally become "cocked" on the knot. At times, when fish are in quiet water, the loop lets the fly vibrate a bit more than one tied in a fixed position and attracts more bites.

BONEFISH AND PERMIT

It was a classic bonefish situation. Tails were popping up five or six at a time and the school scurried about in 10-foot bursts, pushing shock wave ripples as they greedily devoured their prey. This wasn't the classic Bahamas situation, though, this was the Florida Keys. The huge 11- to 13-pound fish were tailing in almost two feet of water. The October full moon rising tide was shoving water across the strip bank so hard it was tough to keep the boat pointed into the current for a cast.

The often-recommended shrimp imitation, tied on a size 4 hook that you'd slaved over last night was supposed to be perfect for tailing fish. The fly landed with barely a ripple two feet in front of the fish as they approached. Surely this would be your day to catch one of these legendary giants. Your jaw dropped in horror as the current quickly dragged your fly from the fish and its v-shaped wake spooked them off the flat.

Florida bonefish are credited with being extremely tough to catch, while bonefish everywhere else in the world are considered aggressive. There is little doubt that Florida fish are a little tougher to catch. They see more boats, are quite a bit more wary, and demand better casting. Our fish are also not as aggressive as they might be elsewhere because they have more food available. Compounding the problem for visiting anglers, though, is that a good part of bonefish lore has been established based on fishing where the fish are small and dumb.

Small makes a big difference in bonefish. In the Bahamas it is not unusual to find hordes of fish in water that barely covers your ankle joint. Keys fish tail in knee-deep water. The best bonefishing in the Keys is often where tidal current is like a river pouring across a sandbar. Flies must sink quickly yet still enter the water with some semblance of decorum.

In jigs, sink rates are controlled by head shapes. Bulk versus weight is evident in the slimmer designed flat-head jigs for bonefish and redfish on the flats, while the same ¼-ounce weight in a round-headed jig sinks much more quickly to plumb shoreline drop-offs or shallower run outs for grab-bag fishing. The same principles apply to flies.

Weight has to balance with the bulk of the fly, and the best tyer's design flies to work like jigs in most situations. Eyes, bead chain, taxidermist's glass, or little lead dumbbells, are used to provide some of the sink needed for our flies. Neither glass or bead chain eyes are heavy enough to anchor flies in stiff currents or sink them to the favored depths of giant bonefish.

We can use flies that are too big. If you tie a bulky fly on a size 1 or 1/0 hook, enough lead to really make it sink will likely make it heavy enough to spook fish on nice in-the- face presentations. At two feet or shallower depths, the entry of the fly can bother the fish. The secret is to tie a small profile fly with enough weight to attack the bottom. I am not happy with size 4 hooks for Keys bonefish but still like a small-ish fly for tailers. An Eagle Claw 254 cadmium or sea guard plated hook in size 2 gives me the extra bite I want, yet lets me tie a small fly.

I only use the size 2 for shallow water tailers, fish crawling on their bellies in a foot or less of water. As the depth increases so does the size of my fly. For fish that can still tail at 18 inches I like a size 1 for Crazy Charlie-looking patterns and usually use a 1/0 for weighted epoxy heads pressed into service as the water approaches 2-foot depths.

We're still talking about classic tailing bonefish depths, considering the size of the fish. Those of you tying flies are at an advantage for this type of fishing. I use twist-ons to weight my flies. You can also find spools of a similar flat profile lead. I like the twist-ons because they provide me a way to measure. For size 2 flies I use a third of a strip and for 1 and 1/0 flies half the strip is just right. I still use some type of eyes on the fly to make me feel like I'm really imitating nature and for the added weight.

Twist-ons are best tied parallel to the shank of the hook on the side opposite the point. Like a jig, if you tie your wing in on the point side, the hook will ride up. Like many bottom feeders, bonefish pin their prey to the bottom, and the up-thrusted hook offers some advantage for hookups, although fish are hooked in all kinds of strange places anyway.

I like size 2 or bigger hooks for my bonefish flies and prefer the shorter shank hook used on the fly in the lower left corner. It's a size 1/0, which lets me tie a fly the same size as the longer size 2 hook shown in the upper left corner. It's easier to hook-up using a hook with a bigger bite.

If you don't tie flies your task is tougher. You might find it hard to locate flies with the sink rates you want. The idea that an epoxy head will sink the fly and is all the weight you need will cause you to waste a fair amount of money. Lead-eyed flies will help if the flies appear small in relationship to the eyes. If the eyes look small on the fly they probably won't sink it at a rate fast enough to make a bonefish eat it. Some anglers might argue with that simply because they always make good enough casts to catch a few fish. As a pro expecting to see only a handful of good casts a week from anglers, I will tell you that poorly weighted flies are crippling.

These flies are going to splash. It should sound like the little plop made by a pebble. It's a sound the fish respond to well. If the weight and size are well balanced using the smallest possible fly, you'll get the sound you want. If it's not a pleasant sound to you it won't sound pleasant to the fish.

Of course there are exceptions. Sometimes you'll find fish just running along shoving wakes with little apparent feeding activity. These fish often respond better to flies slightly higher in the water column. A little bit of flash to give the indication of a small fish doesn't hurt for these flies, either.

If you are going to make a weight mistake with a fly, lean toward the heavy side. You can throw a heavy fly just a little farther away from fish if the splash presents a problem. Actually, the good plop often attracts tailing fish. If you suddenly find a running school, you can strip the fly a bit quicker to get it off the bottom. There is no adjustment you can make when the fish of a lifetime shows up just on the deeper edge and you're stuck with a light Bahamian-style bonefish fly. I can't tell you how many times I've watched paralyzed as a fish waited for a fly to hide in the grass while it floated in their face instead.

Several colors work well for bonefish flies. Some folks like yellows a lot. Bones will usually eat something mostly brown and will take white if they don't like brown. Pink is surprisingly effective and something olive and white works on some spots. Again, barred feathers offer some magic when combined with several body colors.

With some adjustments, the classic Crazy Charlie is hard to beat. Size is a factor as is a weedguard if you weight it enough to fish species capable of tailing in two feet of water. A copper body with a brown wing or a mixed brown and white wing is my favorite all-around shallow water bonefish fly on a short-shanked size 1 hook.

You can change this pattern with a chenille body. Pink and white, green and white, and all white are useful. You can use flashy body material for them, too, and sometimes the fish really prefer some sparkle. These flies tied on 1/0 or even 2/0 hooks work on a variety of species including redfish and pothole sunning snook. The popular bend back series of flies is an interesting alteration, but most of these flies are hope and prayer patterns insufficiently weighted to really fool most fish, even though they do catch some. They work best in the shallowest of water or when tossed against a tree-covered shoreline.

Permit dig, too, and permit became a routine target when folks finally weighted flies to work like jigs. There is little doubt that the best popular pattern for permit is a Del's Merkin. It is not the absolute most definitive crab imitation on the market. It just sinks the best in various sizes and is a great simulator. The fish don't take the time to consider what the fly looks like if it does what a natural does. Naturals dig for the bottom! I tie mine upside down, with the lead eyes on the shank opposite of the hook point and use a weedguard the originator and most imitators do without. You only need this pattern in tan or chocolate. The rubber band legs are neat, but I don't notice the fish missing them very much if you tie your own. One of my customers throws a thumbnail-sized drab pattern he seriously over-weights that permit and bonefish just cannot ignore. He doesn't worry about rubber legs or flashy materials. He just throws his profile fly in their face and sinks it.

Weedless flies help for bottom feeders. You can make a fly weedless by base wrapping the wing, taking a few twists of thread around the wing to stiffen it and stand it up, or by adding a weedguard. The easiest weedguard is a horseshoe-shaped length of stiff mono tied in just behind the eye of the hook with the same x-wrap you use for calftail wings on Wulff patterns. Some folks don't like mono weedguards, feeling they "prick" the fish. The fish eat crabs with serious points on their shells, shrimp with nasty horns, and baitfish with stiff fins. I don't think the fish notice much, and there isn't anything worse than looking at a fish waiting for a fly to move when it is stuck in the grass, unless it is looking at a fly that won't sink to the grass at all. I put weedguards on Clousers, too. A selection of chartreuse over white, brown over white, and white over pink covers most situations. I carry them with 32nd and 16th ounce eyes on size 2, 1, and 1/0 hooks.

There are plenty of other patterns available for bones and permit. Captain Nat Ragland's Puff still works well for permit a couple decades after discovery. Somebody turned it over maybe a decade ago and weighted it with lead eyes. The combo of a tan body, badger tail split, a split cree tail, and some lime or pale orange Krystal Flash is hot. Even hotter is the same fly with a pink body for mudding bonefish, and permit eat it pretty well, too.

The Mother of Epoxy was a proven tournament winner for years when properly tied, but it never translated into a world-beating commercial success. Few people put enough lead into the head to make it work. A medium chocolate body, glass eyes, and the puff tail or a brown bucktail butt worked well throughout the Keys. At times, a white badger tail is hot on some Keys flats.

OTHER FISH

Redfish will eat a bonefish or permit fly much of the time. I prefer something a bit bigger, maybe something on a 2/0, but other anglers think smallish flies are best. Orange bodies and brown wings work well, as do pearl sparkle braid bodies with white wings. You can slave over a justifiable spoon fly, and a shaped hair head or foam-bodied fly will catch you some fish. Silver spoons are a favorite of spin anglers, and you can tie a fly much like them with flashabou. Give a hook a flashabou tail, wrapped body, and a small wing weighted with some oversized silver eyes. They eat it fine, and you can use it to sight fish for trout, snook, and black drum. There is a lot of argument about whether a redfish fly should sink or not. It really depends on the bottom they are using. Redfish act like they don't see a fly much of the time because we fish for them where they can't see. The fly is often on the other side of a curtain of grass they cannot see through!

Cudas like a long pattern resembling nothing much different from a rubber worm. You can braid fish hair or crimped nylon at least six inches long on a size 1 or 1/0 hook for them. I just consolidate the tail with head cement or clear fingernail polish. They'll eat white, red, chartreuse, or something multicolored with a light belly and dark back.

Many offshore species will take a simple white bucktail, as will many flats species like reds, snook, baby tarpon, trout, and ladyfish. The cuda fly works for cobia on rays and larger jacks following rays. I've used pink versions of the cuda fly for tarpon during worm hatches. You can jazz up a bucktail in a variety of colors with lots of flashy material, sometimes leading to a better day.

Sharks like bulk but will take a bucktail. They'll take anything in the right spot and something easily seen helps. Sharks you throw to while free swimming often ignore a fly unless you keep it swimming on their eye. When they are running to chum, sinking it in their face often works best.

Poppers are useful for a variety of species, and the bulk of a spun hair head interests others. Experiment, but realize that there are few colors not duplicated in some forage species. Still, the basics work much of the time.

You can't tell much about flies just because fish ignore them. Until fish run to your fly and say no, it is your cast, and not the fly, that is a problem. A tarpon rolling

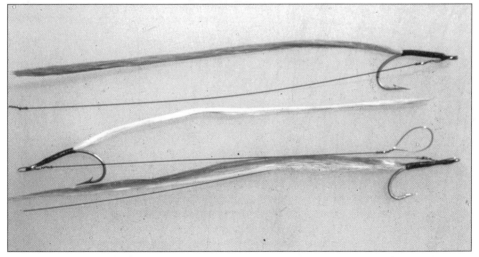

Barracuda flies need be no more complicated than this. Most folks tie them on hooks far too large. A short shank 1/0 is plenty big enough. The fly should be six inches or more long, and they can be soaked in glue or clear fingernail polish so they are easy to cast in the wind with a relatively light rod.

Weight is important on bonefish flies. They need to sink like jigs, with the hook point up. I like a shank-and-a-half length of flat lead, but you can stack round lead effectively as I did on the left hook.

If you buy tarpon flies, make sure the tail is tied in on top of or behind the bend of the hook as it is on the lower fly. The tail on the upper fly is likely to foul on the cast, and tarpon run from fouled flies.

This is a hot orange fly about seven inches long. It's an effective choice for sharks swarming into a chum line.

This is a knocker rig, so named because the egg sinker slides freely on the line. It works well for a variety of bottom dwellers.

If you don't want your sinker sliding on the line, run your line or bite tippet through it twice to secure it.

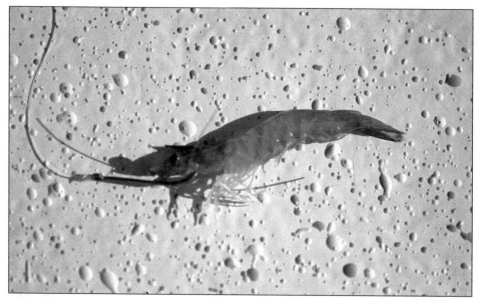

This is a popular head-hooking style for shrimp. It works well for fish capable of inhaling the bait.

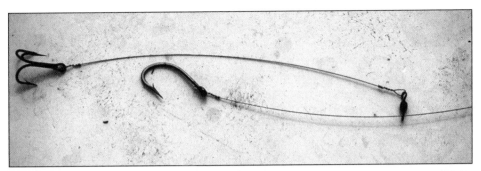

This is Captain Ron Green's ha-ha rig. Many species tend to chop a bait in half on the initial strike. Mackerels are famous for it. Ron's rig allows you to place hooks in the head and tail of a variety of different baits.

This simple pattern consists of a spun antelope hair head with brown and cream craft fur split by some olive Krystal Flash. Tarpon love it and eat it sitting dead in the water.

If you buy leaders with bite tippets attached, avoid those with a gap of double line between the knots. They hinge on the cast and any length lost sacrifices the bite protection of the rig.

up on a fly and not eating it is often rejecting it because it is bouncing too much in the waves. Switch to an intermediate line or put some weight on your leader to keep the fly from bouncing. If it looks like food, fish usually look at it. If they aren't looking, throw it at them until they do!

You can play with all sorts of materials. Craft fur makes great wing material on a variety of flies and good tails, too. Marabou offers a lot of possibilities. A simple shark or tarpon fly can be quickly fashioned by tying a couple of plumes, split in opposite directions on the hook as a tail, and wrapping one or more plumes around the shank.

These are the basics, but experimentation might lead you down another road. Fishing is different every day as fish respond to a variety of food and conditions impact how food becomes available. There is no "best" fly or "best" way to work it. Play with the fish until they respond.

Epoxy flies still catch lots of bonefish. They should be heavy and sink like stones. The fly on the left works magic on mudding and cruising fish. The left fly and the fly on the right came from a mold easily made from oven-baked modeling clay. The middle fly is the classic MOE-Mother of Epoxy-formed by meticulously spinning the hook slowly in your hand until the epoxy sets up. You have to watch the fly on the right, as it will skate if you toss it across the current. The other two are weighted lightly for tailers.

RECOMMENDED FLIES

The following is a short list of reliable patterns that you can fill from home. The size ranges offered for flies is approximate. Other sizes may also prove themselves useful in certain situations.

Bonefish and Permit

For bonefish, sizes 2, 1, 1/0.

For permit, sizes 1, 1/0, and 2/0. Proper weight is crucial.

- Del's Merkin
- Oversized Crazy Charlies
- Mother of Epoxies
- Clousers
- Modified Puffs

Tarpon

For tarpon over 50 pounds, sizes ranging from 2X strong 2/0 and 3/0 to regular strength 4/0 and 5/0.

For juveniles, try 1/0 and 2/0.

- Apte Tarpon Fly
- Apte II Plus (in a variety of colors)
- Cockroach (natural grizzly is famous, but a variety of dyed tails work)
- Apte II
- Lefty's Deceivers (in a few colors and sizes)

Other Shallow-Water Keys Species

For redfish, 1, 1/0, 2/0, and 3/0—weight as needed.

For trout, ladyfish, and jacks, 1/0 to 3/0. Bottom huggers such as redfish eat over-sized Crazy Charlie-type patterns. Fish feeding in muds readily eat a variety of streamers.

Barracuda

Sizes 1 to 1/0 for pencil-shaped streamers. For bucktails, sizes 2/0-4/0.

Any snake-like flies with braided or glued tails work well. Cobia will take similar flies in sizes 3/0 to 5/0.

Sharks

Sizes 2/0 up to 5/0.

Bulky flies with spun hair heads or lots of hackle–orange is often the best color, but they eat everything.

Offshore Species

For tuna and dolphin, sizes 3/0-5/0.

For inshore snappers, try bonefish and redfish patterns around 1/0. For offshore snappers, use 1/0 to 3/0. For inshore mackerel, try 1/0 through 3/0. Offshore, move up to 3/0 to 5/0.

- Lefty's Deceivers (leaning toward white)
- Bucktails (mostly white with some green or blue backs)

Fly Leaders For The Salt

Not a breath of air stirs the calm Florida Keys basin. Schools of giant tarpon are spiked up, sunbathing with their tails and dorsal fins interrupting the calm surface. Any attempt to cast a fly too close to the fish is met with an explosive boil as you disturb their slumber. It's not the fly that bothers them; it's the impact of your 12-weight fly line on still waters. Increasing the length of your leader to 12 feet provides a buffer and with your next cast a fish is on.

Two days later the weather is not so pleasant. Twenty-knot winds challenge your ability to deliver the fly to marauding Oceanside schools. You've read that a shorter leader is easier to cast, but your fly keeps snagging the fly line, spoiling your presentations. Why?

Today's new saltwater fly lines have very short front tapers designed for one reason only: They make you fast with your delivery. They hit the water hard. The abrupt weight change makes it difficult for the running line to support the head as your casts unroll. A 12-foot tarpon leader is becoming the norm, rather than just a calm day necessity. It softens the effect of the short front taper, allowing a much gentler presentation.

There's another good reason to consider using the same length leader all the time. You don't have to make any mental adjustments to properly place your fly as you analyze fishing opportunities. Few of us fish enough that we don't still get rattled when tarpon go by or practice enough to guarantee we can adjust for different length leaders. You might think a long leader presents a problem throwing toward the wind, but we tend to push too hard when we face the wind, aiding "dumping." I have amazed more than a few of my customers having problems with delivery by lengthened their leaders.

For tarpon we're stuck with a bulky shock leader attached to the fly. The class tippet is relatively fragile and should be as short as IGFA rules allow, fifteen inches. That's measured between the knots, by the way. Help yourself and use the material that will stand up to constant casting abuse. The big guns of fly tarpon angling all use the current year's offering of eight kilogram hard Mason. It's durable and relatively stiff. It's hard to find outside of the Keys so you might construct leaders with stiffer single filament lines advertised as tough rather than skinny.

I like a long double line between the class tippet and my leader butt. I don't believe in loops. First, the term "quick change" for loops is a misnomer. Undoing one loop and properly attaching another is a time consuming process. It's much quicker to cut a leader off and retie with a blood or uni-knot. Second, loops that are drawn closed during periods of excitement are often closed wrong and sometimes fail. If you just spent a week trying to get a good hookup, that's a problem. I usually leave two feet of double line at the end of my pre-tied class tippets for leader attachment on tarpon rigs.

I start with a 9 foot 50- or 60-pound butt nail-knotted to my fly line on tarpon rods. This gives me a 12- to 13-foot leader. I like medium stiff mono for butts. Ande or Trilene works well, but I'll admit to often buying an Eagle Claw-100 yard spool of blue 50-pound for $2.00 at K-Mart. Loops on the ends of fly lines, often recommended, are sloppy. They also represent a point of failure as the leader seldom marries to them cleanly.

This same rig works well for medium to bigger sharks if you substitute wire for shock leaders. I forgot to talk about tarpon shock leaders. Two things are important for shock leaders. Abrasion resistance and our ability to straighten them. You can stretch most 80 or 100-pound mono enough to make a reasonable leader of it, but a perfectly straight shock leader, something that looks like uncooked spaghetti, is better.

I fall right back to hard Mason for shock leaders. If I'm fishing for giant fish I use 80-pound. It has to be pre-stretched and precut. Store your cut shock leaders in 1-inch diameter 2-foot-long PVC tube with crutch cap ends, and they'll stay straight. Everyday fishing is covered with 60-pound. It can be stretched perfectly straight while building leaders, even in the boat.

If you use curvy leaders you'll have to use some type of loop knot to attach flies or they'll swim funny. A straight leader allows you to either snell or use a three-turn clinch knot for fly attachment. The fixed knot appears to provide better hook setting than a loop. A straight shock leader is also less visible to the fish. Sometimes the fish eat better with the fly looped to the leader. It makes a difference if you're fishing do-nothing retrieves.

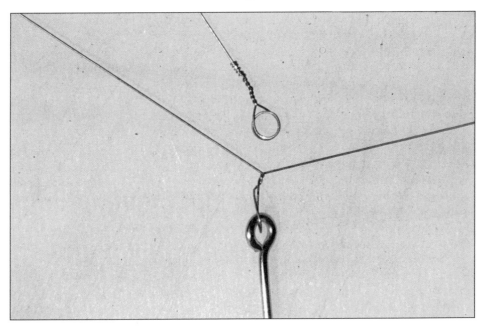

Wire is needed for some Keys species. Getting a good X-series for a haywire twist is easier if you spread the wire wide. Allan Finkelman showed me the hook eye trick. Use a nail and wrap your wire around it twice before making your haywire. You can use any knot you would use to tie a hook on your line when you do this instead of learning something exotic and otherwise useless.

A horseshoe weedguard can be easily added to most bonefish and redfish flies and is usually necessary on lush Keys flats. You just X-wrap thread around it to stand it up and spread it apart.

FOR LESSER FISH

It's hard to call a bonefish a lesser fish, but rigging for fish that don't need shock leaders is much easier than what is required for the big guys. Impact of the line is still a serious consideration for shallow water sight fishing. The very small feeding window of bonefish or redfish place more demands on casting, making it critical to have a well-designed leader that provides consistent delivery.

I use a very simple formula for these leaders. On 7- and 8-weight lines a 30-pound butt is fine. For 9- and 10-weights, utilized for larger flies or windy conditions, a piece of 40 pound works better. I start with a 6- or 7-foot length of Ande or Trilene in the appropriate weight. Next, I add 2 to 3 feet of 20-pound to provide a bit of taper and something to tie tippets to.

Tippets become a very personal matter. I fish heavy flies that work like jigs, so a 3- to 4-foot piece of 12-pound Ande works well for me. If you fish very shallow water tailers with very light flies you many want a piece of finer diameter mono for a tippet. With my stiffer stuff I use a loop knot, preferring a uni-knot loop just to keep the leader from tilting the fly in the water.

As you construct leaders, remember that they have to fish well in your own particular situation. If you have gentle control with your loop a shorter leader may well work for you. Some of the world's best anglers just dribble the fly to the fish, having a perfect understanding of the exact amount of energy needed to just get the fly to them. Others have booming casting styles that require a bit more of a buffer between fly line and fly.

While a lot of anglers write as if there were only one right way to solve any problem, fishing represents a constantly changing set of problems. It's this diversity that maintains our interest. Adjust your tackle and rigging to meet conditions, and you will catch more fish.

Knots For All Reasons

Fishing requires lots of connections, tying lines to hooks and lures in either a fixed or looped fashion, splicing lines together, or attaching shock leaders for fish with gritty lips. There's little agreement about which of the handful of really good knots available is actually the best. Several highly touted connections don't perform well if not tied perfectly, and during hot fishing periods a demanding knot isn't often tied so well.

A guide can't live with poor knots. Customers just don't understand fish escaping for technical reasons. Even worse is fumbling through a set of difficult connections while fish are all around the boat. I decided long ago that simple is better. I needed a knot that would give me a loop for attaching bonefish flies to leaders, put a hook on a hundred- pound shock leader, attach the hundred-pound to a fifteen-pound class tippet, and let me build a leader for my fly rod. Using one knot for everything gives you enough practice to tie it well even if you're in a hurry.

THE UNI-KNOT

I settled on the uni-knot. It does most things very well and if you routinely use if for a variety of tasks, you learn to tie it in the dark. It's a self-securing knot, meaning it will tighten on its own if you're in a hurry and have to throw at fish before you fully tighten all the loops.

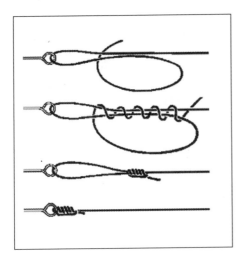
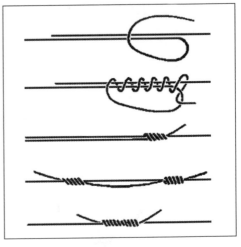

It doesn't get much easier. You fold the tag end back against the standing line then wrap the tag through the loop left by the tag. Five wraps does the trick and you can drop to three wraps with heavier material. To join lines, lay them end-to-end and form knots with both ends.

Hints

When in a big hurry you can use the uni without tightening the tag ends, the knot forms up on its own with the proper number of wraps.

To leave a loop when attaching a fly to lighter lines, just tighten the knot leaving the size loop you want. It will close under the pressure of a fish, giving you a free-swinging bait to fish and the advantage of a fixed connection after hookup. On shock leaders you can form the knot above an overhand knot, which provides a stop when you snug the knot against it.

Drawing on the tag and standing lines in unison is best for attachment when using lines testing over 50 pounds.

When joining two lines of different sizes double the smaller of the two, don't worry about Bimini Twists, and just fold the smaller one back on itself. This is handy for attaching shock leaders without learning any fancy knot.

Lubrication is important in making good knots. Saliva is as good as it gets, just stick the knots in your mouth then tighten.

The uni-knot forms all the connections most needed during a day's fishing. Using one knot let's you quickly become an expert. You can't really use it to form a double line, but you could get by using an extended surgeon's loop. For serious double line needs you should really take the time to learn a Bimini Twist. For low impact species, those that don't jump, a spider hitch works well enough.

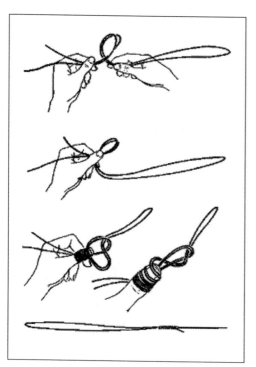

THE SPIDER HITCH

The spider hitch forms a double line more than adequate for most fishing needs and is easy to tie. It does not offer impact resistance equal to a Bimini Twist (required for the biggest fish on the lightest lines).

The spider hitch offers one advantage if you need a double line. It's easily braided. I like a four or five foot double line as a leader for bonefish, permit, or redfish. I make a loop that long and wrap it around my foot. I form a hook on the tag end then twist it between my fingers 20 or so times. I hold it, and then run a hand down the loop. I then let the twisted line spin within my fingers against the untwisted portion. It immediately twists together. I tie my spider hitch with the married lines.

The twisted line idea works with a loop formed by a Bimini Twist, too. In the leader section I said I like a long double line to tie to the leader butt when tarpon fishing. If you cut the loop formed by your double line, you can twist it around a finger and braid it. Oddly, the braid holds. Stick a finger between the legs of the cut double line and twist the pair together.

You'll find uses for other knots, but these give you a good start.

HANDLING THE SHOCK

One innovation stands out in the evolution of fly angling for giant fish. The development of the Albright Knot, furnishing a secure connection of heavy shock leaders to class tippets, eliminated abrasion concerns while fishing for tarpon and billfish. Still considered the ultimate knot for use with wire leaders, the Albright has been replaced for monofilament work in many locales by the Huffnagle.

The Huffnagle is easier for most anglers to tie well. It also offers more consistency in shock leader length. This consistency is difficult to attain with the Albright. IGFA rules require shock leader lengths of less than 12 inches from the eye of the hook to the single line of the class tippet for record consideration. Not fishing for world records? Use the easier uni connection and have fun. As the size of the fish increases a Bimini becomes more important and will actually help in the construction of the connecting knot.

While few of us will ever throw at a 200-pound tarpon, the opportunity to hook a giant permit or outsized shark remains quite real. Even big bonefish will swallow tarpon flies in the right conditions. Many world records are caught simply as a matter of chance, and proper rigging allows anglers to submit outstanding catches.

Shock leaders have a use for smaller species as well. Bluefish often eat flies better when tied to mono instead of wire. Redfish, trout, and ladyfish, for example, have mouths rough enough to justify a 20- to 30-pound trace. While one fish may not work through a leader, fast action finds us forgetting to re-tie flies to leaders, leaving lesser line vulnerable to abrasion.

The accompanying photos show 60-pound hard Mason leader material for the shock leader. It has about the same diameter as 100-pound Ande, a good substitute. I prefer the hard material for two reasons. I feel it is more abrasion resistant. I can also carry it in coils and straighten it in the boat as I construct leaders. Soft material usually requires all kinds of gymnastics to straighten.

I feel perfectly straight shock leaders are important for visibility and fly-riding concerns. A loop does eliminate any problems with fly attitude on less than straight leaders.

THE HUFFNAGLE KNOT

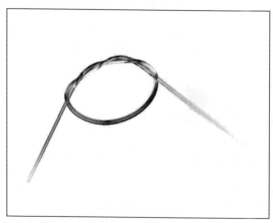

1. *A figure-8 knot forms the basis of our connection. If you're serious about a 12-inch leader, it's easiest to control your leader length if you start with the fly attached to the leader. Start an overhand knot about 10½ to 10¾ inches from the eye of the hook and poke the tag end through it twice like a Surgeons Knot.*

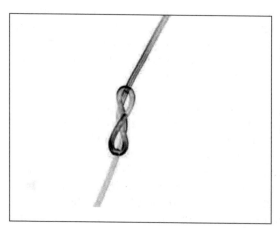

2. *When you snug this up a bit, it forms a nice figure-8.*

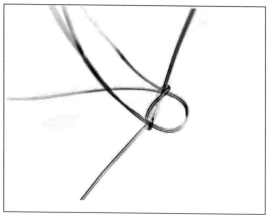

3. *Pass the loop of your doubled class tippet through both ends of the figure-8, headed toward the hook.*

4. *After snugging the figure-8, tie the double line around the shock leader with a pair of overhand knots. A firm and steady pull on the double line while snugging the first overhand knot should close the figure-8 knot. It's helpful to hook your fly or lure around something firm while pulling this together. You might also want to use pliers on the tag end of the shock material.*

5. *The next step is a three turn clinch knot formed by wrapping the tag of the double line between the double line and shock leader. It helps to guide the wraps with one hand while snugging with the other.*

6. *A properly finished knot is very compact with no gap between the wraps of the Bimini Twist and the figure-8.*

THE ALBRIGHT KNOT

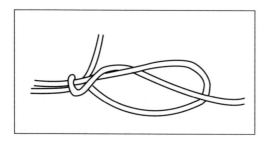

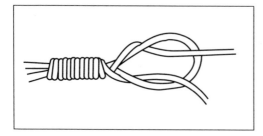

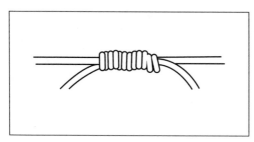

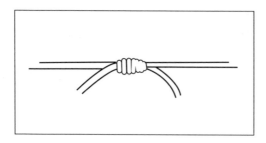

This is the knot that started it all and it has many uses. While the Huffnagle is preferred for serious mono-to-mono work, the Albright is still the best knot for attaching mono to wire when simply folding the wire back or attaching backing to fly line, unless you prefer loops. To tie:

- Simply fold a loop in the tag end of the heaviest material

- Wrap your running line, whether single or doubled, through the loop and then around it

- Make a dozen wraps of running line around the loop headed toward the running line

- Then bring the tag back through the loop. It should look like a square knot

- Draw it tight. Many are convinced the knot will slip with some materials, so they improve it. A couple of half hitches or even a three-turn clinch knot as used with the Huffnagle provides a sense of security

THE BIMINI TWIST

I'm intentionally not providing step-by-step pictures of this knot, as they tend to confuse rather than help. This is a very simple knot to tie if you use just a couple of simple tricks. First, form a doubled line of your desired length and leave about a foot to a foot and a half of tag to work with. Second, hold your standing line and tag together in one, grab the end of the loop with the other, and twist the loop about 20 times.

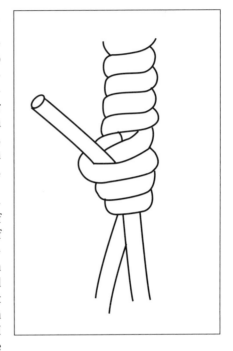

Next, fix the end of the loop to something secure. A knee, or both knees, isn't it. If you're tying a short double line, step in it. If it's too long, put it on a boat cleat, a doorknob, or even a nail. Keep a firm hold on your tag and standing line in one hand, and stick your other hand in the loop. The next step is extra: I like to take the tag in my teeth until I can reach it with the loop hand. I might also wrap the standing line above the knot around my hand, giving me a firm base to work with.

Shove your loop hand toward the knot forming hand. Take a break when you can reach the tag, then grab it with your thumb and forefinger. Now you can snug the Xs up as tight as you want and the tag will wrap over them in a tight barrel for you all by itself. You can guide the wraps with your thumb and forefinger to keep it pretty.

Tie a single overhand knot over each leg of your loop. Tie a three-turn clinch knot over the doubled line and cut the tag. For fly leaders you can draw one of these down about a half-inch with stiff tarpon material, but you don't have to. If you're not pulling tight enough on the tags to break it once in a while, you're not trying hard enough.

Chart Your Way To Success

Charts are maps of the water and you have to have them to find your way through the maze of Keys shallows or to deep-water structure. Their value goes far beyond that for anglers. Once you find fish, you can search for similar chunks of water on your charts and build an inventory of fishing spots.

Before we go too far I have to caution you. No chart in this book is adequate for navigation. They're not big enough to provide any sense of scale. Sadly, when you buy full-sized charts of the Keys, you'll find they don't show a fair portion of obstructions or hidden lakes within many flats.

Expect crowds around many hot spots that are easily identified on the charts. Poking around a bit will turn up more likely bits of structure than you can ever fish. Many "off the chart" sorts of places provide better fishing than some obvious spots and offer a little solitude. A few examples of inshore and offshore terrain should help you figure out what to look for.

The charts are far more helpful in the depths than they are in the shallows, which makes little sense to me. You will find that a variety of important terrain features are not shown on the charts. Prepare for a lot of surprises when you poke your nose into "uncharted" waters. They offer a wealth of fishing opportunities, but without a thorough understanding of how tides work and an ability to read the water, can trap you, too. I once saw a skiff high and dry on a flat that was owned by a guide who only had 51 years of experience at the time! Poke around, but go slow.

Charts provide a lot of clues about where fish forage and where they run into roadblocks. We want to find the roadblocks when fish are migrating seasonally or moving in response to weather changes. We also have to find foraging spots for species we hope to ambush while they feed.

An aerial view of Highway 1.

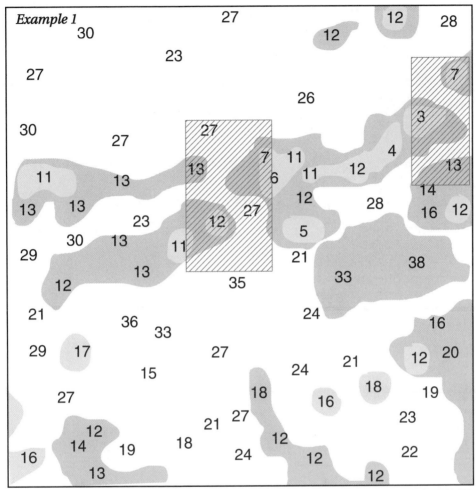

© WILDERNESS ADVENTURES PRESS, INC.

Example 1. A small part of an inner reef reveals all sorts of fishing opportunities. The small circles surrounding numbers indicate steep rises off the bottom. Most hold some sort of fish, but those showing "live" bottom—evidenced by sharply contrasting color schemes while you're on the water—usually hold the most, as well as the most interesting, fish. Groups of numbers on the chart surrounded by odd shaped contours mark much larger areas of raised bottom. Note a couple of obvious funnels through the barrier appearing much like channels. Narrowing passages and rises always focus water flows. They will often concentrate bait and predators. When water flows tumble across the end of the reef they might attract sailfish, kingfish, larger grouper, mutton snappers, and wahoo.

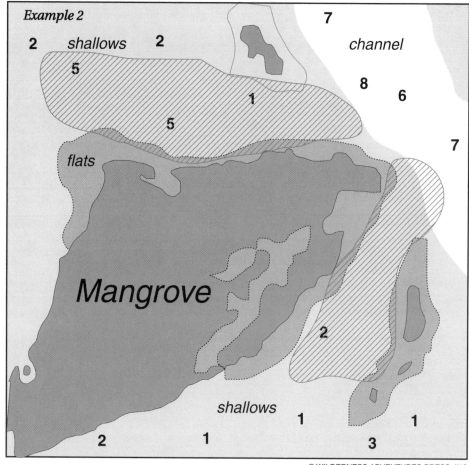

© WILDERNESS ADVENTURES PRESS, INC.

Example 2. *You might "slam," or catch a tarpon, bonefish, and permit in a Gulfside spot like this. Rising water comes from the top of the chart. The left edge of the channel slants a bit across the main flow of current so the current pushes fish toward the shallows. Fish filter past both sides of the point of the island reaching toward the channel. The small basin on the north side of the island is a welcome retreat for tarpon, sometimes big ones. Bonefish and permit flood along the edges. When the tide falls back toward the channel, fish will retreat from the basin along with the water. The shallower area on the south side of the point represents a potential travel spot, too, while the little strip of shallows in the deeper water will concentrate current and likely attract digging fish like bones and permit. The region is loaded with little spots like this. They may not always hold a lot of fish, but those you find will be easy to feed most of the time, and you often have them all to yourself.*

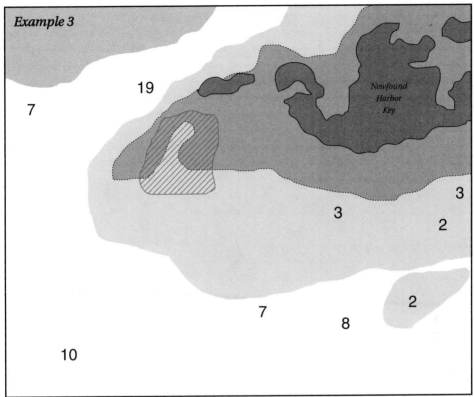

Example 3

19

7

Newfound
Harbor
Key

3

3

2

2

7

8

10

© WILDERNESS ADVENTURES PRESS, INC.

Example 3. *On the west end of Newfound Harbor lies a typical, definitive tarpon ambush spot. It's easily identifiable on the chart. You can see an obvious slot dug into the flat on the chart and on the water. On a rising tide, tarpon are shoved into the slot when routed around the final point if they are headed toward Key West from Miami. The spot is relatively worthless for several reasons. It's best only for westbound fish. It works on only one tide. The boat traffic in the channel behind it is excessive, and most folks can't stand up in a boat once the channel fills with those headed for the reef and beyond. The spot is a good example of what you can look for on the chart and on the water, though. You might catch a fish here, too, if you get out at sunrise or spend the last hour of the day here during the proper tide.*

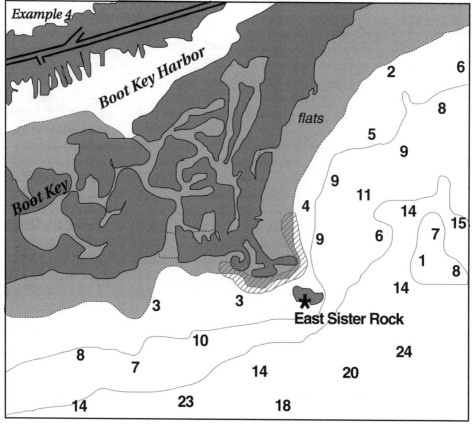

© WILDERNESS ADVENTURES PRESS, INC.

Example 4. *You must use your imagination to find Middle Keys tarpon spots. Little on this chart suggests their presence. A small circle on the chart named E. Sister Rock is a small island. There is a point just to the northwest. A bit of a bar extends between the point and the island. Tarpon cross it only for an hour or two on each tide when headed west and some small fish use it when headed east. The spot will teach you a lot about how tides move fish. The west-bound fish cross the bar when tides are weak, but a hard moving incoming current pushes them far off the obvious edge as the water flows like a river from the west. Schools of fish may roll when they hit the bar from the depths, but you'll seldom see singles and pairs approaching the bank. Odd things happen here, though. There is a ditch against the shoreline, protected by a rock jetty. Some fish hug the Vaca Key Bight shoreline, and then wander through the ditch. When the fish turn around to head east, many of them travel at almost bonefish depths while moving from the Seven Mile Bridge. There are some other secrets here you'll have to discover on your own.*

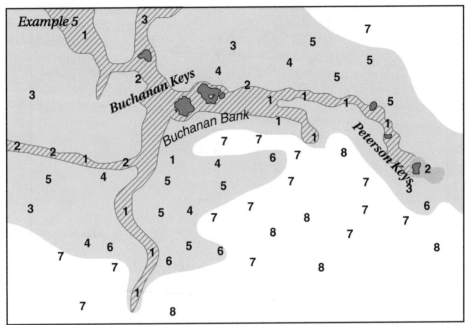

Example 5. *This area on the Gulfside of Matecumbe Key shows a great example of missing or confusing information on a chart. There is an extensive strip bank, a long relatively narrow flat, extending between the Buchanan and Peterson Keys banks. It's shown only as some numbers and not shaded or colored. Just west of Buchanan Keys is another long strip bank extending toward the ocean, also displayed only as a series of small numbers. Connect the 1s in your mind and you've located the bank. There's a bank running off to the left here for about a mile and a half that doesn't even show up as numbers.*

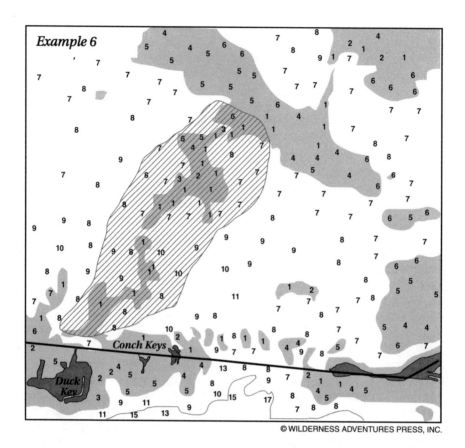

© WILDERNESS ADVENTURES PRESS, INC.

Example 6. *This is a rather bland appearing chart until you take the time to look at the numbers. Behind the bridge, or on the Gulfside, you'll find a series of banks marked by little more than small numbers. Incoming tides come from the Atlantic, at the bottom of the chart, and push tarpon into corners. Permit love the hard charge of water focused against the banks. Since much of the water is relatively deep, you'll find some pretty big barracudas here. The chart may lack color because the bottom seems rather sterile as it is mostly hard cap coral with a minimum of grass cover, but the area still holds good numbers of small- to medium-sized bonefish.*

A Word On Navigation

Navigation in the Keys is a bit tricky. The extent of the shallows is surprising to many visitors and offers serious challenges for even the most experienced boat operators. Some conditions conspire to make travel from point to point downright treacherous.

There is a cute little ditty offering color as a suggestion for avoiding problems in the shallows. It goes something like this: Brown, brown–run aground. White, white–you just might. Green, green–nice and clean. Brown works most of the time, representing the shallowest of water. White could be a bar, but it also could be a deep slot through an otherwise shallow area. Green is rather subjective. Bright green is often a channel or water off an edge. Dark green, like a forest canopy, is more likely a coral head in the shallows, but could represent a lush flat.

The ditty also assumes you can actually see color in spite of the light. When the sun is behind the clouds and viewing is complicated by glare, everything looks the same. There is no substitute for sound preparation and caution. You should never embark on a Keys boating journey without a current chart. Even with a chart you can be at a disadvantage, as it will not reveal every obstacle.

The Keys are very poorly marked, and rudimentary markers placed by well-intentioned folks are often jerked out of the water by those hoping to curtail additional boat traffic. Some think newcomers do not deserve the use of traditional routes if they can't read them. Even our government complicates matters. In the '90s, the U.S. Fish and Wildlife Service suggested they did not want to mark passages in some refuges because too many people might find their way into them. Somehow I thought taxpayers owned those waters. Both sets of folks complain mightily when you run aground, though they refuse you basic navigational tools.

The U.S. Coast Guard is no help, refusing to install affordable markers not meeting their standards or to alter their relatively confusing channel marking system. Even when money exists to install complying markers, they sometimes offer no help. For instance, in my neighborhood the markers at the Gulfside end of the Indian Key channel lie some 300 yards from the actual end of the channel. Slashing toward the west edge marker from the Gulf might put you aground. The markers are poorly placed and too far apart to properly mark the channel. And this is one of the better-marked channels in the Keys.

There are no substitutes for experience and caution. If you're lucky, you'll have a somewhat windy day. If the wind is with the current, channels might appear relatively calm, but waves build in them when the current reverses toward the wind. It's a good clue. The edges should give off a small standing wave pattern. If you have light, you might use the ditty to an advantage. In lakes or broad basins, those deep areas between flats, waves again help. Calming water suggests you are approaching a protected shallow edge. Steepening wave action indicates building water pressure against an edge.

Throughout much of the Keys, you can't reach a destination you can see from where you are by running a straight line. Many boaters head at bridges without aligning themselves in the channels. Cuts through many flats are miles apart. Explore calmly in the Keys. Learning to navigate is much like learning to see fish. It takes time and is never quite mastered.

This mad dog weighed over 140 pounds.

It All Depends On The Weather

The wind howled and the sun gave off little more than a faint glow through the clouds. While we struggled against the elements, the bonefish we sought marched down the edge we guarded as if on a mission. Clouds of glass minnows showered in their path as they hurried toward their destination. As water levels rose, the fish pushed higher on the edge of the flat. Finally, a bit of structure shoved them around the boat at an angle we could handle with a fly rod in the wind. The fish pushed wakes anyone could see once they knew what to look for, and the fish fought over a fly in their face until it disappeared within a hungry mouth.

It was a day when many would consider staying home if they wanted to catch a fish on a fly. The wind blew almost 30 knots, but bonefish often eat like pigs on such days. The day had little to do with catching fish, though. It was a training exercise. At the time I was fishing several Islamorada fly tournaments each year with Allan Finkleman and this was my chance to teach him how to catch waking fish. He fed 34 of them as they charged around the boat, enough to learn the vagaries of hooking fish eating on the run and shoving hard at the boat. It was lesson that served us both well years later.

This was a late winter day set up by pretty conditions encouraging the fish to move in the Upper Florida Keys backcountry. The morning's wind announced an approaching cold front. The fish took heed and headed toward the warmer Atlantic. They were still comfortable, though, and took advantage of every feeding opportunity along the way. There's no way to predict a bonanza like this during fringe periods of the year, for Keys bonefish or other species. This was a random event with slow fishing the day before and after.

Unfortunately, we're often stuck with what we get. Many anglers visit from out-of-state to get away from rotten weather at home. Floridians travel great distances, too, hoping to see new water and catch a dream species. As a guide, I deal with marginal out-of-season days and rotten condition days in season with mixed emotions. I do need to make a living, but expectations are tough to meet with random conditions and many only get a day or two a year to fulfill a dream. Earning money still takes a back seat to considerations of delivering on a promise.

I have a pain quotient during the winter. There are few days you cannot fish in the Keys and expect to catch something if it's safe to put the boat in the water. There are many days when catching the fish of choice is unlikely.

I won't take an angler fishing under several circumstances. If the water is too cold for the only fish you seek, we stay home. Temperatures in the 50s create a real problem on the flats for glamour species the first day or two. In the 60s you may or may not find fish, depending on whether temperatures are rising or falling. Fish flee on the bottom end of temperature ranges, but return more quickly than many think as water warms. Still, returning fish are likely to hang deep and remain a pretty tough catch for inexperienced anglers.

Wind is another factor when it's cool. Twenty knots is a cutoff point for me unless I am reasonably certain my angler can handle it, and I am sure I can provide downwind shots with the prevailing wind and current pushing toward fish I can identify in the water. I've fished with plenty of people who can fish when it blows 30 knots, but they represent a gifted minority. This is primarily a flyfishing book after all, but good bait guides and anglers have more leeway when the weather is naughty. Bad weather sometimes leads to pretty hot bites, though, and often leads to spectacular catches.

One thing to consider is the length and arc of the Keys. What is not a nice day in my Upper Keys neighborhood is potentially fine 40 miles down the road. The broad Gulf does not chill like Florida Bay in the winter and the morning through midday sun angle is better as you head west. Later in the year, with a different wind, the advantage might shift back to the east. During prime time we put up with a bit more wind since we should find fish. I have no mercy when it is warm if I feel I can find downwind fish for my fly anglers and gritty conditions are often great for bait folks.

If you're headed offshore the fishing is often better the rougher it is—within limits. Water never gets so cold fish won't bite and plunging temperatures often stuff fish grocery stores with tons of food.

The toughest questions I get from folks planning trips to my area deal totally with expectations. A common question is: What can I expect to catch on a one- or two-day trip six months from today? I don't have a clue in many cases, as the random date is usually off-season. I drove my tournament customers nuts, refusing to tell them even the night before what the next day might bring.

I need to see the sky, the direction and strength of the wind, water levels, and how hard the tide is pushing, before I know where I'm going. Some factors may suggest I spend the day 20 miles from where I might have started if things were different. A major temperature swing adds to the problem.

Of course, there are many situations throughout the Keys one might consider a lock. Major migrations of favored inshore and offshore species happen with enough consistency that we can believe a trip for them during prime time is a sure bet. In the last five years before I wrote this, though, tarpon have missed the Keys once in May, left well before the end of June in another year, and never showed up at Homosassa on Florida's west coast. Sometimes bonefishing is a better choice.

Kingfish were two months early along the South Florida coast the fall of 1999 for no apparent reason and wahoo fishing was better than ever around the state for an extended period in '97. In 1999 and 2000, we had king mackerel in the Keys during September, and 2000 was the one of the best billfish years ever on record here. We had few kingfish in 1998 and have few again in early winter 2000, but 1999 was a great year for them.

After a December cold front passes in Florida's panhandle, inshore species congregate in the creeks, rivers, and channels. You don't expect tarpon on the beach and immediately head to the creeks for your rod bending exercise. You know the most likely months to find cobia on rays, too, and fish for something else when they're not around. It's typically glamour species and travel considerations that color your judgment.

I'm as guilty as the next angler of bouts of fuzzy focus. It's easy to wake up and remember all the fish you found the day before and plan a rematch. You might fail to notice the wind is now in your face instead of at your back while approaching your magic spot. The shift may add a foot of water to, or blow as much water off, the flat or point you intend to guard. Offshore, it may move bait several miles from a wreck, reef edge, or narrow offshore ledge covered up the day before.

Things do get confusing when traveling to destinations with good weather much of the year. Finding temperatures 30 to 40 degrees warmer than they are at home fools many of us. It may seem like spring or summer to you, but if you need to wear a jacket while running from spot to spot, the fish think it's cold. If you see guides putting on gloves before they leave docks and ramp sites in South Florida, you might expect snook or redfishing to be okay, but forget about tarpon and wait until later in the day or even the week to look for bonefish.

Much of this discussion involves inshore fishing. The offshore set seems less prone to glamour species induced tunnel vision. You might have set your mind on a 15-pound mutton, but a 20-pound grouper seems to ease any disappointment. Thoughts of sailfish easily fade when surrounded by a cloud of slammer dolphin.

It's a bit easier to make a day offshore, too, not that the fishing is any more guaranteed than it is inshore. You have room to carry lots of tackle and you can cover lots

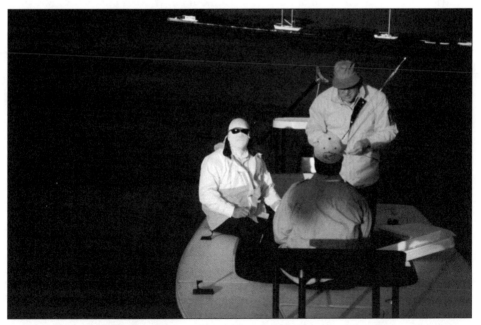

Fishing is pretty tough on days when we dress like this! This was the morning of a Redbone tournament and participants from northern climes laughed about the 55-degree weather until we ran them into a 20-knot wind at 30 knots. The 20-degree wind chill had them begging for more clothes.

of situations with a couple of basic rigs. Twenty-pound kingfish rods do duty on sails, dolphin, and many bottom species. A ten-pound rig provides opportunities to catch and enjoy a lot of lesser species while giving you a shot at a few gamier critters.

Of course, you can play copycat in the shallows. I've knotted 60-pound shock leaders to eight-pound double lines so customers could throw at surprise finds of laid-up tarpon many times. Tying a ¼-ounce jig on the end of a 20-pound spinner you intended for tarpon does not provide the same thrill when all you can find is trout in a mullet mud. Realistic expectations and flexible tackle choices lead to pleasant surprises on many days. Butting your head against a wall of marginal conditions usually produces little more than headaches. Unfortunately, it's common activity.

Bonefish and tarpon are likely the two targets most confusing to anglers. You hit the Keys or Biscayne Bay in February and it sure seems warm to you. It may indeed be 75 degrees and water temperatures may hit 71 or 72 degrees during midday. Talented guides and anglers can find bonefish in this situation if the tide is right. Most of the fish are mudding. If you've never fished for mudding fish, rocket science seems far easier. You may catch a fish or two, though. Unfortunately, many visitors wander home thinking bonefishing is some deep, dark, and mysterious pursuit.

If catching a bonefish or two is your life's goal you might succeed, but you probably missed a great day on the water. With a bit of wire leader, I'd bet you could have thrown to sharks all day with shrimp or a chunk of ballyhoo. A lipless minnow plug or a tube lure hung from the same wire might disappear a dozen or more times within the toothy jaws of barracudas.

Be realistic about your marginal season pursuits. The secret is admitting the weather stinks at home and you need to bend a rod. Take what the day offers you. If your goal is to catch a specific species, don't force the issue. Stay home and save your money for a prime time trip. Many folks, including scribes, will laugh at me for telling you how good summer and fall bonefishing is in the Keys. In the Upper Keys backcountry, it's the best in the world. Give me five days during spring tides, and on at least three of them, I'll show you 100 schools of fish a day as will most competent local guides. Bonefishing is fun, not a chore, under such conditions.

WHEN THE FISH ARE HERE

I had some trepidation about providing the seasonal fish chart at the end of this section. If you're patient and lucky, you can catch the most abundant of species frequenting Keys waters almost any month of the year. There are a few windows of opportunity you should take advantage of both inshore and off, and some sense of season does make things easier.

The largest concentration of tarpon in the Keys filters by during the May and June migration. You may find them coming as early as April and holding on through much of July. A specialist might catch you a fish any time during the year and the summer through fall fishery for smaller fish is pretty good. If you want to fish prime time, you should try to find a guide by August or September a year ahead of your trip, but some great guides have days open longer than you might expect. It is a business, and there is always a turnover of customers.

Bonefish are year-round targets if you can deal with conditions, but prime time is when tides begin improving during late spring and lasts through fall. Prime bone time is also prime permit and redfish season.

Dolphin fishing is hot as early as March and the good bite lasts through June, but you can catch some fish almost year round depending on the weather. Barracuda fishing inshore is often best when there is nothing else to do. They stack up on the flats after the nastiest cold fronts and are hard to find in good numbers when it is pretty.

Late fall through winter is mackerel season. Kings stack up offshore, ceros cover the patch reefs, and Spanish flood the Gulf and are now also congregating around bridges and over some patches.

Tuna join mackerel in a seasonal flood but may hang on for months longer along with bonito. Their season overlaps with sailfish. Sailfishing lights up when cold fronts attack the Keys beginning in October or November in the Upper Keys, though Lower Keys fishing is often best during a spawning migration in April and May.

There are seasons of sorts for grouper and snappers, but one variety or another is available almost anytime. The worse the weather is in the rest of the world, the better it gets for Keys cobia fishing. It is basically a winter pursuit, but as I write this in the fall of 2000, they are everywhere.

Keys weather is not the only determining factor in the quality of fishing for many migratory species. Extended warm spells along either the Gulf or lower East Coast of the United States may hold fish elsewhere for weeks while we wait. On the other hand, early or extended cold can send fish our way or leave them with us well outside of seasonal norms. The fish may lock onto unusual hordes of bait elsewhere, too, and not follow their regular migratory prey.

Just because it's the season and things seem okay to us means little to the fish. May 2001 was an example of things being almost right but never quite making it most of the time. Tarpon tolerate water temperatures about 72 to 74 degrees. They far prefer water temperatures nearer 80 and put up with a bit of extra wind or wind from an odd direction. Add a touch of north or west into the wind and leave the temps barely at 75, and the fish are tough to find on the flats.

While many species have preferred water temperatures, they do have to feed sometime. Bonefish may flee flats when water temperatures sink below 70 degrees, but you may find them warming in corners with water temperatures in the high 50s or low 60s as weather improves. Wintertime stalwarts, such as trout, ladyfish, and jacks, might eat fine in deeper channels on days with 60-degree temperatures.

KEYS FISH SPECIES AVAILABLE BY MONTH

Water type / Species	Jan.	Feb.	March	April	May	June	July	Aug.	Sept	Oct	Nov	Dec
Flats												
Tarpon	A*	A*	A*	A*	PT	PT	A	A	A	A		
Bonefish	A	A	A	PT	PT	PT	PT	PT	PT	PT	A	A
Permit	A	A	A	A	PT	PT	PT	PT	PT	A	A	A
Redfish	A	A	A	PT	PT	PT	PT	PT	PT	A	A	A
Seatrout	PT	PT	PT	PT	A	A	A	A	A	A	PT	PT
Snook					PT	PT						
Ladyfish	PT	PT	PT	PT	A	A	A	A	A	A	PT	PT
Jack Crevalle	PT	PT	A	A	A	A	A	A	A	PT	PT	PT
Variable Depths												
Barracuda	PT	PT	PT									PT
Cobia	PT	PT	PT									
Spanish Mackerel	PT	PT									A	PT
Cero Mackerel	PT	PT	PT									PT
Off-Shore												
Tuna	PT	PT	PT	A	A	A				A	PT	PT
Sailfish	PT	PT	PT	PT	A	A				A	PT	PT
King Mackerel	PT	PT	A	A							A	PT
Dolphin			A	PT	PT	PT	PT	A	PT	PT	A	A
Wahoo			PT	PT	A	A	A	PT	PT	P	A	
Grouper	PT	PT	PT	PT	PT	A	A	A	PT	PT	PT	
Snappers	A	A	PT	PT	PT	A	A	A	A	PT	A	
Amberjack		A	A	PT	PT	A	A	A				

PT = Prime Time (Ideal time to target this species)

A = Available (This species can be found)

*The harbor in Key West holds tarpon in the winter. We get tarpon as soon as the weather warms and turns calm. A blank month, like the stretch of them behind barracudas, does not mean you cannot catch a cuda those months. But the fishing is much better during the winter, and there are other species to target from spring through fall. If you want to have a good time, come anytime. If you harbor dreams of catching a favorite species, come in the prime months.

MONTHLY HOPES

It's been my great privilege to contribute to *Florida Sportsman* magazine since 1990 and share monthly fishing potential with readers since 1995. While there are historically normal patterns to fish movements, some change dramatically from year to year. My monthly column of fishing prospects, written on a relatively timely basis, helps many visitors adjust to and take advantage of changes. As you might expect, I strongly suggest you become a subscriber to the magazine to keep up with current recommendations.

The following excerpts, taken from 1999 and 2000, provide a more thorough idea of what is usually happening throughout the year in the Keys—both inshore and offshore. Of course, every new season brings its own surprises.

January 1999

Occasional chilly weather throughout Florida encourages a wide variety of game species to visit the Keys during January. Even here, a chill may concentrate fish in the warmer depths inshore and off. This leads to great fishing for those prepared to take advantage of the situations weather provides.

We can find some fish on top or at mid-depths, but bottom huggers often provide the steadiest action. A mistake many of us make is not using enough weight to plumb the bottom. Sinking baits into the depths is not the only reason to use plenty of lead. A reasonably tight line allows us to feel subtle takes we might miss on lines bowed against the wind or current.

We do catch a few little bonefish in the Keys, sometimes even when it's cold.

Offshore it may take a pound or more of lead to sink a horse ballyhoo or a whole mullet to structure in lots of current at depths as shallow as 100 feet. You might get by at the same depth with a slab-sided jig weighing half as much if you're sweetening it with narrow profile pilchards or herring. Either way, you need rods capable of supporting the weight of your terminal tackle, with enough reserve butt strength to help you set the hook and get a fish moving toward the boat right away.

You can work offshore with anything from a 12- to 30-pound rod. I tend to avoid rods for any serious fishing work if they bend into the butt at rated line breaking strengths. Rods rated for twice the breaking strength of the line you think you need, typically do the job with appropriate food when you're drifting and jigging, or dropping baits. You can use a rod rated for 8- to 15-pound line as a 12-pound rod if you like, but it will feel mushy and force you to play fish instead of letting you fight them.

Good starting points this month are the numerous public domain artificial reefs scattered the length of the Keys. Most hold muttons and a couple species of grouper during January. In the Middle and Lower Keys a few amberjacks will harass you too. While all species will respond with enthusiasm to live baits, sweetened jigs should catch you a limit.

The ticket to success with jigs in the deep is sweeping them off the bottom then allowing them to flutter back a bit while maintaining a tight line. Bites are often indicated by no more than a different "feel" of the jig as you bounce it. It may get heavier or lighter in your mind. There's no penalty for a false hook set and any odd sensation could be a take.

A bit of lead can play a role in lesser depths. January is often a great month on Keys patch reefs for muttons, mangroves, and junior groupers. While a chum line often gets bait fired up, predators may hold deep, waiting for larger chunks of food to sink or for prey species to rest in cover. A ¼- or ½-ounce egg sinker should be enough to sink your bait to the bottom and let it "tick" along as it drifts in the current on an open-bailed spinning rig.

Live shrimp, ballyhoo, and squid chunks make adequate baits for sandwich-sized keepers. If you hope for something more, any live wiggly critter is usually a better bait. Anchored hoos or pilchards work well for muttons. Kite-suspended blue runners or cigar minnows work for cero mackerels or barracudas on a regular basis and muttons or groupers crawl to the top to swallow them, too.

Mackerels are in abundance this month throughout the Keys at various depths. You'll find kings off the outer reef wherever current flows are concentrated by humps or notches. Fish really worth catching love dorsal hooked blue runners but also respond to cigar minnows and pilchards. You'll catch lots of dinner-sized fish on lesser baits. Expect bunches of ceros on the patches. They'll chomp on the predominate bait in your chum line, a live free lined shrimp, or you can fool them with plugs and flies.

The Gulf behind Marathon was lousy with Spanish mackerel last year and also harbored some bluefish. Moderately discolored water here is home to lots of food most of the time. Bunches of ballyhoo haunt strip banks and wrecks throughout the winter and attract lots of predators. Flipping and skipping baits usually indicate nearby predators.

The bottom here is littered with wrecks attractive to cobia and mangroves. Many wrecks were moved a bit by Hurricane George so you might take advantage of bright calm days to find them again whenever the water is clean enough to allow peering to the bottom. While hunting with your GPS, marking areas with lots of potholes is a worthwhile activity too. Snappers and ceros claim many potholes as home or as ambush sites and more than a few hold legal grouper much of the year.

Weight brings rewards in the shallows, too. In the upper reaches of Florida Bay, snook and redfish prefer jigs bouncing along the bottom in the areas many with run outs and creeks. Sweetened jigs drifted in the current are attractive to bigger mangroves. In ditches with 4- to 6-foot depths, you can fool plenty of fish with ¼-ounce jigs. As depth or current increases, though, you may need ¾- or even one-ounce jigs to properly puff along the bottom.

I suspect we'll have red-hot trout fishing in the Keys Gulf this month. While creeks and run outs will concentrate some fish, time spent in open water may turn up some surprises. For instance the area between Schooner Bank and the southwest Florida coast is riddled with potholes and shallow ridges. Bouncing jigs ahead of the boat as you drift or dragging baits behind you may well turn up some outsized catches. Don't be surprised if you pick up a Spanish mackerel once in a while, either. The scene should repeat itself in 6 to 10 feet of water all the way to Marathon.

Spanish mackerel fishing improved dramatically after Florida's net ban.

If you find lots of bird activity in the area you'll likely find macks and a few blue-fish tearing up baits. The fish will respond to jigs, spoons, or swimming and popping plugs. In open water, the fish are perfect quarry for 8- to 10-pound spinning rigs or 8- and 9-weight fly rods. On great days you may drift in fish for hours.

Best Bet

Sailfish are winter's glamour species in the Keys, exciting visitors and locals alike. There are few secrets for success but some solid preparation often leads to catches while lazy anglers suffer.

Fortunately, Keys fish are not as bait picky as those in other areas. No Keys cap-tain would turn down a bait well full of goggle eyes for sure, but ballyhoo work just as well when they are plentiful. Sailfish are easily fooled by a variety of hand-sized baits, though. Pinfish, blue runners, cigar minnows, large pilchards or herring, and even a grunt, might catch you a fish.

Do not overlook the power of mullet. We often think of them as shallow water baits since we find them foraging in less water than needed to float many skiffs. Sails can't refuse them.

Low light conditions are often best for sails. Baits in the water before about 8:30 A.M. or after 4:00 P.M. typically attract the most bites. Keys sails often corral their own snacks then too, pushing food to the surface. Chasing showers provides us a chance to swoop in and toss baits to fish we can see.

Spinning rigs spooled with 12- to 15-pound line are usually adequate for most fish if they carry 300 yards of line and sport butter-smooth drags. There is a trend in recent years toward lighter shock leaders, with many folks dipping to 40-pound monofilament. It's doubtful sails are leader shy but the lighter leaders may allow baits a bit more freedom. Sails seem to love the chase and lively baits are far more attractive to them.

While you may find fish on top of the inner reef in as little as 10 feet of water, most of the action centers in 120 feet or more of water. The fish usually push along the reef throughout the day and hanging around obvious bait concentrations should lead to a hookup or two.

February 1999

Sometimes it's easy to forget how different fishing is along the 122 mile length of the Keys. Picking the right region frequently has a lot to do with winter success for specific targets. Each area offers different fall-back opportunities. Don't look at the Keys on a highway map to plan a fishing trip. You'll need charts to study watery real estate. If you're planning a trip weeks ahead, go with the generalizations.

A lot of species—most mackerel, a changing variety of grouper or snappers, blackfin tuna, and barracuda—are almost universally available throughout the Keys with small seasonal variations. For others, hot bites might be very localized within seasons or within specific habitat. You can have fun anywhere in the Keys most of the time. When on a mission, do some homework.

Fishing conversations express a lot of "ifs" when we start looking at several thousand square miles of fishy water and dozens of worthy target species. Generally, the Upper Keys are accepted as a best bet for mid-winter sailfishing. Mild cold fronts often shove South Florida fish on their way to the Upper Keys but it might take a smoker to push them to Marathon or beyond. Since the biggest concentrations are coming and going here, you get a few more shots at the fish.

It is possible to find red-hot sailfishing in the Middle and Lower Keys if it stays cold for a while or if bait lures them in. Fishing may well be even better here as fish gang up on hordes of bait as the fishery is somewhat ignored. The locals are ready to help you catch fish, but lots of visitors don't take advantage of it. You can jump on this knowledge if you're fishing at the end of the week and can believe the weather forecast or respond to current fishing reports.

If you want a tarpon, head to Key West for a reasonable shot during most conditions this month and maybe next. Key West fishing often involves chumming with shrimp by-catch, or a well full of white baits. It's typically a deep basin or boat channel game, but nice weather can put fish where the sun quickly warms shallow ledges. In February it takes calm conditions or at least calm edges to do the job.

If it's reasonably warm and moderately calm, you may find fish at any major Keys channel, but Marathon's Seven Mile Bridge is the second choice in winter with other spots far behind. Hot and gorgeous conditions might flood the entire Keys backcountry with fish for fly fishermen. This is a day-by-day thing, not something to plan on months ahead.

Jumping tarpon keep us coming back for more.

It's easiest to find slick warm edges within the vast shallow reaches of the Upper Keys' Florida Bay. It's loaded with broad flats, quickly warming to toasty temperatures. Where wind and current direction match, calm surfaces may form under as much as 15-knot winds coming off an edge. Besides attracting tarpon, rapidly warming water encourages bonefish, reds, and sharks to cruise the edges. In the inner reaches of the Bay you might add black drum, snook, and trout to the mix.

The Bay offers an easily accessed and productive refuge for small boaters unable to get "outside" on the Atlantic in tough weather. Fishing is good enough here to plan ahead for trips, too. While you're unlikely to find a 40-pound redfish you may be run over by 5- to 10-pounders. The deeper channels often hold good numbers of just-big-enough snappers, and a mullet mud can be a day saver or a trip maker. They also provide fun with ladyfish and jacks and offer good trout action.

Because the Bay is so shallow, it also cools quickly. A chill may boot the bones and tarpon but seldom affects other fishing for more than a day or two. Bonefish do congregate on the Upper Keys shoreline when it's chilly, making them easier to find.

The Middle Keys, from the Long Key Viaduct to the Seven Mile Bridge, don't feel the same impact from a winter blast. The relatively deep open Gulf stays warmer, offering choices for small boaters. It's tougher to find protection from the wind in some situations with fewer banks and flats, but they do concentrate good numbers of fish. You start finding good permit action on edges here with lots of good snapper fishing. The long Oceanside shorelines warm quickly and offer good bonefishing. It's also a hotbed for big cudas.

Best Bet

African Pompano are more plentiful than most of us suspect so few target them regularly. They showed up early on a lot of Keys wrecks in 100 feet or more of water in November, likely attracted by large early season schools of white bait. They are a typical midwinter Key West target. We should have fish for a couple more months, and there is at least one secret to success: You have to stick with the program if you plan to catch one, although you will be harassed and sometimes encouraged to quit.

Pompano often circle their "home" wreck instead of suspending on it and might work anywhere from mid-depths to the bottom. You might have to wade through captures of amberjacks, grouper, and big snappers while waiting them out. Tackle choices often have more to do with what else you have to contend with than your target. A 30-pound African on a stiff 15-pound stick may be a fair adversary but a 60-pound amberjack will hurt you when using the same gear.

You've got to use a double line and a reasonable shock leader. A short chunk of 40-pound mono might be enough. Sweetened jigs make good fare for Africans and working them as you would for muttons, with a drop to the bottom and aggressive motions back to mid-depth can be successful. Dropping live pilchards to the bottom also fools fish. A few Upper Keys folks recommend dropping crabs back in the current, and they catch their share of fish.

March 2000

The Florida Keys offer lots of hope for dreamers during March. The official launch of spring promises improving flats action while a wide variety of migratory species bask in the relative warmth of the Gulf and Atlantic. Ever changing weather provides opportunities for those ready to take advantage of them. You may find "best of the year" fishing for some species.

A decent blow or two is rather routine in the Keys during March. In the recent past it has set up some rather hot offshore action. Our sea floor is looser than it was a decade ago and winds kick up lots of sediment. When it flows through the bridges, it often sets up a dynamic edge offshore, corralling bait and concentrating predators.

It leads to hot fishing most of us can easily find. Sailfish, dolphin, and cobia show heated interest in the barrier marked by the color change. If you're lucky enough to be around when conditions are right, you may find all of them surfing the break. They'll eat almost anything lively enough to broadcast a panic scent in this situation.

Trolling a zigzag pattern along the edge will tempt predators, but it is more fun to watch for fish and toss food in their face. It's one of closest things to sight fishing you'll find offshore. The fish are typically far more cooperative and seldom turn their nose up at baits. A well full of serious wigglers is a big help. High action baits like mullet, cigar minnows, speedos, and runners are particularly useful, but you can catch fish on white baits and pinfish.

You can catch a fish or two on flies or hardware, too. The ticket is teasing them up. A runner or mullet under a kite makes a good teaser or you can enlist a friend to toss them a bait and keep it away from them. Such friends are hard to find though

Captain Danny Strub holds a nice cobia for Max Heerman and Melanie Dahlberg.

*When the weather is nicer, March is one of the
better months for dolphin in the Keys.*

and deserve a nice dinner at the end of the day! You do have to show a teased fish
your lure or fly. There's no way for them to find it if it's not on their eyeball.

When the weather is nicer, March is surprisingly one of the better months for
dolphin in the Keys. They range near and far depending on wind direction and velocity, but they travel by in good numbers. It's often too soon for enough days-on-end
winds to build weed or debris lines so you'll have to seek birds to find fish. Fish foraging at random depths do provide opportunities for those trolling while they hunt.
You might run over a school of tuna or bonitos if you're near the Gulf Stream.

You'll still find sails showering baits along the reef this month whenever conditions are right. Cold fronts set up the sail action and also encourage nearby foraging
activity by a typically good kingfish population. The morning and evening sailfish
show is a bit more important this month since things are generally warming up.
Chasing nearby kings between shows is a worthwhile diversion.

There's been a good mix of kings in the Keys the last couple of years. The big guys
show a serious preference for blue runners and cigar minnows. You definitely need
wire for them, but a single hook is usually enough as smokers can swallow a 12-inch
bait with little trouble. Smaller fish habitually cut baits in half, and ha-ha rigs—a pair

of hooks on your wire allowing a head and tail bait hookup—stick more fish. Kings do occasionally relate to grass and weeds, and diving birds not obviously on bait might mark them. Sometimes they are sucking down random shrimp.

Those hoping for flats action will find plenty to do now. We'll have some bluebird days and tarpon will pour into warm backcountry corners after two or three of these days. They come to sun and snack a bit. They respond best to flies but careful anglers can toss shrimp or small lures at them and expect success. If it's almost nice, you can expect some fish around the bridges and in nearby channels. In recent years those willing to make the effort to gather white baits have done best during early season bait trips. Use a few livies as chum and keep the liveliest of baits from your well swimming on a hook in your chum line.

Bonefish spend much of the month during all but the prettiest of days at mudding depths. Over the last several years they have dropped to ever deeper depths and on the chilliest and windiest days you might want to look for them in six to eight feet of water. It takes a bit of weight and a good lead to get a bait in their face at these depths and the fish are hard to see. You can do almost as well or even better by simply dumping a bait on the bottom in the middle of the circles they seem to like to work.

I'm writing this in December and the quality of this month will have something to do with the fishing in March. December calmed measurably and was warm. It lead to clearing waters in much of the nearby Gulf. It indicates good things for March. You should have little trouble finding muds holding trout, jacks, and ladyfish in Florida Bay and nearby waters.

Spanish mackerel fishing was red hot during much of the fall along the Atlantic side but history and tradition suggests these fish should move behind Upper and Middle Keys bridges this month to harass a bounty of bait. They hone in on wrecks and deeper potholes much of the time and quickly find a chum line. They'll eat a shrimp or small livie to be sure, but those fishing Clousers on a fly rod or small pink and chartreuse jigs on spinners will catch far more of them than they can use.

Best Bet

No matter what the weather, Keys wrecks produce in March and often include surprises. In the Gulf shallows you'll find cobia, snapper, Spanish mackerel, jacks, and a smattering of permit and grouper. Jacks and cobia usually ignore shallow Atlantic wrecks, but ceros and muttons shoulder their way into chum lines. On both sides of the Keys you need a healthy chum line to crank things up. Commercial block chum works fine most of the time and attracts the wreck's resident bait hordes to the surface. Showing up with a well full of white baits to use as chum and food almost always leads to catches of better fish.

Over deep Atlantic side wrecks, a livie chum line is almost always the best choice. Depending on where you are, you'll attract kings, an occasional sail, and lots of tuna to baits in the top third of the water column. Dumping weighted baits toward the bottom leads to catches of muttons, grouper, and some amberjacks.

Fishing shallow or in the upper part of the water column in the depths, often leads to spectacular scenes as predators chase prey. At a minimum you'll spot them flashing through your chum line, but they're often boiling on top while chasing skipping bait. Recognizing bites is easy when you're eyeballing your offerings.

Things are tougher in the depths. Fish often eat as food tumbles toward the bottom on a slack or barely tight line. It's sometimes tough to maintain contact across winds or current, but the best at the game respond to any slight increase in the weight they feel on the end of their line or when things suddenly feel light. There's no penalty for attempting to set the hook at the wrong moment, and you'll be surprised how often some odd feeling turns into the hookup of the day.

For those always wondering where to go, I suggest you find the latest copy of new charts available for the Keys showing the most significant wrecks. It's available at Keys tackle shops or online from Waterproof Charts or MapTech.

April 1999

You may have a rock and rolling good time or relax in calm breezes in the Keys this month as the weather alternates between late winter blasts and hints of early summer. Anglers should like weather changes because the fish do. By now, fronts tend to race through the Keys, twisting the wind around the clock in an orderly fashion and keeping fish active.

Bonefish appreciate lots of weather changes. Approaching fronts usually swing the wind from east to south, then eventually to west quadrants before they pass. The fish seem to take this as a sign of a return to cold weather and attack flats edges with a vengeance to gather food. Strong onshore winds shove lots of water down channel edges and over nearby strip banks and encourage heavy mudding activity.

This is not classic bonefishing with polers and anglers whispering to each other as they gently sneak up on prissy tailers. It's war, with the fish charging around like crazed bird dogs on a quail farm. These fish eat anything they see that acts like food. In their two to five foot preferred depths, a size 1/0 fly with 16th ounce lead eyes or a round-headed quarter-ounce jig is a good choice. Of course, they'll eat shrimp if you use a couple of BB shot on the line. White or pink is a good color choice for artificials unless the water is cloudy. In the dust, choose brown.

The fish may be hard to see when they're deep unless you've found a large school. Catching mudders is an art. The fish often mud in a very definite pattern and you can lead them as they charge down an edge. If the wind and visibility is terribly tough though, there's no reason to feel guilty about staking up and tossing baits into the area the fish are using and waiting until they cross the scent trail. It's worth doing as long as you see muds popping off the bottom down current of your baits. You'll get a ray or shark once in a while but will catch plenty of bonefish.

Permit like the month's changing weather too. They often move to inshore patches in April as they think about spawning. Expect them to hold on the up current side so they can rest with structure at their back. You'll likely want to use 15- or 20-pound rods for them so you have some protection against the bottom and enough rod to move them quickly from cover. Free drifted crabs should fool enough fish to make the day interesting.

We often think of dolphin as a late spring or early summer species, but April is one of the better months to catch a big one. Onshore winds are important as they drive the fish toward shore. Even so, they will hang deep this month. Remember the Keys do not run in a straight line and the southwest wind capable of driving lots of fish within reach in front of Marathon is of little use in the Upper Keys. Winds should direct your search patterns.

Most dolphin are found in April by trolling the nearest edge of the Gulf Stream. It's hard to beat a whole rigged ballyhoo, although billfish-sized plastic often interests fish. You won't find many schools now, but some groups may hold a dozen or so fish. Pros resort to heavy tackle, 20- or 25-pound rigs, so they don't spend much time fighting fish. Those carrying pilchards or herring may hold schools close by chumming with livies.

Tom Siska looks a bit more tired than his fly-whipped blackfin tuna.

Those same livies, any sort of white bait caught along the shoreline at dawn, will prove useful for other species too. It's a big month for blackfin tuna throughout the Keys. You'll find them on the Islamorada and Marathon humps, in Gulf Stream rips and over deep Key West wrecks. Nothing turns them on more than a few pilchards or herring struggling on the surface in deep water. You can catch them on anything when they're hot, but a white bait stuck on a strong 2/0 hook at the end of a 15-pound rig is hard to beat.

You can still find some kingfish this month. They love silvery, wriggly baits, so your early morning work is once again rewarded. The fish are often smaller now as the big boys have headed north, but you should have little trouble collecting a limit of fish big enough to grill. They often eat smallish food and you may find them wherever you find terns and gulls dipping into weeds at depths over 60 feet.

You'll find lots of things going on in the Middle and Upper Keys shallows. Trout fishing is vastly improved since the net ban. A five to seven pound fish no longer raises eyebrows, though such a catch was unheard of anywhere in the Keys a few years ago. Trout often like wind and current shoving them against a bank and respond well to jigs or topwater baits. The biggest specimens are suckers for any baitfish under six inches long but you do have to let them mess with it a bit.

Redfish now regularly range as far west as Big Pine Key. They are tough to get to for most of us when they crawl over the hard bottomed lips of many Lower Keys flats. Those doing best to the west use kayaks to reach the skinny water the fish tail in. Here you'll need to throw the lightest possible food, light spoons, skimmer jigs, or weightless shrimp. Back east, in the Upper Keys backcountry, they should began mudding on steep edges this month, and they often tear things up on the windiest days.

Kingfish delight anglers on the end of the rod and on the table.

Redfish tend to dig harder than bonefish and move in bigger schools when they stay deep. If you give the fish room, and fish for them at the outside range of your longest cast, you can catch large numbers of fish without running them off. Round-headed quarter-ounce jigs or slab heavy spoons work best for mudders. With multiple anglers, you can often hook additional fish by tossing toward one on the end of the line. Schooling fish show dolphin-like tendencies as the try to steal food from a hooked fish.

Best Bet

We often ignore the sailfish bite in the Lower Keys. We're long tuned into the winter fishery along points east, as fish move from the southeast coast of Florida to the Upper Keys to avoid winter chills.

The Lower Keys enjoy a very different push of fish and mid to late April often kicks it off. Fish now migrate to the Gulf. Many think they're on the way to spawn. It makes little difference why they are here. The fishing can be red hot and it's interesting fishing to boot.

Sailfish often surf with the current as they slide down the reef. They may be in much deeper water here than some of us are used to. You might want to look in 200- to 300- foot depths, although the fish are often on top.

Every year is different as bait concentrations change. The fish are not adverse to chasing flying fish in 250-foot depths or corralling ballyhoo on a 120-foot deep ledge. The toughest thing about catching them is finding them as they'll eat about anything you throw at them if you can get in their face.

You'll have to troll and seek if it's dark and windy, but the frigates follow and mark fish fairly well when the light is good. We've got lots of ballyhoo in the Keys this winter so the fish may hang shallow this month. You need frisky baits to stop fish on a mission.

May 1999

The world's angling populace is ready to converge on the Florida Keys in May, hoping to experience a fishing extravaganza highlighted by migrating tarpon and rejuvenated hordes of bonefish and permit inshore. Offshore anglers dream of starving schools of dolphin and the potential to encounter some holdover black grouper and migrating sailfish.

These hopes are often warranted, and there sure are lots of other ways to have a good time in the Keys this month. Thanks to the net ban, a number of species provide tons of thrills during May and are often overlooked.

The net ban allowed many species to sneak down the Gulf coast to the Keys during the last five years. We've witnessed a surprising recovery of trout, Spanish mackerel, bluefish, and pompano stocks. A more than decade old regulation protecting redfish and numerous changes in snook rules enhance opportunities for Keys anglers.

During May you'll find numbers of trout stacked against Gulfside banks. The fish are scattered from the coast to the banks behind Big Pine Key. Look for them anywhere the tide shoves bait their way while they can hide with the current behind their backs. You can catch plenty on jigs and they have shown a lot of interest in orange and yellow creations for several years now, many risking confrontation by stealing streamers from tarpon in favored tarpon sunning spots. Bait folks will catch plenty of outsized fish on finger mullet, and pinfish also work well for them.

It's a bit late for Spanish mackerel but a topsy-turvy weather pattern in the Keys this winter might leave a few around. The open Gulf west of the dividing line of the boundary of Everglades National Park might still hold a few. They are pothole or strip bank creatures. If they're not around, many of their favored haunts do hold trout and some interesting snapper gatherings. Some chum will attract them, and white baits, or sweetened jigs, prove attractive to most area predators. You'll have fun working the area with bottom-bouncing baits.

Redfish fled the confines of Florida Bay for several months after Hurricane Irene but returned in decent numbers beginning in February. The northern reaches of the Bay are still by far the best fishing grounds but you'll find decent numbers of fish sulking along the edges of Nine Mile Bank around the bottom of the tide. On the outside Gulf edges, reds often mud in as much as five feet of water. They are suckers for jigs when they do this but spoons or live shrimp make good baits for them in the shallows. It's normal for multiple fish to chase a hooked sibling so boat partners can often hook up by tossing at a fish stuck on the end of a line.

Rapidly improving tide heights and flows encourage bonefish and permit movement this month. Bones jump onto flats edges often a bit too dry during winter and early spring. There aren't more fish but they sure are easier to find. Both the Upper and Lower Keys backcountry comes alive in May with activity peaking around the full and new moon. May marks the beginning of several months when the fish move in large schools at breakneck speed while they chase newly hatched fish fry along flats edges. It seems you have to keep a bait or fly a bit off the bottom in the water column to stop them, but if the front of the school runs over your food, dropping it to the bottom might fool one.

Permit show frequently now along tarpon routes and off channel end points. On dazzling calm mornings you might find them floating up much like tarpon in corners they're pushed into by the current. They can be tough to deal with when it's calm. They're often very aggressive when it's windy and many fly-caught permit fall victim to tarpon flies this month and are real suckers for anything with spun hair heads or crabby looking tails.

If the weather stayed a bit chilly, you'll likely find more than a few holdover black grouper. The fish are definitely drawn to rubble-strewn ledges and move frequently with bait concentrations. You can live bait them with some degree of success, but they often prefer a sweetened jig. You've got to use one heavy enough to fish straight up and down in a stiff chop and current—the best condition for a hot bite.

The sailfish situation is a bit odd this month in the Keys. What seems to be a migration of spawning fish is often well underway along the face of the Lower Keys, but there's no evidence of the same fish moving past the Upper Keys. In any event those seeking sails this month have a good shot at them anywhere west of the Seven Mile Bridge. The fish are often on top surfing along and respond well to lively baits tossed in their face.

Dolphin are where you find them and change depths as the wind shifts direction and velocity. The weather still has some say and alters its moods frequently in May. Be prepared to hunt fish in 300- to 1,300-foot depths. The near side of the Gulf Stream often holds plenty of fish you can easily find by trolling a rigged ballyhoo. There are plenty of big fish around so you might want to run away from schools of small fish before you are stuck with a limit of peanuts.

Best Bet

It's tarpon time in the Keys and while not quite the gold mine of yesteryear, there's still more than enough fish for most of us to catch one. For years we've emphasized hot bites in the evening but these days fishing for a fish or two is often much better at first light unless you're willing to fish in the middle of the night. This depends of course on where you fish. Fishing on both ends of the day is still pretty good where boat traffic is limited.

An early start with a dozen or so pinfish is more important than finding the bait of the day. Fishing on your own you can gather pins the night before or before sunup. If you're not happy running around in the dark, some effort locating a tackle shop selling wiggly critters for a reasonable price at first light makes good sense. The best fishing may be over by 8:00 A.M.

You'll find it relatively simple to hook some pinfish while drifting over grassy bottom along most flats edges. The flats sides of channel end points are often even better. A good rig for them is a couple of long-shanked size 10 or 12 hooks tied on a 6- or 8-pound line above a crappie jig. Sweeten the points with small fingernail sized chunks of peeled shrimp and let the rig bounce in the current. You'll catch lots of other critters and should keep small blue runners and speedos along with the pinfish. Don't tarry on bait fishing sights. Get a half dozen or so and go fishing. The first light bite is a big deal, and you can fish for bait while fishing for poons.

Most Keys channels hold some fish at first light whether the tide is rising or falling. Bridge faces are a focus of activity, but channel bends on both the Atlantic and Gulfside usually hold enough fish to make a day. Often the fish prefer a drifting bait when the tide is rushing. Toss your bait across the current and let it sweep through suspected holding areas.

Pinfish will hold in the current for a while if you find a concentration of rolling fish. It's not a bad idea to hold one bait in the group and let another drift through them with the current, though. Rigging for tarpon is basic and timeless. Stout 15-pound spinning rigs or 30-pound boat rods have their place in the fishery depending on your skill level. A length of 60- to 100-mono shock leader next to the hook defends against a tarpon's raspy mouth. You should choose a hook balanced for strength, the size of your bait, and point setting capability of your rod.

There's lots of talk about circle hooks these days, and they sure have a place if you have the patience to hold the rod still instead of jerking it to set the hook when you get a bite. I've never quite developed the patience demanded for the task, but sometimes leaving a rod in a holder until it seems the fish is stuck overcomes the problem.

You can catch fish all day, particularly if it's gray and windy but it is best to attack the fish early on. May has been by far the best month for tarpon fishing in the Keys the last several years. Now is the time to get yours.

June 2000

During June in the Florida Keys a bust does not describe a bad day or a head and shoulders statue. It's how we refer to a tarpon slapping a bait or breaking the surface as it flees when disturbed while sleeping high in the water in a sunning spot. It's a vision dreamed of by many sight fishing anglers the world over who descend on the Keys with giant dancing silver kings etched in their minds.

Don't let a barracuda fool you when you handle it—it may just be "playing" tired.

We've witnessed a rather startling change in the travel habits of tarpon during the last several years. Ragged patterns led many to give up on the fish entirely and go bonefishing in 1998. The fish didn't move far but if you sat on the same old spot you missed them. They quit rolling as they moved soon after sunrise if they rolled at all. They embarrassed us further in 1999, often traveling farther offshore during rising tides than they did when the tide fell.

Experience tells us tarpon are shoved to and from edges by the current, but if you failed to look over your shoulder last year you missed most of the fish. While tarpon often trace and retrace travel paths when heading to or from Miami along the Keys Oceanside, they did not do it last year. Fish moving in opposing directions often chose wildly varying paths and often swam tighter to the shallows on falling tides than rising. They've always done this in some spots, but they were a bit annoying about it last year throughout the Keys.

To keep things interesting they did just the opposite in much of the backcountry, sticking their noses into currents usually shoving them off of banks while fighting the current to sneak by in the depths when expected at bonefish depths. It did eliminate a lot of crowding problems as folks sought more sensible fishing.

This tells us only one thing, you have to adjust your fishing depth until you get in front of fish. If the water is moving, the fish usually are too. If they are not hitting your boat, you're too shallow or too deep. I suspect the fish are moving deeper to avoid boat traffic, but in some cases the fish shoved shallower last year on the falling tide than I have ever seen them and I move my boat a lot. I told customers a couple times that we sat where fish could not get by us, but they did by just going around us. Move, move, move!

For many anglers, June offers a first shot at the dolphin fishery as you finally get the kids out of school. You're not too late and can usually catch all the fish you can stand. Wind or lack of it often dictates where you'll find fish. Ideal much of the time is any south quadrant breeze. It sort of shoves the fish inshore along most of the Keys.

With brisk winds you might find fish in as little as 300 or so feet of water. Early in a calm cycle you may have to move out to 600 to 800 feet of water and move 20 miles offshore if a calm continues. Weed lines are not what they once were, as NOAA, the folks who think catch and release fishing is a bad thing, allows commercial harvest of sargassum for sale as chicken feed even though it is critical habitat for pelagic fish fry.

We search for birds now. Frigates often mark spawning pairs or small groups of slammers while diving gulls and terns most generally haunt schools of smaller fish. Flotsam typically holds fish but you might be surprised to learn the fish aren't always right under it and might hang 100 yards or more from it until it attracts food. If you don't get a bite right away around some boards or floating timber, don't give up on it, widen your trolling circle.

Yellowtail anglers are on equal footing this month throughout the Keys as the fish return to most reef ledges from east to west. This has been a constantly improving fishery for a handful of years now and flags are increasingly common. The ticket for success is a free drifting bait if you can get the fish off the bottom. You know soon after you get a chum bag in the water as smaller members of the clan show up at your transom.

The bigger family members hold farther behind the boat and sometimes deeper. There's no rule forbidding you from adding a bit of lead to your line to sink your bait below a school of small fish while you search for some bigger ones. Don't use so much that your bait sinks instead of drifts.

Lots of creatures hang below chummed up yellowtails, most seeking a snack. It's always a good idea to anchor some sort of bait to the bottom on a 30- to 50-pound conventional rig. Most often some color grouper grabs your bait, but muttons aren't shy about snacking on their smaller cousins.

Sometimes June is an interesting month for holdover blackfins. The fish are often on the small side but sure make good dinner. You might troll for them with black and red feathers or black eels while searching for dolphin. Very small fish can make effective baits on Middle and Lower Keys wrecks for leftover amberjacks.

Best Bet

June is one of the best months to bonefish in the Keys as the flats come alive with happy fish and you often have many prime spots all to yourself as the rest of the world chases big scalies. The backcountry in both the Upper and Lower Keys comes alive with roving packs of hungry fish. Long time readers know I am a fan of mudders, but summer tailing and waking activity is truly what bonefishing is all about.

There are few sights in fishing more fascinating than a school of slowly moving, happily slurping bonefish. It is seldom easier to find than it is this month. If you can ignore the tarpon action off the banks, the crack of dawn is by far the best time to find large concentrations of bones.

You can take your pick between tailers and spot tailers. For continuous tailing activity, choosing a spot with water levels around the bottom of the falling tide or start of the incoming is best. Very early in the day, these fish won't be too hard to feed as long as you don't hit them on the head.

I prefer fishing spots were the tide is just falling from its peak water level. It's a bit tougher to keep track of the fish in the water, but they do eat if you get it right in their face much of the time. We have fish in the Keys capable of tailing in two feet of water and they are the ones I want to catch.

Later in the day, a flush of water onto a flat from cool depths will encourage fish activity and may keep them active for hours. Contrary to popular belief, bonefish seldom move higher onto flats as water levels rise. They often drop off onto the edges and cruise or mud. They are much easier to feed in three feet of water than they are in one. Use a fly capable of diving to the bottom. You can always work it faster than normal if the fish are in a rush, but you can't make a light fly sink if the fish insist on eating bottom-seeking food. Make sure your shrimp sinks if you choose to spin fish.

July 2000

Success in the Florida Keys often depends on the horizon in July. Low light conditions around sunrise and sunset offer the best chance at many species. You've got to catch bait around sunup or you may never catch it on bright calm days. A few of our favorite targets spend much of their time far from land this month.

Keys summer sunrises are beautiful whether we find fish or not but also lead to unusual and exciting fishing opportunities. Typical calm weather encourages some odd bait behavior and predators quickly hone in on schools of everything including glass minnows, pilchards, and mullet scattered inshore and off. Exploring obvious concentrations of terns and gulls bouncing on the horizon might turn up a few surprises.

We often ignore birds in the shallows but anglers smart enough to take a few bird flagged detours while headed to bonefish or redfish flats last July found good numbers of tarpon sucking down glass minnows and very small pilchards on a number of Gulfside flats edges. Typically, current shoved bait into corners it could not escape. It's a Keys-wide event happening mostly where hefty bridge currents feed basin corners. You can enjoy it with any kind of tackle and almost any food if you stumble into it.

If you're caught unprepared, bonefish rods with ¼-ounce popping plugs or white bucktails are fine for lethargic summer fish up to 50 pounds or so if you add a short 40- or 50-pound shock leader. It's too hot to deal with 100-pound fish on such tackle but a 15-pound rod lessens the pain if you plan ahead. Smaller fish are a riot on a bonefish fly rod. July usually offers good sight fishing opportunities here and there for laid-up fish in more classic situations with a decent number of fish still pushing on migration spots in the Upper and Middle Keys. The fish respond better to bait and lures in July than they did in June.

Some concentrations of smallish inshore baits attract lots of other predators. Trout, ladyfish, and jacks are often on the fringes of obvious tarpon activity. I'd guess they don't want to become a meal so they wait for leftovers. They can provide additional action for several hours after the tarpon give up, though, so they are worth looking for if you want to bend a rod without working too hard. The tarpon typically quit when the birds do.

Offshore at sunrise, bouncing small birds are most likely on frisky pilchards washed around by the tide. Baitfish find comfy conditions everywhere so go with the flow when it's pretty. Depending on water depth, you might find small blackfin tuna, a mix of dolphin, or even some snappers feasting with the birds. You might want to use a 12-pound rig in the depths but small plugs, bucktails, and streamer flies will all fool fish.

Concentrations of small predators often attract larger ones. Dropping a two-pound blackfin into the depths if you're over a wreck might fool an amberjack while a legal snapper may do the same or fool a grouper. Schools of small dolphin, especially those on a feeding binge, may represent a feast for a marlin.

Lots of you want to catch dolphin this month and with typical weather, calm waters provide a chance to range far and wide looking for them. Heading for the horizon is often the only hope we have and you may hit the Gulf Stream before you find fish. While small diving birds can mark fish of any size, frigates often mark the slammers and super slammers most of us hope to catch.

Don't get trapped with preconceived notions about where the fish will be. Weather is not always typical and cooling breezes can shift the fish for miles. Remember, the Keys don't run in a straight line and wind shoving fish offshore in the Lower Keys may not move the fish at all in front of Key Largo.

Heading for the horizon makes sense for bonefishing too. Our tides are better this month and we're not stuck fishing channel edges for the next several months. Fishing away from the crowds can remind us of the good old days or surprise us with new discoveries. Many summer schools are pushing with the water and throwing wakes as they chase glass minnows. They do stop and tail here, and there and you can find creepy-crawler tailers if you insist.

Waking fish are far easier to catch, and some mornings they can wear you out. Besides lining the boat up for good shots, the toughest thing about catching them is getting food where they can see it. If you fish defensively, hoping fish will swim to a shrimp or a fly, you might as well forget it most of the time. Stick it in their face when they're moving fast. If I must fish for tailers, I prefer to hit them early in the day at the top of the tide. They're urgent to feed then, yet relatively comfortable with their surroundings.

An angler waits for a big lemon shark to reach casting range.

It's not too late to catch a tarpon around many of the bridges. Pinfish make reasonable food and are easy enough to gather; small crabs might be better. You'll have to drift them in the current or drift with the boat if the fish ignore you. Fish do stack up in basin corners behind the bridges on the rising tides, particularly during the dark of morning. You might have them all to yourself if you float or pole in for them just before sunrise.

Best Bet

We're seeing profound changes in the amount and types of bait and game species in the Keys Gulf. We have acres of bait where there was none before the net ban. Suddenly there are concentrations of trout and redfish along banks behind the seven Mile Bridge and points west. July is a pay-off month, providing some opportunities anglers should pursue here.

There are many small wrecks scattered in 8- to 12-foot depths you can easily spot on cloudless days. They hold fish in the summer but the real value of finding them is saving GPS numbers for the winter and spring. Catalog a few and stop to catch enough snappers for dinner if you must.

July's improved tides kick off several months of heavy mudding activity by rays, bones, and redfish on the deeper edges of many banks. The rays attract all sorts of passengers and most will hit a jig or weighted bucktail streamer. You can throw shrimp, but you don't have to.

The bones and reds sneer at conventional wisdom on many days, staying off the flats and digging in the cooler water flooding them. Both species tend toward dumb in this situation and once you find them, may offer multiple hookups before they move off a short distance. It's fun fishing and also provides good training for spotting and tossing at mudders when conditions are tougher in the winter.

With good visibility, now is not a bad time to search for pothole-laden corners along flats edges well flushed by the tide. They hold some trout and maybe jacks and ladyfish now, but again we're cataloging them for the winter. Good corners might have some permit on them for the next few months.

You'll find a fair parade of marauding sharks along most of these edges. Lemons and blacktips from 50 to 100 pounds represent the norm, but you might see anything. A 15-pound spinner rigged with a swimming plug tied to a couple feet of wire gives you a good shot at a few. Dancing the plug in their face or swimming it on their eye should trigger a strike.

August 2000

A couple of hours or so after a gorgeous August sunrise, many eagle-eyed Florida Keys species become a bit hard to fool. The weather is typically calm and hot and there's no rush to fatten up for winter. The easy fishing is over on many days if you miss the low- light bite. It takes a bit of extra effort to make things happen, but you can still catch plenty of fish with some work.

If you're late to an August party you have to bring good treats and offer them with some sensitivity. Midday fish tend to turn down yesterday's stale snacks and get really hostile about it when it's offered on the end of handline dimension leaders. Try to find some live bait or at least fresh dead stuff. What you thawed and froze again last night often won't work even to hold a hungry horde of dolphin at the transom. If you're having problems feeding fish using no leader might help when you're fishing dead in the water.

Things aren't so critical if you're trolling. Speed masks some bait shortcomings and leader diameter. If you're new at this you may not understand speed. Dolphin and tunas are content picking off lures and baits chugging along at eight miles an hour or so. If you're lucky enough to watch them work flying fish, you'll often see busts where flyers hit the water. The fish scaring them up in the first place swam along with them and grabbed them when they could reach them. Skipping ballyhoo or houndfish aren't fast enough to escape either!

You can double your speeds for wahoo and marlin. Both are frequent visitors in August, enjoying a bounty of small dolphin. It means you can keep some lures working while you race to the horizon searching for birds, boards, or weed. You may find some good marlin fishing this year. During April and May it was excellent. There's no guarantee for August, but the number of smaller fish caught in the spring is encouraging. Rigged small bonitos or tunas make good skipping baits for them. A hooked schoolie dolphin serves double duty, decoying a school of siblings around the boat and as a potential meal for a blue suit.

Dolphin at the transom, once you find a school, offer lots of diversions depending on their size. Bigger fish are often screaming along into the current and don't hang around long even if you try to decoy them. They might stick around if you offer live chum. Smaller fish will mess with chunks for a while, at least long enough to tease a few with jigs or flies. If they're picky you need help. Get someone to reel a bait away from them and try to get your artificial between the fish and meaty teaser. At times you have to crank a chunk along to fool fish when they get tired of drifting ones if you continue to baitfish.

It's impossible to suggest how far you'll need to range to find dolphin. The wind dictates everything, though once you get to the Gulf Stream you should bump into a fish or two often enough to keep things interesting. With luck, onshore winds will cut your travel times.

There's no such thing as a normal month in the Keys even in relatively stable August. Last year blackfins turned on the last two weeks of the month. I noted in 1998 that a bunch of kingfish in the 8- to 10-pound class harassed yellowtail fishermen for several weeks while wahoo stole the stage for a couple weeks in 1997. Fishing inshore and off for traveling species is often hours of rather quiet searching interrupted by intense action. Those ready with a variety of gear and food do best. Twenty-pound spinners and 30-pound conventional gear meet most needs for offshore trollers who stop to mess with sighted fish.

There are less strenuous ways to have fun. You'll find a mix of dinner-sized critters on the patches. Early and late is still best, but through the middle of the day baits ticking along the bottom with the current fool enough fish to keep things interesting.

An 8- or 10-pound rig adds to the sport while providing a fair shot at an occasional outsized specimen. A standard knocker rig (see page 65) with the smallest egg sinker that will do the job is fine, and light jigs tipped with flesh work well, too.

In the extreme flows of the cuts through the narrow strip banks of the open Gulf, tipped jigs attract all sorts of fish in a scent trail. You can use standard chum or rig a chum pot and break up a few shrimp in it. Jacks and grunts you'll likely catch while doing this make workable baits for sharks that are sure to search the scent line. Hang one below a cork on some #7 or #8 wire tied to a 15- or 20-pound rig and just dump the rig in a rod holder.

Best Bet

The Lower Keys backcountry offers some of the best flats action in the Keys this month. Big tides around the full and new moon push small and medium size tarpon into some interesting corners along with good numbers of permit. Bonefishing early and late, or on gray days, is often hot during the same tides. Fishing is protected throughout much of the area by tough navigation. The U.S. Fish and Wildlife Service

Jack crevalle are plentiful in much of the Keys backcountry.

basically refuses to mark "their" refuges because they don't want casual boaters in the area. It works.

Fishing here is sometimes better a little later in the morning for flats species and may last through midday or later. The fish are not more tolerant of the sun but the best floods of Gulf water peak well after dawn. The off moon tides are best for those wanting off the water when it gets hot as they peak early. Plan your trips based on how much time you're willing to spend in the sun. Fish the days you have based on the tides, and you'll do well.

You have many ways to start a search. Water coming onto flats from wide expanses is the coolest and most fish prefer the incoming side when the sun is up. When water is uniformly cool across a flat, they do use both sides. A channel bend often concentrates cool flows a little higher, or farther, onto a flat. Such spots attract more fish if boat traffic is a problem. Bends dumping into a bit of a depression or against a gradually sloping ledge leading to an island could attract small tarpon along with permit.

Rigging for every species with one rod is possible if you understand you'll find yourself overmatched from time to time. A 10-pound rod matched with a reel spooled with some skinny high tech 10-pound or some low-tech 8-pound mono should do the trick. Most species will take a small shrimp or crab at the end of a 20- or 25-pound leader on a smallish size 1 or 1/0 hook. In stiff current a split shot might help for bones, although permit and tarpon should eat baits skittering on top. If they don't, let baits drop in their face. There's always a place for a 12- to 15-pound rig aboard with some larger crabs and heavier leader.

The same scenario with strong flooding tides later in the day offer rewards in the Upper Keys backcountry with fewer permit and tarpon but lots of redfish.

September 2000

September is no longer a best kept secret for flats anglers seeking hot Keys action, yet it offers much of the charm of days gone by. Fishing pressure is still relatively light and random non-fishing boat traffic is almost nonexistent throughout much of the Keys. The month also ushers in a series of astronomically strong tides lasting through November.

The big tides put water on many flats that bonefish, permit, and redfish often can't use the rest of the year. They crawl up on them with enthusiasm and tail right through the hot midday sun. Hard charging water helps keep flats cool and provides lots of scent trails for eager fish. The big water confuses many anglers if they stick around when water levels are too high.

Contrary to popular wisdom many species don't move higher onto flats as water levels rise unless they remain too shallow for larger predators. The fish get off them and either forage on the edges or migrate to the next flat with the right water level for tailing. Like most rules, this one has an exception. While the biggest family members may move on, youngsters often hang around and mud or simply run along with the flow of tide and chase glass minnows on many backcountry flats in the Lower and Upper Keys.

Smallish bonefish are often scarce or at least hard to find much of the year. You'll bump into them now in surprisingly stiff water flows. The giants like to move along with an edge next to them—much like tarpon—unless they can find tailing depths. They will spot tail, hitting a high spot here and there as they travel.

Fall tides offer lots of versatility since you can find the water level you want within a relatively short ride. Study the tide adjustment tables for the area you intend to fish. You might note mid-falling levels on one flat within 15 or 20 minutes of one with mid-rising levels. Once you find a pattern, you can follow it throughout the day in the Upper and Lower Keys by running back and forth under the bridges or from one side of a large basin to another.

Permit pop up on both sides of flats, but you may find more where they are comfortably protected from the rear too. While crabs are by far the best bait for the season's biggest bones and most permit, a shrimp works fine for both. If you're lucky enough to hit a day with a bit of wind you can often fool permit with a shrimp by swimming it a bit, taking advantage of their jack family roots. Just like with the hot flies of the day, dropping it to the bottom when you have their attention usually triggers a bite.

The tides leading into the full and new moon often carry surprising numbers of tarpon with them. You'll find them in many spring-type lay up spots, corners with the tide pushing them against the bank. You won't find spring-like numbers, but you might get to throw at fish by yourself. While you may not think of it, more than a few random fish track along traditional Oceanside migration routes. You won't see many but might throw 20 or 30 times at singles and pairs. They're happy now and eat with gusto. A fishy looking fly is often the best food for them. A streamer with a bit of Krystal Flash in it works well for both laid-up and traveling fish.

Small groups of reds and singles tend to work as shallow as they can get. Don't ignore churning muds in three to five feet of water just off Gulfside edges, though. You may find it full of double-digit reds you can't run off. These fish are suckers for jigs so you don't have to get too fancy with them. You might fish anywhere from the southwest coast to Big Pine these days. The fish have returned in force to Florida Bay's Gulf edge flats following the storms of last fall.

It's almost never the wrong time to do some snapper fishing, but it might remain a low light or nighttime activity through much of the month. Yellowtail fishing should hold up from Key Largo to Key West on the steepest drop-offs in 60 to 120 feet of water. You might have to "sand ball" them if you intend to fish during the day. It requires a sort of messy mix of masonry sand, glass minnows, and menhaden oil to turn on the fish. Pack a ball of "chum" around a hooked shrimp and wrap your line around it a few times. Drop it toward the bottom and break your bait free when you think you're deep enough. You might still keep your bait in the current until you get the classic run off signaling a bite.

In the last two years we've had lots of under-10-pound kingfish on deeper Keys wrecks. They're following tremendous early bait migrations and the fish responded well for those gathering enough pilchards to use as chum and bait. The fish put on

Mangrove snappers do eat jigs.

quite a show if you pick gear suited for them. Eight and ten pound spinning rods are often stout enough. If your pilchards are big, you'll need a ha-ha rig (see page 67)— a nose and a tail hook on your wire leader.

We saw a lot of early blackfins last year. In the Upper and Middle Keys they love sea mounts but find deeper wrecks around Key West to their liking. You might troll for them with low light conditions. Otherwise, you'll need lots of live chum. Don't risk them on 10-pound rigs unless you're in lots of small fish. They are much easier to deal with on 20-pound gear.

Best Bet

There's too much to do in the Keys this month to send you off in one direction or another, although a lot of folks haven't gotten their fill of dolphin yet. This isn't prime time, but finding fish is still a reasonable expectation. Some skippers don't chase anything else for another couple of months, as long the weather stays reasonable.

You may find fish anywhere depending on the winds. The most dependable action, though, is often from the edge of the Gulf Stream to 10 or so miles into it for fish from 15 to 30 pounds. Weed lines are typically scarce so you have to seek birds and watch for random bait activity. You might as well troll as you go and sailfish-sized plastic or plastic guarded rigged ballyhoos work best. The fish are quite happy chasing them down while they skip in your wake.

Leaning toward heavier tackle is helpful this time of year. Twenty-pound gear is minimal and 30-pound rigs might be better. You can land the fish on lighter tackle, but they are on the march, charging along hunting food. They are very hard to hold around the boat unless you have a good supply of live chum. Even then they bore rather quickly, having seen the game for months. You don't want to spend a lot of time fighting fish. You need to keep chasing them!

You'll run into some smaller fish. Please remember that these are next year's most prolific spawners. Let them grow.

October 2000

While weather may change the mix of early arriving species to the Florida Keys during October, we have seen one constant over the last several years. Our bait migrations continue to improve since the net ban and more species find cause to move along with it. October is a bit of a bonus month for anglers as crowds are sparse and fish cooperative. Weather might range from chilly and damp to summer-like calm. A range of weather offers an abundance of opportunity.

If you prefer anything to sight fishing flats species, you might hope for slightly blustery weather. Days on end with north or west winds cool things off and provide an early season push of fall favorites. It makes it a bit chillier than it might be on either coast north of the Keys, and bait often concentrates nearer the reef than the shoreline.

We've seen earlier migrations of both small kingfish and blackfin tuna the last several years, along with an improvement in early season mutton snapper and black grouper fishing. The fish don't share common water but are sometimes within reasonable distance of each other.

The smaller macks begin where bigger family members leave off, where concentrated current caused by breaks or rises in the reef corral bait. Chumming with livies is a great way to play with them. You can anchor down and draw them to the transom with a flow of freebies. Spin anglers need only a bit of wire on the end of a 10- or 12-pound rig to enjoy the bite and capture a meal by nose-hooking a small pilchard and floating it back with your freebies. You may find the fish on shallower wrecks this month, too.

Depending on how steep your ledge is, and the makeup of the bottom, you might find enough muttons or grouper in the area to spice things up. Muttons like to suspend over relatively clean bottom while black groupers prefer rough bottom and often hide in it. A pilchard-sweetened jig makes good food for either species. You can plumb the depths for both by fluttering your jig to the bottom and lifting it a step at a time back toward the surface until you find a taker. This is something like work if you hope to succeed. It demands a relatively stiff 20- or 25-pound rig and some concentration. The fish usually take as the jig flutters back and you need to fish a jig heavy enough to keep a taut line in the current. Respond to any odd sensations at the end of the line.

Tuna are found around the sea mounts or deeper wrecks, wherever current is shoved toward the surface by the structure. You owe it to yourself to chum for them and do some lure or flyfishing when you raise them. You can land a chunky fish on a 9- or 10- weight fly rod but using a 12-weight might save some hand and arm cramps. They are not the easiest fish to deal with under the boat!

The year 2000 is one of the best on recent record for blue marlin and October is traditionally thought of as hot month for them. If the season brings along a bunch of bonitos when the tuna come, the bite will surely remain hot this month. While the Keys provide an occasional big fish, many are small enough to fool with sailfish or big dolphin-sized plastic or whole rigged ballyhoos. You can troll too fast for them, but you have to work at it. Covering lots of water around the sea mounts, including Key West's infamous wall, may turn one up. You might find one anytime you find a school of small dolphin, and if you hang out with the school for a bit sticking your decoy dolphin on a 30- or 50-pound rig may attract one.

Whatever phenomenon brought the marlin also held a fair amount of sailfish in Keys waters through much of the summer. It wasn't a wholesale fireworks display like after a smoking winter cold front, but it was good enough to justify some early morning trolling in favored areas this month. Sails often like the same current concentrations attractive to kingfish but demand a bit more water. Depths of 110 to 200 feet make a good starting point.

There's more to do than run offshore searching for glamour species. Patches start loading up with smaller muttons and grouper this month along with a good mix of mangrove snappers and cero mackerel. You can capture plenty of these fish by using commercial chum to attract them and a variety of cut baits to feed them. It's hard to beat a livie chum line, though, along with tethered live bait. Little pilchards are top baits but finger mullet might fool the biggest fish on the patch. If you think your bait is a tad oversized you might give fish a second or two to turn it around in their mouth before you smack them.

The fall live bait tarpon fishery differs quite a bit from the late spring. Far fewer boats on the water make for happier fish and an abundance of bait makes the fish fairly aggressive. The fishing is often easier as they follow mullet into the channels as current drives them in from the ocean. Bridge faces and flats just behind the bridges concentrate prey and predator. The fishing is by far the best under low light conditions early and late in the day or when it's a bit cloudy and rough.

You can get by with lighter tackle this time of year as few fish exceed 100 pounds and you don't have many boats in the way. A bit of practice with a 12- or 15-pound rod now will make you tough to deal with next spring when you go back to 20- or 30-

pound gear. You still need a shock tippet and a maximum amount of double line allows you to put some extra pressure on the fish next to the boat.

Sometimes the mullet run doesn't reach the Lower Keys until next month but you should find plenty of small to medium-sized tarpon there this month anyway. They like the maze of creeks and channels and are somewhat less molested here because the backcountry is a bit tougher for casual boaters to navigate. The fish respond well to flies, crabs, shrimp, or small swimming plugs along with jerk baits and plastic grubs.

Best Bet

October winds down the classic bonefishing many anglers prefer. It's sometimes several months before good numbers of tailing and waking fish are easily available for casual anglers again. They are typically plentiful now and a bit greedy. You can bet the locals chase them early and late whenever they can this month. As always, there is a best time to chase them, depending on your goals.

The biggest clan members show a marked preference for the strong tides building into the full and new moon. You can find a few anytime this month but they tend to gang up and are far easier to feed under the cover of extra hard charging water. You'll find some fish high on the flats as water levels rise, but the largest groups, and those easiest to feed, often hover on the edges.

Giants are especially fond of edges with hard flows shouldering them against the bank. It doesn't matter if it's a defensive measure or because food tumbles in the extra current. They like it and feed aggressively.

Smaller fish run all over the tops of flats this month. The bait migration can cause some confusion as the wakes of smaller bones sometimes remind us of schools of mullet. In some situations you won't find many bonefish around mullet. They don't like all the noise and extra predatory activity. In any event, it's best to throw first and ask questions later.

November 1999

Visions of sailfish, blackfin tuna, king mackerel, mutton snappers and myriad lesser players fire the imaginations of those planning offshore fishing trips to the Florida Keys in November. Typically, good numbers of fish delight anglers often enough to keep them coming back for more. The spoils go to those understanding the conditions contributing to a hot bite and knowing how to respond to them.

The Florida Keys is one of the world's most unique fishing destinations. I often feel like a broken record as I describe the hoped for hot bite of the month. Hot bites for some species last for extended periods and some species are available almost every day of the year. Quality bonefish guides won't back away from a "got to catch one" charter about 330 days a year. I've caught tarpon every month of the year. I'll bet a bunch of charter boat captains can say the same about dolphin and sailfish. There are peaks here but responding to conditions leads to great days for many visitors.

November kicks off our usual hot winter season when conditions are right. We hope for horrible weather along the Gulf coast and lower East Coast. The colder things get elsewhere, the better. Such conditions force bait and predators our way.

Nasty cold fronts we refer to as "smokers" lead to the best bite. A hard charging front crisply turns the wind around the clock, blows wind from any direction for a day or less, and rapidly chills the water before clearing the area. In the shallows the bite is typically hot as the front approaches and while it sits before things get too cold. Offshore the bite is hot from "in town" fish, the grouper and snapper clans, and a variety of mackerels as the season progresses. Sailfishing heats up as a front clears but still raises a decent chop.

Quickly swapping winds create color-change edges offshore. Westerly winds leading into fronts often shove lots of sediment from the Gulf to the Atlantic and wind swapping back to any east quadrant stacks it until it settles. The distinctive edge confuses bait and attracts many of our favorite predators. Sailfish and dolphin haunt

White not prime time for bonefish, winter can still offer some great fishing when conditions are right.

these edges over the next several months whenever conditions build them. In February and March, they are often joined by cobia.

Experienced anglers can sight fish the edges. Sails often surf them and look almost like tailing permit as the move along seeking food. Dolphin flash in and out of the edge and their almost fluorescent powder blue color contrasts sharply in a dusty edge. Tossing either species a lively bait almost guarantees a hookup.

There is nothing wrong with trolling the edges, either. A live bait is still your best choice. Mullet are an often-ignored offshore bait but their vitality makes them a great bait. They are usually pretty easy to find in November. Any white bait or a blue runner makes good food, though, and most of us can catch pinfish. Everything eats a pinfish. The edge is important but predators sometimes move into the dirtier water so a zigzag trolling pattern often works best.

Weather constantly changes in November and it's just as likely you'll find gorgeous blue-bird conditions. Heading for the Gulf Stream opens up some interesting possibilities. Slammer dolphin are often attacking bait this time of the year, charging into the current and driving hapless prey to the surface. Diving birds headed toward Key West often mark roving schools. They stay topside longer this time of year since water temperatures are comfortable. Trolling rigged ballyhoos around surface activity should catch you a fish or two. You should also be ready to toss a live or fresh bait to sighted fish.

Bird activity might indicate tuna action. We start seeing lots of blackfins in November. It's hard to find a better live bait for them than a pilchard, but they'll take a variety of plastic if you want to troll for them. One of the secrets for succeeding while trolling is keeping lures in the clean water behind your wake. You sometimes need to drop back as much as a hundred yards so fish can settle down after you pass over them.

November provides plenty of inshore activity too. It's a much better bonefish month than you might suspect. Pre-frontal conditions, as the wind starts around the clock, usually encourages tons of mudding activity if it's chilly and lots of tailing action if it's warm. November tides are the last really strong tides we'll see for several months. The fish know it and take advantage of it. You should too.

If it gets really cold, look for fish to drop off flats edges and mud in as much as six to eight feet of water. They are stupid here! Shrimp and jigs work great for the spinning clan. I like flies for these fish with 16th ounce eyes. Bright jigs and flies work best if the water is clear and brown works best if it's dusty.

It's not really a tarpon month but it only takes a couple of really pretty days to encourage a few fish to show up here and there. Early season lay up spots attract a few fish if it's really calm and many Keys bridges hold fish anytime the water is warm enough.

If you just want to play and gather a bit of supper, mullet muds in the Upper and Middle Keys Gulf will hold good numbers of trout for the next several months. The open Gulf behind Marathon should turn on this month with Spanish mackerel and bluefish. Look for bird activity and flipping bait to mark fish.

We do have seasonal activity in the Keys but the weather here, and the weather in the region around us, often determines fishy activity. Picking the fish of the day based on conditions rather than the calendar leads to the most fun.

Best Bet

Conditions forming offshore color-change edges often cloud the reef, wrecks, and patch reefs. Many of us fish in boats too small for happy reef or wreck fishing while the water is bouncing, but the patches can be red hot when dusty. They are sometimes hard to see, though. You can often get into fish by using a line of lobster trap floats as a marker. Don't mess with the traps. It's a serious criminal offense and the owners are a hard working bunch just trying to make a living.

Aggressive use of chum should crank up the area's bait population and predators won't ignore them for long. If you throw a net, gathering enough resident ballyhoo or cigar minnows should be easy, and they are the bait of preference for the mackerel, muttons, and grouper sure to sneak into your chum line. If you don't throw a net, a peeled chunk of shrimp makes a good ballyhoo bait on a hair hook tied to a light spinner when free floated in the current. Ballyhoo plugs on the bottom work for grouper and muttons, but both will smack a livie on top and the wiggler is attractive to mackerel. Last winter many Oceanside patches held both cero and Spanish mackerel.

If you prefer hardware to bait, several lure types work in a chum line. In the Upper Keys, snappers will respond to jigs while jigs or top-water baits work fine in the Lower and Middle Keys. Mackerel and groupers like swimming plugs and macks also like jigs. In dusty water something chartreuse and pink is particularly effective for Spanish and ceros.

December 1999

Many offshore anglers dream of white-capped, wind-swept waters this time of the year. Cold fronts push bait our way, whetting the appetites of favored wintertime game species. Last winter the offshore set suffered the indignity of rather comfortable weather. The inshore crew cheers such weather, but they get their turn in the summer and fall.

I judged last December as an exception. We have pretty days to be sure this month, but December often provides some of the coldest weather of the year. It's needed to really crank things up and set up good fishing for the months to come. We want to see cobia and kingfish driven from the Gulf, and more kings along with sailfish and tunas pushed our way in the Atlantic.

The best days offshore typically start within half an hour of sunup, while pelicans still harass pilchards and herring on the shoreline. A couple nets full of white baits, puts you ahead of the game. Most channel end points hold some bait though you might have to move along the shoreline of some Keys to find them. Meaningful concentrations are almost always marked by pelicans.

Sometimes you'll need ballyhoo, cigar minnows, or blue runners. You can hook and line all of them on patch reefs. Many folks don't stop for hoos until they shower

Diving pelicans mark bait for anglers early in the morning.

a few while running. It's not a bad plan. Once you stop, you can toss small, sweetened jigs for runners while you wait for the ballyhoo to crawl into your chum line. A small bait-catching jig is something around a 16th or 8th ounce. Adding a couple of hair hooks on the line above your jig gives you a shot at cigar minnows and pinfish while you fish for runners.

You may never escape your patch reef. Flashing schools of bait often attract predators. December is typically a great cero mackerel month. They love the patches, and last year they were joined by Spanish mackerel on the Oceanside for the first time in years. Both species demand a bit of wire in front of hook or lure. Tiny connections are important as jealous family members often hit bulky leader knots or swivels, thinking they are food. They'll eat almost anything fitting in their mouths.

You can often find legal-length snappers and grouper on many Keys patches, too. You may have to experiment to fool them. Some days, baits floating in the current with the chum do the trick, while it has to tick bottom while drifting at other times. Anchoring a bait might lead to the fish of the day, but you might catch a monster willing to crawl to the surface for a hotly vibrating livie. Play the game!

Sailfish and kingfish water is not the same, but the species are often not too far apart. Breaks or rises in the outer reef concentrate baits attractive to both. Reef lights in the Keys are popular fishing spots since they mark steep rises concentrating food. If you don't mind fishing in a crowd you can catch enough fish to make a day by varying trolling depths offshore of the lights. You could hide from the world if you sought similar but less obvious structure elsewhere along the reef. Sails are typically going to hang at 110-foot depths or deeper, and kings stay shallower. You might cheat and try to find the break between them. Sailfish know nothing about wire so you could zigzag at a common depth and harass both species.

Inshore fishing is far from dead this month. Plenty of bonefish are caught in December. Conditions favorable for the offshore clan put bones at mudding depths. Mudding fish are a riot and the preference for folks wanting to catch lots of fish. They are tough at times. You can't see them much of the time but watching a string of muds popping off the bottom gives you an idea about where the fish are heading. Tossing a bait in their path should lead to a hookup. If you find fish working tight circles, back away from them and leave a bait on the bottom in the circle. They'll find it! You all know how to fish tailers and wakers. You'll find lots of them on bluebird days.

The Spanish mackerel fishery really lit up in December last year. It focused from roughly a couple of miles behind the Long Key Viaduct and Seven Mile Bridge out past Schooner Bank. You're going to have to hunt a bit, but flipping bait and diving birds mark fish often enough that most of us can find them. They are great fly and jig targets in a chum line. Clouser minnows on a fly rod or a bucktail jig for the conventional set work fine. The fish tear these offerings up badly. It's best if you find some nylon jigs or tie your flies with some nylon. The fish don't care, and they'll last longer.

Take a hard look at muds along banks in this area too. The trout fishery became spectacular last year. A two-pound fish we looked at as a decent catch a couple of years ago is a release critter today. We may see double-digit fish here in a couple more years. The wind and current driven edges typically hold the most fish. They get to hide with shallow water protecting their backs while food floats their way.

Best Bet

There are plenty of bottom fish in the Keys and chilly, windy conditions concentrating bait typically makes them easy to find. Wrecks are an obvious starting point for anglers seeking muttons and a mixed bag of grouper. Jigs heavy enough to fish straight up and down in the current, sweetened with a fresh ballyhoo or white bait, make good food. With large baits and stiff current, you might need anywhere from 4 to 8 ounces of weight or more to hit bottom and provide good bite warning tension. Little white baits or even shrimp might fish fine on ¾- or one-ounce jigs on risky 12-pound rigs.

For serious work in rough weather you're likely better off with some 20- or 30-pound gear. Bottom fishing pros are pretty serious about making fish move off structure once they're hooked. They may well set the drag at half or slightly more of the breaking strength of the line. They want something to break, hopefully the fish's will to dive into cover.

Deep-water bites, even with big jigs, are not often announced with much fanfare. Your jig might feel somewhat heavier, or a bit lighter when a fish grabs it. Fish often bite as the jig falls back toward bottom while you work it with up and down strokes. If you've found fish on the bottom you might simply lift the rod, then let your jig fall back to tease them while keeping a tight line. Suspended fish often demand a pumping and reeling action, but you still have to allow your food to fall back between strokes. The lift in both cases should be somewhat aggressive.

Groupers typically hold tight on cover while muttons often suspend. You'll have to plumb from bottom to mid-depths to find fish. Don't be surprised if your wreck coughs up an occasional king, and sailfish will sometimes find a sweeping jig makes a good snack. On nice days, tease these fish with a livie chum line. Many wrecks host blackfins now, too, and getting them on top is a sight to see.

A cloud of mud like this might hold anything.

Tides Are the Key

We'd left the dock in a hurry. I knew exactly where I wanted to be, and we didn't even bother to thread fly lines through rod guides. We were paying for it now, though, as we fumbled for flies and mis-threaded rods. School after school of fish were waking off the flat in front of us. We had hurried too much and shut down just a bit too close to suit the fish. It was the other side of the 300-yard-wide flat that really interested me but the sight of those fish leaving had me alarmed.

My partner had come to the Keys on a mission. He wanted to catch a 10-pound bonefish. The day was calm and destined to become hot. I needed to get him hooked up early. I shoved the boat vigorously toward my goal, the opposite corner, insulated from our noise by all the shallow water between the fish and us. Twenty-odd schools of fish were still happy where two tongues of current met. Ignoring several schools of fish barely able to tail on top of the flat, I worked toward a school that was raising quite a fuss in the deeper water just off the edge. They easily tailed in twice as much water, indicating they would all be 10-pounders.

I was surprised as I witnessed a perfect cast. A couple small boils indicated interest, then a take. Huge washtub boils marked a hookup and a panicked school of big bones. The fish made a mistake. Spooked by fish between it and deeper water, she headed toward the crown of the flat and ran out of water. Exhaustion compounded by no maneuvering room gave me a netting opportunity only minutes into the fight.

A school of fish slowly works its way into the shallows on a gorgeous Key's summer morning. Sometimes the wake is all you see.

Coral beds at low tide.

The fish was just ounces short of 13 pounds. I suggested we go home, suspecting it would be all downhill from there.

Of course we intended to keep fishing, and as I poled back to the edge another school began flashing silver. A second perfect cast resulted in an 11-pounder. Now I knew it was all downhill. As the water began to flow toward the bridge the fish disappeared. We'd found a brief 30-minute feeding frenzy encouraging us to search for other flats at the same tidal stage.

Understanding tides provides a huge advantage in finding fish anywhere and is critical throughout the Florida Keys. Within 45 minutes of Islamorada or Loggerhead Key in the Lower Keys, you can find low incoming water, low falling water, or any stage in between—all occurring at the same time. It's a simple matter, sort of, to fish a productive tidal stage throughout the day much of the year. The complexity of Keys tides is compounded by vast shallow stretches acting as dams. Seasonal tidal weakness also allows weather conditions to drastically alter water levels. June through December marks the most consistent tides with August through November being prime time for tailing flats dwellers.

Use of a tide chart will quickly reveal the advantages of late summer through early winter tides. While the time of tide changes is useful, the critical information is the tidal range, the difference in water levels between high and low tide. Spring tides, the tides occurring around periods of the full and new moon, have ranges at times a foot and a half greater in the fall than other times of the year. Fish can grocery shop at all kinds of new malls.

Tide charts provide a correction table for each location's tides. This helps you determine the tide on the spot you want to fish. What does that mean? If you pick up a tide chart in Islamorada to use for your Upper Keys trips, high and low tide times are for Alligator Reef Light. This tide level projection is good for most Oceanside and nearby bayside flats surrounding Islamorada.

The most confusing aspect of dealing with tides is understanding when high and low tide occurs. Predicted tide schedules have nothing to do with current direction, water apparently running to or from a flat. They predict when the most or the least water stands on any given spot. Many locations have a two to three hour overlap, the period when the current looks like it is rising or falling while the water level is doing the opposite. About 2½ hours is a fairly average overlap between water level and current changes.

Tradition says low incoming tide is the tide to fish for bonefish. I think many prefer the low incoming tide because the fish are easiest to see as they crawl up into super skinny water. If you think about low tide experiences though, you'll often remember single fish, sometimes pairs or a trio, and lots of fish paranoia. Most of us have a tough time getting a shrimp, or even a fly, into the water with extreme low water fish.

The absolute top of the tide, maximum water depth with the water level just starting to fall, with incoming current, is often the best tide for bonefish. It's normal to see much bigger groups of fish at this tide stage. The fish are usually running amok. They are digging hard, blowing all kinds of mud, and tailing activity—when the depth and size of fish allows—is aggressive. Low water tailers barely show tail corners and are almost stately or elegant as they crawl from morsel to morsel. I like to fish for aggressive fish. The crawlers drive me nuts as they flee from baits or lures still in the air.

Higher tide levels offer an important benefit. Lots of boat traffic much of the year limits flats edge fishing to early and late hours of the day unless the weather is bad. When fish can get away from channel and lake edges they settle down. When I'm having a tough time finding or feeding fish I usually head for a flat near the top of the tide. I like to think the fish are comfortable with all that water over them, yet feel the water escaping, providing them a sense of urgency to feed. Top of the tide fish just seem happier.

Of course there are plenty of situations when low water is just right. During really big tides fish often flood flats along with the tide. A few flats never have bonefish at high water but look like conventions the last couple hours of the fall and the first couple hours of the rise.

Another common misconception is that fish move farther and farther up on a flat as the water level increases. They do to a point. With a lot of water, eventually predators can reach them and they are at a disadvantage. They often drop off to the edges and don't come back up until the water level starts to fall.

Another confusing truism associated with tides is the claim that fish always feed into it. It's not so. At least half the really great bonefishing spots I fish are populated by fish that feed across the current. There are several good reasons for this. The fish are seeking an ideal water temperature. When it's warm, a few hundred yards up the flat the fish aren't comfortable. They come in on the cool side of the flat at the depth where they are happy and work across the current. At higher water levels bonefish will pick a depth, sometimes using as much as 3 or 4 feet of water for defensive reasons, and again work across the current.

Big bones, fish over 10 pounds, seem to take particular pleasure being shoved against a flat by the current. They have immediate escape in front of them. It's also possible that the tide shoving against the flat dislodges food. If you pole out of fish, look behind you. If you see more tails or muds, the fish have picked a depth and are working across the current.

Where birds stand, you can't run a boat and probably can't even pole one.

Putting It All Together

The practical range for Upper Keys bonefish is within the second set of banks behind Islamorada. It starts at Cross Bank, runs to Crab Key, out to Panhandle Key, then all the way to the third point of Nine Mile Bank. There are lots of fish on the Oceanside.

Okay, so where do you fish today? I could tell you all about fictitious Bookmark Key. It's great! If you come in February and the wind is out of the north, the flat won't float most skiffs or harbor any fish. I'll tell you that six days before I wrote this there were tons of fish on the flat west of Tea Table Channel. The tide was a weak high incoming. It was hot and bright. We had a great 20-knot east wind helping shove water and bonefish and permit up against the bank. There were no boats running over the fish. Two days later at the same tide stage but with calm conditions and some boat activity, it was a watery wasteland.

I am writing this to help you, though, so here is an example of what I look for in one area of the Keys. A good portion of the second tier banks have no fish much of the year. They require a few days of a good spring tide. If you get a good 2.8 to 3.0 high tide for a couple days, fish will start using them. They will vanish as tides wane with a few exceptions. This is warm weather fishing and some of these flats will have uptide side fish if there's enough water for them to use the edges.

In the middle of these banks the tide is about 3 hours behind Islamorada. As you work back to the east you find spots 4 or 5 hours behind Islamorada. A lot of these flats have bonefish through both tides as long as there is enough, but not too much, water and good current.

Heading west to Nine Mile Bank, we find water doing all kinds of strange things. On the south and west side of the bank out to the second point, the tide is about three hours behind Islamorada. Just past the second point the tide starts to rise about 1½ hours after it starts to fall in Islamorada, and it does about the same thing in most of Rabbit Key Basin. Tides can be hours off at any location depending on the wind and barometer.

Second tier banks share a common problem. The fishing is good because the fish are relatively undisturbed. Few boaters besides guides and serious anglers use these waters and the fish are not accustomed to engine noise. You absolutely must stay away from boats and flats with your engine running. If you idle up to the bank and the fish are there, say good-bye to them. When these fish leave they will swim leaving major wakes until you can't see them with binoculars. Pole three or four hundred yards to your chosen flat and you'll find it worth the work.

Islamorada provides a year round fishery for bonefish. One is safe assuming every flat connected to the main islands of the Keys from Marathon to Tavernier Creek on the bayside has some fish most of the time. Simply getting away from boat traffic and into tailing depth, if you have current, will find you some fish. Except during extreme high tides, you will find some spots on most local bayside flats shallow enough for big fish to tail, or they are easily spotted as they mud.

Midday you can look for mudding fish on channel edges and where the tide pushes up against the bank between Oceanside points, at channel corners, or the down tide end of the many lakes surrounding Islamorada. On bigger tides a shift to the second tier banks will often produce plenty of shots for tailing and waking fish. You should stay away from Nine Mile near high water on bigger tides. Even the experts on the bank find this a crap shoot.

Telling you exactly where to fish is a nightmare. I have no idea what wind or tide or temperature condition you will have when you visit. I can narrow your search, but you will have to buy a chart. Edges leading to corners are almost always better than straight edges. Corners are important to your fishing. One edge usually will have current running straight down it for fish that want to work into the current. The other will have current on it at a right angle holding fish that want to work a specific depth across the current.

With light to medium winds I like slick protected edges if the current is average or better. At higher water levels look for ridges, spots where gradual slopes of flats become shallow quickly. On weak tides, edges with the wind helping to push the water are preferred. When it's really windy I like spots with the wind and tide banging into the bank together. Bonefish are very aggressive in this situation. When it's warm, I spend most of my time on the side of the bank deep water is coming toward. I do the opposite when it's cold, as water is warmed as it moves across the flat and fish move toward it.

Creepy crawler bonefish are hard to catch but fun to watch.

There's nothing like a big bonefish to bring on a smile.

THE BIGGEST FISH

Fall bonefishing is spectacular to say the least. Half the existing bonefish line-class world records are fall Islamorada fish. When you get into fish you'll swear you're in one of the world's best locations, and the truth is you are. The numbers of fish seen can be startling. Other than rival Biscayne Bay, nowhere else on earth has fish that match these in average size.

A few adjustments of tackle and technique help in the fall. Hard charging water may sweep a fly, jig, or bait at fish even though you intended to fish it on the bottom. Change to a round-headed jig if you're having trouble with a skimmer. Adding another split shot may help with a shrimp. If the extra splash bothers fish go back to the single shot and try ending your casts with the rod high, then dropping the tip to let the bait fall back a bit. A fly you might normally use for mudding fish may be more appropriate for hard current tailers.

Always search for good tidal flows. On big tides fish will most likely be where the current bends the grass to the bottom. On weak tides you may have to search hard to find any current. That's where you'll find fish. It doesn't take long to find a few good spots providing some success. Every fish will teach a lesson and provide some clue for the future.

Much of the time you'll find scattered opportunities, a few tailing singles, a couple of schools here, and three or four groups of mudders there. Keep poking away. You will hit spots exactly right, when the combination of wind, tide, and sky meet all the fishes' needs. When things are perfect fish may well come for hours. Keep records, you will want to repeat this pattern. There will be surprising similarities in spots holding fish, providing you clues for chart research. It won't take long to master Keys tides and develop a nice inventory of productive spots.

Tides don't always do what we expect them to, especially on weaker phases. We might expect tarpon to run an edge because the tide should push them there but a wind shift might move them off the beaten path. An east wind might push fish perfectly against an edge jutting north to south into the ocean. A wind shifted 45 degrees toward the south will likely lead fish around the bank instead of against it. The fish push in again as they round the point. If they are headed west, they are pointed the wrong way for easy fishing but you might be better off fishing for fewer fish headed the other way that are shoved against the bank.

Starting in about 1996 fish became far less predictable than they once were. During a week in 2000 I sat on a spot I've long loved. The current indicated tarpon should push into a nice corner before rounding a short point for a perfect downwind shot. I thought I might get some rest here, but the fish moved across a path over 300 yards wide and I poled helter-skelter after them, as no two shots were the same among the first 30. Some pushed into the corner and continued to shove over the bank. Others randomly turned and crossed the point from one end to the other. Almost as many sometimes used the point as some sort of street sign as they approached it from deep water and more than a few turned before they reached it. I only fished the spot when I could see well and could move for each shot. A decade earlier, the point was a dependable spot for waking and rolling fish.

To fish successfully in the Keys, you have to study the tide charts, and adjust each day to wind caused changes in the direction of water flows. Tides are severely impacted by the direction and velocity of wind. Sometimes they move for hours longer than expected or don't fulfill their promise when fighting the wind. Winds can hold water on one side of bridges or the other. An understanding of flats edges might put you in a well-flooded corner holding starving fish while helping you avoid one lacking current.

We've talked a lot about Islamorada in this section, but all the hints have meaning throughout the Keys. The distance between Atlantic and Gulf points are much shorter in the Lower Keys, although the tides are almost still opposite each other. The differences between tidal levels are often less between opposing points but the differences still exist and provide opportunities. The ditches are narrower in the

Lower Keys and the dams higher. When the water moves, it moves en masse. The windows close quicker, demanding more knowledge. At the same time, the fish are "happier" and more apt to reward anglers that find them.

You will not do well anywhere in the Keys without mastering the tide. Once you do, you will find plenty of fish when conditions put them on the flats. Take advantage of local tide charts by making sure you understand the point they reference and by using the adjustment tables for the flats you want to fish. The tide changes are surprisingly varied over rather short distances. You might find an extra hour or two of water movement within a five to ten minute boat ride.

New England striper guide Jeff Northrup is pretty handy
on the tarpon flats.

The Options Are Endless

There is no simple way to mark spots on charts pointing to the "big three" of Keys sight fishing: tarpon, bonefish, and permit. While some roughly defined areas traditionally hold fish they seldom fish the same year after year. Others get hot for days or weeks at a time. The fisheries change constantly and finding fish is in many ways only a small part of the catching equation. Lesser fish move a lot, too. The random activity of tournament anglers might provide some clues to the problem.

Tournament teams fishing, as much as 100 miles apart during an Islamorada fly tarpon event is fairly typical. Some might guard a shoreline within sight of the Miami skyline while others pole sheltered Lower Keys basins. A 100-mile gap isn't unusual during bonefish events, either. A few boats will always fish Biscayne Bay while others prefer bridge channel flats around Marathon. These folks all must leave the same dock and have only so much fishing and travel time. Late returns to "weigh ins" result in lost scores. It's a serious trade off to sacrifice fishing time for travel time.

They travel for a variety of reasons often unrelated to the number of fish they might find. Some feel tarpon resting in dirty water are far easier to feed than those skulking across a white hole on the Oceanside as they travel. Others can't see fish in dirty water or make the quick cast often required when you stumble onto a fish at 30 feet on the wrong side of the boat. The predictability of fish crossing where they are easily spotted, with the wind from just the right direction, is helpful if things are tough. If catching a fish rests more on luck than skill, numbers of fish become important. Only a few shots at fish in spots where they always seem to eat is worth the torture of long dry spells between shots if the angler is dependable.

Tournament folks aren't alone as they range far and wide. Conditions demand everyone play a moving game much of the time. You might start tarpon fishing at the crack of dawn next to a busy channel edge five minutes from the ramp during a tide change. In the right spot you're often greeted by happy hungry fish putting on a show worthy of the most remote backcountry edge or lake. You can bet if it's a pretty day the fishing won't last more than an hour or two.

You'll still have fish coming by the boat if the water is moving, but they can be boat harassed or simply turned off by a bright sun. It's time to move and find some fish with better attitudes. You might find a stretch of Oceanside shoreline relatively unmolested by boats where the fish might still eat just fine. Running to a remote spot is usually a better bet. The tangled web of Keys channels and flats offer a wide range of tidal conditions within relatively reasonable boat range.

The beginning of the tide on a flat 15 miles away might provide the ticket to midday success. With luck you'll find some fish, far from the drone of passing boats, just stirring from end-of-the-tide naps and eager for a snack. You might guard a migratory edge or pole for a few fish, finding a quiet corner full of bait a nice place to camp.

Bonefishing is much the same. Sometimes the fish only use a small part of the tide and follow changing water from flat to flat. You might also have to move to find fish you can see. Some days no one can see mudding fish, so we look for tailers. At other times tailers are tough to feed, but if you can see, mudders are often pigs.

Pick your Keys destination based on your desires for convenience, solitude, and ease of access—to an abundance of your favorite target species.

Heather, the author's daughter, shows off a permit.

Finding Fish
AN ADVANCED DEGREE

You could easily spend a flats fishing career fishing within a few hundred yards of the well-marked major channels in the Keys. There are also hundreds of unmarked ditches in the Keys. Channels are nothing more than rivers or creeks through shallow flats. They serve as highways, funnel food for feeding fish, and shelter resting fish.

Channel edges are one of the three critical basic magnets concentrating shallow water fish activity. The focused current from channels affects fish far removed from them, too. A flush of water banging against a flats edge several miles from a channel end may hold resting tarpon in season and concentrate feeding activity of other species. Remember this—it is important and will lead you to somewhat quieter fishing spots if you'll hunt flats edges fed by seemingly distant flows.

The Lower Keys shallows are very congested so that much of the fishery is impacted by immediately direct water flows. In the Middle Keys, many flats are somewhat removed from focused currents so any hard charging flows of water concentrate fish. Upper Keys waters are almost equally divided between broad basins and focused flows.

The other two easily located critical hot spots are the corners where terrain turns to form points, and the points themselves. You can and will find fish on long stretches of flats edges between the obvious corners and points. Over time, you should explore them and learn them. You'll have to, as hapless boaters tend to bounce all over the longest points in their travels and disturb lots of fish! Many times, along the longer edges, small jutting points or recesses into a flats edge focus fish activity and aren't shown on a chart.

Stream anglers should have a pretty good idea about how water flows position fish when they feed and rest. Our favorite shallow water species in the Keys react much the same to current with a major exception: They don't hide behind anything to break the flow of water. They want it in their face with structure protecting them from the rear. Few saltwater fish are big enough to frighten every predator so they practice defense.

The biggest freshwater trout often sit in the stiffest flows offered by an undercut bank. Bonefish, tarpon, snook, redfish, and permit are often in corners you could visualize as an undercut bank if the flats edge wasn't under water. Some rest there while others visit only to forage. Common sense suggests food is washed off a bank on the down current side while washed toward it and concentrated on the up current side. The fish know it. Anglers often ignore it.

I've read, sometimes with astonishment, how one flat holds fish on a rising tide while they move to another nearby when the tide falls. It's no surprise, which is what astonishes me. Our rivers change directions four times a day. One popular misconception leads to the confusion over why fish pick different flats when the tides change. It is generally suggested that fish such as bones or reds constantly feed into the tide and tarpon move with it. It's only partially correct and in many instances totally incorrect.

Example 7. The chart on page 139 illustrates how over time many larger channels dumped sediment along their edges, building long points near the ends. Both sides of the points serve as barriers to fish migration. In this example the deep corner formed by the point corrals tarpon when they're shoved into the shallows by the tides. They still usually hit some part of the point or the end of it when the tide switches direction. Rising bottom serves as some sort of navigational aid for them.

Bonefish and permit move toward the corner too, pushed by the tide when it rises and attracted by the scent of prey when it falls. Fish push along the channel edge side of the point, seeking deep enough water to cross or to crawl up on the bank to feed. At other times the edge is the only part of the flat with enough current to attract fish.

You'll find corners like this one throughout the Keys. I can think of hundreds of them, and this type of example is one of my favorites when tarpon are moving from right to left and are pushed toward the flat by the tide. There's the hint of a question mark along the left edge of our corner. You can adjust right or left to take advantage of the wind and sun if you set up at the little point formed where the semicircle becomes a straight edge. Lots of folks fish this at the end of the point. It's a mistake as many fish jump the bank before they get to the point, although it is a hot spot during a small portion of each tide. You do have to work the fish "on the pole" inside and can "sit" on the point.

An X on our little point down the bank is worthless. A stiff breeze blowing toward the channel edge pushes water hard enough to shove fish over the bank before they ever think about turning to the point during a good part of a spring tide. They'll miss you by 300 yards on this particular spot. Wind directed flows paralleling the channel edge often turn the fish off the bank before they reach your side of the semicircle. They still follow the edge but usually travel deep enough that you won't see them if you're not in their path. Either way, if you don't adjust, you'll think there are no fish.

The breeze shoving the fish over the bank is often not fishable for most right-handed fly casters but a delight for left-handers. There's far more to picking spots than knowing where the fish are. On a day when the right-handers can't fish here, I'll be half a mile to the right on another point the fish can't cross that turns them back toward the wind.

Bonefish often come with the tide in the hottest areas of the Keys, on flats in the Lower Keys backcountry and within their range in Everglades National Park. Redfish do the same in much of their range. Most bottom foraging species spend a lot of time feeding across the current elsewhere, shouldered against flats rather than crawling onto them from the down tide side. I've had a lot of great days fishing on the wrong side of the bank. It's often easier to fish on the so called proper side of the bank as fish

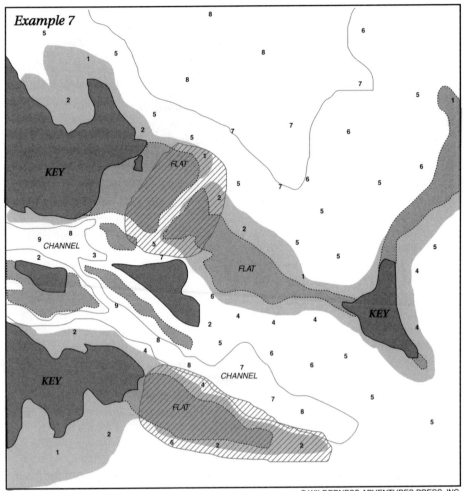

Example 7

© WILDERNESS ADVENTURES PRESS, INC.

poke their noses into the shallows, but the fish almost always eat our offerings better on the wrong side though they are sometimes harder to see as they forage in deeper water.

Weather makes a difference. When it's cold, water warmed after traveling over a flat attracts fish. When it's hot, fish spend more time where cool water approaches the flat. It seems basic, but we become fixated on spots and sometimes forget.

When tarpon fishing, you should be throwing at fish or hunting for them almost constantly. You won't find fish all the time, but there's a reasonable trade off between guarding a spot that should produce for most of the day and wishfully hanging out. To make a day you almost have to start throwing at tarpon at sunup unless waiting a short while will provide a bonanza or the weather is so tough you can only fish where you're parked.

Example 8. *A common mistake is to think fish will move predictably through the course of a tide. This is a typical terrain hook useful when tarpon are moving from left to right on a rising tide. Spots like this exist all over the Keys. The point in this example is about 200 yards long but relates well to other similar spots.*

With a hint of current, the fish may barely scrub the point on their way by if the wind is shoving water at a right angle across the bank. They might crawl the edge early in the morning, though, hoping to escape if the flow is barely noticeable. They'll fool you. As the tide freshens it shoves them toward the long edge to the right if the current flow matches the arrows. Once they get into the corner they typically try to find a way across the point. If they can, they'll cross the point until the tide softens again. You might think they'd hug the point if they can't cross it, but most of the time the flow of water shoves them off the point instead, and they won't test the point again until the tide weakens.

The hot spot is the corner if they can cross, but if they can't you'll probably do better if you fish the outside of the point. Once the fish come around the point, the current shoves them against it again. You don't have to make this adjustment if visibility is good. You can still see the fish as they travel in deep water inside the point, but they are usually easier to deal with when shoved against the bank on the other side.

When guarding a long point resembling this one with a current running parallel to the right edge, tarpon are often shoved high onto the bank after they make their turn. Such a spot is a valuable find as the fish often give themselves away as they travel whether you can see well or not. They're very easy to feed with the current across their face, too.

Sadly, some use a head start in the morning to protect a tarpon spot for the day instead of finding fish to throw at during the magical first hour or so. Worse is sitting through an entire tide knowing the fish won't be there until the tide changes. During "season," if fish are moving and the water is moving, there's seldom a reason to wait endlessly for fish to come by. The fish are not usually too far away. In the shallows, wind velocity and direction easily alter the direction of water flow. The shift may seem subtle, but traveling fish may miss your idea of their expected path by several hundred yards. This may not sound like much, but there are plenty of days when missing the path by 25 feet is about as productive as sitting at home. We spend a lot of days on the water with miserable visibility.

Sometimes current has little impact on fish and they are on some inexplicable mission. During the 1999 tarpon season, the fish confounded us with rather bizarre travel patterns. They often ran traditional falling tide routes on the rising tide and fell into deeper water when it seemed the current should push them toward the edges. Tarpon don't always ride the current. At times, they shove into it. I have guessed they

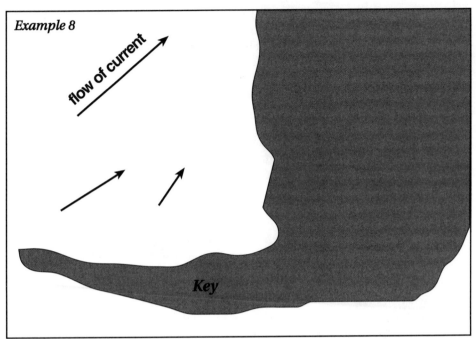

Example 8

flow of current

Key

feel a concentrated flow of water indicates deeper water to them as current flows are often halted when flats act like dams as water levels fall. It adds to our confusion but demands consideration in some parts of the Keys.

Tarpon get to you again when you think you've figured them out on falling tide spots where they nose into the current. During super low spring tides some flats dry up. Without a flow of water over them tarpon seem to lose it and wander aimlessly in deeper water.

Species we typically fish for as they forage, such as bonefish, redfish, and permit, might use the same flat you found them on yesterday but might move a quarter or half a mile down the edge if the wind shifts as little as 45 degrees (if water levels don't change much). There are widely published generalizations about foraging species that hold little water.

I've mentioned that many anglers believe they always push higher onto flats as water levels rise. Single redfish and small groups of bonefish might seek the shallowest water they can find. Large schools of redfish, most bonefish, and permit often fall off flats as water levels rise. They push along or feed on the edges many days. I've guessed they feel better able to defend themselves against predators with deep water all around them. You'll understand this better when you see a shark or two pin prey against a shallow edge. Once sharks can reach any part of a flat a bonefish can reach, the bonefish will move to areas providing 360-degree escape routes.

Speaking of sharks pinning prey, I must say pictures of folks standing in the water reviving an exhausted tarpon, while seemingly heroic, show some lack of intelligence. The first time you see a 12-foot hammerhead or 10-foot bull shark catch and destroy a 100-pound free swimming tarpon, you will understand.

Bonefish do rush the shallowest portions of the flats during the transition period at the top of the tide. There is an hour or two when the direction of the current indicates the tide is still rising even though the water level is falling. They feed aggressively during this part of the tide; the grocery store is about to close while water flows still broadcast the scent of food. You'll find them crawling pretty shallow at the bottom of the tide, too. It's the easiest time for them catch a crab. They are easier to feed at the top of the tide and much of the year you'll find more fish around the peak.

Redfish are difficult in that they feed on falling tides where only a handful of boats manage to float. They seem quite content in little more than potholes at the bottom of the tide, and you may sit aground with no water under you if follow them too aggressively. Plan your escape while chasing them during strong spring tides.

Foraging fish appear lost without water flows across flats just like tarpon. They seek the last piece of flat with current on falling tides, and the first piece with moving water on the rise. At times, water rises without obvious current for a short while. If water exceeds tailing depth before you note any current, it's unlikely you'll have many fish through most of the tide. Move until you find a spot with good water flows.

While it's safe to assume fish at some time or another have to pass along every shallow edge, the hot spots focus activity. They also provide an advantage since we can adjust to conditions by picking bends we can guard depending on wind and light.

There's not much in the sea more sinister than a big bull shark.

Bonefish are seldom this easy to see.

Spotting Fish

Flats fish are notoriously hard to see unless they are tailing or rolling. It's best if we learn to deal with them under the toughest conditions so it seems easy when conditions favor us. Another story will provide clues, and I will give you some more at the end.

A voice from the poling platform calmly announced a good push about 200 feet out at 10 o'clock. I had no idea what push meant, and as I stood staring at the water the voice became more frantic, "Point your rod, right there, look at the shake, the shake." There it was, more of a thump than a shake as water appeared to back up on itself, but obviously something was swimming at us. The voice from the platform conveyed panic now, "Cast 10 feet to the right of the push!"

When the fly hit the water the voice announced I was behind the fish, but evidently I was not behind all of them. As I raised the rod, hoping to begin another cast, the tip reversed course, resistance against the line announcing my fly was captured by a tarpon. My rookie status extended to fish fighting, however, and the 150-pounder landed on a tight tippet that immediately parted as I failed to bow when she jumped. A stiff chop and a dark sky had covered my sloppy presentation, but without Homosassa guide Alec Williams' ability to read wakes, I would have never had a shot.

The lessons Alec taught me served me well. Learning to recognize wakes adds a lot of shots to a day of sight fishing, and in many conditions often leads to the only good shots of the day. Conditions that force us to read wakes to make presentations often provide us some advantage over otherwise spooky fish. Wake watching is almost always easier when conditions are toughest for seeing fish in the water. A stiff chop reverses with more intensity than calmer water and wake edges tossed by moving fish often appear more distinct in flat light.

Anglers will find plenty of opportunities to tangle with pushing fish. You'll be surprised, too, by species not often associated with sight fishing yet capable of providing a lot of sport and some meaningful experience. Have you ever considered sight fishing for roving jack crevalles? They often terrorize baitfish and launch very pronounced wakes.

Jacks respond well to most lures and flies useful for other fish. You might throw as much as 15 to 20 feet in front of the obvious wake. The fish are always a bit in front of the most active water and move at a good pace. They are not hard to feed and offer quite a challenge on a 10-pound spinner or 8-weight fly rod.

Snook are available to anglers seeking waking fish, too. In the uppers Keys backcountry, schools of 4- to 8-pound fish seem particularly attracted to flats edged by long white potholes. Schools of finger mullet and glass minnows add to the attraction. The fish typically push on the shallow edges of the potholes and throw a short lumpy wake. A ¼-ounce white jig tossed 10 feet in front of the school then bounced just enough to puff dirt as it falls back attracts a lot of bites. Poppers or streamers work well on fly rods.

A blacktip shark slices through the water.

Florida Bay redfish may not compare in size with those in other parts of Florida, but they provide lots of action for anglers in the Upper Keys or those fishing from Flamingo. The fish often gang up into big schools in late spring and begin moving into the interior of the Bay where they throw very distinct lumpy wakes as they work on flats edges or chase bait on top of flats. The fish are often very shallow and respond well to spoons, flat-headed jigs with bait tails, or flies. The fishing continues through summer and fall and the range continually moves west along the Keys as fish numbers increase.

Bonefishing is definitely easier whenever you can find waking fish. Lots of situations set up waking conditions for them. On slightly cold winter mornings in Miami or the Upper Keys, the north Key Largo to Elliot Key shoreline can be lousy with fish cruising at 2- to 4-foot depths. The big balls of fish usually move fairly fast and throw very thumpy wakes that often look like two boat wakes coming together. The fish push with enthusiasm during similar conditions in front of Marathon and in some of the Lower Keys backcountry.

Several flats in south Biscayne Bay entertain hordes of pushing fishing as they fall out of the bay with the tide. These fish thump along edges and occasionally pause to tail or mud whenever they find food. You can use the wakes as an alarm and position the boat for shots as the fish pause to feed or try to feed fish as they cruise. Cruising fish are usually off the bottom a bit and can see baits placed a bit farther away than you might throw them for tailers or mudders. It's tough to stop them long enough to feed them, but they respond very well to a bait, jig, or fly worked off the bottom. A shrimp or small crab without weight or a fly that drifts rather than dives to the bottom can help fool-pushing bones.

There are a lot of flats in the Keys backcountry where fish push very steady wakes over long distances, never seeming to pause and eat. On some broad shallow flats or along edges too shallow for the fish to cross, you can easily see these fish 300 to 400 yards away. When you get close to the fish you'll notice frequent flashing and occasional mudding in the school. The fish eat as they move with glass minnows making up much of their diet, but they still pick up the occasional worm, crab, or shrimp in their path. Fish in the front of these schools often prefer a retrieve up in their face; farther back in the school, slowly hopped offerings may attract more takers.

In the Lower Keys, Cudjoe Key guide Andy Brackett locates lots of bonefish by searching for wakes. He states that here the bigger wakes are most often large schools of 3- to 4-pound fish. On shallower flats, narrow vees he describes simply as water going the wrong way are bigger fish, often exceeding 10 pounds. Andy cautions his anglers about the wake being behind the fish and has them cast aggressively, especially when fish are shallow.

Tarpon also push, of course. The key to finding waking fish in most conditions is a lot of current shoving them against a flats edge and into very shallow water. In some bays it is not unusual to find 100-pound fish crawling along edges in 18 inches of water. Somehow they are able to navigate long stretches at this depth while showing not much more wake than a large mullet. Hope for a dorsal fin to pierce the surface occasionally to help you lock in on the fish.

Reading water is also important over short distances. Tailing species often move farther than we'd like before they tail again. In a nice chop the water will often bounce a bit without having time to form a wake. It can at least provide a clue to where they might show next. Some species, and reds in particular, will bounce off and on flats with some regularity, grabbing a few morsels before returning to deeper water. This activity is marked by very localized violent thumping of the water.

You can drive yourself crazy looking at wakes since many non-target species disturb the water enough to attract our attention. Mullet and needlefish are the most common offenders. A half-dozen finger mullet may radiate a nice little vee at bonefish or redfish depth. A larger school can look a lot like gamefish. Usually, though, their wakes have a somewhat fragile look to them. Wakes from small fish often seem to ride up and down on waves, while target wakes crash on through. The vibrations of bait wakes are very short and much more rapid than a target species in most cases. All bets are off when you run into hordes of 2- to 3-pound mullet!

On very calm days slow moving fish may barely provide a vee as they move, and you may mistake them for mullet or smaller baits. If the wake moves faster than its size might indicate it is likely bait, but look at one once in a while until you're sure you've learned the difference. It costs nothing to throw a cast if you're not sure.

Guides I've talked to all recommend throwing some distance in front of wakes. Wakes are often set up by the dorsal fin and sometimes the tail. At least the business portion of the fish is almost always in front of the wake. Fish tend to move higher in the water when pushing wakes unless they are at tailing depth. Because of this they can see a bit farther. It's not so important to hit them in the face with their increased ability to see, and giving them a bit of room eliminates some of the risk of spooking them.

A lot of edges offer a spot or two encouraging fish to do something to your advantage. Fish may shove very tightly against a bank, then obviously fall off of it as they hit a corner or some obstruction. This may slow them down a bit and give you a better shot. You may also find fish pushing an edge without showing until they hit an obstruction. Guard those spots.

The size of a wake is determined by a lot of factors: size of the fish, how close they are to the surface, how fast they are moving, and the action of the water. Big sharks, tarpon, and permit are capable of moving without disturbing much water, but they do disturb it some. Even species at typical tailing depths can move without showing us much. Learn to look at any unusual water activity even if it's only a funny little crease in a wave or water that just humps up slightly. It often indicates fish below.

You can get an idea of what pushes may look like by looking at choppy water bouncing off fixed objects. Waves build their own reflective patterns as they bounce off sea walls or the side of a boat. The movement of fish just exaggerates the waves' own tendencies. It might actually help during the course of a trip to note how waves are reflecting around you as they bounce off the boat, a clue to how fish may appear in your particular wave pattern.

When it is very tough to see, wakes may be our only clue that fish are using a flat. If you sight fish you've likely heard the term "nervous water" to describe fish wakes. My good friend Woody Thrasher doesn't believe water has anything to fear from fish. He likes to think the water is excited. Learn how to spot and feed fish in wakes and you'll be excited, too. You'll catch a lot more fish.

Spotting fish is a very subtle thing. Fish digging on the bottom often raise clouds of mud, but sometimes their mud pops up as little more than an orange- or grapefruit-sized puff. Feel blessed if you are looking at the puff as it pops from the bottom. The fish has his nose right there. If your guide has time to point you to the puff and describe it, the fish is gone, and you can only hope to see the next puff. Rooters often move in a relatively straight line and you can guess about where they are. You can see muds on surprisingly dark days if you concentrate your fishing over dark bottoms or close to shorelines cutting glare.

Tailers are easy for most to see but only provide good opportunities if you have learned to cast well enough to get the fly or a bait in the water while their tail is up (if you cannot see them otherwise). The same goes for rolling tarpon. They are worthless to you if you can't get the fly in the water while their nose is up unless they are suspending exactly where they rolled. Long strings of tarpon present another problem. The rollers are often "tail-end Charlies," rolling because there is a traffic jam in front of them. Tossing at cruising rollers on days when large schools are moving is often fruitless unless you throw back along their line of travel. You typically spook the unseen fish in front of rollers if you have not read the pattern and throw across their path. There is no mercy on the flats.

No sight is quite as thrilling for a flats angler as a tarpon at the surface.

Good sunlight makes things better but not always simple. Our favorite targets are reflective and pick up the color of the surrounding bottom. The fish darken up in schools as they block reflections from each other, but small groups, small fish, and singles can remain a bit transparent. Permit always seem transparent, and you hunt them by seeking their jet-black edged fins or clown-like white lips contrasting against the bottom.

While fins punctuating the surface are easy for many anglers to spot, fin edges are a big give away below the surface, too. Tarpon fins range from dark blue to black or purple with good light. Over dark bottom they might contrast like a white hanky with just the right sun angle. They show at times as pink or orange in slightly muddy water.

Redfish fins are often tinged in blue as are those of some smaller bonefish. We do occasionally sight fish for trout, but they usually show nothing more than a very thin gray back line. Cuda fins are dark, and the dark edges appear slightly boxy looking. Smaller pushing snook look a lot like bonefish, but their shadow is often olive colored, while their dark lateral line is visible when they are resting.

There is a cast of supporting characters on the flats seemingly put there just to confuse you. What we call boxfish share some of the coloration of a bonefish and even appear to tail. It's usually their dorsal fin waving in the air, and it buzzes like a helicopter rotor. Head on, barracuda look much like bonefish. Small sharks might pop a fin while cruising and look like tailing fish. If it's obviously a dorsal cutting the water it's almost always a shark, as bones have to show some tail when their dorsal is up. Bonnet sharks possess relatively huge dorsals for their size, and they look like tails far too often. Little rays mud as do bonnets and boxfish. I've chased my fair share of far off cormorants that splashed below the surface more than above.

Good sunglasses are critical for success. Good does not always mean expensive, but a quality lens sandwich and the right color are important. There is a lot of debate over the advantages between plastic and glass lenses. Some prefer a lighter-weight offering. I like the long life of glass, but I haven't lost a pair of glasses in 15 years and tend to stick with my favorite colors. Color is the toughest part of the choice once you find something with a comfortable frame within your budget. Most of the time on the flats I prefer brown with a vague hint of green and yellow.

I lean toward more yellow on darker days, but not so yellow that the glasses offer an obvious color change. Good yellow is hard to find. I feel any glasses that change the natural color of your surroundings eliminate a lot of contrast. I've taken glasses off customers and found I couldn't see anything in them! Muddy brown, any reddish sort of brown, and too much yellow are all culprits. Check out the quality of the lens sandwich by wearing one pair of glasses and looking through another. If you note rainbow star bursts in the lens you'll get headaches as your eyes fight to adjust to the flaws. Sometimes a slight tilt of your head can change the alignment of polarization just enough to help you see a difficult fish.

Side shields can help if there is a lot of glare, but they cut down your peripheral vision. A hat offers a lot of help with overhead glare and many feel hats with dark under-visors help more. There are a number of oversized designs on the market, and they certainly can't hurt.

Seeing fish is in art form and doing it well takes time. Don't be afraid to throw at anything suspicious. It's often a fish!

A happy angler shows off a redfish.

It's The Shot That Counts

There's nothing like a seductive tail to get you into trouble and I'd done it again. Crawling into the shallows to throw at a single redfish left us hopelessly out of position for the school now chugging down the edge. I could get the boat close enough to try a shot but wouldn't have time to get past them on the upwind side. We faced a 20-knot wind. While only five feet short, the cast may as well have been in a bathtub for all the good it did.

Plenty of fish rested on our edge, most lay buried in the grass as they often do while waiting for a little more water and better current. Bad light made them tough to see, although a couple tailed. Finally I woke up and positioned us upwind of the path used by our sporadic schools. We could see better here and found some slowly cruising singles. This was better. We caught some fish.

Given time, most of us can find fish, but I'd failed my basic responsibility. I didn't consider how I'd arrange the boat so my pal could identify a few fish and make good casts. Keeping the boat off the bank in the wind wasn't fun but was our only hope. Over the course of a day, most of us are better off if we get a few really good shots while flats fishing, instead of many bad ones.

For good shots, we have to find fish we can identify in the water, throw at accurately, and that are actually willing to eat. It sounds simple enough and with some basic understanding it can be. Note I didn't say we had to see fish, only identify their location. We can do this by positioning the boat where we can see fish do something to disturb the surface. If you worry too much about "seeing," you may ignore other

An angler waits for some bonefish to show over the light bottom.

important factors. Concentrating on seeing fish is okay if watching fish is your goal. The quality of the shot almost always is more important than easy sighting.

Most of us throw baits, lures, or flies best at slightly down and slightly across wind angles. If you can find fish pointed at the wind this angle is easy to get—the boat stopped bow downwind with the fish at 11 o'clock for right-handed casters, or one o'clock for left-handed casters does the trick. It also gets the boat out of the angler's way. Excited spin and plug anglers wrap string around misplaced rods or upright push poles often enough to worry about this. Polers only stand in the way of a fly caster once.

The tougher conditions are, the more important this angle gets. Luckily for us, while lighting and wind conditions change daily on Keys flats, the edges are not straight. Thousands of bends, curves, and points provide all sorts of opportunities to position fish where we want them. It's human nature to want to go where we think we will find the most fish. You have to ask if you can effectively fish there with the conditions you have.

One of my favorite fly tarpon spots involves an edge shaped like a giant reversed question mark and it offers myriad opportunities. Fish push into it from the east with a rising tide, but as they come around the C portion of the edge, they line up into the morning sun. I can set the boat up to handle winds from northeast to due south by only adjusting over a 100-foot path. I can move to the far left or west side of the C if the wind comes up from the north for right-handers. With north winds, the fish may be tough to see for a while early in the morning, but we can throw at those we can identify and leading into the C is a small point where the fish often roll or shake water.

I have to leave here with lefties when the wind turns north, but half a mile up the edge my flat again points toward the sun. We hide behind a small point where the fish bounce water so we know where they are and have a head-on shot. Little of this path offers good visibility without some sun unless you use the shallow points. My lefty point is a pie wedge only about 50 feet long. A white spot at the end of the entire right-handed trail suckers many anglers. But most fish cross the bank before they get there, the feeding angle is poor, and the wind is seldom right for casting there without a struggle.

I didn't always have my question mark spot figured out. The light bulb finally lit for me when I realized some of my less experienced clients caught more fish there than my more competent ones. With fly anglers capable of handling a bit of wind on the wrong side of the boat I tended to take a position where we could reach every fish we could see. One of my best anglers spent two days here without touching a fish many years ago.

After he left I had some first timers who could not deal with any hint of wind. I made the 100-foot move to put their fish perfectly down and across the wind. In two days they hooked nine fish and landed three. It was a rude awakening for me, but the revelation that great shots were more important than covering all the fish served me well a few weeks later.

Angie Lucas and I faced a 20-knot north wind and no light on the second day of the 1990 Women's World Invitational Fly Tarpon Tournament on our way to becoming the first ever guide and angler team to win three straight major Islamorada fly-fishing tournaments in a row. There are only a few good north wind migrating tarpon spots for fly tossers in the Upper Keys. We had to have a spot giving us a downwind shot at some fish we could identify in the water. We sat upwind of a ditch tarpon use to cross a bank oriented north to south.

It's a horrible shot at right angle fish, but a patient angler throwing a fly into the middle of a school and letting the current do all the work of dancing the fly has a chance to catch a fish here. Helplessly watching a fly sweep and hoping for a take requires a bit of dedication, but the fish Angie caught that morning won the tournament for her.

Corners are the gold mines of flats fishing and you're wasting them if you pick a favored spot to guard without exploring the entire edge they establish. A shallower edge like my question mark works magic on bonefish, redfish, and snook where they push, too. Various parts of the edge provide easier angles for chasing critters taking a nap, and as winds change, for those feeding. You might also consider that current attacks the various edges at different angles. It may be straight down one edge and across another. Depending on wind and visibility, fish may work into the current or across it if feeding.

You won't find spots like my question mark by looking at charts. They're small chunks of much larger edges. You've got to pole and search them out, although sometimes fish give them away. Redfish or bonefish running edges in a hurry may turn to travel around what seems an insignificant mound of grass, just inches shallower than surrounding water. It might turn them into the sun and wind for you and they'll likely hump water so you can identify them.

As you search edges you'll recognize all types of terrain positioning fish for you. Many are obvious barriers, some only the fish understand. Many submerged terrain features serve as edges. Oyster bars, grass beds sprouting from light bottom, interconnected potholes, flats, shorelines, or even jetties might all define a path. If you're in an area of broad flats you'll likely find a variety of depressions and shallow ridges on top of the flats funneling fish.

The searching is not endless but your discovery may be. Learning how fish use a few edges provides clues to others. It gives you confidence to adjust the boat a bit if the wind or visibility is a problem. You've arrived and will have the most fun when you realize how all the spots you know fit the day's conditions. When you do you'll head for the best spot to catch fish, not just see fish, if they're moving.

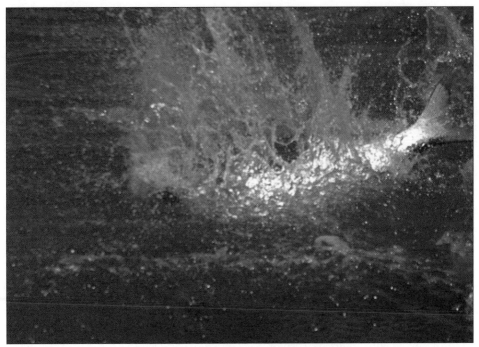

It's a lot of fish splashing lots of water.

BACK TO BASICS

Terrain features help us identify fish under low light conditions, but as we discussed in the last chapter actually seeing fish is a big help. Reading a wake is not always simple but a bronze or bluish ball of fish at its head makes pinpoint casting easier. Your new understanding of how fish use edges simplifies lining them up in available light too. When married to spots, you might stare at the sun for no good reason. With knowledge of how fish use terrain you may pole a hundred yards for a better angle or start somewhere else first.

We all have some order of preference for seeing fish. With or without light most of us see tailing fish pretty well and casting angles are more important for them than light. Besides being fun to watch, fishing for tailers represents classic flats fishing. Fish don't always tail, though, and in some conditions tailers may be tough to feed, but I sure can't tell you to stay away from them. I can't do it either. When they're stubborn, you might seek spots where you have some combination of activity. I guess I'm hung up on edges. Give me a few tailers, a few waking schools, and some mudders, and I'm a happy camper.

There are advantages to this, too. First, the deeper you can recognize fish, typically the easier they are to approach and feed. Many of us find our boats constantly dragging bottom while chasing reds, and sometimes bonefish, while fishing tailers. A hull-dragging bottom makes getting a good angle tough and alerts fish. In many situations I find more fish close to deep water.

In bonefish tournaments I seldom fished for tailing fish unless they were on the edge, there were tons of them in deep enough water to easily fish them, or they were the only fish I could actually see. Sometimes you have to fish the only fish you can see. Remember that edges might be defined by a depression in a big flat or a shallow ridge surrounded by deeper water. Fishing edges is a confidence builder. If done enough it becomes natural and you'll fish well when edge fish are all you can find. If we can't find tailers or wakers, we need cruisers or mudders, our other edge targets.

With fish positioning basics in mind it matters little what species we fish for. We'll adjust depths for migrating tarpon, cruising reds or bones, or tailing fish. We can fish down sun for pothole huggers and most of our shots should be at good angles. We've got to protect what we've found, though. The tougher conditions get, the more important it is to protect our good shot.

Some anglers poke fun at folks preferring to stake up, but if fish are hitting the boat perfectly and they're eating, there is a lot to be said for a consistent shot. We sometimes fish in stupid conditions, and you might sit on what you believe are the only fish you can see and cast to. Understanding the basics may help you catch fish when you really shouldn't be able to, even if fish are moving.

We can get more aggressive as conditions improve. Every fish won't be on the same highway and angles aren't so important when wind isn't a problem if we can see and throw at fish head on. Part of aggressive boat work is staying away from fish. I crowded my redfish earlier so got out of position for fishing the majority of the fish using my edge. If you're on the proper side of the fish, your light and wind help you move to fish a bit out of range.

Leaving maneuvering room provides a few extra seconds to point out the fish, talk about the shot, and perhaps move the boat a few feet, and could make all the difference. Lots of time for shots is a seldom-found luxury while flats fishing. We can make time if we don't crowd the fish.

So far we've put all the pressure on whoever is picking spots and poling the boat. Anglers have to participate, too. Polers are terrible mind readers and fish never provide enough time for poor communication. The angler's first job is finding announced fish around or approaching the boat. If the boat is moving, the poler is often already swinging the boat for your shot or to give chase. You have to agree where 11 o'clock is while he works you into position.

A trick or two helps. I like my partners to point rods at suspected critters. We can talk left and right then, or maybe add a descriptive color, wave bounce, or terrain feature to the discussion. On close fish, distance is often a problem. With some of today's quietest boats, fish swim under rod tips. Don't keep secrets. If you can't see the fish, say so. Added description may help or you may cast in a general direction and let the poler adjust you from there. You may have time for another cast, or simply moving your food a bit may get it in a fish's face.

Good communication allows the poler to keep you away from fish until you can deal with them. Once he thinks you've gotten them, the boat's going dead for the shot as soon as it makes sense. You have scant seconds when things will work and typically if you miss, the shot is history. Why the rush? Unless you're dead downwind, the boat won't sit still long, and you may lose your angle. Current is also a factor. A swinging boat may drag a bait or throw too much slack in a line to work it.

Poking around in the shallows reveals all kinds of surprises. You may sit a little deeper on a tailing edge and find more fish migrating with the current than tailing into it. The muds you can suddenly see now may be loaded with starving fish. The puzzle snaps together far easier when edges are well defined.

Poking around in the shallows reveals all kinds of surprises.

Presentation

I came to flats fishing from the black and white world of bank lending. There, one could take all the time needed to analyze a situation and deal with it leisurely. Flats fish go by the boat quickly and offer a wide range of opportunities with little time for analysis. Still, each chance offers some options. There is no absolute correct way to handle every shot on the flats.

I am surprised whenever I read about the "correct" fly strip for tarpon. I am even more surprised when I hear how well fish eat at a hot spot during one tide when they won't eat on the other. It indicates inflexibility to me, an unwillingness to learn. Saltwater fish are often thought of as greedy, but they are not much different in many ways from their freshwater cousins. They have a pretty good idea what the food of the day can and cannot do in the prevailing current, and they ignore poor offerings.

Fly anglers should pay more attention to what naturals do than to what they look like. A silver dollar-sized crab, a favored June tarpon food, does not dart into the current. It floats in the current and wiggles its legs. In calmer water at bonefish depths, it dives into the grass. The favored retrieve of flies emulating crabs, though, is often a hectic series of jerks. It usually doesn't work.

The best retrieve for a permit is just to let the fly sink once you are sure the fish knows it is there! Permit became more routine fly rod catches when folks finally weighted flies so they attacked the bottom like jigs. They still bang a crabby looking offering that only suspends if it is windy enough.

Flies dead drifted in the current often attract more fish than those jerked along. At other times, some movement is needed. A fly sweeping across the current might work if stripped a bit but sometimes works dead drifted. If the current is running at you, you may not be able to strip a fly fast enough to maintain contact with it. If you are fishing down current, a fly suspended in the current is most likely to fool a fish. Don't be fooled when you read about "the" one correct strip for a tarpon fly.

The best fly anglers tease their fish, stripping or allowing the fly to settle, as the fish responds. There are a number of acceptable ways to fish for bonefish. Some prefer to throw a fly along a hoped for path and begin working it when the fish are in the neighborhood. They are unwilling to spook the fish with a cast. This is tough as it is easy to start a retrieve too soon and have the fly too far from the fish when they get to where it was. You might also end up behind the fish or across their path if you wait too long when they decide to turn before they get to it.

I feel the best cast at any bottom feeding species is one they see hit the water, leaving the fly to dive to the bottom right in their face. Don't get nervous about scaring the fish. A fish will never eat a fly it doesn't see but might still eat a fly that momentarily alarms it. I've seen plenty of tarpon turn around to eat flies landing on their tails when laid up, and bonefish reconsider and turn around to eat a fly landing a bit too close. But I've never seen a fish eat a fly it did not see!

We get in hurry on the flats, wondering what the fish thinks of our cast. Sometimes doing nothing is the best approach. If you throw across the path of the fish, any movement of the fly is likely to scare them. Their food never swims at them. If you are very short with your cast, you might work a fly back in front of them. If you cannot adjust, you are better off leaving the fly alone until they swim by it before trying another cast.

There is an exception to every rule, of course. A current charging hard at a fish will carry food toward it. Saltwater fish look toward the current for food. You might attack a tarpon with a fly if you are moving it with the current. There are also odd occasions when they will eat a fly stripped aggressively into the current. They eat a fly best when it is sweeping naturally across their face with the current, though. It's important to cast on their down current side when they are traveling. They won't often chase a fly thrown where the current takes it away from them.

We hope to deal with fish head on, but it is sometimes impossible. Typically your only chance at fish offering a poor angle comes with a cast next to them. You might make them turn to the fly, turning the opportunity into a head-on shot. On desperate days, you take the shots you get. When fishing is decent you try to maneuver the boat and wait for the fish to give you a good angle. You might miss some shots, but you are better off taking the best shot you can by waiting.

Fish don't always move as you expect them to. Tailing species sometimes move with the tide. If you watch and follow them, they often turn back toward the current to feed, giving you a great shot. It takes some courage to wait out the shot, and sometimes you don't get a shot. I've been rewarded time and time again by waiting, though, and feel it's worth the risk.

Never pray for a bad cast to work out. It might, but if your guide is hollering at you to pick up and throw again, it is for a good reason. Guides make mistakes, but they have a pretty good handle on where the fly will or won't work. The advantage of a fly is being able to toss it right in the fish's mouth. Sometimes you will pick up a fly too soon. Even your eagle-eyed guide may miss a fish a bit away from the core group. It's the breaks of the game. If you're a good team, you share in your mistakes and triumphs.

The Roadblocks Between Fish And Angler

Teasing and catching Keys flats fish is a bit different than succeeding with fish living in shallows elsewhere. The fish are less than tolerant of flies tossed across their path most of the time. An abundance of food also makes them lazy. They don't chase out of the way food much on a normal day but may become quite aggressive before approaching fronts or when conditions put them on a tear. Calm days are tough for feeding but fun for fishing, while a day or two of decent winds is often a boost for the ego if you can deal with the wind. Everything happens in quick time on Keys flats.

A lot of little and not so little complications stand between anglers and fish. Some are simply a product of human nature. For instance almost everyone suffers for a while with impatience. Once the fly is in the water, we've got to move it to see if the fish will run over and eat it. Other complications are mechanical, like digging a soda out of the cooler before getting a rod ready to fish when you reach a flat.

Great anglers share some common traits. Foremost is a constant focus on the task at hand. Guides lean toward impatience, too, and often crowd spots to see if fish are there. It's amazing on slow days how often the only shot or two on a flat happens within moments of shutting down the motor. Digging for a drink may well cost you the shot of the day.

Keys fish tend to surprise you, as visibility is often tough, and fish plot ways to sneak around you. I swear tarpon sit on the other side of white holes and wait until an angler is somehow in trouble or not paying attention before they attempt a crossing. You can't stay awake all the time, especially if the day is boring. If you insist on practice casting incessantly, though, you're likely to miss a lot of shots as fish crawl between you and a fly too far from the boat to prove useful.

Moving a fly too far, too soon, or too fast is a real problem shared by many anglers. We talked some about this in another section, but it deserves a second mention. Guides are often limited in how much they can help you with retrieves if you don't understand the drill. They are focused on the fish and often can't see your hands. I remember a tournament when my angler was throwing very well and had tarpon after tarpon behind the fly. They were running in panic from his fly no matter what fly I tied to his line. On the fourth day of the tournament I found myself beside him pointing out fish because visibility was so tough. I could see his hands just fine. His "twitch" of the fly was an almost two-foot-long jerk! When I explained a bare flick of the wrist moved the fly enough, he hooked the next fish he threw to. He catches fish pretty well now.

You also have to control a fly line when you cast. The trick is to form a circle with the thumb and forefinger of your line hand to cast through. Searching for the line at the end of a cast may cause you to miss a fish eager to see the fly move. Don't get confused, though. Sometimes you don't want to move the fly the moment it hits. Analyze the situation first.

The next couple of problems arise because seeing fish is just not easy. I've fished my regular customers for 10 to 15 years so we talk pretty well by now. We try to understand what each is going through as we struggle to catch fish as a team. The first and worst error is ripping the fly from the water if you don't see a fish behind it when it lands. I hate to tell you how often anglers make great casts then try to "improve" them if they don't see a fish run right at it. It's a horrible mistake and takes years to overcome. The worst example I saw of it in 2000 involved a wonderful cast at a permit in perfect feeding conditions.

I did manage to stop my angler from jerking his fly from the water, but he had moved the rod enough to leave a lot of slack between him and the fly. The cast had looked short, but the fish was high in the water and saw the fly just fine. It raced 20 feet to eat it, but we could not set the hook because of all the gyrations. I beg my customers not to lift the fly from the water if they can't see fish, but it's a tough thing for all of us to overcome.

The second sighting problem pops up when you have a perfect line on hard to see fish and a fish somewhat off the flow suddenly becomes very easy to see, such as with rolling tarpon or tailing bonefish. I've watched in horror as anglers redirected casts toward easily seen fish they cannot possibly catch because of the odd angles between them and the fish. No amount of urging is ever enough to prevent it!

I've found, after talking to anglers when this happens, that they are so focused on the moment they cannot hear my gentle pleas (also known as screaming) to leave things as they are. There are a number of places in the Keys where this is a common event. Years ago, when hundreds of hundred-fish schools of tarpon filed through Sandy Key Basin, boat teams often agreed at the end of a day to never fish there again. It was a place where the most experienced anglers lost their minds and turned great head-on shots into impossible right angle ones. Lead fish turned as they hit the boat. They were easy to see when they did so but wouldn't eat. Seeing fish there was a bit of a nightmare.

No one wants to let fish get by the boat without showing them a fly, yet in schools some fish can't eat no matter how much they want to. A right angle retrieve doesn't leave a fly in a fish's face very long. Facing and casting at fish still pointed at the boat is the right way to fish for them, but human nature gets in our way. Watch tarpon cross a hole. Once a fish turns, every fish turns in the same place most of the time. You'll do a lot better throwing at the fish still headed at you. Dealing with such situations is very emotional, though.

Mechanically, when your guide or trusty poler jumps off the platform to move, they are ready to go. Focused anglers reel up and join their partner. Those more relaxed usually make a practice cast or two to straighten out the line or fulfill some casting fantasy. It's your fishing time, spend it as you like, but if you're in no hurry you tend to temper the enthusiasm of your partner.

Being late to start the day cuts the legs out from under your guide, particularly during tarpon season. Daylight fish are by far the easiest to feed. Fifteen or twenty minutes rigging gear at the dock may not seem like much, but someone chomping at the bit to go finds it a significant inconvenience.

I have to speak up for guides here a bit. Sure, we're hired help. Starting a bait fishing day at 8:00 pays the same as poling your brains out starting at sunup, though. Guides do the sunup thing because it's magic. String your rods the night before and get to the dock on time. If you want to catch serious fish, Keys flats species, you must get serious about the fishing.

Rolling Stone *writer Erik Hedegaard shows off a nice summer snook.*

The Bite and the Fight

On the flats, you get no fight until you learn how to recognize and respond to a bite. Bites from some species are mysterious, seldom felt, and hard to read. Bonefish, tarpon, and permit, our glamour quarry, all eat best when the fly moves straight away from them. Important but somewhat lesser species, like redfish and snook, do the same thing. Since they rush the fly head on, they often push the line toward you and eat on the end of a slack line. It's rare to feel the initial bite of a bonefish as they keep moving along with the school when they eat. Permit are often found alone and pin baits to the bottom. Reds and snook often stop to chew.

Tarpon often announce a bite with an easily read flashing side and occasional huge boil. Seeing a tarpon bite is a problem for most of us. There is no doubt when a fish responds, but a mouth offers little resistance if the fish are not properly pointed before we attempt to set the hook. Tarpon mouths hinge like the loading ramp of a cargo plane, the upper lip is much like the top of a tunnel. If you pull on the string while the fish is pointed at you, the fly usually pops right out of their mouth.

You have to strip until you feel the weight of a tarpon in your hand or against the rod tip to make sure some of the fish is between you and the point of the hook. Reaching for the sky before you feel the fish in your hand leads to failure most of the time, a trait called "snatching." Moving the rod to set the hook is a mistake with most Keys flats species.

You must also learn to respond to a bottom feeder running to a fly and stopping where you think the fly is. The stop is the only obvious sign of a bite since you will seldom feel the take and they usually eat the right fly in the right spot. The fish grab and spit quickly, and if you raise the rod you move the fly too much for the fish to find it again if it doesn't have a mouthful of it. The fish will eat time and time again until it gets stuck if you just bounce the fly along by feeling with the line and a series of strips.

For years I've chuckled at those suggesting bottom feeders are nipping at flies or spitting out flies with weedguards if they are feeling ticks on their lines. They are feeling the fly popping out of the fish's mouth. Flats species inhale the fly. They don't taste the tails or respond to an unnoticeable prick of a little piece of monofilament used for a weedguard. Flats fish eat all kinds of critters capable of causing harm to humans without consideration of the perils. These folks are just missing the fish by raising the rod tip, they are feeling the fly pop out of its mouth.

In most cases you are best served by trying to strip tight to the fish before you do anything with the rod to set the hook. It is not natural since we raised our rods tips for years to hook many other fish, and we also think a broad sweep of the rod provides real hook-setting power. Pulling on a tight line sets hooks far better.

Flats fish often stun us when finally hooked. You sort of hold on for dear life the first few times you hook up. Even with experience you let a big tarpon have its way with you through a jump or two. Your first mission is looking at the line on the deck and making sure it will clear the boat. Many anglers point the rod toward the horizon and start really banging on the fish to set the hook when the line comes tight to the reel. You have to stay alert. Tarpon tend to hit the air with shocking speed and you have to reach to them to get the pressure off the tippet and the hook when they do.

You fight saltwater fish, not play them. A constant give and take of the line shortens the battle. If the fish isn't running, it's time to pull it back to the boat. You'll face a standoff or two but just holding on increases the risk of failure and harm to the fish. The well popularized "down and dirty" technique works well with many Keys species. We fight fish with rather low rods and constantly pull them away from their intended line of retreat.

Some situations demand a high rod on initial runs. Bottom feeders tend to flee with their bellies dragging, and we risk cutoffs without raising the rod some. Bonefish and permit tend to fall off if you get the rod too high, though. I don't why, but I've seen it enough to feel the rod angle creates a problem.

There is a cute tactic for dealing with confused fish. Once in a while a fish will run the wrong way on a flat, heading for the shallows instead of the depths. They run away then turn and run right at you. The natural inclination is a futile attempt to maintain a tight line by raising the rod when they turn around. It only works for second or two. The best response is dropping the rod tip so the fish pulls a circle of line behind it. The drag of line against the water maintains enough pressure on the hook most of the time to firmly hold the fish.

I'm not going to go into all the "don't reel against the drag" and "pump and reel" stuff you can read anywhere. I will caution you about considering a direct retrieve fly reel as a winch. There is a pretty good chance you'll snap the handle off your reel if you try to hold a fish by the handle. If you're buying new gear you'll end up with rim control spools most of the time. If you get some of the fine old stuff or a reel without a rim control spool, you'll have to figure out something else, like lots of pressure on the line or using fingertips against the inside of the spool.

Tom Siska bowing to a far off king. You've got to reach to a jumping tarpon.

Tom backing up the tarpon. A low rod and lots of back pressure puts the hurt on a tarpon.

Tom shows perfect form while bowing to the king.

Chumming

Chum is anything you put in the water to attract fish to your boat. It can range from a handful of shrimp bits used to attract bottom feeding shallow water species, to live baitfish fed to schools of migratory fish to hold them around the boat. We use chum to attract fish from the depths toward water where we can see them or to lower their inhibitions toward taking baits tethered to hooks and wire leaders.

Sometimes we use chum to attract unseen fish. Other times we use chum to position fish we know are there so we can see them and cast to them easily in the prevailing light and wind. In the shallows, shrimp bits or shrimp bits in a tube or chum pot are often used to attract bonefish to sight fishing depths. It doesn't take pounds of chum to attract a school of bonefish. Too much chum is actually a problem as it attracts many unwanted species.

The best chumming days are those with a good wind pushing along with the tide, widely broadcasting scent. On these days, a couple of shrimp busted into chunks is often enough. There is an advantage to freely tossing shrimp chum toward a light bottomed spot where you might attract a favored inshore species. The fish hang around longer when they find chunks they can eat. However, free chunks encourage munching by undesirable species and will sometimes disappear before working their magic. A tube full of shrimp bits puts out scent longer, but desired species won't spend much time circling a tube. Fish eat pretty good over a tube, though, as your offering is all they can find to eat when they are tricked by the scent trail—if you cast quickly.

Bonefish, redfish, permit, and small sharks will crawl into a shallow water scent line put out by a tube or pot. They'll eat almost anything tossed into their face when they do. Live chum or major scraps might attract tarpon over a long distance, raise offshore species to the surface in the depths, and keep schools of migrating fish within casting range. If you try to feed some fish by throwing something at them before they reach the chum, they usually run right over it. Throw to the chum, not to the fish. There is an exception: Sharks will usually eat everything in their face so you can fish them as soon as you can see them.

Upper Keys backcountry guides routinely use chum lines fed by stunned and struggling white baits to draw snook and redfish from mangrove lairs. A few white baits tossed into the current can draw tarpon within easy reach. They certainly work magic for pelagics hanging around wrecks or steep reef drop-offs anywhere in the Keys.

Those lucky enough to find a bunch of ladyfish will find chunks of them a great attractor for sharks or in-season tarpon. Perhaps the greatest attraction for sharks, though, is a barracuda or some barracuda chunks. We'll talk more about sharks, but for now I'll say barracuda chum is by far the best shallow water teaser you can find for them.

On the patch reefs or along shallow water backcountry strip banks, commercially ground chum works magic on many bait species. Worthwhile gamefish may not respond to the chum but certainly like the concentrations of bait attracted to it.

You put the chum in a wide mesh nylon bag and let chunks of it fall into the current. Sometimes there is not enough current to move the trail into or across the wind and fish show up where you cannot reach them. Lighter chum, such as widely available menhaden oil, floats with the wind and attracts plenty of bait.

You can fill your live well with live chum quickly if you can toss a cast net. Many pros prefer some hook-caught baits to those they net. A string of hair hooks, light wired, long- shanked small hooks about size 12 or 14, baited with shrimp chunks, fool lots of chum- line bait when fished with light tackle. The drill is to loop several hair hooks on the end of a 6- or 8-pound rig, and drifting them baited with peeled shrimp in your chum line. I like to anchor my string of hooks with a 16th or 8th ounce crappie jig, and the jig is often eaten by a grunt or blue runner. Both are useful baits. A Sabiki rig, a series of gold hooks dressed with plastic or hair referred to as quills, is quite attractive to white baits when they seek shelter around deepwater structure, including a bridge face, channel marker, or reef edge drop-off. You anchor the chain of hooks with a teardrop sinker offering enough weight so you can jig it near the bottom as dictated by the prevailing current and wind. Some white baits eagerly latch on to undressed gold hooks.

Chum is not magic. You might move a bonefish or school of bonefish several hundred yards or raise some bottom dwellers a hundred feet or more off a wreck so you can fly fish for them. Sharks might find you from a mile or more away, though. Pelagics often feed at the surface in 1,000 feet of water and willingly stop for freebies.

You can use a very simple technique to excite bait inshore. Cheap cat food in a can works for grunts and pinfish. Punch a few holes in the can and hang it from the transom on a piece of mono. They'll find you. Oats might raise white baits within cast net or hook range if scented with fish oil. Chum puts fish where you can reach them and often puts them in the mood. Learning how to use it will save or improve many days on Keys waters.

A butterfly-filleted barracuda is the hot chum for sharks.

Blacktip sharks are spectacular fighters and eat a wide variety of offerings, including flies.

Chasing Jaws

One thing you can do inshore and offshore during most of the year in the Keys is chase large sharks. I'll whet your appetite a bit with a story I wrote about a day of chumming for sharks in Key West with a butterfly-filleted barracuda. Then I'll provide some clues about catching sharks on your own on flies, or with other offerings on light tackle.

The outsized dorsal fin cutting a hot trail through our chum line unmistakably belonged to a hammerhead shark. Few critters hone in on a struggling victim with more speed and purpose, and while we had a few seconds as he closed the last couple hundred yards between us, we panicked. We'd just stowed our gear, exhausted from a day of fighting hammerhead pretenders. This wasn't a sea monster either, but a perfect world-record-sized fish for our tackle of choice, a 12-weight fly rod and 16-pound tippet.

A Chinese fire drill ensued as we rushed to take advantage of our good fortune. Most underwater visitors to our scent trail during the day left in boils and blurs when they encountered the boat. This one fully intended to eat our chum, rope and all. The casts involved little more than dumping the fly on the water at the cuda's tail. Finally the hammer ate, but the leader parted, tangled in the chum's teeth. Somehow the fly popped loose, miraculously floating within reach, and we tied it on as the hammer again attacked the chum. Three more bites resulted in a pulled hook. The fifth led to a perfect hookup.

The angler was Tom Siska, the guide, Key West's legendary Ralph Delph, the first charter captain/guide to lead anglers to 100 world record catches. I had joined Tom for pictures and lessons.

Delph convinced Tom it was a perfect day to attract monster sharks to the boat in the shallows along the eastern edge of Boca Grande Channel. We talked of the possibilities of fly rod record hammerheads, although we realized one might never appear in our chum line. Delph promised plenty of encounters with big bull and lemon sharks.

Delph quickly outlined his routine for sight fishing shallow water sharks. "We'll butterfly a barracuda and hang it half in, half out of the water so wave action continuously washes scent off it as the boat bobs up and down. With this 20-knot wind against the current we'll have plenty of chop helping send the message. We're going to drift so the scent line is erratic like a struggling fish. The sharks will come in hotter than they do to fixed chum spots."

On the way out he explained the fun part—the bite. "Sharks are stuck with a prehistoric instinct playing into the hands of anglers. When excited they have to test possible food. We only move the fly enough to make sure they see it then let it sit. They'll eat it dead in the water. If we were using plugs, we'd want something we could swim on their eye. It's important when we drift to stay aware of the scent trail. You can spot it by watching grass floating by the chum."

Delph uses cable type wire leaders for light tackle work. He finds 40- to 60-pound test wire cable adequate. For flies and 16-pound tippet he's happy with a Mustad 3407 size 5/0 hook. "It provides a good compromise for hook setting and is strong enough to withstand the pressure of a prolonged fight."

Very few visitors to our chum line were small enough that we might actually land them with our tackle of choice. Finally, a "smallish" 225-pound lemon shark inhaled a fly. A pretty good tarpon fisherman, Tom put plenty of pressure on the critter.

The shark was in trouble when Tom pulled it within Delph's gaffing range. Ralph prefers to hook release category sharks in a pectoral fin. He feels it gives him plenty of control over the ever-dangerous mouth, minimizes much of a shark's tendency to roll violently on the gaff, and does them minimal harm.

I was grateful for the pictures. Between you and me, I would have cut the leader. I do not, however, possess Delph's experience or physical strength. His largest Boca Grande capture is a former all-tackle world record hammerhead. The 976-pounder possessed 36-inch pectoral and dorsal fins. Hammerheads are the only sharks with equal length fins and the high dorsal cutting the water adds tension to their sinister looking approach.

While waiting for our hammerhead, other critters provided plenty of entertainment. We had plenty of big sharks to throw at, and they also brought company to the party. Several times we hooked big jack crevalles hounding our quarry. Cobia hounded them, too. They readily ate our 7-inch streamer, but of course they took their lives in their hands when tethered to a 12-weight rod in front of the roving sharks.

I also talked to Captain Kenny Harris. Kenny guided Rick Gunion to the largest hammerhead on fly capture in 1995, a 154-pounder on 20-pound tippet.

"Flyfishing for these guys is a waste of time," said Harris, "but this is an incredible fishery. The problem is not feeding them or being able to put enough pressure on them. The mouth of record sized critters is simply far enough behind the snout that it's tough to protect the tippet.

Me, Delph, and a handful of other dedicated guides have hooked hundreds of hammerheads between us but there are few light tackle catches. A hammer's skin is much rougher than that of most other sharks. The fight is more erratic too, since they are so athletic. You must crowd the fish during the fight, keeping the class tippet off them. Positioning the boat for the chase is easier when knowing where the hook is."

Both captains wish the IGFA would allow some sort of chafing gear over fly rod class tippets so they could catch more hammerheads. Maybe a soda straw or a piece of vinyl tubing would get the job done but it doesn't meet the rules.

Harris also notes, "Plug and spin anglers have it a bit easier and can catch plenty of sharks simply conforming to Metropolitan Miami Tournament rules allowing 18-inch wire leaders and rod length double lines for shark fishing. Catching 250-pound hammerheads is not routine, but this rig will do the job at the end of a 15-pound outfit."

Both suggest chum line sharks respond well to large swimming plugs you can dance on the surface or drag along their eye. Bomber Long A's or Creek Chub Broken Backs account for plenty of fish but brutes occasionally crunch them. Magnum Rebels hold big sharks without such risk according to Ralph.

Rick Gunion, holder (1995) of the 20-pound fly rod world record for hammerheads, has hooked bunches of them and understands more than a bit about the obstacles. He's obviously also in awe of the sharks as he discusses their speed, the super rough skin, and erratic behavior.

"In my experience most hammers are far less aggressive than the one you met and are usually quite boat shy after a first or second pass at the chum, but nothing attacks the boat with the speed of a hammerhead," says Gunion. "Fly anglers in particular but all anglers, have problems protecting line from hammers. The tail and dorsal fins are huge compared to their body size and those of other sharks, and constantly attack the line. They also have trouble getting a lure or fly in their mouth because of their eye placement so many are foul hooked. Any fish is much tougher to control when you can't pull their heads off balance."

Gunion also says that "hammerheads might respond to different or less stimulus than other sharks because of their increased radar. While the many bulls and lemons Key West sharkers will see often crawl straight up the chum line, hammers come from everywhere."

We discussed our jobs when Tom could move the hammerhead toward the surface about 30 minutes into the fight. Of course, Ralph was on the gaff but hammerheads are mean twisty critters so I would tail rope it and try to help. Tom would

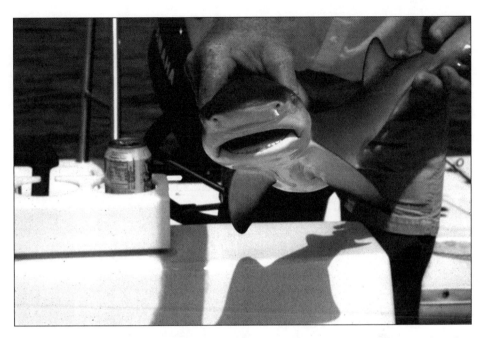

Small lemon sharks are great fun on bonefish gear. They are often confused with blacktips, as they both have black fin edges. But blacktips are shaped like footballs and are far more muscular.

loosen his drag so the shark could not saw through the class tippet and disqualify our catch.

Suddenly the shark oddly rose to the surface 15 feet in front of the boat. Tom attempted to raise his rod to protect the tippet and it held during the surge. Ten minutes later, with the shark almost within gaffing range and perhaps tired enough to safely handle, a second surfacing surge broke the leader.

Of course the leader looked like it was attacked with a file, something no one could do anything about. I left with a new respect for a magnificent creature and the difficulty of capturing one that met IGFA or Met Tournament rules.

*We saw this hammerhead almost a quarter-mile
away as it sliced through our scent trail.*

A New Hammerhead Legend

Many of Florida's hot tarpon spots host big hammerheads that often rob anglers of fish. Perhaps the next location for a prolonged series of tarpon snack stories will be the Long Key Viaduct in the Keys. According to Marathon guide Captain Butch Hewlett, the bridge is currently host to a trio of critters quite capable of snacking on 100-pound fish.

Hewlett lost half a dozen tarpon to the group in 1995. He's sure one is over a thousand pounds and the other two weigh maybe 600 to 700 pounds. He tried once to save a fish by running over its attacker, hitting it twice with his motor.

He says it didn't phase the shark a bit. If you've ever seen a big shark, and particularly a large hammerhead, attack a tarpon it will keep you out of the water. My last encounter involved a 125-pound fish and a pair of 14-foot hammerheads. The fish quivered at the surface much like the mullet it ate on our hook. One shark head butted it about 5 feet out of the water.

I put the boat between the sharks and the fish. They simply swam under the boat to complete their attack. The tarpon disappeared amidst a stream of blood and a cloud of scales in less time than it took you to read this sentence.

Hewlett figures the Long Key group ate at least 18 tarpon off anglers' lines at the bridge last year, but that was not the full extent of their destruction. During tide changes Hewlett says they pursued resting fish with a vengeance. You could easily spot the biggest shark feasting on fish a quarter of a mile away.

EFFICIENT HUNTERS

Hammerheads are definitely prehistoric, like most sharks they are thought to be unchanged for 350 million years. They grow to frightening sizes, thought to attain lengths of 5.5 to 6.5 meters or about 22 feet.

The huge elongated head houses a magnified version of shark prey-seeking radar, the Ampullae of Lorenzini. This sophisticated set of organs is capable of locating struggling fish by reading variations of electromagnetic pulses over large expanses of water. It is a feature most developed in the hammerhead.

Harris offers another theory for the hammer configuration. He thinks they use it like an airfoil on a race car or a hydrofoil on a boat. He notes the hammerhead can do things no other shark can do as it turns an ultra-tight radius in pursuit of its prey.

No doubt hammers are fast. While eating lots of tarpon, they also love rays. One specimen documented by the IGFA had more than 100 ray spikes in its head. This is minor league prey for the shallow water speedster, though. Many have witnessed hammerheads wearing down bonefish and barracuda, some of the faster fish in the sea.

PREPPING FOR A RECORD

You don't guide to Delph's 1996 total of 107 light tackle world records by accident and a day spent in his boat quickly confirmed it. A current copy of the IGFA World Record Book fills recognize patches a prominent spot on his console. Knowing the species one might come across during the day and rigging to fill a void in a particular line class enhances record-breaking opportunities.

It helps to know a trick or two to deal with a specific target, too. Long before we ran into Tom's hammerhead, Ralph drilled him on the hook-setting technique he hoped would leave enough wire outside the shark's mouth and over its snout to provide abrasion resistance. A solid lifting move seldom recommended for fly rod targets did the trick.

Delph rigs like every bite could lead to a record class hookup. For a fly rod you get a foot of bite leader, typically wire or heavy mono, measured between the eye of the hook and the class tippet. The foot includes connections so he ties them as cleanly as possible.

There's no advantage in extending the class tippet much past the minimum required 15 inches between knots. It does not last long stretched across the back of fish and lasts shorter still across the rasp-like back of a shark.

DOING IT ALONE

While hammerhead light tackle and fly captures will likely remain rare, South Florida and the Keys offer a wide variety of spots where cuda drifting might provide thrills and a few chills. Some things quickly come to mind and a local chart will provide more ideas. Two factors stand out for great conditions leading to success. Wind against or across the current offers the most erratic scent trail, increasing shark aggression. Huge volumes of water through relatively narrow funnels carry and concentrate scent trails.

The huge flush of water off the South Florida tip between Flamingo and Cape Sable harbors some bona fide monsters but also lots of more reasonable blacktips and smaller lemons. Many of the banks on the Gulfside of the Long Key Bridge are home to large numbers of blacktips and a few hammerheads.

The open water between the Arsnicker Key and Adams Key in south Biscayne Bay harbors plenty of large sharks. The Oceanside of the northernmost reach of the Keys is home to impressive numbers of hammerheads. Miami guide Captain Mark Krowka says you'll know it's a hammerhead day when most rays are scraping their bellies on the coral while barely covered with water, needing to feed but defending themselves from attack.

Sharks deserve a lot of respect around the boat. Besides all the teeth, their jaw muscles are impressive and many species bite with 5000 or more pounds of pressure per square inch. You might imagine such force by considering the full weight of a loaded half-ton pickup truck parked on the tip of your thumb. Teeth only add to the problem.

Sharks are cartilaginous fishes. Their skeletons are like our noses, firm but flexible. Most have no trouble biting you if you only have control of the tail. Hooks, plugs, and flies are cheap and cutting leaders to release sharks is the safest way to end most encounters.

You can chum plenty of smaller sharks within fly rod range with handfuls of shrimp or shrimp bits in a chum tube. They are not picky about food, but you have to get it in their face. You can find sharks perfectly sized for 8-weight rods and others that are more than anyone can handle on a 12-weight. On appropriate gear most will surprise you. When you are overmatched, they will stun you.

You can chum for sharks from a fixed position or toss at those you find while poling, but they really do light up in an erratic scent trail. I have customers who specifically book days of wave bouncing current for chumming. It's quite a sight to see and you simply cannot take well-placed food away from a hot shark.

Don't try this at home. Captain Ralph Delph is an expert at handling sharks, but they can bite their own tails. This lemon is big enough to hurt someone.

A Basic Primer
for the Deep Blue Sea

It's a mistake to visit the Keys and not spend a day or more offshore if you have the chance. At times, fishing opportunities in the depths, ranging from the near shore patch reefs to the broad expanses of the Gulf Stream, far exceed what is available in the shallows. Those fleeing cold weather during winter months and harboring a dream of an outsized catch are often far better served heading deep. Even when flats fishing is good, the depths offer an exciting change of pace.

Water temperatures are seldom altered enough in the depths to hurt the fishing, and bumpy weather turns fish on instead of running them off. Tough conditions on the flats often lead to hot bites offshore. The vitality and attitudes of the fish are also very different. The offshore glamour species, such as billfish, dolphin, tunas, and mackerel, are constantly on the move. Most grow quickly and have not been pressured as much, often offering novice anglers a good chance at catching nice fish.

Most inshore species live far longer than their offshore cousins. They've seen it all. A six-foot tarpon is in its thirties, if not older, and is a fly or bait refusing veteran. Your rigged offering tossed to a six-foot sailfish may be the first rigged bait it has ever seen, as they can sometimes attain this length during their first year. A four-year-old sailfish is a very old sailfish. The same is potentially true for a 60-pound dolphin, while a 10-pound bonefish has likely seen the whole routine several thousand times.

We attack fish in the depths with a different attitude. Chumming is the norm on the patches as is the use of live bait as food, teasers, or chum as we move deeper.

When a pelagic swims up to a bait, it eats it more times than not. (Oddly, tarpon that swim past baits still may inhale perfectly presented flies.)

Offshore fishing is a bit more work. No matter how you fish, using flies, lures, or bait, most days start with bait gathering. It's not totally necessary, but the time is usually well spent. Live chum is a big deal over wrecks or reef ledges. It helps, too, when you find roving schools of fish charging along in the Gulf Stream. In a fixed situation you use the livies to fire up the resident fish. When fish are moving, you use livies to hold them around the boat while you try to feed them.

Having an abundance of lively baits aboard opens up many opportunities for fly anglers. Livies have no place to hide when you toss them overboard as chum miles from shore. They try to hide under the boat, attracting predators within easy fly range. They also tend to stay near the surface so you can fish with a floating or intermediate line. Fish chasing live chum tend to eat everything they see without question if it makes sense. There are moments when they play hard to get, though, and demand a fly change or two.

Some species run through a chum line so quickly you cannot get a fly in their face. You can deal with them in a couple of ways. Many suspend a very hardy bait from a kite and blind fish the area around it. If you can see well, a good friend might help by teasing fish within casting range. This is accomplished by your partner tossing an interesting bait to your prey and keeping it away from them, while you put your offering right in its face. This is highly charged fishing and you should ignore the fact that partners sometimes cannot resist the hot predator chasing their teaser!

There are good reasons to lean toward heavier gear for these games. On anything much less than 10-weight fly rods or 15-pound spinning rigs, the fish will defeat you unless you are playing with babies. You never know what you might find offshore. A school of "peanut dolphin" is often hounded by 30- to 50-pounders or a 40-pound wahoo.

Your first few casts at suspected tuna might result in hookups with bonitos appropriate on a 9-weight as they often show up first when you begin chumming, but you could also snag a 20-pound blackfin or 60-pound yellowtail tuna in the same chum line. Twelve-weight fly rods or 20-pound spinning and conventional rigs lead to more reasonable battles with these fish.

Keys pros go out of their way to add to the challenge of the day, using gear providing a fair chance for fish and fisherman. Sometimes, lighter gear offers the only hope for a hookup if you have to toss a bait to sighted fish or if the fish are picky.

Some members of the snapper clan often refuse baits tied to anything heavier than a single strand of 10-pound line. The bait has to drift freely in the current to fool them in many cases. On a cloudy day, you might hook some while working a streamer through a chum line, but on other days a fresh bait, dumped off the spool of an opened-bail spinning rig and naturally drifted with the current, is the only thing they will eat.

The typical routine for yellowtail snapper when they respond well to chum near the surface is free lining an unweighted bait in the current. Line suddenly accelerating off your spool announces a take and setting the hook after a quick three to five count usually leads to a hookup. At times, this popular snapper family member refuses to climb from the depths. Then we "sandball" for them, packing a baseball sized ball of sand around the bait to plunge it toward the bottom. You wrap your line around the ball several times then jerk on the rod tip to break it free and expose the bait when you feel it hits the proper depth. The sand is juiced by adding fish oils, commercial chum, glass minnows, and sometimes cooked macaroni.

A chum line at yellowtail depths attracts a variety of species. In season you may run into kingfish and certainly can expect some barracudas. A variety of groupers willingly take baits fished under the yellowtails. Mangroves and muttons might show up too, but they respond better to baits weighted to tick along the bottom with the current. While shrimp are the easiest bait to use for most of these fish, a small white bait or pinfish attracts the largest specimens.

The same techniques work on the patch reefs. Patch reefs are steep rises off the bottom between the Keys and the outer reef. Not all hold fish but most do hold at least some. The best are marked by lots of bottom cover, including grasses and sponges. It's here you'll catch bait, and patches offer realistic fishing opportunities on the roughest days as they are somewhat sheltered. They are fun and productive any time, though, offering many ways to bend a rod and capture dinner.

You recognize patches by lots of color changes. On days when it is hard to see you can get in the neighborhood during the prime late fall through early spring months by lining up with trails of lobster traps. It's not perfect, but if you're chumming you can move the fish where you can use them.

Electronic toys help on the patches and in deeper water when used in conjunction with a chart. Most Keys tackle shops carry the chart of significant features within the boundary of the Florida Keys National Marine Sanctuary. The chart provides GPS locations for most known wrecks, artificial reefs, and meaningful live bottom. Manufacturers of GPS receivers provide reasonably priced units capable of getting you close to hot spots. Even so, you often need a fish finder or bottom reader to lock onto the best structure. You might see it on the patches without mechanical help, but you won't in the depths.

A number of offshore favorites don't hug structure, although they relate to it because it attracts bait in some way. The current shoving across the reef is concentrated by rises or slots and both areas focus feeding activity of sailfish and kingfish during their seasons. Sails tend to hang deeper than kings, but the two are often not very far apart. Both species eat best early and late in the day and might eat all day if it's gray and a bit rough. Major reef features are relatively easy to find so they often attract a lot of boat activity. Even though crowded, you'll bump into fish around easily identified hot spots.

Some anglers anchor and chum for kingfish, but most slow troll for them as they do for sailfish. You just barely maintain headway as you drag baits around suspected hot spots. Kings might hover in as little as 40 feet of water in some parts of the Keys but usually hang out a bit deeper. Sails spend most of their time in 100 feet or more of water, though they are known to crawl on top of the reef at times to chase food. If you do chum for kings, they provide a reasonable fly target. A Hi-D line and a bucktail is the rig of choice.

You'll find some interesting targets chasing baits near the surface all the way into the Gulf Stream. Dolphin and tuna-type fish constantly focus on easily found forage. Both species spend meaningful time around Keys sea mounts. From Islamorada to Key West there are sharp rises off the bottom in 1000 or so feet of water which direct water flows toward the surface when Gulf Stream current hits them. The rips are somewhat obvious, and if they are not you can still likely read them by bird activity.

It's interesting to watch birds forage for food a dozen or more miles offshore. Frigate birds, or Magnificent Man of War birds as they are more properly called, often hover over larger predators, waiting for them to drive bait to the surface. Petrels join the hunt in spring and summer. You'll sometimes find plenty of diving species along with them. Gulls and terns often work the surface when fish drive bait within easy range. They sometimes indicate the size of predators beneath them by their action. Terns won't sit on the water over large predators, probably feeling some fear for their own lives.

You will occasionally snag a bird. They deserve your best efforts to recover the hook and untangle them. Most are easily handled and you can calm them by covering them with a towel. You may never retrieve a frigate bird if you hook one. They soar too well. Other common species don't put up much of a fight. Many of these birds

Discarded fishing line keeps on fishing with occasional bad results. Dispose of it properly and don't leave it in the water.

have razor sharp beaks and don't understand your friendly intentions. Handle them like a dangerous fish.

Dolphin often hold bait near the surface for some time and low hovering birds mark them. Tuna rise and fall so birds rising and dipping more accurately reflect their presence. You can find both dolphin and tuna by paying attention to flying fish. Those you kick up with the boat tell you nothing but any you see taking off independently should alert you. They seldom fly around randomly! If you see boils when they hit the water you had best get your lures in the neighborhood. You can troll for both species a bit faster than you think. They have little trouble catching lures chugging along at 8 to 10 knots.

At times, both species hover under random offshore weed lines, though weed lines are most frequently linked to dolphin. There is a richness of food associated with floating sargassum. Floating bladed grasses usually don't indicate a concentration of food, but they sometimes shelter some forage of interest to mackerels. Take the hints the seas offer you and always pay attention to birds.

You can always stop around suspected food concentrations and do some blind casting or bait fishing. A chumming opportunity might surprise you miles from shore. Any time you find floating debris, you can expect to find some fish. Boards or other floating items often shelter species looking for a bit of shade or looking for bait hiding under free floating cover.

Much of the year, dolphin seek food and shelter around floating debris. However, wahoo might rest in the depths below waiting for young-of-the-year dolphin. Cobia constantly hunt shade, and there are times a marlin may focus on debris seeking any bite-sized morsel, which might mean just about anything when they are in the mood.

You should constantly seek debris while trolling and troll around it expecting a bite if fish aren't readily spotted. Sometimes you can stop and toss lures and flies to it, or sink a bait below it. Begin by trying it with flies or artificials, then resort to bait if you get no response. Not every floating board hides worthwhile fish. You need to test every floating board, though, and work a circle several hundred yards around it.

Many roving species operate at a "depth of the day," which changes often depending on conditions. The biggest factor is the direction and velocity of the wind. Remember that the Keys face the ocean in a gentle arc so the wind moves forage differently from one end of the island chain to the other. A northeast to east breeze pushes bait toward shore along the Upper Keys but slides parallel to the Middle and Lower Keys. South-oriented winds are far more helpful there. If there is a lot of wind from the east it may push bait far enough inshore to help everywhere.

Sailfish in their various modes of bait or spawning migration travels tend to relate to the reef, and a base depth of maybe 80 to 120 feet of water is a reasonable starting depth for them. You might have to look for dolphin in anything from 300 to 1,000 feet or more of water. The calmer it is, the farther you have to range to find them. During the calm days of summer you may never find any fish between the Keys and the Gulf Stream.

Sometimes extreme weather conditions set up similarly extreme fishing opportunities.

You Should Have Been Here Last Year

We all know the most often heard line in fishing is "You should have been here yesterday." The best time to go fishing is when you have the chance, of course, but a set of seldom seen circumstances combined last year in Islamorada for sailfishing, the likes of which few people will ever see.

Skip Nielsen's boat, *How 'Bout It*, was one the three Bud and Mary's marina that combined for 77 fish in four days. He caught over forty while the blitz was on. According to Skip, conditions are right about every 8 to 10 years to make the fish so accessible. It usually happens in March or April.

The Gulf Stream has to bend in and push within about 300 feet of the reef and the current must run at least 4 knots to the northeast. A couple weeks of south to northwest winds ending in several days of high northwest winds are needed to push filthy water out of the Gulf of Mexico. When the Gulf current loop turns milk white in 150 to 200 feet of water, most conditions are favorable for the event.

The wind now has to turn to an east quadrant, anything from northeast to southeast will work and it has to blow hard enough to build 4- to 8-foot seas. This provides three distinct color changes from the dirty water beginning with yellow-green, changing to powder blue, then dark blue. The powder blue band will ordinarily cover a 100- to 200- yard-wide swath. Everything in the ocean—marlin, dolphin, tunas, and particularly sailfish—swims to the powder blue change. They all swim right on top in the powder blue water.

Sailfish, like this rocket-launcher, know how to entertain.

The sailfish are already here swimming against the stream on their way to Gulf spawning grounds for May rituals. Skippy described the event as pure sight fishing, casting to tailing fish that are visible up to 100 yards away. They even found a swordfish and managed to hook it. After it jumped off on the second jump it went right back to tailing, but they could never get another bait to it.

Now that you know what conditions are required, watch the weather. When it has been nasty long enough in late spring check your favorite Islamorada source of fishing information for Gulf Stream conditions. Maybe you can hit the blitz and tell everybody they should have been here last year.

Since the 1994 event, more people have honed in on these conditions, and they are a bit more common than once thought. The variety of fish is broader than thought too, and you might find cobia or huge sharks in the mix. Conditions are usually somewhat uncomfortable and most folks just ignore them, preferring to fish more sheltered waters. It does take a bit of a breeze to maintain the sediment line. If you have the chance to do this–go! It's awesome to watch the wide variety of fish surfing the color change, which looks just like a wall in the water. The fish are on top. You can stop them easily with a bait and many will take a fly if you use the bait to tease them. Any nasty mid to late winter cold front muddying the Gulf and near shore Atlantic can set this up. If you can't deal with the wind using a fly, enjoy the bonanza with bait. For most of us this situation is a once in a lifetime event.

Rob Delph prepares to release a bonito.

If you troll, you have no need to worry about capturing bait. Fresh ballyhoo are a staple in all Keys tackle shops and are even available at most grocery and convenience stores. You can rig them alone. They last longer and are somewhat more attractive when dressed with a rubber skirt. You can use something with a bullet head or a flat head in front of them. The plastic comes in a wide range of colors. Dolphin seem to prefer green and yellow and also eat pink and white or blue and white.

Blackfins readily eat a rigged hoo also, but they lean toward black and red skirts. Both species will attack small bullet-headed plastics or weighted feathers. Feathers are a wahoo favorite. Tuna eat a lead-headed eel-shaped black rubber lure with enthusiasm. A cedar plug that looks much like a fat cigar is also a popular trolling bait. The fish seem to like it in wild colors bearing no resemblance to nature.

A ballyhoo-sweetened jig is a favorite offering for many bottom dwellers.

Bonito, and sometimes tuna, hone in on some surprisingly small baits and a length of soda straw on a hook is often all you need to fool one if you weight it with an egg sinker. Straws come in handy for quickly rigging ballyhoo, too. Feed your line through a short piece before tying your hook on the line. You can then slide the straw over a hoo's bill to hold it on a hook instead of wrapping it with rigging wire.

Shock leaders are routinely used when trolling artificials. You move along fast enough that the fish don't have time to check things out. Something around 40 to 60 pounds is usually enough, but if you drag large baits meant for billfish you might want to use something far heavier. You can land most Keys billfish on something under 200-pound test. The use of larger hooks, starting with maybe a 3/0 in a soda straw, is normal when trolling. Keep them sharp.

In many ways, fishing offshore is far closer to the "good old days" of fishing in the Keys as the mix of fish is farther removed from the bounds of civilization and anglers can still base in the Keys and enjoy the best of accommodations at the end of the day.

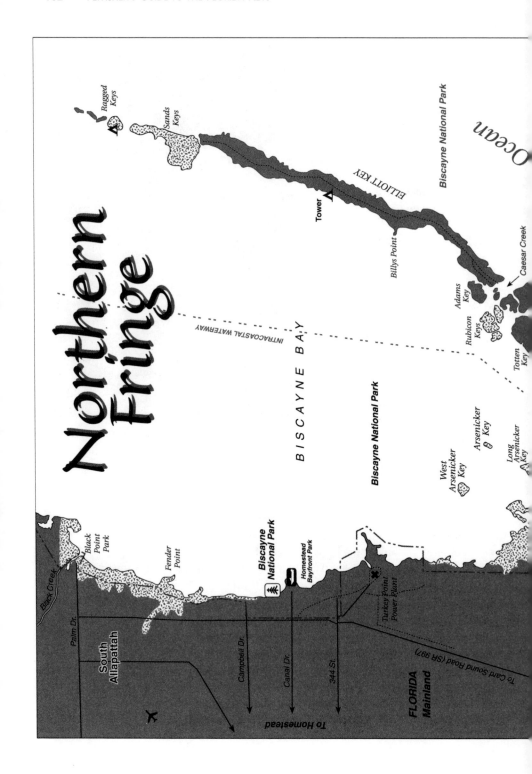

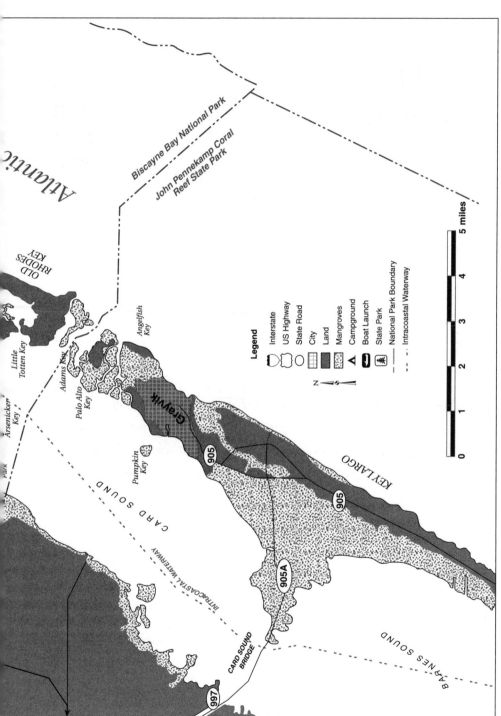

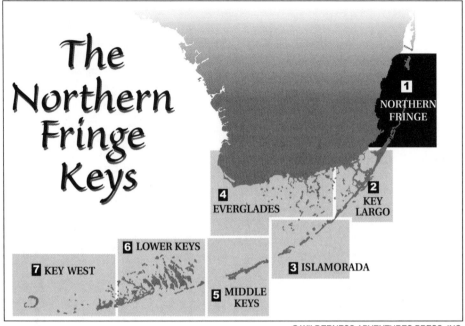

© WILDERNESS ADVENTURES PRESS, INC.

Civilization failed to fill a large gap on the shorelines of South Biscayne Bay and the far northeastern reaches of the Florida Keys island chain. Those rushing toward widely known hot spots like Islamorada, Marathon, and Key West miss some great fishing when escaping the mainland.

Much of the area is protected within the boundaries of the Biscayne Bay National Park or by areas of critical concern purchased by the state on Key Largo. Launching access is limited so there's not much random boat traffic.

Access is good enough for serious anglers yet many flats see relatively little fishing pressure compared to those around more famous Keys destinations. They're easily reached from the south coast of Florida or approachable from Upper Keys ramps as weather allows. Often during the winter, bonefishing is better here than anywhere else in the Keys if you're intent on catching a bonefish in classical stalking fashion. When it's cold, fish gather in numbers along the warmer shorelines, fleeing rapidly chilled Gulf water pouring through Upper Keys bridges to the west. For shots at the region's big cooperative fish, boat teams fishing famed Islamorada spring and fall fly tournaments often risk long boat rides in the dark and potential missed afternoon weigh-ins.

While there's much to do within sight of the Miami skyline, the more wild and wooly northern reaches of the bay are best marked by a line from Black Point on the mainland, to the Ragged Keys on the eastern side of the Bay. The water is reasonably fished if you're visiting Miami on business or want to stay in the city for other reasons. Florida City, at the southern end of Florida's turnpike, offers fairly priced accommodations and good fishing access from the last Atlantic side ramp on the mainland.

The lack of boats contributes to a calm experience. Perhaps more important for the fish is the huge mostly unrestricted flush of Gulf Stream warmed water shoving back and forth through the core of the bay from the north. The shorelines are also well protected from winter's coldest blasts. The narrow gaps between the islands bordering the Atlantic focus flows like fire hoses, offering additional attractions to fish. Members of our favorite flats fishing target species respond well to stout current and relatively consistent water temperatures. Folks just normally gravitate toward the famous areas of the Keys, not understanding how remote and productive this part of the world is.

The area is probably most compelling during the winter, but this is also when it is most crowded. You face a migration of anglers from other parts of the Keys and a concentration of tourist activity by those seeking a winter respite while clinging to city- style accommodations. The action really comes alive after a smoking cold front, one dropping temperatures 15 or 20 degrees and bearing 20-knot north quadrant winds. The Oceanside shorelines typically load up with bonefish fleeing chilly Upper Keys waters.

This is fairly simple non-spot specific fishing. The fish run the outside shoreline in the lee from the upper end of Key Largo all the way to the Raggeds. They often travel high in the water and push very obvious wakes. They tend to ignore baits and flies if they're not in their faces and fished to suspend. "Wakers" usually show best on rising tides and tend to stall frequently when the tide weakens on the coldest days. You're most likely to find stalled fish around the top of the tide as water sits and warms during the afternoon.

Stalled fish are a real treat. You won't find them all the time and may not recognize them until you've seen them a few times. Bonefish often stall in corners or off points where the water is a bit warmer than it is elsewhere on the shoreline. I usually find them a little offshore in six to eight feet or more of water and scattered from top to bottom. It's a strange encounter as the fish typically swim in a slow spiraling circle with some fish mudding on the bottom and others in the school finning on the surface in the sun. In this situation, a bait, fly, or lure fluttering in the school attracts more bites than one weighted to attack the bottom. A cloud of muddy water in the distance, interrupted by occasional white or silver flashes as fish turn on their side to feed, is your clue to this activity. You might find bones doing this anywhere around in the Keys, but it happens most from Key Largo north.

While bonefish flee colder Upper Keys waters along the Atlantic shoreline post haste, they often move along at a more relaxed pace in the bay. To be sure, they are

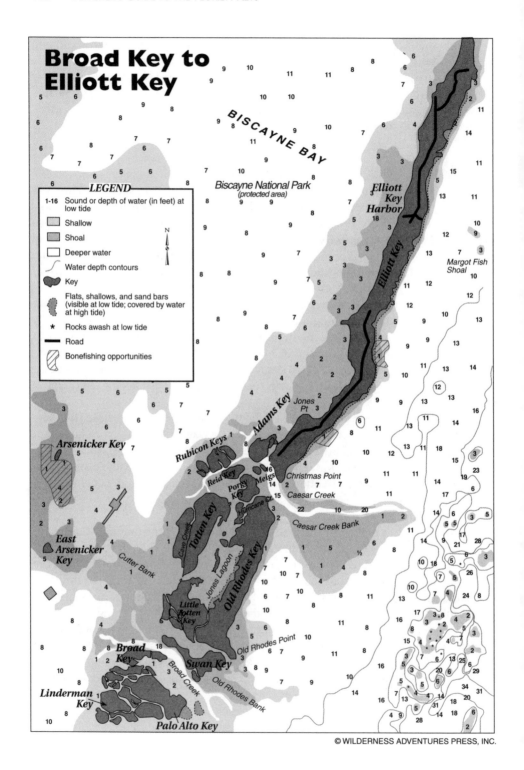

Broad Key to Elliott Key

BISCAYNE BAY

Biscayne National Park
(protected area)

Elliott Key Harbor

Elliott Key

Margot Fish Shoal

LEGEND

1-16   Sound or depth of water (in feet) at low tide

Shallow

Shoal

Deeper water

Water depth contours

Key

Flats, shallows, and sand bars (visible at low tide; covered by water at high tide)

*   Rocks awash at low tide

Road

Bonefishing opportunities

N

Arsenicker Key

East Arsenicker Key

Rubicon Keys

Adams Key

Jones Pt

Christmas Point

Caesar Creek

Caesar Creek Bank

Reid Key

Porgy Key

Meigs

Hurricane Cr.

Cave Creek

Totten Key

Jones Lagoon

Old Rhodes Key

Little Totten Key

Cutter Bank

Old Rhodes Point

Broad Key

Swan Key

Broad Creek

Old Rhodes Bank

Linderman Key

Palo Alto Key

Broad Key to Elliott Key—Some of the best flats here show up only as numbers. Study Arsnicker Key for an example. It's a great spot for tailing bones and attracts a few permit. The Elliott shoreline looks pretty clean on the chart, but it hides lots of short bottom rises and our favorite species cruise it regularly. Because things aren't obvious here crowds tend to stay light.

still on the march when it's cold but they stop to feed in more typical fashion as the day warms. You'll find them digging more actively on flats shelves or within depressions on top of the flats. There's not as much shallow real estate here as there is around Islamorada, making it a bit easier to figure out where to sit. I like to guard flats points while the fish are moving in response to the weather. It gives you shots at fish moving deep and those bumping into the banks and detouring around them. The coastal or inside shoreline holds bonefish although they're often tough to spot, preferring slightly deeper water. They are goofy, though, and seldom refuse the proper food.

Bonefish are not the only wintertime attraction. There's a surprising amount of "pop up" tarpon activity along the coastal shoreline whenever the weather is reasonably warm. The area is loaded with creeks hiding some small to medium-sized fish most of the year. They cruise on nice days and you'll find smaller family members hiding in ambush under mangrove roots at other times if you pole the shoreline. They often share space in the most attractive corners and run outs with snook. The cooling canals from the Turkey Point Power Plant offer a respite from the winds and chill for both anglers and fish.

There is no telling what species you'll find scattered in the central reaches of the bay during cool weather. Spanish and sometimes cero mackerel find their way into mullet muds along with good numbers of trout and the odd concentration of bluefish. Any obviously cloudy water deserves a look. It's best to stay off of them with your motor and drift or pole toward their edges. At times, random muds are loaded with small bonefish too. Shrimp or jigs work well for spinfishing folks plumbing muds, while fly anglers do well with Clousers and other similarly weighted offerings.

Biscayne Bay is relatively deep when compared to many other Keys basins. It holds a good population of resident seatrout often suspended over grass beds rising from the bottom. Barracuda fishing here is some of the best in the Keys, comparable with the dominant world record fishery around Key West. More mixed-bag action is available around myriad ditches and flood control canals draining the mainland.

There are plenty of reasons to fish here the rest of the year. Bonefish are abundant on the area's flats spring through fall. Early morning tailing activity on bayside flats can be as good as it gets anywhere in the Keys during the summer. The spring and fall fishery is fabled for numbers of large fish.

Permit fishing rivals all but the very best offered in the Lower Keys. Permit are where you find them, here as elsewhere in the Keys. While you'll stumble upon fish

Old Rhodes Key to Key Largo—All those creeks are something good, folks! They offer a hiding place on windy days when you just want to latch onto supper. You'll also find little tarpon in them much of the year along with a bunch of snook. The inlets and outlets concentrate good flows of water favored by bonefish and permit.

in corners of the grass flats, the raging currents of the narrow funnels seemingly stupefy the fish. They usually sample reasonable offerings properly presented in their feeding windows.

Significant numbers of big tarpon winter in the warm waters of southeast Florida's deeper shipping channels and flood the outside shoreline when beginning their migration toward the west as spring fulfills its promise. The inside coastal shoreline fishery is slightly ignored and seldom discussed. It's a bit ignored by the fish too, but you can often find just enough fish of your very own here to make a nice day. You may face a crowd outside if you try to fish around channel-end points. The obvious channels are bordered by structural obstacles, making fish easy to spot. The concentrated current helps us feed them. For tarpon, it's often best for newcomers to seek somewhat less exciting spots on the long shorelines that are frequently ignored.

Card Sound seems a natural extension of the bay, although currents are lazier and the edges are steep, not shelving. It's far less attractive for both bonefish and permit, but tarpon and snook filter along its edges. Trout fishing remains good here. During windy winters the Macs make their way into the sound, too. The Card Sound Bridge might well be one of the best spots to try your hand at trolling for tarpon and, considering its proximity to the Miami metropolis, offers surprisingly uncrowded and consistently good live bait fishing.

Barnes Sound, while not a logical extension to the bay, is a tempting target from the good public ramp on Card Sound Road. It's fishing changes drastically from year to year as salinity levels rise and fall depending on flood control demands and natural rainfall. While random fishing may prove difficult here at times, tarpon and snook tolerate a wide range of salinity and follow bait captured by the flow of the tide. You may find fewer fish, but again you'll often have them to yourself. Big tides pushing both prey and predators can provide some hot action at times.

Jewfish Creek provides the first meaningful access to Florida Bay and the Gulf for fish migrating along the coast. Tarpon and snook fishing can be awesome here at night if you can convince the bridge tender to keep the lights on to attract bait. If not you can provide your own miracle with a live well full of pilchards you might offer to the fish. This end of the bay is easily fished from ramps on Key Largo if you seek a quick few hours respite early or late in the day.

There are two ways into the Keys from Florida City. Least inspiring is U.S. 1, and I caution you to drive it carefully. On Card Sound Road, you get some view of the Keys as they were before becoming overwhelmed by modern civilization, along with a glorious look into the reaches of Biscayne Bay from one of only a handful of meaning-

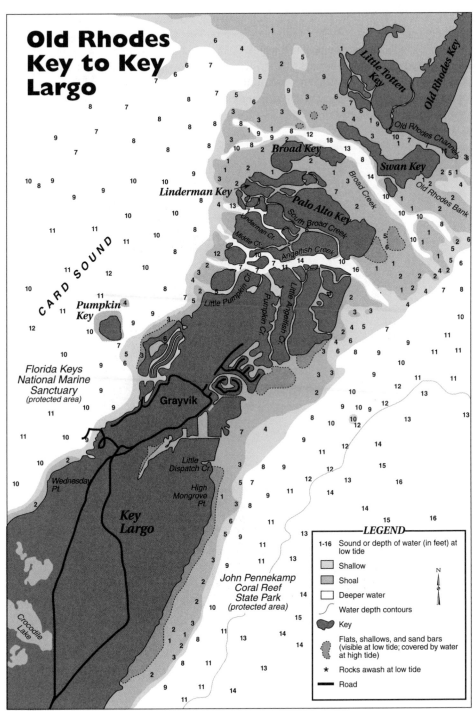

Old Rhodes Key to Key Largo

CARD SOUND

Pumpkin Key

Linderman Key

Broad Key

Palo Alto Key

Little Totten Key

Old Rhodes Key

Old Rhodes Channel

Swan Key

Old Rhodes Bank

Broad Creek

Linderman Cr.

Middle Cr.

South Broad Creek

Angelfish Creek

Little Pumpkin Cr.

Pumpkin Cr.

Little Angelfish Cr.

Florida Keys National Marine Sanctuary
(protected area)

Grayvik

Little Dispatch Cr.

Wednesday Pt.

High Mongrove Pt.

Key Largo

John Pennekamp Coral Reef State Park
(protected area)

Crocodile Lake

LEGEND

N

1-16   Sound or depth of water (in feet) at low tide

Shallow

Shoal

Deeper water

Water depth contours

Key

Flats, shallows, and sand bars (visible at low tide; covered by water at high tide)

★   Rocks awash at low tide

Road

© WILDERNESS ADVENTURES PRESS, INC.

fully elevated Keys bridges. The look may prove useful if you take the time to buy the charts you need to properly attack Keys waters. The charts will make more sense if you have a feel for the reach of the water.

The end of the road here is littered with well-known food and hotel chains. The best launching site is within the boundaries of Biscayne Bay National Park and the road to it is well marked. It is surprisingly far off the highway but worth the trip. Contact the Florida City Chamber of Commerce at 305-247-2332.

This permit fell to a tarpon fly on a windy morning.

Northern Fringe Hub City Information

You can make either of these cities your headquarters while fishing the Northern Fringe Keys if you trailer your own boat. At the first light at the end of turnpike, (if you're headed to the Keys) you can turn left to reach a good boat ramp at Biscayne Bay National Park. Turn right if you prefer to launch in Everglades National Park. Both ramps are a bit of a ride from the highway, but both offer good fishing within sight of land.

If you decide to fish the Everglades, you can stay at Flamingo Lodge in Everglades National Park at 941-695-3010. Take lots of bug spray if you intend to wander outside.

Florida City

HOTELS AND MOTELS
Baymont Inns & Suites, 10821 Caribbean Blvd., Cutler Ridge / 305-278-0001
Best Western Gateway, 411 S Krome Ave. / 305-246-5100
Comfort Inn, 333 SE 1st Ave. / 305-248-4009
Econo Lodge, 553 NW 1st Ave. / 305-248-9300
Hampton Inn, 124 E Palm Dr. / 305-247-8838

RESTAURANTS
Mutineer Restaurant, 11 SE 1st Ave. / 305-245-3377

RV PARK AND CAMPGROUND
Florida City Camper Site, 601 NW 3rd Ave. / 305-248-7889

Homestead

HOTELS AND MOTELS
A-1 Budget Motel, 30600 S Dixie Hwy. / 305- 247-7032
Anhinga Motel, 250 S Krome Ave. / 305-247-3590
Days Inn, 51 South Homestead Blvd. U.S. 1

RESTAURANTS
Redland Rib House, 24856 SW 177 Ave. / 305-246-8866
Golden Corral Family Restaurant, 350 N Homestead Blvd. / 305-245-2406
Capri Restaurant, 935 N Krome Ave. / 305-247-1542
Kim's Cupboard, 36650 SW 102 Ave. / 305-247-0844
Gusto's Bar & Grill, 326 1st Ave. / 786-243-9800
City Grill, 545 West Lucy Street / 305-248-1993

RV PARK AND CAMPGROUND
Southern Comfort RV Resort, 345 E Palm Dr. / 305-248-6909

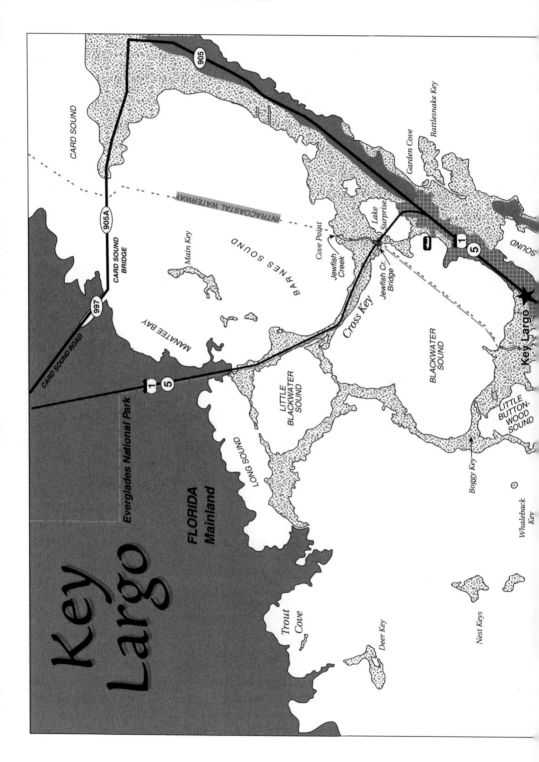

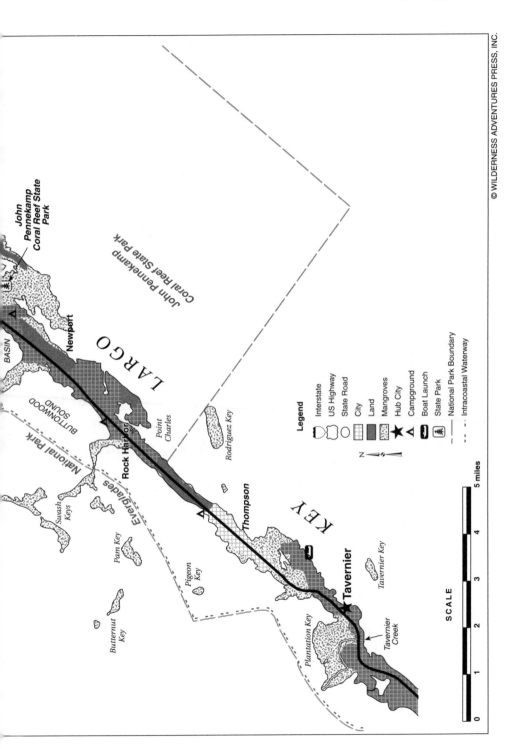

Legend

Interstate
US Highway
State Road
City
Land
Mangroves
Hub City ★
Campground ▲
Boat Launch
State Park
National Park Boundary
Intracoastal Waterway

John Pennekamp
Coral Reef State
Park

John Pennekamp
Coral Reef State Park

LARGO

Newport

BASIN

BUTTONWOOD
SOUND

Point
Charles

Rock Harbor

Everglades
National Park

Swash
Keys

Pam Key

Pigeon
Key

Butternut
Key

Rodriguez Key

Thompson

KEY

Tavernier Key

Tavernier ★

Tavernier
Creek

Plantation Key

SCALE

0   1   2   3   4   5 miles

© WILDERNESS ADVENTURES PRESS, INC.

Rumor has it that when Bogey and Bacall filmed the 1940s movie, "Key Largo", you could sleep in the middle of the highway from dusk to dawn without fearing the impact of a traveling vehicle. When you hit Key Largo's divided highway while approaching the Keys today, you might shed a tear for days gone by. There's no reason to.

From the highway, Key Largo resembles bustling far outlying suburbia, yet it takes only a few minutes to find a corner of the world all your own once on the water. It's also easy to find a quiet out-of-the-way eatery and a spectacular sunset view.

You'll never feel guilty leaving non-fishing family members ashore here as they'll have no problem finding ways to stay entertained. The region can meet the needs of the most demanding among us whether you seek world-class luxury or simple solitude. The wealth of activity within easy reach of good fishing becomes particularly endearing once you realize that you have the choice of enjoying it or escaping it. We're not going to talk much about offshore fishing in regional sections, but Key Largo offers the longest consistent season in the Keys for sailfish, along with great wahoo fishing, and is widely recognized as home to some of the largest cubera snappers in the world.

A quick glance at charts of the Key Largo Oceanside shoreline might suggest it's a bit sterile when compared to the mazes of flats around Islamorada and the Lower Keys. You have to take a closer look. Charts for the Keys really do not accurately illustrate the fishing opportunities and require the use of some imagination. While shoreline shallow waters are depicted as only a couple colored bands of water, a glance at the numbers marking the depths shows a wide variety of ridges and grass beds rising from the bottom.

It takes a serious cold front to push all the fish from the shoreline since it is virtually isolated from the chilling impacts of Florida Bay waters with the exception of the southwest end. The effect of Tavernier Creek is not felt far, but it is worth noting on the coolest days. While a positive during the winter, a lack of stiff channel flows influences fishing the remainder of the year.

The bonefish working the long shorelines average smaller than those nearer Miami or Islamorada, maybe something less than seven pounds, but they are typically cooperative. You'll find them bouncing around or tailing on the unmarked shallows on both sides of the bottom of the tides and mudding on them at the peaks. In between they cruise and are somewhat hard to spot. It's not a place to be on a cloudy day with lots of water. The fish are almost translucent against the light bottom on the best of sun days unless they're in big schools.

Search a bit more and you'll find a few broader flats tucked away in corners or jutting from an offshore island. Double-digit fish are common here. Big and small fish mix up their chosen habitat as the weather changes. I'll admit I've never met a bonefish I didn't like, whether it weighed two pounds or twelve.

Although bones use the entire shoreline at one time or another, any spots offering increased water flows hold them longer and encourage more feeding activity. If you study the chart thoroughly you'll find a few outlets from residential canals and a couple of natural ones to boot. They're worth an extra look.

Plenty of permit ply the long shoreline. A lack of current sometimes makes them hard to feed when it's calm, but they eat quite well on windy days. Both bones and permit will hound rays whenever you find them in good current so don't ignore the obvious plumes of a ray mud. At least a couple of fly rod world record mutton snappers were Key Largo fish caught while they tracked rays. Fish here spend more time with rays than they do in many other parts of the Keys.

Tarpon have to sneak by here too, and they do so in droves. You'll find the usual crowds around the obvious areas of congested pathways with high water flows. With a bit of work you could find several miles of shoreline all your own. While Key Largo is not noted as a tarpon hot spot there are many advantages to finding slightly out of the way fish. Fish unmolested for miles during their travels are a joy to watch. If you do the right things they usually eat pretty well, too. You can find solitude on this island's long shoreline, something missing around many hot spots. The vast majority of fish moving between Key West and Miami travel the shoreline so you're bound to find some, though a few fish find ways to fool you.

Key Largo, Southwest End—This chart of the southwest end of Key Largo shows little in the way of obviously interesting terrain, yet local waters harbor a solid year round population of bonefish that increases dramatically during cooler months. The fish are often on the move, although they tail dependably at the bottom of the tide. You'll find large marl flats, but the fish move frequently over relatively hard clean bottom. They are more aggressive when they do. It's a tough area to fish when you cannot see well, as the fish are often deep unless tailing conditions are good.

Earlier, I suggested a decent amount of tarpon filter through Card and Barnes sounds. They're frequently pushed through the Jewfish Creek Bridge and into the confines of Blackwater Sound. They track edges here like they do every place else. At the top of the tide you might find some sleeping against the western shoreline. Big tides eventually push them through the handful of creeks connecting the sound to others. They might find a corner to their liking and spend several days resting and feasting, or find an outlet leading them to further travels.

Any of the obvious drainages should hold a few fish during most of the tarpon migration and it only takes a few resting fish to make a day for a good fly caster if you pole likely spots. There are often some small fish in Blackwater Sound most of the year.

I've skipped by Largo Sound, but it does offer some interesting fishing for bonefish and permit along its uncivilized shore. It can be a wintertime hot spot and also has a few scattered fish during prime early and late tailing hours when the tide is right. You'll find little tarpon in here, too, some under the shadow of docks along its developed shore.

There are myriad creeks branching off from the sound, and they hold some surprisingly large snappers along with snook. You can reach them on the worst days if you need a place to hide from the weather or catch a quick dinner when you don't have a lot of time to spend on the water. On the Gulfside of Key Largo, the creeks separating the basins offer the same escape, although

The size of the fish has nothing to do with the size of the grin.

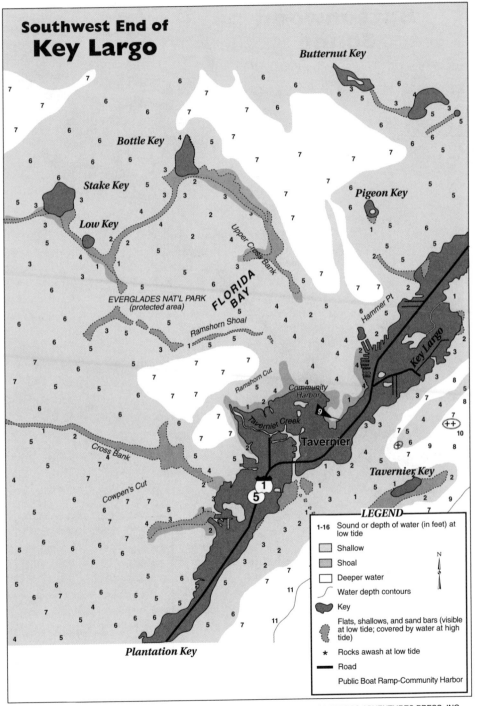

Southwest End of
Key Largo

Butternut Key

Bottle Key

Stake Key

Low Key

Pigeon Key

Upper Cross Bank

EVERGLADES NAT'L PARK
(protected area)

FLORIDA BAY

Ramshorn Shoal

Hammer Pt

Key Largo

Ramshorn Cut

Community Harbor

Taverniet Creek

Tavernier

Cross Bank

Cowpen's Cut

Tavernier Key

LEGEND

1-16	Sound or depth of water (in feet) at low tide
	Shallow
	Shoal
	Deeper water
	Water depth contours
	Key
	Flats, shallows, and sand bars (visible at low tide; covered by water at high tide)
*	Rocks awash at low tide
—	Road
	Public Boat Ramp-Community Harbor

N

Plantation Key

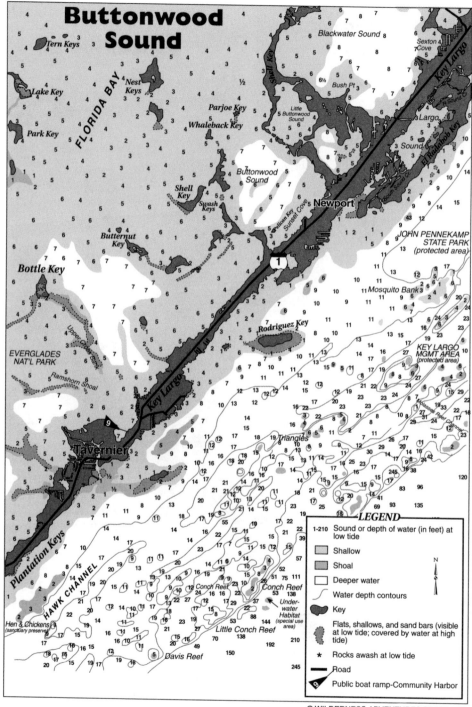

© WILDERNESS ADVENTURES PRESS, INC.

fishing in those used for navigation is better at night or before and after the crowds come and go throughout the middle of the day.

The Gulfside offers numerous unpublicized fishing opportunities. Schools of small to medium-sized jacks search the shorelines for hapless prey. There are enough random redfish sunning when it is cool, or tailing when it's warm, to deserve some attention. Wherever you can find a good flow of water pushing under mangrove prop roots you can expect to find a snook or baby tarpon if there is enough water for them to hide while waiting for food to wash by. Deeper holes under the mangroves or blow downs hold some surprisingly large snappers.

There are few bonefish or permit along most of the Gulfside of Key Largo, but as you near the flow of water from Tavernier Creek their numbers increase. During the late 1980s and early 1990s this may have been one of the best bonefishing areas for big fish in the Keys. It was sorely impacted by algae blooms in the mid '90s. While not fully recovered in 2000, the strong flow of summer and fall water along with vastly improved water conditions now make it an area worth prospecting. The flats are best during spring tides.

The near side of Everglades National Park is surprisingly quiet yet offers good to occasionally excellent fishing. The bay is broad here with large basins. The scattered flats all concentrate food and game species. There's much to be said about fishing a mile long length of flat by yourself. I often like to park on an unfamiliar edge and watch it through a tide. Boredom is seldom a problem on area flats if you pick an edge with obvious water movement.

Many basin flats without great flows of water seem rather featureless, almost scrubbed in appearance, as they lack the lush grass cover we see elsewhere. You might overlook them. They do hold food and even if they don't attract feeding fish, still serve as a barrier to migration. During summer and early fall you might find large schools of redfish randomly running some of them. If you do, keep in mind that they often use them for a number of days.

Any muddy areas you find demand attention. Mullet are the usual culprits, and they attract a variety of predators interested in eating either them or whatever critters they stir from the bottom as they dig. Wind can raise fishy looking muds against a flat or shoreline edge. If you don't get bit right away or see some obvious fish activity, move on.

Buttonwood Sound—This doesn't look like much as there is far more deep water than shallow. Still there are lots of nooks and crannies hiding a variety of fish. Any migratory fish are stuck here for quite some time since there is such a gap between outlets once they are driven into the bay by currents. The basins hold good populations of fun fish you can find in muds, such as trout, ladyfish, and jacks. The redfish population is continually increasing on the flats. The creeks offer good fishing for snappers and snook, along with some tarpon much of the year. Much of it is close at hand, too, offering good access for a quick trip.

Key Largo Hub City Information

Key Largo

HOTELS AND MOTELS

Anchorage Resort/Yacht Club, Jewfish Creek / 305-451-0500
Bay Cove Motel, 99446 Overseas Hwy. / 305-451-1686
Baywood Villas, 104250 Overseas Hwy. / 305-451-3595
Bay Harbor Lodge, 97702 Overseas Hwy. / 305-852-5695
Best Western Suites-Key Largo, 201 Ocean Dr. / 305-451-5081
Blue Lagoon Resort, 99096 Overseas Hwy. / 305-451-2908
Coconut Bay Resort, 97770 U.S. Hwy. 1 / 305-852-1625
Family Paradise Island, 107900 Overseas Hwy. / 305-451-1133
Florida Bay Club, 103500 U.S. Hwy., 1 / 305-451-0101
Gilbert's Holiday Island of Key Largo, 107900 Overseas Hwy. / 305-451-1133
Holiday Inn Sunspree Resort & Marina, 99701 Overseas Hwy. / 305-451-2121
Jules Undersea Lodge, 51 Shoreland Dr. / 305-451-2353
Kelly's Motel on the Bay, 104220 U.S. Hwy. 1 / 305-451-1622
Key Largo Inn Travelodge, P.O. Box 2843 / 305-451-2478
Marriott Key Largo Bay Beach Resort, 103800 Overseas Hwy. / 305-453-0000
Lona Kai Resort, 97802 U.S. Hwy. 1 / 305-852-7200
Largo Lodge Motel, 101740 Overseas Hwy. / 305-451-0424
Marina Del Mar resort & Marina, 527 Caribbean Drive / 305-451-4107
Marriott's Key Largo Bay Beach, 103800 Overseas Hwy. / 305-453-0000
Neptune's Hideway, 104180 Overseas Hwy. / 305-451-0357
Port Largo Villas, 417 Bahia Ave. / 305-451-9212
Ramada Inn Resort & Marina, 99751 Overseas Hwy. / 305-451-3939
Rick's Place, 104300 Overseas Hwy. / 305-3287
Rock Reef Resort, 97850 Overseas Hwy. / 305-852-2401
Seafarer Fish & Dive Resort, 97684 Overseas Hwy. / 800-599-7712
Sheraton Key Largo Resort, 97000 Bayside Hwy. / 305-852-5553
Stone Ledge Motel/Apartments, Rt.. 1, Box 50 / 305-852-8114
Suites at Key Largo, 201 Ocean Dr. / 305-451-5081
Sunset Cove Motel, 99630 Overseas Hwy. / 305-451-0705
Westin Beach Resort - Key Largo, 97000 Overseas Hwy. / 305-852-5553

RV PARKS AND CAMPGROUNDS

Florida Keys RV Resort, 106003 Overseas Hwy. / 305-451-6090
Holiday RV's Inc, P.O. Box 1546 / 305-451-4555
Calusa Camp Resort, 325 Calusa St. / 305-451-0232
American Outdoors Camper Resort, 106003 Overseas Hwy. / 305-852-8054
Key Largo Kampground/Marina, 101551 Overseas Hwy. / 305-451-1431
Rock Harbor Marina & RV Park, 36 East Second St. / 305 852-2025
Kings Kamp, 103620 Overseas Hwy. /Mm 103.6 BAYSIDE / 305 451-0010

VACATION RENTALS

All Star Vacation Rentals, 500 Burton Drive / 888-249-1779

Florida Bay Club, P.O. Box 2520 / 305-451-0101

Freewheeler Vacations, P.O. Box 1634 / 305-664-2075

Moon Bay Condominium, 1850 NE 18th Road / 305-893-3566

Port Largo Club Condo Assoc., P.O. Box 1290 / 305-451-4847

Vacation Properties in the Florida Keys, 230 Homestead Ave. , Ste 301 / 305-453-9062

Century 21 Keysearch Realty, 101925 Overseas Hwy. / 305-451-4321

Schmitt Real Estate Co, 100430 Overseas Hwy. / 305-451-4422

RESTAURANTS

Alabama Jack's, 58000 Card Sound Rd. / 305-248-8741

Anthony's Italian Restaurant, 97360 Overseas Highway / 305-853-1177

Arnie's Café & Marina, Mm 107 5 Overseas Highway / 305-451-1929

Ballyhoo's Grill & Grog, Mm 98 Median / 305-852-0822

Bayside Grill, 99530 Overseas Highway / 305-451-3380

BJ's BBQ, 102570 Overseas Highway / 305-451-0900

Bogie's Cafe, Mm 100 Oceanside / 305-451-2121

Cactus Jack's, Mm 103.9 Bayside / 305-453-0249

Cafe Key Largo @ The Sheraton, Mm 97 Overseas Highway / 305-852-5553

Cafe Largo, 99530 Overseas Hwy. / 305-451-4885

Cheng Garden Chinese Restaurant, 101443 Overseas Hwy. / 305-453-0600

Coconuts @ the Marina Del Mar, Mm 100 Oceanside / 305-451-4107 / Fine dining with a fishing theme

Crack'd Conch Restaurant, 105045 Overseas Hwy. / 305-451-0732 / Once a fishing camp now with great seafood and local cuisine

Craig's Restaurant, Mm 90.5, Plantation Key / 305-852-9424

Crazy Flamingo, 45 Garden Cove Dr. / 305-451-8022

Danny's Waterway Restaurant, 106690 Overseas Hwy. / 305-451-1929

De Mares Restaurant, 1 Seagate Blvd. / 305-453-9337

Denny's Latin Cafe, 99600 U.S. Hwy. 1 / 305-451-3665

Doc's Galley, 522 Caribbean Dr. / 305-451-5652

El-Rouby's Restaurant, Mm 99.5 Bayside / 305-451-4000

Fish House Restaurant, Mm 102 4 / 305-451-4665 / The finest in "Conch Style" cooking in Key Largo.

Frank Keys Cafe, 100211 Overseas Hwy. / 305-453-0310

Ganim's Kountry Kitchen, 102250 Overseas Hwy. / 305-451-3337

Gus' Grille at the Marriott, 103800 Overseas Hwy. / 305-453-0000

Harriette's Restaurant, Mm 95.7 / 305-852-8689

Hideout Restaurant, Mm 103.5 Oceanside / 305-451-0128

Hobo's Restaurant, Mm 104.2 Bayside / 305-451-5888

Island Seafood & Spirits, Mm 97.6 / 305-852-4888

Italian Fisherman Restaurant, 10400 Overseas Hwy. / 305-451-4471

Key Largo Ocean Resort Cafe, 94825 U.S. Hwy. 1 / 305-852-1168
Keys Palm Restaurant, 106690 Overseas Hwy. / 305-451-6059
Makota Japanese Restaurant, Mm 99.5 Bayside / 305-451-7083
Mandalay Marina Tiki Bar & Restaurant, 305-852-9019
Marlin Restaurant, Mm 102.7 / 305-451-9555
Mary & Stan's Restaurant, Mm 99 / 305-451-2947
Mexican Plaza Restaurant, Mm 103 / 305-451-3490
Mrs. Mac's Kitchen, Mm 99.4, 99336 Overseas Hwy. / 305-451-3722 / A true down-
   home meal just like Mom makes
Oceanside Cafe & Marina, 94825 U.S. Hwy. 1 / 305-852-1168
Parrot Head Cafe, 100-A Ocean Dr. / 305-451-4703
Pilot House Restaurant & Marina, 15 N Channel Dr. / 305-451-3142
Port Largo Coffee Shop, Mm 99.5 Port Largo / 305-451-2999
Quay Restaurant, 102050 Overseas Hwy. / 305-451-0943
Senior Frijoles Restaurant, Mm 103.9 Bayside / 305-451-1592 / Mexican dishes
   and Caribbean style seafood.
Snapper's Saloon/Raw Bar, 139 Seaside Ave. / 305-852-5956
Snook's Bayside Restaurant, Mm 99.9 / 305-453-3799
Sundowners On The Bay, Mm 103.9 Bayside / 305-451-4502 / Fresh seafood with
   an unbelievable sunset view. Inside and outside dining
The Quay, 102050 Overseas Hwy. / 305-451-0943
Treetops Restaurant At The Sheraton, 9700 Bayside Hwy. / 305-852-5553
Snappers Waterfront Saloon & Raw Bar, 139 Seaside Ave. , Mm 94.5 /
   305-852-5956

FLY SHOPS/BAIT AND TACKLE
Bill's Bait & Tackle Shop, Mm 99.5 Bayside / 305-451-0531
Bluewater World Corp., 100460 Overseas Hwy. / 305-451-2511
Boater's World Discount Marine Center, 105660 Overseas Hwy. / 305-453-9050
Cross Key Bait & Tackle, Overseas Hwy. / 305-451-0051
Grand Slam Outfitters, 40 Fishing Village Dr. / 305-367-3000
Key Largo Bait & Tackle, Mm 101.5 / 305-451-0921
M & M Rod & Reel Repair, 103530 Overseas Hwy. / 305-451-0442
Ocean Reef Clubs, Inc.,1 Service Village Dr. / 305-367-2611
West Marine, 103400 Overseas Hwy. / 305-453-9050
Yellow Bait House, Mm 101.7 / 305-451-0921
Zappie's Bar & Tackle, Mm 99.5 Bayside / 305-451-0531

BOAT RENTALS
Caribbean Watersports, Westin Beach Resort, Mm 97 / 305-852-4707
Club Nautico Of The Florida Keys, 527 Caribbean Dr. / 305-451-4120
Cross Key Inc., Overseas Hwy. / 305-451-0051
H20 Adventures, Mm 94.5, 829 Bonita Ln, Rock Harbor / 305-853-0600
Hobo's Boat Rentals, Mm 104.2, Bayside / 305-451-4684
Holiday Isle Watersports Inc., Mm 84, Holiday Isle / 305-664-5390

Island Style Water Sports, 104100 Overseas Hwy. / 305-453-4359
Italian Fisherman Marina, Mm 104 / 305-451-3726
It's A Dive, 103800 Overseas Hwy. / 305-453-9881
Ocean Bay Marina, Mm 100, 5 Seagate Blvd. / 305-451-3109
Sea Elf's Reef Rentals, 2 Fishing Village Dr. / 305-367-4391
Island Style Water Sports, 104100 Overseas Hwy. / 305-664-3636

MARINAS

Garden Cove Marina, 21 Garden Cove Drive / 305-451-4694
Italian Fisherman Marina, 10400 Overseas Hwy. / 305-451-3726
Markey's Marine Service, 98250 Overseas Hwy. / 305-852-3337
Pilot House Marina, 13 Seagate Blvd. / 305-451-9985
Port Engineers, P.O. Box 2768 / 305-451-1864
Rowell's Marina and Boat Sales, P.O. Box 1661 / 305-451-0295
Travis Boating Center, 106280 Overseas Hwy. / 305-451-3398
Key Largo Harbor Marine, 305-451-0045
Molasses Reef Marina, 305-451-9411

CAR RENTALS

Just Jeeps of the Keys, 305-367-1070
Avis Rent A Car, 800-452-1494 / www.avis.com
Dollar Rent A Car 800-800-4000 / www.dollar.com
Alamo, 800-327-9633 / www.alamo.com
Hertz, www.hertz.com
Enterprise Rent A Car, 31 Ocean Reef Dr. / 305-367-4226

EMERGENCY INFORMATION

Coast Guard, 305-664-8077 or VHF 16
Seatow, 1-800-4-SEATOW / Key Largo / 305-431-3330 / 24 hour dispatch
TowBoat/U.S., 800-391-4869 / 24 hour dispatch

Tavernier

Hotels
Bay Breeze Motel, 160 Sterling Rd. / 305-852-5248
Conch-On-In, 103 Caloosa St. / 305-852-9309
Island Bay Resort, 92500 Overseas Hwy. / 305-852-4087 / 800-654-Keys
Keys Motel, 90611 Old Hwy. / 305-852-2351
Tavernier Hotel, 91865 Overseas Hwy. / 305-852-4131
Tropic Vista Motel, 90701 Old Hwy. / 305 852-8799

Vacation Rentals
Ocean Pointe Suites and Condos, P.O. Box 442, 92 Oceanside / 305-853-3000 /
   Condominium resort
Prudential Keyside Properties, 91951 Overseas Highway / 305 853-1100

Restaurants
The Frog And The Fly Cafe, 91200 Overseas Hwy. / 305-852-8584
Great Wall Chinese Restaurant, 91200 Overseas Hwy. / 305-852-8508
Greek On The Creek, 901 U.S.Highway 1 / 305-852-3103
Tropical Cafe, M.M. 90.5 Overseas Highway / 305-852-3251
The Copper Kettle, 91865 Overseas Hwy. / 305-852-4131
Country Gulls, 91260 Overseas Hwy. / 305-852-8244
Craig's Restaurant, 90154 U.S. Highway 1 / 305-852-9424
Old Tavernier Italian Restaurant, 90311 Overseas Hwy. / 305-852-8106
Old Tavernier Restaurant Bar, Mm 90.1 / 305-852-6012

Boat Rentals
Tavernier Creek Boat Rental, Mm 90, 90800 Overseas Hwy. / 305-852-3894
Oceanside Watersports, 90511 Overseas Hwy. / 305-853-5899
Sundance Charters, 368 S Coconut Palm Blvd. / 305-852-8895

Fly Shops, Bait and Tackle
Plantation Fisheries, 305 248-4043
Roberts Bait Supply, 305 248-4043

Marinas
Mangrove Marina, Mm. 91.7 Bayside / 305-852-8380 / 130 wet slips, 30/50 amp
   service, gas & diesel, ship store and dry storage.
Tavernier Creek Marina, 90800 U.S. 1 Box 6 / 305-852-5854 / Dry storage up to
   36', wet slips with security / Fuel dock / Parts / Ships store & tackle shop.
Blue Waters Marina, 230 Banyan Ln. / 305-853-5604
Campbell's Marina, 200 Florida Ave., / 305-852-8380

Hospitals
Mariners Hospital, 88.5 High Point Rd # 50 / 305-852-4418

Key Largo Marina Services

Marina	Phone	Slips	Tackle	Gas	Groceries	Public Ramp	Restrooms	Restaurant	Repairs
Garden Cove Marina	305-451-4694	6	Yes	Yes	Yes	Yes	Yes	Yes	Yes
Italian Fisherman Marina	305-451-3726	0	Yes	Yes	No	No	Yes	Yes	Yes
Key Largo Harbor Marina	305-451-0045	80	No	Yes	No	Yes	Yes	Yes	Yes
Markey's Marine Service	305-852-3337	0	No	No	No	No	No	No	Yes
Molasses Reef Marina	305-451-9411	16	No	No	No	Yes	Yes	No	No
Pilot House Marina	305-451-9985	15	No	Yes	Yes	No	Yes	Yes	No
Port Engineers	305-451-1864	0	No	No	No	No	No	No	Yes
Rowell's Marina	305-451-0295	0	Yes	Yes	No	Yes	Yes	No	Yes
Travis Boating Center	305-451-3398	0	No	No	No	No	No	No	Yes
Tavernier Creek Marina	305-853-5854	0	No	Yes	Yes	Yes	Yes	Yes	Yes
Blue Waters Marina	305-852-5141	19	No	No	No	No	Yes	No	No
Mangrove Marina	305-852-8380	20	Yes	Yes	Yes	Yes	Yes	Yes	Yes

Islamorada

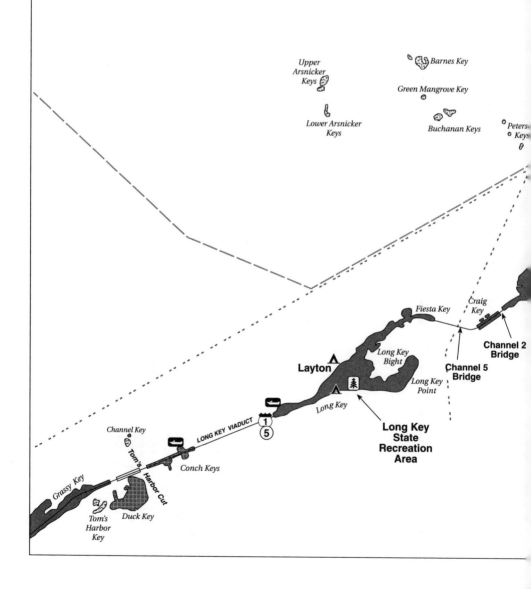

Upper Arsnicker Keys

Barnes Key

Green Mangrove Key

Lower Arsnicker Keys

Buchanan Keys

Peters Keys

Craig Key

Fiesta Key

Channel 2 Bridge

Long Key Bight

Layton

Channel 5 Bridge

Long Key Point

Long Key

Long Key State Recreation Area

LONG KEY VIADUCT

Channel Key

Conch Keys

Grassy Key

Tom's Harbor Cut

Tom's Harbor Key

Duck Key

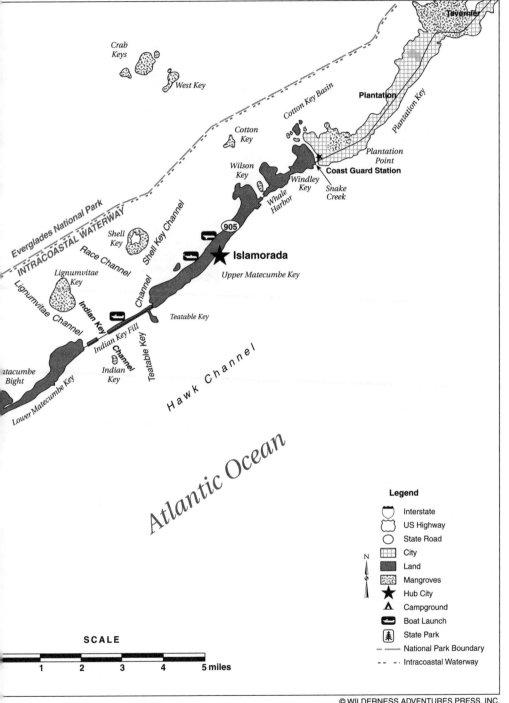

Crab
Keys

West Key

Cotton Key Basin

Plantation

Plantation Key

Cotton
Key

Plantation
Point

Wilson
Key

Coast Guard Station

Windley
Key

Snake
Creek

Whale
Harbor

Everglades National Park

INTRACOASTAL WATERWAY

Shell Key Channel

905

Race Channel

Shell
Key

★ **Islamorada**

Lignumvitae
Key

Channel

Upper Matecumbe Key

Lignumvitae Channel

Indian Key

Teatable Key

Indian Key Fill

Channel

Teatable Key

atacumbe
Bight

Indian
Key

Hawk Channel

Lower Matecumbe Key

Atlantic Ocean

Legend

N

	Interstate
	US Highway
○	State Road
	City
	Land
	Mangroves
★	Hub City
▲	Campground
	Boat Launch
	State Park
– – ––	National Park Boundary
– – –	Intracoastal Waterway

SCALE

1   2   3   4   5 miles

© WILDERNESS ADVENTURES PRESS, INC.

© WILDERNESS ADVENTURES PRESS, INC.

The Sportfishing Capital of the World, Islamorada may be the best known sight fishing destination within comfortably civilized confines. However, the area's self-proclaimed fame is based on an offshore fishing fleet regarded as the largest in the Keys.

Discovery of the inshore fishery came later, when outboards finally made exploration of the surrounding 1,500 or so square miles of water practical. While few secrets remain, fishing on area flats is still pretty good. This is the birthplace of much of what we consider flats fishing standards and legends.

Islamorada was long considered the commercial settlement on Upper Matecumbe Key. It's now the name of the Village of Islands, which added Lower Matecumbe, Plantation, and Windley Keys to newly incorporated city boundaries in 1998. You might expect crowds here, and as one of the Keys' most developed areas, things might seem a bit touristy to some. The business district is bustling, masking the ease of finding serenity on the water. It's a great place for non-fishing travel companions, though, with good shopping and waterside eateries along with numerous dive and snorkeling concessions. Random boat traffic, including jet skis, can be a problem at times, but you don't have to fish congested areas.

Within the traditional boundaries of Islamorada, skiff guides routinely cover the Key Largo to Grassy Key Oceanside shoreline and the majority of Florida Bay from popular docks and ramps. The best sight fishing water is almost all within a 45-minute boat ride and the many flats offer sheltered lee side routes to good fishing during most reasonable weather conditions.

Quick and comfortable access to so many fishing opportunities is Islamorada's real claim to fame. Anglers throughout the Keys often descend on the area's protected flats when conditions are tough since there's almost always some way to line up shots at fish coming toward the wind or sun.

It's a toss up whether the nearby shallows are more famous for bonefishing or tarpon fishing. Bonefishing is pretty much a year round activity, tipping the scales slightly in its favor. Often, at any given time, over half of current line and tippet class bonefish world records come from within the normal travel range of local anglers. Fish weighing double digits are routine catches for visiting anglers. Summer and early fall provide the best fishing for sheer numbers of fish, but fall has long been regarded as the best time to catch a "slob," slang for chubby fish weighing more than 12 pounds. Since the late '90s, March and April have offered an additional shot at record-class fish.

Nearby flats, those within sight of the highway, tend to hold the biggest fish on a year round basis. The area features lots of soft grass flats and enjoys a strong flush of water during new and full moon tides because of the numerous constricted channels. The biggest fish are often found in the main flow of water whether it's along the channel edges or where current narrowly focuses at right angles across rises.

You may never need to pole more than 100 yards from the edge of one of the area's bridge channels to find fish. Doing so for much of the day is often a waste of time anyway. Nearby fish face significant pressure, and creepy crawlers in the shallowest of water are a bit twitchy to say the least. They do eat well early and late in the day, and fishing before the last couple of hours before sunset in the fall is a real treat. Otherwise, channel edge fish tend to eat far better, though the flies you read about for the Bahamas won't work at their preferred depth of two to three feet. You'll need a BB shot or two on the line to sink a bait in the current, too. The best bonefishing (for sheer numbers of fish) moves to the backcountry, within Everglades National Park boundaries, once things warm in the spring. It lasts through the fall with occasional wintertime flurries when the weather is mild. Many of the prime spots still fall within sight of the Overseas highway.

The main tarpon migration starts and ends here as the fish go by on their way to Lower Keys worm hatches in the spring and head toward points unknown on the Gulf and Atlantic coasts when the hatches end. It's also not unusual for them to find a comfortable lake corner and hang out for a week or two when conditions are prime. The Lower Keys may have better concentrations of small and medium fish later in the year, but holdovers here are often 100-pounders.

The local backcountry sees some of the earliest "shows" of tarpon in the Keys for sight fishermen. Three or four days of glorious weather, providing temperatures in

Matecumbe Key to Plantation Key—*It's likely that several of the next line and tippet class world-record bonefish are feeding on flats illustrated in this chart. It is something I'd like to hide and most of those in the know would prefer I did. It's easily visible from the road, though, and we need to talk about it. The high level of activity is hard to hide.*

Nearby water is crowded, as you might imagine, for a couple of reasons. It's in the middle of a hot pleasure boating area and a lot of the traffic is uninformed. Because of the size of the fish, there's lots of fishing activity. I mastered this area years ago and have won tournaments here, but I drive by it more than I fish it these days. I find it useful only on short day trips, when there are few boats on the water, or during the worst weather days when the fish are the happiest.

I don't like the crowds. The fish are educated beyond doctoral level and are not particularly anxious to accommodate anglers. There's also the constant threat of being run over by a random vessel. You only have to run to the fringes of the chart to find happier fish and a sense of calm. You're only a couple of miles from Everglades National Park, a mysterious trip for most without fishing intentions, and where jet skis seldom roam.

Much of the area on the lower left end of the chart is off limits to motor operation. Expect to do a lot of poling (and please do). The fish eat best in two to four feet of water, demanding flies with 32nd-and sometimes 16th-ounce eyes. You may need a round-headed jig here instead of the skimmer design often recommended for bonefish so you can sink it to the feeding zone. Hugging the channel edges turns up plenty of fish, but exploring with a push pole reveals a number of ridges and depressions attractive to fish and not obvious on the charts. The channel edges hold permit and the channels can hold lots of tarpon during season.

This chart once again illustrates why Keys charts are only slightly useful. For instance, on the Oceanside of this chart you'll see a couple of little circles with (+) signs in them, offshore to the northeast of the "MICRO Tr" designation. These are coral heads. They are only a couple of a bunch and part of a very shallow flat reaching the shoreline, navigable only around the tops of the tides. If you can't read water, you'll often run into this flat when you move. If you don't investigate it you'll miss some fishing opportunities. The flat is a major barrier turning tarpon toward the sun and often-prevailing wind during their major migration and provides some year-round bonefishing.

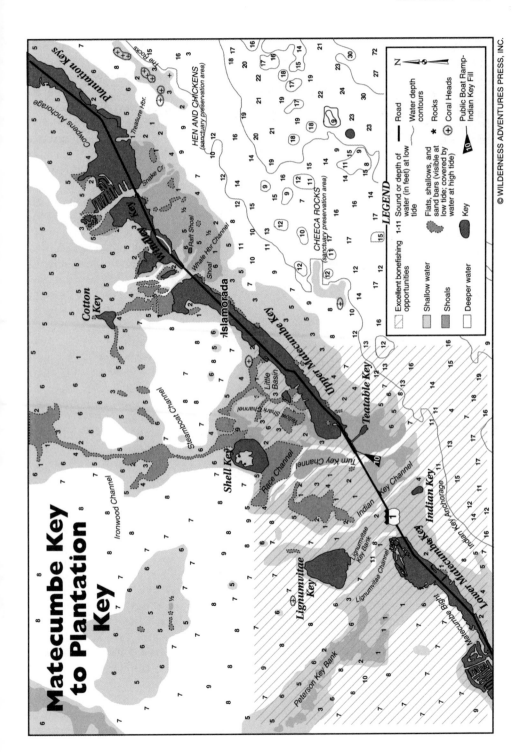

Matecumbe Key to Plantation Key

LEGEND

1-11 Sound or depth of water (in feet) at low tide	
Flats, shallows, and sand bars (visible at low tide; covered by water at high tide)	
Excellent bonefishing opportunities	
Shallow water	
Shoals	
Deeper water	
Key	

Road
Water depth contours
Rocks
Coral Heads
Public Boat Ramp-Indian Key Fill

Plantation Keys
The Rocks
Cowpens Anchorage
Treasure Hbr.
Snake Cr.
HEN AND CHICKENS (sanctuary preservation area)
Raft Shoal
Windley Key
Whale Hbr Channel
Cotton Key
Shoal
Islamorada
CHEECA ROCKS (sanctuary preservation area)
Cotton Key
Steamboat Channel
Ironwood Channel
Little Basin
Upper Matecumbe Key
Yellow Shark Channel
Shell Key
Race Channel
Turn Key Channel
Teatable Key
Indian Key Channel
Lignumvitae Key Bank
Lignumvitae Key
Lignumvitae Channel
Indian Key
Indian Key Anchorage
Peterson Key Bank
Lower Matecumbe Key
Matecumbe Bight

Bill Wilson hoists a tarpon.

the 80s with no wind, attract surprising numbers of fish. It's thought tarpon travel thousands of miles to hide for the winter, although it certainly does not take them long to return to backcountry lakes to bask in a warm winter sun. It's nothing to plan for as it happens randomly, without warning or reason.

Sight fishing routes get crowded and bad weather during the peak of the season might demand a bit of imagination. If you can't get on the proper white hole when the sky is dark, you could look for a place where the fish habitually roll or throw a bit of a wake as they go by. Oceanside fishing can be awesome when the weather is tough, but it is often a waste of time on a gorgeous day more than an hour after sunrise or before sunset. There are just too many boats on the water when the weather is nice. A quick trip into the Gulf should turn up good fishing.

While not noted as a permit destination you can still find more than a few here and there depending on the time of year. Some of the craggiest inshore patch reefs hold fish in the late spring or early summer along with the reef itself and many of the area's wrecks. These fish are best fished with live crabs. Flats anglers will find fish spring through fall, pushing flats edges on both sides of the Keys, hanging off of channel end points or occasionally sunning where current pushes them into a comfortable corner. The inshore fishery has displayed steady improvement since Florida's inshore net ban and should only get better with time.

Islamorada offers an interesting diversion on its shallowest flats, many in park waters. In the 90s anglers witnessed a wide-ranging return of redfish and you might find them anywhere. They share a number of flats with bonefish. During days when you can't see into the water below a wake, you're often not sure if the school of fish attacking you includes bones or reds. Most of the time it doesn't matter. Both will eat a shrimp, crab, jig, or fly. Those rigged with double lines on spinning and conventional rigs will be okay, but fly anglers not using a shock leader might lose a redfish once in while. Checking for abrasions after any capture makes good sense and you can use a light shock leader for both species if they're working deeper edges. Most shared bonefish and redfish activity is on what is considered Islamorada's second tier of banks. This is a huge connected strip of flats and islands between Arsnicker Key and Plantation Key.

Finding inshore species is not difficult around Islamorada. You can start within a few hundred yards of the highway on either side of Matecumbe Key. The bridge channel edges and the points leading from them are good beginning jump-off spots. Water may be crowded because it's handy, and random boat traffic during peak vacation periods or on weekends will force you to learn more remote waters.

AROUND THE VILLAGE

Islamorada proper as defined by tradition is "town," with all the accommodations and conveniences any traveling angler might hope to find. The fishing around the four islands making up the village of Islamorada is not the same. The feel of each island is very different from the highway and so is the boat traffic. Plantation Key is a mix of small commercial concentrations and residential areas. It's relatively calm and offers many of the comforts of home. The best flats are on the ends of the island, but you'll find a few interesting corners on the shoreline if you look.

Windley Key feels totally commercial and is covered with quality motels. Highly popular party spots make it an area to avoid on holiday weekends, yet when boat and Jet ski traffic is light, fishing is surprisingly good here.

Lower Matecumbe Key is tame in comparison to the rest of the area and provides fewer conveniences. The shoreline is sadly a shadow of its former self, although tarpon do push the "beach" in good numbers. While not offered as a premier destination area, it is a nice area with some quiet motels offering good access. If you seek some solitude this is a handy place to stay, and you have good access to the famed live bait tarpon fisheries at the Channel Two and Five bridges as well as excellent backcountry action.

There are real advantages to concentrating on the hub of the village for flats fishing. From the Gulfside, you have a choice of comfortable routes to the hottest area fishing grounds and can easily pop out to the ocean if necessary. There are days when running some area lakes is just no fun from Plantation or Lower Matecumbe Key, even if fishing might be good on the other side. You're closer to options in the hub, too. Tarpon do run the entire Oceanside of the Keys, but there are more ambush spots for them within the couple mile stretch between the Matecumbe Keys than there are on the long face of Plantation Key. On the other hand, fewer anglers tossing at fish and less boat traffic often means happier fish and a better day on the water.

Bonefishing is good throughout village boundaries wherever flats edges provide funnel- type boundaries toward bridge channels. You have to pick your moments for success on some flats, though. Between Snake Creek and Whale Harbor channels, you should never be surprised by Jet Ski and recreational boat harassment unless you're there early and late in the day. Fishing can be great during tough weather as you might be on the water alone.

There's good bonefishing on the second tier flats behind Plantation Key in late summer and fall. It's a function of higher water levels. Flats here and farther into the bay are attracting increasing numbers of redfish and the area is much quieter than the center of the village.

LONG KEY: A CHANGE OF PACE

Long Key almost feels out of place when you head to the west. It is relatively undeveloped thanks to some tough terrain and a mile and a half square state park, the Long Key State Recreation Area. There is a settlement at Layton in the middle of the island offering convenience store shopping and bait. The shoreline is almost unspoiled along much of its length. It's more like some of the Lower Keys than the Upper Keys. If you're not lucky enough to get a room or find a campsite locally, the shoreline is easily reached from Islamorada area ramps or Duck and Grassy Keys.

Fiesta Key at the end of the Channel Five Bridge, leads to the island and offers a KOA campground. There's plenty of fishing within sight of the campground for tarpon, bonefish, and permit. Wade fishing for bonefish in front of the state park is very good around both sides of the bottom of the tide.

Thanks to a relative lack of boat pressure and little shoreline development, fishing the Long Key shoreline is often as good as it is in far more remote Keys locations. It's a definite tarpon hot spot and the fish usually eat flies here all day long except during very bright and calm conditions.

If we hope to maintain this great fishery we have to use very good manners when fishing here. At the height of season you may find as many as a dozen boats scattered along the various underwater ridges waiting for fish with a few other boats poling. Fitting in line is confusing. The fish wander farther from shore than you might think. It's a place requiring a lot of poling as you set up and a wide berth when you travel.

You'll find a lot of small tarpon scattered here until the middle of the fall. Bonefish range the shoreline in good numbers, tailing in the shallows on the low ends of the tide and mudding on the shelves the rest of the time. Water moves hard here on both tides, making fish aggressive. With some searching you'll find a few interesting points within Long Key Bight deserving some attention along with some pretty good corners. The bottom is tough in the Bight, making fish hard to see at times.

Duck Key to Long Key—*Fortunately much of the boat traffic here remains in the major channels, although a boat or jet ski now and then makes its way through the fishiest areas. The chart, at least of the Oceanside face, is one of the worst. Just off the right edge of the island you'll note some small numbers like ½ and 1. This is a hard ridge you'll run into if you don't pay attention. Fish run into it all the time in their travels, and it's the kind of spot we want to find. There's a bunch of these scattered along here. You need to run around the area to protect your boat and the fishing. There's a lot of deep water close to shore not shown on the chart, too. You could run your boat there and sadly some do. The deeper runs are important areas that allow fish some time to relax, and they stop to sleep on this shoreline. There is no reason to disturb them here.*

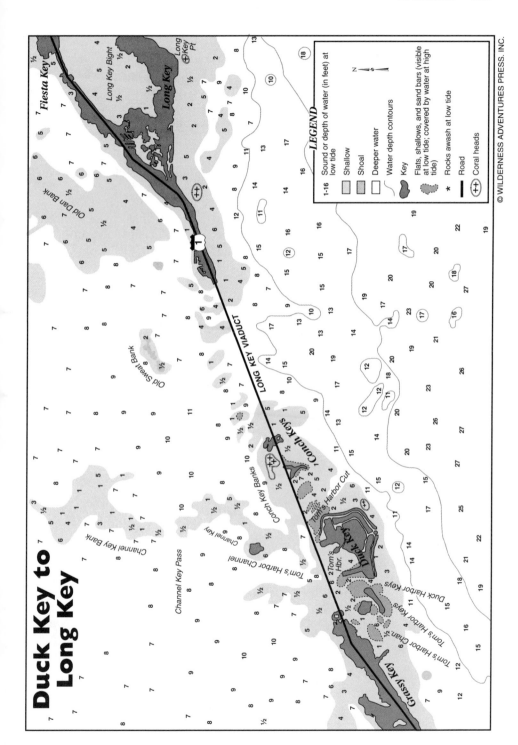

Duck Key to Long Key

LEGEND

1-16 Sound or depth of water (in feet) at low tide

Shallow

Shoal

Deeper water

Water depth contours

Key

Flats, shallows, and sand bars (visible at low tide; covered by water at high tide)

* Rocks awash at low tide

Road

⊕ Coral heads

© WILDERNESS ADVENTURES PRESS, INC.

Fiesta Key

Long Key Bight

Long Key

Long Key Pt

Old Dan Bank

Old Sweat Bank

LONG KEY VIADUCT

Conch Keys

Conch Key Banks

Channel Key Bank

Channel Key Pass

Channel Key

Tom's Harbor Channel

Tom's Harbor Cut

Tom's Hbr.

Duck Key

Duck Harbor Keys

Tom's Harbor Keys

Tom's Harbor Chan.

Grassy Key

Long Key Viaduct is one of the better live bait tarpon sites in the Keys with some fish hiding in its shadow much of the year. It comes alive during season with the fish migrating the Gulf face on rising tides and the power poles on the fall. Plenty of fish find cause to take a break here to the delight of anglers hanging baits around the pilings. On the other end of the island, the Channel Five Bridge offers good fishing, but the fish are just settling in from their travels and not quite as aggressive.

Behind the west end bridges–on the Gulfside–you'll note lots of little numbers on the chart and even some hints of flats. The area is riddled with flats. Tarpon use them as resting spots on the rising tides and they mark migration routes. The shelves attract lots of permit and mark the beginning of great permit water extending through the Lower Keys. They oddly don't get much attention from bonefishermen, but chumming often leads to some pretty good action with small to medium-sized fish. The cuts through the banks are loaded with snappers and offer a nice diversion if you just want to bend a rod.

***Long Key to Lower Matecumbe Key**—This is a pretty fair illustration of the Long Key Bight. It's a surprising place so close to civilization. The chart does not show several long shallow points harboring both permit and bonefish. They also turn migrating tarpon. The Gulfside might look a bit sterile but don't be fooled. You'll have to look for little numbers again. If you take the time to do so you'll find a series of shallow ridges in the middle of the chart. Permit like them, bonefish and tarpon visit them, and you'll find snappers and trout in the cuts through them. They concentrate tremendous water flow, making sharks easy to chum. The Lower Matecumbe shoreline once offered tremendous bonefishing, but the addition of a bunch of long docks disrupted their travel patterns and forced them offshore. You'll still find the occasional tailer here if you time the tide just right.*

Note the hinged jaw. It's the cargo-plane mouth causing all our hookup problems with tarpon.

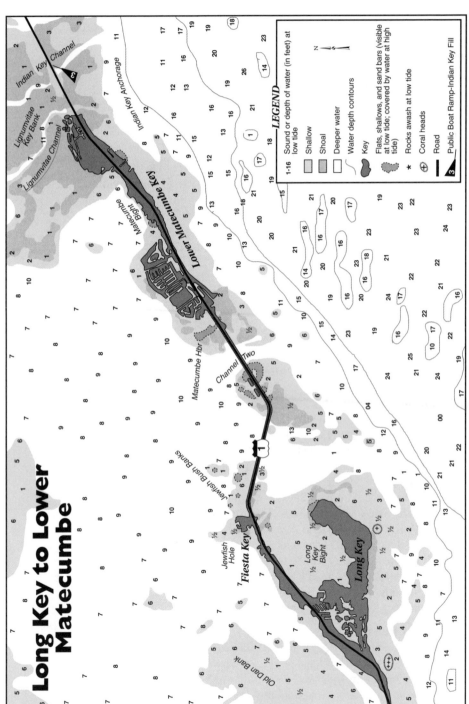

Long Key to Lower Matecumbe

Islamorada Hub City Information

HOTELS AND MOTELS
Breezy Palms Resort, Mm 80, P.O. Box 767 / 305-664-2361
Casa Morada, 136 Madeira Road / 888-881-3030
Cheeca Lodge, Mm 82, P.O. Box 527 / 305-664-4651
Coconut Cove Resort And Marina, 84801 Old Hwy. / 305-664-0123
Conch Restaurant, Mm 83 / 305-664-3391
Coral Bay Resort, Mm 75.5 Bayside / 305-664-5568
Chesapeake Resort, Mm 83.4 Oceanside / 800-338-3395
Days Inn And Suites, Mm 82.5, 82749 U.S.Highway 1 / 305-664-3681
Drop Anchor Resort Motel, P.O. Box 222, Windley Key / 305-664-4863
Golden Key Motel, P.O. Box 710, Mm 81, U.S. Hwy. 1 / 305-664-4418
Hampton Inn & Suites, 80001 Overseas Hwy. / 305-664-0073
Harbor Lights Motel, Mm 84.9 Oceanside / 800-327-7070
Hibiscus Resort, P.O. Box 85 / 305-664-8787
Islamorada Motel, 87760 Overseas Hwy. / 305-852-9376
Islander, P.O. Box 766 / 305-664-2031
Kon-Tiki Resort, Mm 81, Rt.. 1, Box 58 / 305-664-4702
La Jolla Resort, Mm 82.3, Rt.. 1 Box 51 / 305-664-9213
La Siesta Resort, Mm 80 Oceanside / 800-222-1693
Matecumbe Resort, 76261 U.S. Hwy. 1 / 305-664-8801
Ocean Dawn Lodge, 82885 Old Highway / 305-664-4844 / Apartments with 2-3
  night minimum stay
Oceanside Isle, 69500 U.S. Hwy. 1 / 305-664-0706
Ocean View Inn & Pub, 84500 U.S. Hwy. 1 / 305-664-8052
Ragged Edge Resort, 243 Treasure Harbor / 33036 305-852-5389
Sea Isle Resort/Marina, 109 E Carroll St. / 305-664-2235
Shoreline Motel, Rt.. 1 Box 57 / 305-664-4027
Siesta Motel, 7425 Overseas Hwy. / 305-743-5671
Smuggler's Cove, Mm 85.5 Bayside / 305-664-5564 / 800-864-4363
Star Of The Sea, 77521 Overseas Hwy. / 305-664-2961
Sunset Inn Resort, Mm 82.2 Bayside / 800-558-9409
Topsider Resort, 75500 Overseas Hwy. / 305-664-8031
Tropic Air Resort Hotel, 75780 U.S. Hwy. 1 / 305-664-4989
Tropic Dive Resort, Mm 90.5 Oceanside / 1-800-537-3253
Lookout Lodge, Mm 87.7 Bayside / 305-852-9915
Tropical Reef Resort, 84977 Overseas Hwy. / 305-664-8881

VACATION RENTALS
American Caribbean Real Estate, 81 Bayside / 305-664-4966
Anglers Realty, Mm 81 Oceanside / 305-664-9166
Freewheeler Realty, Inc, Mm 86 Bayside / 305-664-2075
Houseboat Vacations, Mm 85.9 Bayside / 305-664-4009
Island Villa Properties, Mm 81.6 Oceanside / 305-664-3333

Paradise Connections, 89 Oceanside / 305-852-2405
Century 21 Keysearch Realty, 86000 Overseas Hwy. / 305-664-4637
Schmitt Real Estate Co., 82205 Overseas Hwy. / 305-664-4470
Tropical Diversion, Mm 77 Oceanside / 954-474-2406 / Waterfront homes, all amenities, vacation rentals
White Gate Court, Mm 76 Bayside / 305-664-4136 / Exclusive, quiet resort / Architect-designed cottages / Fishing pier / Weekly rentals
The Mooring Village Mm 82 Oceanside / 305-664-4708 / Very secluded luxurious beachfront cottages / Weekly rates available
Sea Isle Resort, Mm 82 Oceanside / 800-799-9175 / 1,2, & 3 bedroom houses, villas
Shady Palm Villa Motel, Mm 76.7 Oceanside / 888-664-8389
Port of Call Townhomes, Mm 88.5 Oceanside / 305-232-3569 / Luxury oceanfront townhouses
Palms of Islamorada, Mm 79.9 Oceanside / 888-554-KEYS / Condo units with ocean exposure, monthly rentals only
Madeira Bay, Inc., Mm 82 Bayside / 305-664-4748 / Property management & development.
Lindo Mar Apartments, Mm 75.1 Oceanside / 305-664-9504 / Yearly or seasonal rentals.
Island Villa Properties, Inc., Mm 81.6 Oceanside /305-664-3333 / Full-service realtor, Vacation rentals.

RV RESORTS AND CAMPGROUNDS
Fiesta Key KOA, Mm 70 Bayside, Long Key / 305-664-4922

RESTAURANTS
Atlantic's Edge Restaurant, Mm 82 Oceanside / 305-664-4651
Bentley's, Mm 82.8 / 305-664-9094
Coral Grill Restaurant, Mm 83.5 / 305-664-4803
Craig's Restaurant, Mm 90.5, Plantation Key / 305-852-9424
Green Turtle Inn, Mm 81 / 305-664-9031
Horizon Restaurant At Holiday Isle, Mm 84 / 305-664-2321
Hungry Tarpon, Mm 77.5 Bayside / 305-664-0535
Lazy Days Oceanfront Bar/Seafood Grille, 9 Overseas Hwy. / 305-664-5256
Lovin' Dough Restaurant & Bakery, Mm 81.5 / 305-664-2310
Lorelei Restaurant & Cabana Bar, Mm 81.9 Bayside / 305-664-2692
Manny & Isa's Kitchen, Mm 81.6 / 305-664-5019
Morada Bay Cafe, Mm 81.6 Bayside / 305-664-0604
Ocean Terrace Grill, Mm 82 Oceanside / 305-664-4651
Papa Joe's Landmark Restaurant, Mm 79.7 / 305-664-8109
Rip's Island Ribs 'N' Chicken, Mm 84 / 305- 664-5300
Plantation Yacht Harbor, Mm 87 Bayside / 305- 852-2381
Paul's Beach Bar and Grill, Mm 84.8 / 305- 664-0123
Rumrunners Island Bar & Deli, Mm 84 / 305-664-2321
Smuggler's Cove, Mm 85.5 / 305-664-5564

Squid Row, Mm 81.9 / 305-664-9865
Whale Harbor Raw Bar & Grill, Mm 84 / 305-664-9888
Willy's Tiki Bar, Ocean 80 Resort, Mm 80 / 305-664-0855
Woody's Italian Garden, Mm 82 / 305-664-4335
Ziggie's Conch Restaurant, Mm 83.5, 33036 / 305-664-3391

BAIT AND TACKLE

Abel's Tackle Box Marina & Deli, Mm 84.5 U.S. Hwy. 1 / 305-664-2521
Bass ProShops Outdoor World, 81576 Overseas Hwy. / 305-664-4615
Bonefish Bob's Used Tackle Shop, Mm 81.9 / 305-664-9420
Florida Keys Fly Fishing School & Outfitters, 81888 Overseas Hwy. /305-664-5423
Islamorada Bait &Tackle, 81650 Overseas Hwy. / 305-664-4578
Sandy Moret's Florida Keys Outfitters, 81888 Overseas Hwy. / 305-664-5423
Papa Joe's Marina, 81576 Overseas Hwy. / 305-664-5005

BOAT RENTALS

A B C Watersports, 85500 Overseas Hwy. / 305-664-5549
A-1 Wave Runners Inc., 85401 State Road 4-A / 305-664-9914
Abels Marina, 84341 Overseas Hwy. / 305-664-3380
B & M's Boat Rentals, Mm 79.8 Bayside @ Papa Joe's Marina / 305-664-4864
Estes Fishing Camp, Mm 84 / 305-664-9059
Florida Keys Kayak & Sail, 77522 Overseas Hwy. / 305-664-4878
Florida Keys Sailing School, Inc., 85944 Overseas Hwy. / 305-664-8718
Lime Tree Water Sports, 68500 Overseas Hwy. / 305-664-0052
P J's Boat Rental And Repair, 79851 Overseas Hwy., Upper Matecumbe /
    305-517-9746
Paradise Watersports, 80001 Overseas Hwy. / 305-664-2300
Pier 68, Mm 68.2, Long Key / 305-664-9393
Rent A Boat At Robbie's, Mm 77.5 / 305-664-9814
Sea Bird Marina, Mm 69.5 Overseas Hwy., Long Key / 305-664-2871
Treasure Harbor Marine Inc., Mm 86.5, Plantation Key / 305-852-2458

MARINAS

Bud N' Mary's Marina, Mm 80 / 305-664-2461
Cobra Marine, Mm 85.9 Bayside / 305-664-3636
Coral Bay Marina, Mm 81.5 Bayside / 305-664-3111
Holiday Isle Resort and Marina, Mm 84 Oceanside / 305-664-2321
Matecumbe Marina, Mm 80.5 Bayside / 305-664-2402
Max's Marine, Mm 80.5 Bayside / 305-664-8884
Smugglers Cove, Mm 85.5 Bayside / 305-664-5564

EMERGENCY INFORMATION

Coast Guard, 305-664-8077 or VHF 16
Seatow / 1-800-4-Seatow / 24-hour tow service
TowBoat/U.S. / 800-391-4869 / 24-hour dispatch

Islamorada Marina Services

Marina	Phone	Slips	Tackle	Gas	Groceries	Boat Ramp	Restrooms	Restaurant	Repairs
Abels Marina and Tackle Shop	305-664-3380	0	No	Yes	No	No	No	No	Yes
Bud N' Mary's Marina	305-644-2461	0	Yes	Yes	No	No	Yes	No	Yes
Caribee Marine	305-664-3431	Yes	No	Yes	No	No	Yes	No	Yes
Coral Bay Marina	305-664-3111	5	No	Yes	No	No	Yes	No	Yes
Holiday Isle Resort & Marina	305-664-2321	18	Yes	Yes	Yes	Yes	Yes	Yes	No
Mangrove Marina	305-852-8380	20	Yes	Yes	Yes	Yes	Yes	No	Yes
Matecumbe Marina	305-664-2402	5	No	No	No	Yes	Yes	No	No
Max's Marine and Boat Yard	305-664-8884	0	No	Yes	No	No	No	No	Yes
Plantation Yacht Harbor	305-852-2381	88		Yes	No	Yes	Yes	Yes	No
Robbies	305-664-9814	5		Yes	No	Yes	Yes	Yes	Yes
Treasure Harbor Marine	305-852-2458	24	No	Yes	No	Yes	Yes	Yes	No
World Wide Sportsman Bayside Marina	305-664-4615	60	Yes	Yes	Yes	Yes	Yes	Yes	Yes
Smuggler's Cove Marina	305-664-5564	30	Yes	Yes	No	Yes	Yes	Yes	No
Cobra Marine	305-664-3636	71	Yes	Yes	No	No	Yes	No	Yes

Alone With Tarpon

Both angler and guide were moist with perspiration, although the first pink glow of the sun only now warned of its arrival. The humidity was stifling, forcing each to gulp repeatedly for air. Even so, they mentally held their breath, hoping they had found the final channel leading to the quiet basin corner they felt held fish. The blending of sky and water provided no clue of their location, and the guide navigated from memories of dozens of similar mornings.

The silence was more deafening than the roar of the outboard had been as they swapped to the gentle gurgling of a hull designed to become one with the water when powered by a push pole. They had at least found the lake corner they'd sought. Would they find fish? Not wanting to wake the fish with the motor, they left a fair margin between themselves and the suspected resting site.

A cormorant in the distance, a turtle just behind the boat, and a diving pelican mimicked activity of rolling or busting tarpon. The weight of their anticipation increased with each false alarm. Suddenly and unmistakably a fish announced its presence. It wasn't much of roll, just one of those barely nose and dorsal-up actions marking a fish just stirring from a nap and going nowhere.

It was, however, what they'd hoped to see, and the action of the stretching fish woke others nearby. The first trickle of incoming current also woke up the mullet and a few disappeared in gaping foaming holes as tarpon punished them for staying too close. Whether the fish were hungry or angry at being disturbed didn't matter. They would likely eat a fly.

Expecting nervous fish because of the calm conditions the angler had rigged accordingly. He'd threaded an 11-weight line through the guides of his 12-weight rod that morning to lessen the impact of his casts. He extended his leader to 14 feet and hoped the bushy pattern crafted on the undersized 2/0 hook would intrigue, not scare, the fish.

Angler and guide whisper across the boat. Talking would not disturb the fish, but it would disturb the moment. It was too early to see fish in the water suspended over the lush green bottom. They would have to wait for a fish to roll in range to provide a target. The fish suddenly wiggling in front of them only showed the slightest tip of his tail, perhaps floating up seeking the warming sun.

As the angler began his cast a second fish offering a better angle stuck his nose out for a breath of air. The cast was quick and sure. As the fly settled a series of bubbles rose below it indicating he'd hit the fish's nose. On the first gentle strip of the fly line, a small boil 7 feet behind the fly might have been a tail kicking the fish forward to investigate. A bigger boil might have been a strike.

Still the angler stripped line searching for some sign of life. He didn't wait long, as the tarpon turned after capturing its prey. His hands, one controlling the line, the other clutching the rod, moved apart with a practiced fury designed to sink steel into gristle. The angler, an obvious veteran, switched his attention to the deck and did not look up even when hearing the fish jump. He was more concerned with clearing the remaining fly line from the boat. If he could, he'd have plenty of jumps to watch.

The pressure on the fish increased as the line came tight to the reel. Now the angler participated, reaching the rod vigorously toward the fish to relieve stress on hook and leader as the fish greyhounded in the distance. The tarpon's sprint and aerial gyrations quickly exhausted its first wind. Knowing the battle could last indefinitely if the fish rested, the angler went to work.

Initially, the fish resisted little as he was pumped to the boat, but after recovering the backing and half the fly line the angler felt renewed efforts from the fish, which chose to jump not run. The angler, a little tired from his own efforts, responded slowly to a furious headshake. The hook fell out of the fish's jaw. Later they found the point of the fly's hook slightly bent.

There was no reason to rush their preparations for the next fish. The flooding tide would wash schools into their corner for several more hours, and both knew summer's heat made it unlikely they would be interrupted by other boats. While many choose to pursue tarpon during the peak of the migration in May and June, these men preferred the quiet yet riskier prospects of summer.

They fished together often, and naturally took advantage of conditions encouraging tarpon to lay up throughout the year. The first few warm and calm days of late winter accompanied by the increased water levels of full or new moon tides mysteriously flood Florida Keys backcountry spots with fish too. There was never a way to predict when the weather would be right, again ensuring uncrowded fishing.

Laid-up fish were worth the risk. While large migrating schools throughout the Keys provide tarpon finicky about eating flies on occasion, laid-up fish seldom say no. Anglers might have to change flies once or twice and adjust their teasing technique, but good casts were usually rewarded.

Migrating fish were fun, though. During tough weather condition they ate flies well. Ambush spots could be chosen to take advantage of the wind, and a contrasting bottom highlighted fish as they traveled. On calm days migrating fish were often nearly impossible to feed. Catching a really big fish, even a 100-pounder, on a travel route was an unusual event, however, even in tough conditions favoring their willingness to eat.

The biggest fish caught each year were always laid-up fish usually caught in March or April. Hundred-pounders were common during prime laid-up fish conditions throughout the upper Keys backcountry until September most years. Lots of smaller fish flood the Lower Keys then, too. But the odd 170-pound fish caught each year almost always fell to a spring angler.

Fishing laid-up fish offered other enticements, as well. Their haunts were often the most remote and scenic corners of the Keys backcountry. Some notable exceptions were giant fish spots within sight of Islamorada, Sugarloaf, and Big Pine Keys, but the fish there were so big at times the distractions were easily ignored.

The hunt for these fish added to the overall experience. They often slept over dark bottom, and early morning fish were only recognizable by fin edges reflecting white in the sun. Mullet muds attracted lots of fish too. Here an eerie pink or orange glow from fins assisted anglers in connecting dots from dorsals to tails and the more critical eating end. Illuminated by a midday sun on lighter bottom, a head-on fish stood out like the proverbial floating log, but sideways to the viewer only a thin line of the fish's back, easily overlooked, announced the fish's presence.

They showed up like ghosts, appearing by magic at boat side. If you remembered to fish to their closest eye you could actually turn them around to pursue and eat a gently stripped fly. It was surprising how close they would eat to a boat, especially in a mullet mud. The angler remembered one 125-pound fish hitting the boat with her tail as she captured the fly.

They had the situation they wanted now. Several hundred fish were basking in the mullet mud hidden in their remote backcountry corner. They checked the leader. The shock tippet was unscarred indicating some sort of lip or cheek hookup. The bent point was perhaps a tad long and was quickly cut back with a file. It was time to look for another fish.

The nearest roller was a couple hundred feet away. They moved toward it slowly, scanning their limited field of vision, as they seemed to crawl. It was still tough to see and running over fish even with the poled boat would move other fish. For the moment the fish also had an advantage. The tide was running toward the sun, they would be facing into the current, leaving the boat behind them.

An impatient fish provided the angler another break as she rolled toward the boat perhaps seeking a more comfortable spot for a nap. She couldn't ignore the little shrimp seductively fluttering in her path, planted deceptively with a quick and quiet cast. She protested her error as steel sunk home by thrusting her bulk skyward. She surprised the angler with the suddenness of her response, and he was startled by her size. Failing to react to her jump he could only groan as the tippet parted. While there would be many more hookups in his life, this one—like most others before it—would never be forgotten.

Such days happen frequently in the Keys with a bit of luck and some intelligent planning. Many species provide similarly dramatic moments. You might find a tide-long bonefish feast or permit tails punctuating the surface as far as you can see along an edge. A horde of tuna and bonito chummed to the surface will raise your hackles and bunches of sailfish showering bait along the reef should, too. A couple days before writing this I found well over 600 snook scattered in potholes along a quarter mile edge. Few weighed less than ten pounds and it was a heart-warming sight, knowing how scarce they'd once been. Clouds of mudding redfish or large tailing concentrations raise the same emotions. This is what we dream of.

Bonefish do not have inferior mouths.

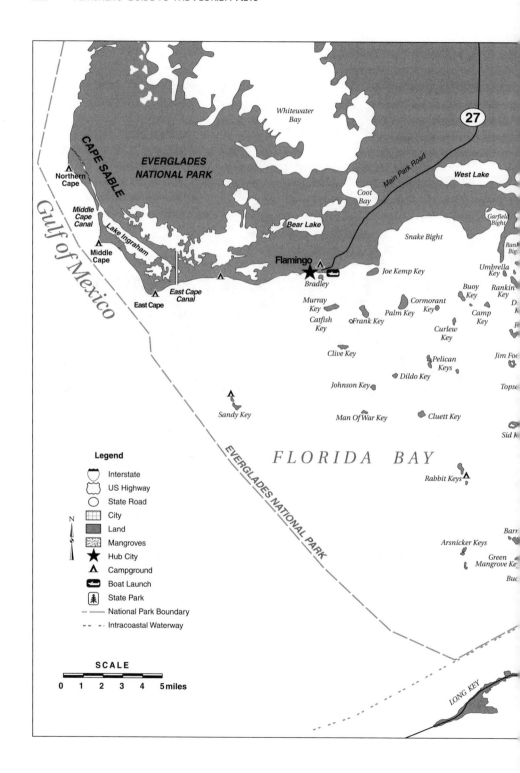

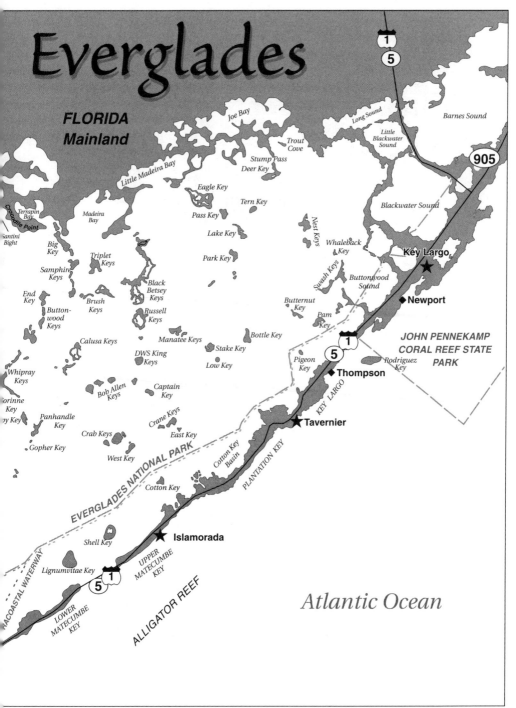

Everglades

FLORIDA
Mainland

Joe Bay

Long Sound

Barnes Sound

Trout Cove

Little Blackwater Sound

Stump Pass
Deer Key

Little Madeira Bay

Eagle Key

Tern Key

Blackwater Sound

905

Terrapin Bay

Madeira Bay

Pass Key

Nest Keys

Crocodile Point

Santini Bight

Big Key

Lake Key

Whaleback Key

Key Largo

Triplet Keys

Park Key

Swash Keys

Buttonwood Sound

Newport

Samphire Keys

Black Betsey Keys

Butternut Key

End Key

Brush Keys

Russell Keys

Pam Key

JOHN PENNEKAMP
CORAL REEF STATE
PARK

Button-wood Keys

Calusa Keys

Manatee Keys

Bottle Key

Stake Key

Rodriguez Key

Whipray Keys

DWS King Keys

Low Key

Pigeon Key

Thompson

Corinne Key

Bob Allen Keys

Captain Key

KEY LARGO

my Key

Panhandle Key

Crane Keys

Tavernier

Crab Keys

East Key

Gopher Key

West Key

Cotton Key Basin

EVERGLADES NATIONAL PARK

Cotton Key

PLANTATION KEY

Shell Key

Islamorada

UPPER MATECUMBE KEY

Lignumvitae Key

LOWER MATECUMBE KEY

ALLIGATOR REEF

Atlantic Ocean

INTRACOASTAL WATERWAY

© WILDERNESS ADVENTURES PRESS, INC.

Everglades National Park—A Step Back In Time.
Anglers throughout the Keys find excuses to take advantage
of the easy access the Upper Keys offer to the waters of
Everglades National Park. The majority of the extensive
shallows of Florida Bay, protected within park boundaries,
offer more than just great fishing,

A Note to the Reader

There are not enough pages available in this book to teach you all you need to know to fish in the Everglades. The following section provides good information on fishing the open water portion of Everglades National Park easily reached from the Upper and Middle Keys. The entire Everglades is another story, requiring another book by someone more competent than myself.

We're talking about nearly three million acres of wilderness. It's laced with thousands of miles of natural streams, manmade ditches, and sometimes large pockets of water. It is rich in fish life and home to a wide variety of wildlife. Probably of most interest to anglers seeking saltwater fish is the portion of the swamp easily reached by penetrating coastal rivers or by launching on the inland side of the "plug" separating the Gulf from Whitewater Bay at Flamingo. Flamingo is reachable by boat from much of the Keys or by road from Florida City.

The "outside" of the Everglades, the coastal reaches along the southern end of Florida, are fished successfully with many techniques already discussed in the book. There is also a hoist available at Flamingo to lift your boat over the plug, allowing you to spend a day exploring a different type of fishing.

The southwest coast is littered with rivers and smaller outflows, all attractive to fish. Some, such as Shark and Lostmans rivers, harbor tarpon of one size or another almost year round. The coastal beaches of the southwest coast are famous for traveling snook, reds, and tarpon. There is good reason to follow streams for miles into the interior of the Everglades, too. The fish do, and you often find deep pockets so loaded with fish that you can wear yourself out fighting them on fly gear (with streamers and poppers) or conventional and spinning tackle (using jigs and top water baits).

The larger reaches of water are reasonable well marked. You can get in and out of the larger rivers and sneak your way carefully through Cape Sable's Lake Ingraham. Whitewater Bay is much like a large lake. Almost any fish you care to catch short of offshore pelagics, bonefish, and permit, are available in the coastal streams and interior lakes.

Deep holes often cough up jewfish, now called Goliath grouper, up to several hundred pounds, along with a variety of other groupers and snappers. These holes, of course, are also loaded with backcountry favorites such as trout, ladyfish, redfish, and snook. In season, you may encounter mackerel or bluefish. Black drum are common visitors and a hundred pound tarpon might surprise you in the tiniest hole.

Water in the interior tends to move in a rush. It is usually best to avoid the shallowest reaches that only flood near the top of the tide. Water will fall out from under you before you know it and leave you stranded where no one can help you. Along the south coast, many of the barriers are soft mud, but the southwest coast has firmer bottom and oyster bars as hard as concrete.

The stiff flow of water may require some sinking lines, particularly when it's chilly and the fish hug the bottom. The traditional saltwater nine foot rod is fine in broader reaches but you might want beaver-pond type gear elsewhere. It will prove inadequate for a lot of fish but fun for many others. Folks using conventional gear often drop down to convenient 6 or 6½-foot rod lengths. You're often not casting far and room for a back cast is a luxury.

Much of the interior water is stained from brown to black. Darker patterns and lures tend to work better here. The fish take advantage of obvious holes where the flow of water slows somewhat, and you'll often find them backed up to structure with the current in their face.

Besides carrying a GPS, you should consider other preparations for serious interior exploration. Carry far more food and water than you need for a day. Mosquitoes might carry you off without the lavish use of repellents. Radio and cell phones signals do not travel far through mangrove forests. To reach for help, equip yourself with an antennae you can attach to the end of a push pole. Some extra flares could prove handy, too. You might need warmer clothes than you think if you're stuck overnight. Even pros get stuck here, so take your time.

This book covers the best fishing in the Everglades that is easily reached from the Keys, but if you have the time and inclination, a trip into the interior is well worth the effort.

Anglers throughout the Keys find excuses to take advantage of the easy access the Upper Keys offer to the waters of Everglades National Park. The majority of the extensive shallows of Florida Bay, protected within park boundaries, offer more than just great fishing, they provide an escape from the modern world as rules ban or restrict most water contact activities like diving, water skiing, and Jet Ski use. All commercial fishing activity is banned, too. The rules, along with tough navigation, keep random non-fishing boat activity to a minimum. It's still possible to fish a day in the park without hearing another boat, but you're sure to see some on the horizon.

From Key Largo to Lower Matecumbe Key, park waters are only a couple of miles away. They're also within reasonable reach of anglers fishing from Long, Duck, and Grassy Keys. There's more to the park than the bay, too. A broad swath of water in the open Gulf of Mexico holds a wide variety of fish, and fishing around a couple of coastal drainages is routine activity. In this book, we're going to concentrate on areas easily and customarily visited from the Keys by the average angler.

Florida Bay is loosely defined as the water bounded by the Keys, the Florida coast, and the long ridge of flats running from Lower Matecumbe Key toward the northwest, reaching almost to the southwest tip of Florida. It's a year round fishing wonderland covering some 1100 square miles of shallows averaging just 39 inches in depth. The ridge of flats separating bay and Gulf are a bonefisherman's dream near the Keys and a redfisherman's delight as they approach the mainland. In between, some areas hold populations of both species and numerous channels hold snapper and trout much of the year, along with tarpon in season. Cobia and tripletail visit park boundaries and occasionally Gulf edges. There's a hot Spanish mackerel bite in the park's slice of the Gulf during the winter.

The park is a mystery for many, even those who fish it often. Fish we sight fish for might use a particular spot for days, months, or seasons in a row, then vanish. Sometimes it's easy to figure out what changed, but often it makes no sense at all. There are constants offering obvious references and we'll talk about those. Charts of the area are only partially useful, showing some of the channels and showing none of the contours on top of flats. They'll get you back and forth if you stay on established paths, and you should do so to start. Don't head into the bay without a chart and compass.

There is something for everyone in the park. Sight fishing folks need to find fish in shallow water where they're easily seen and willing to please. Lots of visitors just want to see the sights and catch something. Others, willing to use the bait and tackle of the day, have a good shot at the species of their choice much of the year, within reason. If you're going to do this on your own, be patient as you gradually learn routes to fishable water. Also realize, even pros sometimes only find scattered fish of selected "glamour" species, and "home runs, " or great days of fishing, are sometimes more luck than skill.

Prospecting is fun in the park and provides lots of opportunities to learn. A sight fishing angler using fly, spin, or plug tackle and interested in whatever species comes down the edge will find plenty to throw at. In clear water, a slightly weighted white streamer, a Clouser Minnow, or a ¼-ounce white jig behind a short 30-pound shock

Kathryn Spencer seems happy with her bonnet shark.

leader is appropriate food in predominately redfish country. If the water is a bit dirty but you can still see into it, switch to something brown and orange or yellow and orange. Almost any species you find in the area at sight fishing depth will eat these simple offerings. All you need is a likely looking edge. In the winter fish may use the edge of a flat to hide from wind or take advantage of water warming as it crosses a flat. Spring through fall they're often actively feeding, although you'll find some fish just hanging out. Good water movement is usually most attractive to a wide variety of fish.

This isn't home run fishing, it's fun. Your edge should show some life, the occasional flipping bait, a mudding ray, or a shark crawling along. Concentrate your focus from tailing depth to perhaps three feet of water. Potholes are important as they might hold resting fish and several species use them as highways while moving along a flat. Fishing for fun, you can throw at anything. Small sharks are fair game and if you set the hook quickly on the bite, you might get a lip hookup so you can land them on a mono leader. It's no big deal if they bite you off.

Throughout much of the northern reaches of the bay, mudding rays almost always have some fish hovering between their wingtips, waiting to steal food. Small jacks are the most common species, but you might find a big one with them in some areas. In redfish country, reds follow rays along with trout, snook, ladyfish, and snappers. The fish stare at the ray looking for food and many sit right on top of them. A direct approach, tossing your food at the ray, usually works best.

This is what tarpon are famous for!

If you're lucky with your choice of spots, you'll see a redfish tailing here and there if it's warm or sunning in a pothole if it's cold. Snook might push along an edge if there is lots of bait. They may share a pothole with some trout. Jacks almost always push. In season you may find a small tarpon or two. All are fair game for your fun rig.

If you find nothing of interest in 15 minutes or so, it's time to leave unless you've missed the tide. Moving water is important. Some of the interior of the bay is rather dead, however, and a lack of activity while you run for miles or pole several hundred yards of bank is a bad sign. An unmarked cut through a bank or deeper ditch around an island is often worth a few casts. You might be surprised by what you find.

Do this often enough, particularly around full and new moon tides, and you will hit a home run now and again. A school of a 100 to 500 redfish intent on harassing mullet in a mud or an acre-sized gathering of tarpon can show up on any edge spring through fall, sometimes miles from where you might expect them. You could just stumble into a seasonal or tide-induced migration of seemingly endless schools of bonefish anywhere in their range. Concentrations of trout, redfish, and snook lying in warming water flows are no surprise in the winter. If you find a few fish on an edge, the edge will likely hold some fish when the weather and tide is the same for some time—maybe. There is little accounting for home runs, although conditions may hold fish in a specific spot for days or weeks.

You'll find mullet muds, areas of discolored water usually marking bait and likely predators, scattered throughout the bay. In the winter they typically hold jacks, trout, and ladyfish in many areas. You can jig in them or work a topwater bait over them. Sometimes a shrimp suspended below a popping cork is the right food. Finger mullet and pilchards make good food, too, while flyfishing folks should do okay with a popper or streamer. In season, a mullet mud might hold tarpon in the bay or macs in the Gulf.

WHERE TO BEGIN

I can tell you a little more about fishing in the mixed bag reaches of the park than I can about fishing some other Keys spots. A 25-boat bonefish tournament around Islamorada often clears the flats of fish by the third day or at best they just quit eating. Piling 100 boats into a five-mile circle around Flamingo, with some jigging in channels and others plying edges for redfish, typically has little impact. You'll seldom see more than a dozen or two boats here except on the prettiest winter weekends.

An area bounded by Roscoe Key to the east, Clive Key to the south, and Bradley Key to the west, provides all the backcountry fishing opportunities anyone might dream of. Area flats are loaded with redfish. Snook sun in the area's potholes during winter and spring. Trout flood shallower ditches in the winter on the falling tide, spreading into the basins and onto the tops of flats as the tide floods.

I suggested earlier there are some "constants" in the park and this is a good place to learn how they work. Channels and run outs throughout the bay and the strip banks scattered in the Gulf provide meaningful starting points for a variety of fishing.

Fish settle into the ditches to feed as the tide falls and pop out of them to hunt the flats when it begins to rise.

In dead end channels, they may crowd the end until there's enough water for them to get onto the flat. Snook, in particular, like to wait with their tails against the edge while the tide floods, bringing them a snack now and then. While bait and jig fishermen hold the upper hand in deep, fast moving flows, fly anglers will find plenty of action using weighted streamers on sinking or sink-tip lines.

Sight fishing folks will do best working the smaller side channels and run outs. While fish pop out of the larger ditches regularly, smaller cuts into the flats lead to shallower water often preferred by tailing and sunning species, and they are buffered from passing boat traffic. Many of the smaller ditches are shallow enough to reveal ray muds, where they feed while waiting to climb onto the flats. It's usually worth throwing at the mud. If the water is fairly clean you can spot individual fish staging for their attack on the flats.

Very few of these smaller channels are marked. They usually appear as pale green ribbons twisting through the flats. If it's been windy enough to stir things chocolate, you'll need a new plan, as everything will look the same. When you start prospecting in the shallow and muddier parts of the park, the multitudes of mullet will drive you crazy. Many are big enough to push a decent wake or leave a mud easily confused for one kicked up by a feeding fish. You might as well take a shot if you suspect predators. You'll find one often enough to make it worthwhile.

Watch yourself here on the falling tide. Redfish tend to do okay in wet grass and it's easy to forget where you are if they're tailing well. Pay attention to your escape route. If you get stuck, take your shoes off before you jump overboard to shove yourself to deep water. The mud seems only slightly firmer than quicksand, and you may not get your shoes back if you leave them on.

You don't have to run all the way to Flamingo to find decent fishing. The area is rich with life, though, and sometimes it's easier to learn what good geography looks like when fish are abundant. You can find many of the same species in varying numbers within a couple miles of Key Largo and Plantation Key. Anything to the west and the north of Captain Key is a good starting point, although fish move even closer during the summer and stay through the early fall.

Snake Bight and Dildo Key—*Tides move briskly here much of the year, moving lots of forage attracting favored backcountry species such as reds, snook, trout, jacks, ladyfish, and lots of sharks. The flats are broad and one should use caution to avoid tides falling out from under the boat. The deeper basins hold tarpon, sometimes as much as eight months of the year. The channels offer great mixed-bag fishing with baits and lures. You can reach this area in about 45 minutes from anywhere in the Upper Keys, and it offers more fishing than you can learn in a lifetime.*

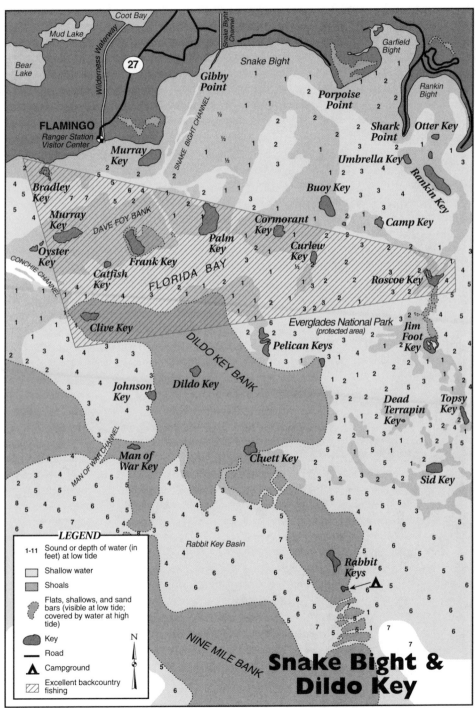

Snake Bight & Dildo Key

© WILDERNESS ADVENTURES PRESS, INC.

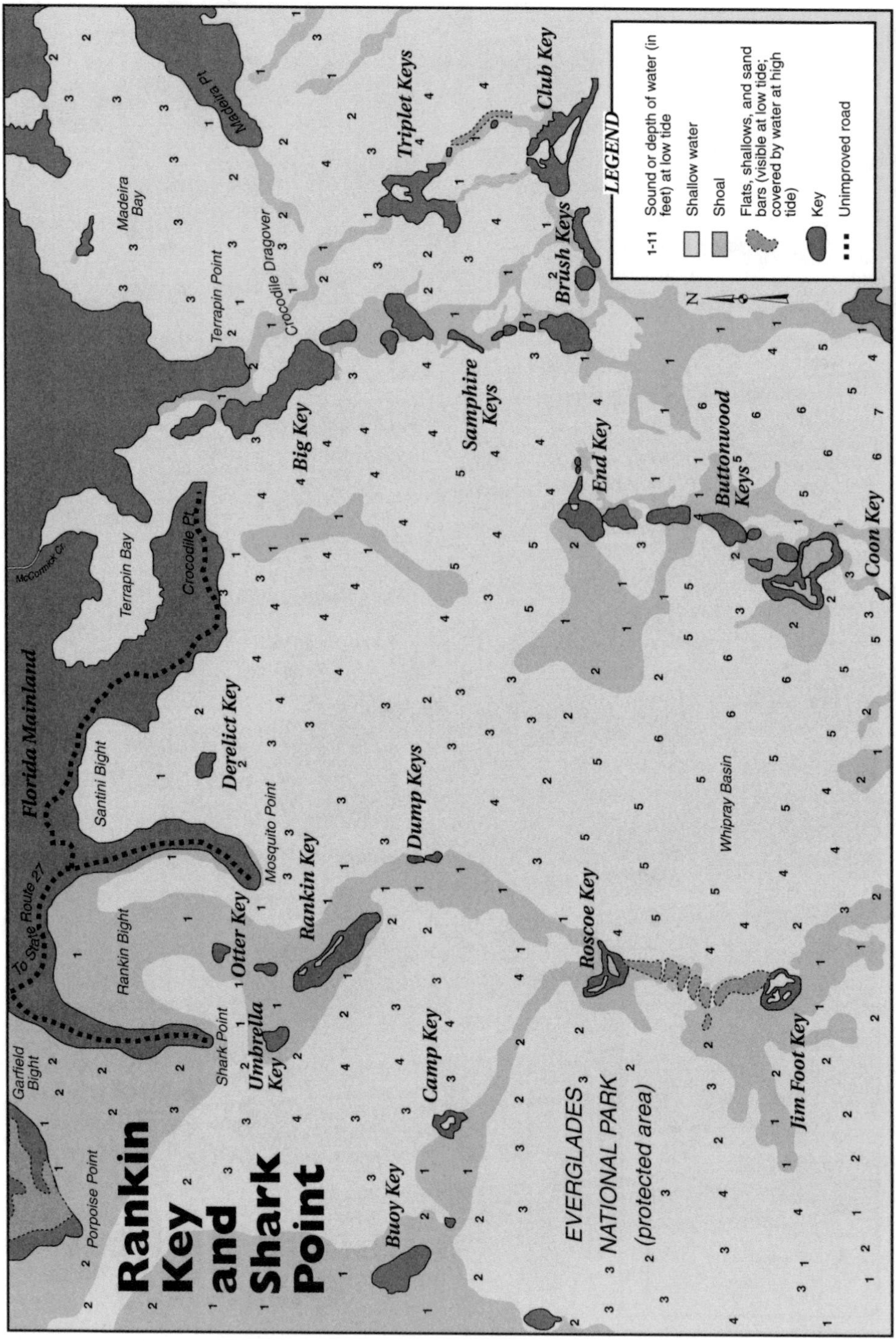

Rankin Key and Shark Point

LEGEND

1-11	Sound or depth of water (in feet) at low tide
	Shallow water
	Shoal
	Flats, shallows, and sand bars (visible at low tide; covered by water at high tide)
	Key
┈┈	Unimproved road

N

© WILDERNESS ADVENTURES PRESS, INC.

Florida Mainland

Madeira Bay

Magdaleine Pt.

Terrapin Point

Crocodile Dragover

Terrapin Bay

McCormick Cr.

Triplet Keys

Club Key

Brush Keys

Samphire Keys

Big Key

End Key

Buttonwood Keys

Coon Key

Santini Bight

Crocodile Pt.

Derelict Key

Mosquito Point

Dump Keys

Whipray Basin

Rankin Bight

Shark Point

Otter Key

Umbrella Key

Rankin Key

Roscoe Key

To State Route 27

Garfield Bight

Porpoise Point

Buoy Key

Camp Key

Jim Foot Key

EVERGLADES NATIONAL PARK
(protected area)

The flats are not quite as expansive here, and you'll find some strips narrow enough to see across. This can be a bonus as fish sometimes work both sides. Roving fish often like to run with the current pushing them against a bank while those coming in from the depths to feed might work onto the flat facing the current.

You might check out island edges anywhere in the northern reaches of the bay. A large majority of islands have moats on one or more sides, dug out over the years by tides. They're split between deep rushing channels and gradual depressions slightly deeper than the surrounding flat. The depressions are the most fun for fly fishers. Fish sun in them, tail in them, and use them as migration routes.

Surprisingly few boats pole much of the coastal shoreline east of Rankin Key, maybe thinking they might as well complete the run to Flamingo. During higher water periods in summer and fall, you will run into some interesting fishing in scattered corners. The shoreline holds some reds and snook, occasional pockets of small tarpon, and roving schools of aggressive jacks. A rising tide is safest until you have a good feel for escape routes when the tide falls. In the winter and early spring muds often mark trout and ladyfish concentrations. Reds, along with sheepshead, work some of the isolated strip banks in deeper water.

Rankin Key and Shark Point*—This is a vast area harboring almost all year-round species common to Keys shallows, except bonefish and permit on a seasonal basis. Where water flows are good, many flats see lots of tailing reds and some sunning snook. Most of the basins offer pretty good mixed-bag fishing for trout and ladyfish in mullet muds during the winter. Migratory species such as mackerels and cobia seldom reach the area. Be careful here as the bottom is very sticky. Tides are weak here much of the year.*

The Everglades is rich with life.

THE FINAL FRONTIER

Anything I tell you about the southern and western reaches of the bay gets me in trouble. Here you'll find some of the best bonefishing anywhere and some of the best tarpon fishing in the Keys. Every new boat on the scene jeopardizes the quality of the fishing, but I believe adventurous folks will stumble into it on their own and might fit in if they recognize what is at stake for the fishing community. None of this stuff is really secret, though, and much is marked on charts already available.

Bonefish here eat as well most of the time as they do at widely recognized "easy" spots in the Bahamas. Good manners are important. You have to pole on and off the banks or risk running fish off the flats. If you might recognize the occupants of a boat or the brand of a boat, you're far too close while fishing park flats within sight of civilization. When civilization becomes a mere outline on the horizon, too close is often defined as being able to determine the color of the closest boat. Realize that giving space works both ways. There's no reason to stalk used fish if you don't have to, and there is lots of room in this end of the bay.

I can tease you with some Xs on the chart, but suggestions about where you might find fish are likely useless because the area is so vast I can only vaguely guess where some species might feed on the day you visit. I have no intention of scaring you away, but I'll try to explain what you face fishing here on your own. You can't see across the flats. It's not just that you cannot see into the water on the other side of the flats, the flats extend beyond the horizon. They are not well marked and the fish concentrate in rather small areas that change daily with no more than a subtle wind shift.

Since 1984 I've spent over 3,000 days fishing the area for bonefish or where I could watch bonefish while I tarpon fished. If I get the bonefish thing right two out of three times I feel pretty good about it. Sometimes I'll miss three or four days in a row, then hit it right every day for a week. Weather alters the area dramatically. Between the summers of 1995 and 1998 I fished a stretch on the rising tide that produced 75 to 100 shots a tide at schools of over 100 bonefish with a nice mix of redfish and the occasional permit tossed in. It has not reoccurred since the tropical weather events during the fall of 1998.

Enough with the caveats! On nearby park flats you can find some fish a good part of the time after tides begin improving in the spring and good fishing lasts until tides weaken in early winter. I call this area the second tier of Islamorada banks. It's the strip of flats and islands running from Plantation Key in the east toward Arsnicker Key in the west. These are typically spring tide fish and they tend to migrate toward the east as the tides build. It's possible to find plenty of fish without ever leaving the sight of civilization.

Heading north toward Rabbit Key and west along the Nine Mile Bank, the fish are wilder and much harder to find. When you do find fish, they are some of the easiest fish to feed in the Keys. Bones range as far north as Man of War Key during parts of the year in this end of the bay and the farther north you go, the more redfish you'll find sharing flats with them. It's challenging fishing and a bit confusing at first as they typically tend to run over boats. They do stop and tail at times but are often chasing glass minnows when they're feeding the best. They do toss nice wakes most of the time, and it won't be long before you get a handle on where they are in relationship to their wakes. You have to lead them more than you think and the bottom rises and falls enough to make breaks in wakes a normal part of the drill, so all of us miss plenty of fish. Once you do figure it out, you can catch a bunch of fish if you learn how to feed them. Most of the time you have to keep a fly up in their face, but sometimes you have to drop it to the bottom to get a bite.

While Keys bonefish tend to feed into or across the current, they often come with the water along many edges in this part of the bay. The fish are usually running and the current is shoving the fly at you if you keep it off the bottom. You have to strip fairly quickly to move the fly along and maintain a tight line so you can hook a fish. Though they often eat a fly up in the water, it's a mistake to use one too small and too light. You can always move a heavy fly a little faster to get it off the bottom, but you cannot make one sink if it's too light. If your fish are digging as much as running you will need a fly you can get to the bottom a good part of the time. My favorite fly for the neighborhood is a fairly heavy size 1 copper-bodied Crazy Charlie alteration. Flies with white wings over a pink or olive body are hot at times. The fish do lock onto crabs once in a while, and a thumbnail-sized Merkin is just right.

Sheepshead are tasty critters but a bit tough to clean.

Tarpon use both sides of the Bay Barrier Bank during their migration. The area also attracts early season sunning fish on the prettiest of days. Things become a bit hectic here during the height of the season. Everybody wants to fish for tarpon in May and June. It's hard to blame them, but sometimes a July trip provides decent fishing without the hassle, and you see scattered fish along the bank until at least September. They're friendlier when the crowds are gone, too!

This side of the bay is full of lakes and basins long famous for holding laid-up tarpon when moon tides shove them over the bank or through the channels. I'd gladly name spots if I knew they'd be worth fishing when you got here. For instance I almost lived in Palm Lake for over a decade. There were plenty of fish between the lake and

Pompano fight hard for their size and are prized
on the table.

me, but I could catch almost anyone a fish there seven or eight months of the year. A huge mullet mud harbored seemingly starving but lazy fish during the1980s and much of the 1990s. The majority of fish disappeared toward the end of the '90s along with the mullet. Some return now only on a random basis, mostly in late winter when this is one of the warmest areas in the Upper Keys backcountry.

The loss of the mullet seems an obvious factor in the disappearance of the fish, but it might not matter at all. Equally famous migration and resting spots directly to the west suffered similar declines on both sides of the bank. At the same time fishing improved a bit toward the south. Don't worry though, the fish range throughout Florida Bay, and it won't be long before we stumble across their new routes through the Gulf.

Tides mean everything to tarpon and throughout the course of the season they move both ways along the bay barriers, idling along with the water flow much of the time but fighting it now and again. The best fishing for inbound fish, those coming to the Keys along the Atlantic coast, is often on the rising tide behind the bridges. Lots of fish filter through the channels and are shoved against the banks behind them by the current. They don't all make it to the park and might hide in any good flow of water holding food and providing shelter. Fish find their way in from the Gulf, too, so basins near any of the park's fringes almost always have stray fish during the season.

The best fishing for migratory fish occurs in this part of the bay after Lower Keys worm hatches in late May or early June. As many tarpon seek their escape to points north, they are driven by rising tides from Middle Keys bridges toward the southwest Florida coast. If they want to travel up the Eastern seaboard, most are stuck filtering past one side or the other of the Bay Barrier Bank while headed toward the ocean.

Laid-up fish are the real prize of tarpon fishing, as they are famous for their willingness to eat. You can find a few of them in this end of the bay anytime of the year when the weather is spectacular. You will almost always find some during the migration by searching corners toward the end of the rising tide and while the tide is slack before it begins to fall. Tarpon do tend to roll more on the slack tide and as currents weaken. The absolute best condition for this is sunrise in a calm corner at the end of the tide. You might run into them anywhere current pushes hard against a bank. It's not a bad idea to stop once in a while and watch corners and edges for telltale rollers. They often stop wherever the tide dumps them and might sit out slack tides miles from where you expect them.

Our bay barrier makes a hard west turn at Man of War Key. The bank between the Gulf and coast is huge here. It's difficult to fish so attracts surprisingly limited attention. Tarpon come with a screaming current when they come, so it's tough to keep the boat pointed at them when they turn. Numerous cuts dissect the bank and hold a wide variety of species. The truly adventurous might seek one of the many depressions on top of the bank offering something unique to the area. Opportunities include a good wintertime pompano fishery and the odd flounder catch. Both sides of the bank often offer spectacular fishing for big sharks.

A line drawn from the middle of the Long Key Viaduct to a few miles offshore of Cape Sable marks the western reaches of the park. Between this boundary and the Gulf barrier bank, you'll find fisheries lost then recovered in the '90s. Many think the late fall through early spring Spanish mackerel fishing here is some of the most consistent light tackle fishing anywhere in Florida. The fish are randomly scattered in relatively open water from between Arsnicker Bank and the Cape. It helps if you can see the stretches of potholes and use them as a starting point for chumming, but bird activity and flipping bait mark fish often enough.

Some days you can drift in concentrations of fish and catch plenty by blind casting a pink and chartreuse nylon jig or a weighted streamer like a Clouser. You don't need anything fancy but eight inches or so of #4 wire is helpful. You also need to tie a rather small knot. The little macs are famous for grabbing anything looking like food following a hooked sibling. A bubble trail from a sloppy tag end attracts unwanted attention.

You may well pick up some snappers and trout if you're drifting along an edge fed by current and wind or in an area with lots of potholes. Stopping to chum could lead to some action for both, and chumming could improve the mackerel fishing if it's slow, as well. In recent years bluefish joined the macs for a few weeks on their way through the Keys, adding a bit of spice to the fishing when bait concentrations were best.

If you spend any time studying charts of the area, you'll note some random banks scattered in the open Gulf. They concentrate a number of predatory species and tarpon find them attractive in season. There are a number of interesting and seldom visited bits of structure scattered in the neighborhood.

Understanding tides is critical to success with many species. In the bay, it is possible to sit on a narrow strip where water is rising on one side and falling on the other. Water rises from the Gulf in about half of the bay while it's fed by the ocean elsewhere. Much of what you read about tide adjustments is based on Key West tide tables, but you're usually fishing park waters from the Upper Keys and should learn to time tides from Miami or Islamorada tide charts. Alligator Reef is a good reference point for tides since much of what you can see from civilization fits within its pattern. Over the years I've found some spots work only on the tide changes most of the time, while it makes little difference on others. Tide changes almost always spark some interesting fish reactions, though.

The tide around Islamorada coincides pretty well with published tide times for Alligator Reef, which is about 45 minutes later than published times for the Miami Harbor entrance. The published tide times reflect minimum and maximum water levels and have nothing to do with the direction of the current. The current on Islamorada Oceanside flats and nearby Gulf flats consistently changes about 2½ hours later.

While the tide at Buchanan Bank is much the same as it is around the bridges, the tide changes an hour or so later at Barnes Key, an hour later than that at either Twin Key, and as much as four hours later between Panhandle and Crane Keys. It's worth your time to carry a pad and pen to record the time of current changes, as fish often don't do much until they get the water they want. For years tarpon poured from the west end of the Long Key Bridge starting about 3 hours and 43 minutes after the published high tide at Alligator light.

The current swaps along First National Bank almost exactly on published tide change times for Alligator while it's about 1½ hours later in Sandy Key Basin or along Man of War Bank. Add another hour for a swap on top of the Bay Barrier Bank and almost 3 hours for the flats just east and south of Flamingo.

A range of creeks drains the south Florida coast. All are attractive to fish and may hold anything from jumbo jewfish to huge schools of jacks over the course of the year. A favorite target of many Uppers Keys anglers is the East Cape Canal draining almost land-locked Lake Ingraham. The mouth of the canal concentrates significant bait activity and attracts tarpon as many as 250 days a year. Snook fall into the ditch on falling tides and crawl onto surrounding flats during the rising tide in large numbers much of the year.

While this is almost a year-round fishery, much of the best fishing coincides with the worst possible weather in the rest of the world and only marginal weather in the Keys. The canal holds fish almost every day. It's not really flyfishing country, although you might do okay with sinking lines and bulky streamers. Meat and jigs rule in the often discolored ditches. I like to run to the southern reaches of the lake when it's really cold.

Fish jam into the warmest currents and sweetened jigs bounced along the bottom fool a wide variety of species ranging from fish-for-fun jacks, trout, and ladyfish to more intriguing species like tarpon, redfish, snook, and black drum. You want to be careful here. The ditches are narrow and might be too shallow for jumping a boat up onto plane at the bottom of the tide, and the poorly marked flats are quicksand sticky. You can be sorry you're here if you're faced with running home with the tide running into the wind. The chop is brutal on a chilly day.

Most of us will never live long enough to learn all there is to know about park waters. Just when you think you have some small portion of it figured out some vagary of weather or regulation changes it enough to demand you learn it all over again. It's a constantly changing environment, fortunately full of fish and providing some bit of escape from a crowded world.

The Big Bay—*The chart on the following pages does this area little justice, and the expanse of flats is huge. The long shallow ridge beginning at Matecumbe Key and running to the mainland serves as an almost impenetrable barrier between the open Gulf and Florida Bay, although some years migrating tarpon crawl through one of the dozens of ditches leading to the interior of the bay. If a fish swims in Keys waters you'll probably find it here. Folks have even seen sailfish and marlin on the edges. I've caught dolphin running across the flats. The area is "tender," as the fish simply won't tolerate engine noise. Few navigational aids exist. If you can't read water, you'll likely bump into something.*

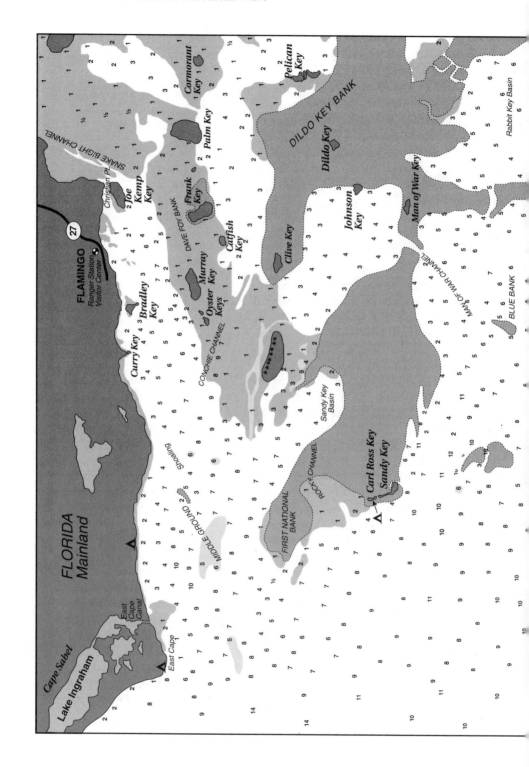

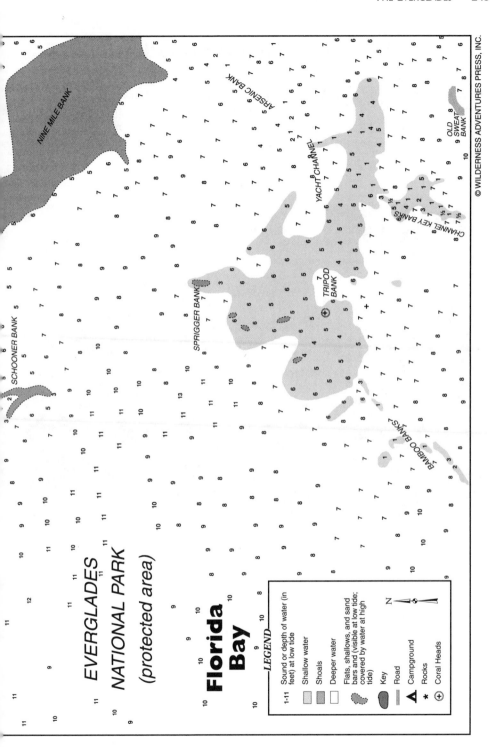

Everglades Hub Information

For more information on Everglades National Park, call 305-247-6211, or write to: Everglades National Park Information, P.O. Box 279, Homestead, FL 33030. Camping is available at Flamingo, and the Flamingo Lodge and Marina offers all the comforts of home. Call 941-695-3101 for more information. The park entrance can be reached from U.S. 1 in Florida City by turning west onto SW 344th Street. Continue on the park road to reach Flamingo.

Everglades Marina Services

Marina	Phone	Slips	Tackle	Gas	Groceries	Boat Ramp	Restrooms	Restaurant	Repairs
Flamingo Lodge Marian & Resort	941-695-3101	46	No	Yes	Yes	Yes	Yes	Yes	No

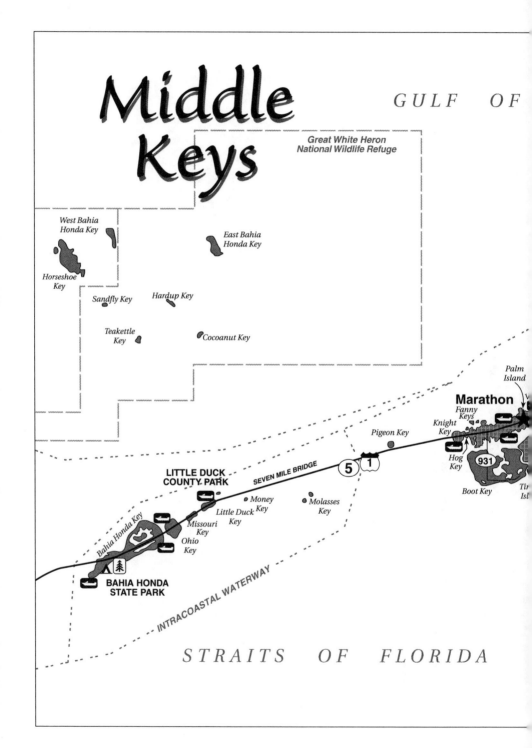

Middle Keys

GULF OF

Great White Heron
National Wildlife Refuge

West Bahia
Honda Key

East Bahia
Honda Key

Horseshoe
Key

Sandfly Key

Hardup Key

Teakettle
Key

Cocoanut Key

Palm
Island

Marathon

Fanny
Keys

Knight
Key

Pigeon Key

LITTLE DUCK
COUNTY PARK

SEVEN MILE BRIDGE

5 1

Hog
Key

931

Money
Key

Molasses
Key

Boot Key

Tir
Isl

Little Duck Key

Missouri
Key

Ohio
Key

Bahia Honda Key

BAHIA HONDA
STATE PARK

INTRACOASTAL WATERWAY

STRAITS OF FLORIDA

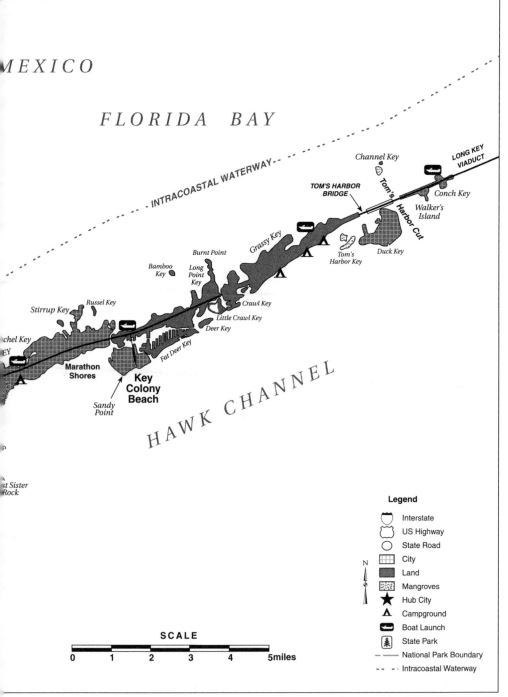

MEXICO

FLORIDA BAY

INTRACOASTAL WATERWAY

Channel Key

LONG KEY VIADUCT

TOM'S HARBOR BRIDGE

Tom's Harbor Cut

Conch Key

Walker's Island

Grassy Key

Burnt Point

Duck Key

Bamboo Key

Long Point Key

Tom's Harbor Key

Stirrup Key

Russel Key

Crawl Key

chel Key

EY

Little Crawl Key

Deer Key

Fat Deer Key

Marathon Shores

Key Colony Beach

Sandy Point

HAWK CHANNEL

st Sister Rock

Legend

Interstate
US Highway
State Road
City
Land
Mangroves
Hub City
Campground
Boat Launch
State Park
National Park Boundary
Intracoastal Waterway

N

SCALE

0   1   2   3   4   5miles

© WILDERNESS ADVENTURES PRESS, INC.

© WILDERNESS ADVENTURES PRESS, INC.

The Middle Keys offer some sense of calm compared to the islands toward the mainland, as the tourist activity is not so pronounced since much of it is somewhat removed from the road. There is also a different feeling of community when you are hemmed in by civilization.

Much of the bulk of the stretch of islands between Conch Key and the end of the Seven Mile Bridge lies roughly halfway between where U.S. 1 hits Key Largo and ends in Key West. This stretch is also middle of the road in other ways. A glance at charts of the Keys, not a road map, offers another perspective.

The Middle Keys are somewhat like the bar between the weights of a barbell. Broad expanses of impassable flats lie behind, or on the Gulfside, of both the Upper and Lower Keys. The Middle Keys are instead surrounded by vast expanses of open water with scattered flats. During one phase of Keys development, this area was the focus of much of the water flowing around the southwest tip of Florida. The Upper Key's Florida Bay was dry around 1500 B.C. The Oceanside of the Lower Keys was somewhat removed from the often too chilly and silty Gulf flow.

Historically chilly and silty Gulf flows impeded or arrested more recent coral development in the Middle Keys, and the stiff flow of water continually scrubbed potential silt gathering dams, leaving this area with far fewer extensive flats than the weighted ends of the barbell. Since the time when water levels rose throughout the reaches where the Gulf meets the Atlantic, coral development slowed. Today, coral thrives only in areas far removed from meaningful Gulf flows, along the Oceanside of Key Largo and the Lower Keys.

There are plenty of fishing opportunities in this region, though it might not seem obvious when you look at the charts. Water often trickles across areas of broad flats and through numerous channels elsewhere. Not here. When shallows rise abruptly from the bottom and channels are few, the sudden focus of waterflow offers easily found concentrations of eager predator species. Permit seem more numerous here than in the Upper Keys, and tarpon migrating on the Oceanside at least appear to eat flies much better. This is also due in part to less near-shore boat traffic.

Local water is big. It is certainly home to a wealth of "traditional" sight fishing skiff operators, but many pros run "jack of all trades" businesses from larger vessels. A larger boat you use at home, whether considered a bay boat, family boat, or reasonable near-shore boat, suits the wide variety of fishing in many ways. It's not unusual to see someone guarding a tarpon migration route or chumming for bonefish in a center console suitable for sailfish on fair days.

There are plenty of poling opportunities, but travel through the region is seldom sheltered and some of the best fishing demands long rides in open water. Tarpon runs are not well protected due to a relative lack of long Oceanside points. We might describe some of the best spots as rough when the tide shoves into a 15-knot wind. It's a bonus, as it cuts down much of the random boat traffic common in parts of the Upper Keys. Fish are also generally friendlier in such conditions.

ON LAND

Marathon is typically thought of as the "Middle Key." Like Islamorada, Marathon was a settlement, not an island. What is traditionally thought of as Marathon grew around a commercial fishing village on Vaca Key. Today, Marathon is an incorporated city bounded by Tom's Harbor Bridge to the east and the Seven Mile Bridge to the west, excluding the city of Key Colony Beach.

Outside of the "business district" of Marathon, there is a nice feel on the road through the Middle Keys. Even within the heart of town, traffic seems to move with a purpose unlike what you find on much of Key Largo or in Islamorada proper. There is a variety of marinas, accommodations, and restaurants along the road to Marathon, but they don't seem to intrude. You'll find everything you need here to keep your boat running or to keep non-fishing family members entertained, along with plenty of competent professional help if you seek it. You can also find a little bit of peace along with some great fishing very quickly.

While there are a handful of bridges and channels in the region it feels rather homogenous or all somehow connected. Conch and Duck Key are somewhat off by themselves, but the rest of the chain of islands might be one. We'll start at Conch Key.

My frame of reference is sometimes distorted, as I have not seen much of the rest of the world beyond the Keys for two decades as I write this. To me, Conch Key feels like a tucked-in commercial fishing village hidden somewhere else in my memory. I have the impression residents live much from the sea and not from tourist traffic. I couldn't tell you the name of a single resident of the island, yet in some ways the island epitomizes what the Keys and its residents must once have been. Here they deal with life head on.

Things are a little less direct on Duck Key. There is a sense of isolation from reality. The island attracts those of more comfortable means and offers upscale accommodations. Don't be fooled. They cater to fishermen here in style and the island provides easy access to a wide variety of fishing opportunities, as does Grassy Key. Grassy Key feels somehow in the middle, offering modest appearing yet excellent restaurants. The few accommodations, though close to the highway, feel remote because of their intimate contact with the water. There is some feel of yesteryear here. It continues as you travel across Little Crawl, Crawl Key, and Fat Deer Key.

This is Bill Driscoll's first tarpon—it's smaller than it looks.

ON THE WATER

Long stretches of water without an outlet to the Gulf provide an almost captive audience of favored Keys species along the Oceanside of the Middle Keys. If the fish are pushing it's simply a matter of getting in their face. Flats are still numerous here and hold or route lots of fish. Flyfishing for tarpon is as consistent as it is anywhere in the Keys and sometimes better. There is some indication a good part of the inbound migration of fish in the spring comes down both coasts, down the Atlantic side and out of the Gulf. It's not unusual for the early season westbound migration to be far better at Long Key than it is in Islamorada. It gets even better at Conch Key as Gulf fish pop through the Long Key Bridge. Once the fish are stuck on the Oceanside, they cannot escape until they hit Vaca Cut. Most stay in the ocean until they hit the Seven Mile Bridge.

You do face a bit of a challenge here early in the migration. The fish are coming from the sun and often with the prevailing wind during prime morning hours as they head toward Key West. There is less terrain here turning them back into the sun and wind. The schools are large enough to see most of the time, but early in the season you must possess the skill to toss a fly into the wind or with the wind on the wrong side of the boat if you cast with your right hand. Left-handers have an advantage in the predominately onshore wind.

The need does not last long. Perhaps the greatest concentration of tarpon during the heart of the season is between the Long Key and Seven Mile bridges. Once the fish settle in, there's a lot of bridge jumping and the fish move both ways along the face of the Keys. There is a period during the season where the numbers going both ways is almost equal, and you'll see a certain amount of Sunday driving as the fish circle the islands seeking comfortable resting spots and concentrations of food. You don't have to get all the shots, just good ones.

Spots are not quite as obvious as they are where you find more flats. The fish spend more time running black and white edges between grass beds and clean bottom. They bounce off of random structure. One of my favorite spots in front of Grassy Key is an odd coral head rising from the bottom in 4 to 6 feet of water depending on the tide. There is little geography to suggest the fish will use it, but they gravitate toward it like a homing beacon on falling tides. There is a bit of a bottom rise inshore of it, but there is plenty of water for the fish to use to sneak by. The coral head is maybe 100 feet in diameter with a brilliant white edge.

Grassy Key Area—Is my coral head on the chart? Not really. There is a lit-tle 5-foot bump shown on the chart in front of Grassy Key that is close. The chart does not show what amounts to an 8- to 10-foot deep trough inshore of the bump that is used by the fish on the rising tide and occasionally by giant fish on the fall. This chart does show a pretty good tangle of terrain around Tom's Harbor. Note the banks on the Gulfside.

Anglers possess a different attitude about what is too close when tarpon fishing this part of the Keys. Some of the white spots are rather large and the fish travel on fairly wide paths. You may end up guarding a spot with another boat or two. Don't crowd in second if you don't know where you are, but don't feel bad about talking to someone if they cut off your fish, either. It's seldom intentional and some days the fish are moving a bit differently than people suspect. I've found some local folks more married to spots than they are elsewhere, too.

Tom's Harbor was the scene of one of the most bizarre spot guarding scenes I have ever witnessed. On the final day of a tarpon tournament in the mid '90s, my angler needed a couple of fish to place. We had no business setting up there, as the water was far too rough, but we had a handle on the fish; Allan Finkelman, my angler, knew the drill. We arrived just as the tide began to fall and the fish started to move.

A pair of anglers in a large center console slid into the rising tide spot between the island and us a few minutes later. They disappeared! They went to sleep, likely thinking no fish would hit their boat for six hours. The fish poured by our boat, and we hooked five or six. The anglers in front of us got up twice during the tide and even adjusted the boat once, but they sat the majority of the day on a dead spot. We were the only two boats on the horizon, and they could have easily set up in a great flow of hungry fish. They popped up and started fishing when the tide changed in the afternoon, but they were set up for the spot and not the fish, as most were coming from behind them. It was their spot, though, and no one else was going to get it.

We find some interesting geography as we move toward the west on the Oceanside. You can do okay just by recognizing that the fish tend to use the slight bottom rises marked by grass beds as reference points as they migrate along much of the shoreline. Traditionally they swim on the white side of the edge, tucking into the slightly deeper troughs. In the late '90s more fish learned to swim on the dark bottom. As elsewhere, the tarpon are pushed toward shore on the rising tide and fall away with the current when it swaps most of the time.

While we often have to bust our rears to "match the hatch" in the Upper Keys, the tarpon eat some flies you might not try without encouragement as they move along local routes. All black works surprisingly well even during the brightest and calmest conditions. It works even better when it's rough. Apte IIs, rust rabbit strip flies, and a vivid olive with a chartreuse collar fool lots of fish where you find reasonable current. A royal blue and orange is hot in bridge flows. There is still plenty of reason to use more natural appearing flies at times.

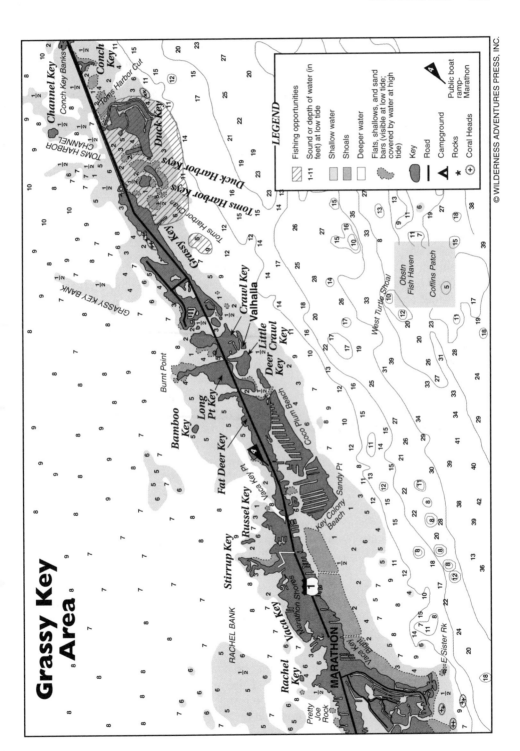

Grassy Key Area

LEGEND

Fishing opportunities

1-11   Sound or depth of water (in feet) at low tide

Shallow water

Shoals

Deeper water

Flats, shallows, and sand bars (visible at low tide; covered by water at high tide)

Key

Road

Campground

Rocks

Coral Heads

Public boat ramp-Marathon

© WILDERNESS ADVENTURES PRESS, INC.

Channel Key
Conch Key
Conch Key Banks
Toms Harbor Cut
Duck Key
TOMS HARBOR CHANNEL
Duck Harbor Keys
Toms Harbor Keys
Toms Harbor Chan
Grassy Key
GRASSY KEY BANK
Crawl Key
Valhalla
Little Crawl Key
Deer Crawl Key
Burnt Point
Bamboo Key
Long Pt Key
Fat Deer Key
Coco Plum Beach
Russel Key
Vaca Key Pt
Sandy Pt
Key Colony Beach
Stirrup Key
RACHEL BANK
Rachel Key
Vaca Key
Marathon Shores
Vaca Key Bight
MARATHON
Pretty Joe Rock
E Sister Rk
West Turtle Shoal
Obstn Fish Haven
Coffins Patch

Because the Middle Keys shelve so steeply into the ocean, some bonefish flats come and go with the weather, occasionally silting over after a hard storm and later cleansed over time by the action of the tides. There are plenty of marl flats scattered along the Oceanside. Most attract some tailing bonefish around the bottom of the tides and mudding fish at the top of the tide.

The fish move all the time, but you might have to chum a bit to get a handle on them. Much of the water at cruising depths is hard to see into. The fish average a bit smaller than they do in the Upper Keys, and schools are sometimes small, too. Much of the bottom is light, offering little contrast. There's nothing wrong with attracting them to a spot where you can easily see them.

While flats flushed by channels are the easiest to find they also attract a lot of attention. The fish make do on plenty of more isolated spots along the face of the islands. You'll have to dig for these a bit as fish use some more than others on a seasonal basis. With rare exceptions, most hold some fish when the tide is right.

Plenty of permit frequent tarpon runs and eat subtle tarpon flies just fine. There are enough fish around the bridge flows to justify a day or two chasing them. They are creatures of edges for the most part, popping up while facing the current in flats corners or digging into a hard charge of water coming off a flat. Don't overlook the abundance of near-shore coral heads rising steeply off the bottom at 10- to 20-foot depths. In good current flows many hold a fish or two waiting for a hapless crab. Spin anglers have an advantage with these fish that they can capitalize on by drifting a crab or live shrimp in the area.

In the late '90s redfish began pushing along the Oceanside, and the fishery should only improve over time. Big schools of reds often hang out for days on spots they like as long as conditions stay roughly the same. In 2000, the fishery is still relatively undiscovered and may remain so for a while. For now, the fish eat almost anything resembling food if you get it in their face.

ON THE OTHER SIDE

The Gulf is broad and relatively deep behind the Middle Keys, yet its depth is interrupted by a wealth of strip banks and a few broad flats. As often noted during other chart discussions, much of the useful terrain is not easily found on a chart. You have to look at the depth numbers to locate the banks on the charts if you can locate them at all. It is worth the effort to find them, though, as the fishing is often reminiscent of the good old days for a variety of species. There are a number of strip banks in the neighborhood holding lots of fish. It's a fun fishing area for a number of species but demanding for some of our favorites. You'll find many of the most important area strip banks just behind the bridges between Long Key and Duck Key.

Tarpon are shoved against them as they move and sometimes find them a nice place to rest. The shelves harbor many of the area's largest bonefish, and permit haunt the edges. All species eat well in the heavy current. It's not easy fishing here. You have to work hard to control your boat on the end of a push pole. But it is worth the effort as fish reward good casts so much better in a hard charging current.

Bonefish are not as obvious on top of the flats as they are elsewhere in the Keys. The hard flow of water makes them easier to chum, though. Chumming here is sometimes different from what is done in other parts of the Keys. You can broadcast free chunks of food or use a chum pot. Either way, locals do a lot of blind casting in the scent trail seeking any species they might attract. I'm told the fish will eat any jig or fly as long as it is mostly pink with a hint of white.

The stiff flows make chumming for sharks easy. You'll find lots of athletic black-tips and lemons of impressive size that you can easily fool on a variety of tackle. The cuts through the banks hold good numbers of snappers and seatrout, and Spanish mackerel use the nearby banks during season.

The area is littered with old wrecks and man-laid trash piles. You won't find them on the charts and have to seek them on calm, high-visibility days. When you find them, mark them with your GPS so you can find them again during the winter. In season, fall through spring, they attract lots of cobia and might hold swarms of jack crevalles year round, along with plenty of wintertime macs and snappers. Some offer sensational permit fishing.

During the winter you will find a variety of scattered muddy areas between the bridges and the mainland. Some are tossed up by bait, but many harbor a variety of interesting predator species attacking bottom-dwelling food. Trout and ladyfish are the most common occupants, and they are joined by jack crevalles and sometimes redfish and Spanish mackerel. It's really jigging country, but fly anglers often do well using a sink-tip line dragging a buoyant fly beneath the surface. Clouser minnows are also very productive.

For fun days out here you can run from bank to bank, stopping if you find a mud or some bird activity around flipping bait. Mullet and pilchards use the banks and flats much of the year. Ballyhoo swarm into this part of the Gulf in the winter. Lots of flipping "hoos" usually mark worthwhile fishing. You'll find a fair scattering of large potholes along the western boundary of the park, too. Chumming in them might raise some big snappers. It also works for macs in season. You have good access to park water from the eastern end of the Middle Keys, but you need to show some restraint and watch the weather. A big wind into the current can make a crossing toward the mainland or some of the remote scattered banks a bit uncomfortable.

THE BIG BRIDGE

The Seven Mile Bridge is actually 684 feet short of claimed length, but it crosses more water than most anglers will properly learn in a lifetime. If you do learn it all you may find you never need to leave the area to have at least some sort of shot at a majority of shallow water Keys species along with more than a few deeper-water stragglers. The huge flow of water through the bridge moves a lot of food in both directions and attracts predators. The channel also serves as the most important Keys funnel between the Atlantic and Gulf.

Seven Mile Bridge Area—We typically think of bridges crossing deep water. There are flats, bars, and islands under this one. Many hold tailing and mudding species, and all serve as barriers for traveling fish. The deeper ditches hold lots of tarpon in season and a few most of the year. The deeper slots between pilings give up grouper and snapper while snook take up residence where food is easily captured and they can find some relief from the current. The banks scattered behind the bridge see their share of pushing tarpon and some rest on the edges. You'll find trout back up against a few and redfish on others. Realize, though, that you can't just run toward any hole in the bridge and get through.

Fly anglers find almost as much tarpon-turning terrain under the bridge as they do along the face of Vaca Key. The west end of the bridge, starting at Molasses Key, offers numerous snags for fish moving along the face of the Atlantic side of the bridge. Many of the edges show only as numbers on the chart though some of the shallower ones are shaded.

You'll find good numbers of bonefish here off and on and there are some wading opportunities with designated parking for road-bound anglers. Waders have a shot at a grand slam, as the area is justly famous for abundant and relatively cooperative permit. A lot of fish move too deep for waders to easily spot them so some angler's resort to fishing off short stepladders to enhance the view.

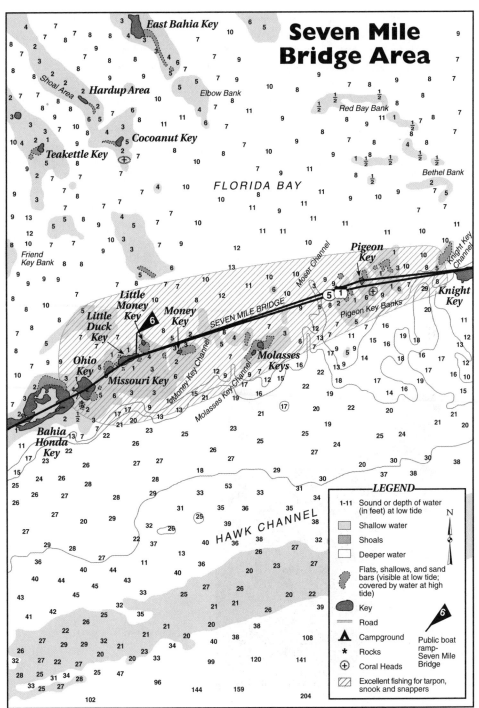

Seven Mile Bridge Area

East Bahia Key

Shoal Area
Hardup Area
Elbow Bank
Red Bay Bank
Cocoanut Key
Teakettle Key
Bethel Bank

FLORIDA BAY

Friend Key Bank

Pigeon Key

Knight Key Channel

Moser Channel

Little Money Key
Little Duck Key
Money Key
Ohio Key
Missouri Key
Molasses Keys
Pigeon Key Banks
Knight Key

SEVEN MILE BRIDGE

Money Key Channel

Molasses Key Channel

Bahia Honda Key

HAWK CHANNEL

LEGEND

1-11	Sound or depth of water (in feet) at low tide
	Shallow water
	Shoals
	Deeper water
	Flats, shallows, and sand bars (visible at low tide; covered by water at high tide)
	Key
	Road
▲	Campground
★	Rocks
⊕	Coral Heads
▨	Excellent fishing for tarpon, snook and snappers

N

6 Public boat ramp- Seven Mile Bridge

© WILDERNESS ADVENTURES PRESS, INC.

There are some tarpon around the bridge much of the year. The current is pretty stiff to say the least so fooling them with a fly is pretty tough. You can resort to high-density sinking lines and big whistler-style patterns for them, or you can fish around the ends of the tides. Fish are easy to find on calm days, providing a couple hours of opportunity around the tide changes.

You'll find lots of other species around the bridge including decent numbers of Spanish mackerel in the winter and some very big crevalles year round. Obvious ledges rising out of channels are a good place to start looking for them.

At the turn of the century, the banks bordering the broad channel on the Gulfside represented the western boundary of good seatrout range. The fish use the potholes in open water and let current back them into banks. You'll find some redfish scattered here and there. They often mud on the deep edges like bonefish.

This part of the Gulf is also loaded with old wrecks, and piles of litter dumped as fish attractors. Fly anglers can chum over them and raise a variety of fish. Those looking for sharks will find some true monsters on both sides of the bridge. A hundred-pound tarpon is a good bait for some of them! It is easier, however, to just heat them up so you can hook them on a 6-inch streamer.

Overall, the Middle Keys offer good facilities, a somewhat calmer feeling than the Upper Keys, and lots of fishing opportunities.

Max Heerman shows off a Spanish mackerel.

Middle Keys Hub City Information
Marathon

HOTELS AND MOTELS
Anchorlite Motel, 11699 Overseas Hwy. / 305-743-7397
Banana Bay Resort, 4590 Overseas Hwy. / 305-743-3500
Bay View Inn & Marina, Mm 63, Conch Key / 305-289-1525
Blackfin Resort Motel & Marina, 4650 Overseas Hwy. / 305-743-2393
Blue Waters Motel, 2222 Overseas Hwy. / 305-743-4832
Boathouse Fish Camp & Lodging,12501 U.S. Hwy. 1 / 305-743-4922
Bonefish Bay Motel, 12565 Overseas Hwy., Mm53.5 / 305-289-0565
Buccaneer Resort Hotel, Mm 48.5, U.S. Hwy. 1 / 305-743-9071
Cocoplum Beach Villas, 133 Coco Plum Dr. / 305-743-9106
Coral Lagoon Resort, 12399 Overseas Hwy. / 305-289-0121
Crane Point Resort & Marina, 7200 Aviation Blvd. / 305-743-5463
Crystal Bay Resort & Marina, 4900 Overseas Hwy. / 305-289-8089
Duck Key Motels, Rt.. 1 Box 1128, Greenbriar Rd., Duck Key / 305-743-2800
Fanny Key, 2 Fanny Key Rd. / 305-289-0001
Faro Blanco Marine Resort, 1996 Overseas Hwy. / 305-743-9018
Flamingo Inn, Mm 59.5, 59299 Overseas Hwy. , Grassy Key, 305-289-1478
Grassy Key Beach Motel, Mm 58.5, 58182 Overseas Highway, Grassy Key / 305-743-0533
Gulfview Motel, 58743 Overseas Hwy. , Mm 58.5, Grassy Key / 305-289-1414
Hampton Inn & Suites, 1688 Overseas Hwy. / 305-743-9009
Hawk's Cay Resort/Marina, Duck Key / 305-743-7000
Hawk's Nest, Mm 31 Kyle Way-South / 305-743-6711
Hidden Harbor Motel, 2396 Overseas Hwy. / 305-743-5376
Holiday Inn And Marina Of Marathon, Mm 54 / 305-289-0222
Key Lime Resort/Marina Club, 11600 1st Ave. Gulf / 305-743-3505
Kingsail Resort Motel, 7050 Overseas Hwy. / 305-743-5246
Knights Key Inn, Mm 47 By 7 Mile Bridge / 305-289-0289
Lagoon Resort/Motel, 7200 Aviation Blvd. / 305-743-5463
Longhorn Lodge, 12550 U.S. Hwy. 1 / 305-743-2680
Marathon Key Beach Club, 4560 Overseas Hwy. / 305-743-6522
Overseas Motel, 3600 Overseas Hwy. / 305-743-6843
Pelican Motel/Trailer Park, Rt.. 1 Box 528, Grassy Key / 305-289-0011
Ranch House Motel, 7251 Overseas Hwy. / 305-743-2217
P&P Bonefish Lodge, P.O . Box 500937 / 809-345-5555
Royal Hawaiian Motel, Mm 53 / 305-743-7500
Sandpiper Motel, 2443 Overseas Hwy. / 305-743-2244
Sea Cove Motel, 12685 Overseas Hwy. / 305-289-0800
Sea Dell Motel, 5000 Overseas Hwy. / 305-743-5161
Sea Shell Beach Resort, Grassy Key / 305-289-0265
Seahorse Motel, 7196 Overseas Hwy. / 305-743-6571

Seascape, 1075 E 75th St. Ocean / 305-743-6455
Seaward Motel, Mm 51.5 / 305-743-5711
Sombrero Resort, 19 Sombrero Blvd. / 305-743-2250
Tropical Cottages, 243 61st St. Mm 50 / 305-743-6048
Vaca Cut Motel, Mm 53 / 305-743-5214
Valhalla Beach Motel, Grassy Key / 305-289-0616
Valhalla Point Resort, 56223 Ocean Drive / 305-289-0614
Wellesley Inn, 13351 Overseas Hwy. / 305-743-8550
Yardarm Motel, 6200 Overseas Hwy. / 305-743-2541

VACATION RENTALS
Bonefish Towers, 2000 Coco Plum Drive / 305-289-0488
Fish N' Fun Vacation Rentals, 1299 Copa D'Oro / 305-743-2275
Casa De Addison, 1501 W. 63rd / 305-743-6463
Continental Inn, 21 West Ocean Dr., Key Colony Beach / 305-289-0101
Dolphin Vacations, 11199 Overseas Hwy. / 305-743-9876
Key Colony Point, P.O. Box 510099, Key Colony Beach / 305-743-7700
Key Colony Beach Realty, One 7th St. / 800-766-5033 / Luxuriously appointed
  condominiums
Keys Island Realty, Inc., 309 Key Colony Beach Shopping Center, Key Colony
  Beach / 305-289-1744
Sea Isle Condos, P.O. Box 510151, Key Colony Beach / 305-743-0173
Sunset Villas, 100 West Conch Ave. / 888-658-8924
Escape to the Keys Realty, 80654 Overseas Hwy. / 800-327-4836
Schmitt Real Estate, 11100 Overseas Hwy. / 305-743-5181
Conch Vacation Rental W/ Boats, 9583 Overseas Hwy. / 305-743-8877

RV RESORTS, RENTAL
Fiesta Key KOA, P.O. Box 618, Mm 70 U.S. Hwy. 1 / Long Key / 305-664-4410
Sunshine Key RV Resort and Marina / 800-852-0348
Jolly Roger Travel Park, 59275 Overseas Hwy. / 800-995-1525
Lions Lair Travel Park, 58950 Overseas Hwy. / 305-289-0606
Key RV Park, 6099 Overseas Hwy. / 800-288-5164
Knights Key Campground, Mm 47, P.O. Box 525 / 800-348-2267

RESTAURANTS
Adventure Island, 12648 Overseas Hwy. / 305-289-1742
Angler's Faro Blanco Resort, Mm 48.5 Bayside / 305-743-9018
Anthony's Ristorante, 4290 Overseas Hwy. / 305-743-2990
Banana Cabana Restaurant, 4590 Overseas Hwy. / 305-289-1232
Beach House The, 401 E Ocean Dr., Key Colony Beach / 305-743-3939
Brian's In Paradise, 11050 Overseas Hwy. / 305-743-3183
Buccaneer Resort Hotel, Mm 48.5 U.S. Hwy. 1 / 305-743-9071
Castaways Restaurant, 1406 Oceanview Ave. / 305-743-6247
Chef's Sombrero Resort, 19 Sombrero Blvd. / 305-743-4108
China American Garden, 1622 Overseas Hwy. / 305-743-2140

Cracked Conch Cafe, Mm 49.5 / 305-743-Cafe
Crocodile's On The Water, 1996 Overseas Hwy. / 305-743-9018
Don Pedro Restaurant, 11399 Overseas Hwy. / 305-743-5247
Driftwood Cafe, 10877 Overseas Hwy. / 305-289-1662
El Castillito Restaurant, 2438 Overseas Hwy. / 305-743-7676
Gallagher's Little Gourmet Restaurant / 305-289-0454
Galley Grill, Mm 25, Summerland Key / 305-745-3446
Gators Food & Spirits, Mm 47.5 Gulfside / 305-289-7332
Golden Palace Chinese, 10877 Overseas Hwy. / 305-289-0880
Grassy Key Dairy Bar, Mm 58.5, Grassy Key / 305-743-3816
Grassy Key New York Pizza & Deli, Mm 59.5, Grassy Key / 305-289-0001
Herbie's, 6350 Overseas Hwy. / 305-743-6373
Ideaway Cafe, Mm 58, Grassy Key / 305-289-1554
Holiday Inn & Marina Of Marathon, Mm 54. / 305-289-0222
Hurricane Restaurant, 4650 Overseas Hwy. / 305-743-5755
Jo-Jo's Restaurant, Mm 60, Grassy Key / 305-289-0600
Kelsey's Fine Dining, 1996 Overseas Hwy. / 305-743-9018
Landing Restaurant, Key Colony Beach Causeway / 305-289-0141
Latigo Dinner Cruises Marina, Mm 47.5 / 305-289-1066
Locals Only Sports Bar & Grill, Mm 52.5 / 305-743-8729
Pancho Villa's Steak House, 2010 Overseas Hwy. / 305-289-1629
Panda House Chinese Restaurant, 5230 Overseas Hwy. / 305-743-3417
Porky's Too, 1400 Overseas Hwy. / 305-289-2065
Porto Cayo At Hawk's Cay Resort, Mm 61 Duck Key / 305-743-7000
Quay Restaurant The, 12650 Overseas Hwy. / 305-289-1820
Royal Pelican, Holiday Inn, Mm 54 / 305-289-0222
Ship's Pub & Gallery, Mm 61, Duck Key / 305-743-7000
Shuckers Raw Bar & Grill, 1415 15th St., Oceanside / 305-743-8686
Silverado Steak House & Saloon, 1477 Overseas Hwy. / 305-743-5600
Stout's Restaurant, 8349 Overseas Hwy. / 305-743-6437
Stuffed Pig, 3520 Overseas Hwy. / 305-743-4059
Subway Sandwiches & Salads, Mm 53 / 305-743-2219
Sunset Cafe, Mm 48.5 U.S. Hwy. 1 / 305-743-9071
Takara Japanese Restaurant, 3740 Overseas Hwy. / 305-743-0505
Village Cafe, Gulfside Village / 305-743-9090
Wobbly Crab Restaurant, 5230 Overseas Hwy. / 305-743-7469
Wooden Spoon, 7007 Overseas Hwy. / 305-743-7469

FLY SHOPS/BAIT AND TACKLE
Baitrunner Charters, 1060 52nd St. Gulf / 305-743-7548big
Kahuna Bait & Tackle, 3580 Overseas Hwy. / 305-743-4500
Bonefish Bay Junction, 12565 Overseas Hwy. / 305-289-0920
Captain Hook's Marina, 11833 Overseas Hwy. / 305-743-2444
Drag-N-Bait, 1250 Oceanview Ave. / 305-743-2817

Fish 'N' Fun Waterfront Tackle, 12501 Overseas Hwy. / 305-743-2275
Footless Fishing And Chum Co., Inc., 1337 Ocean Breeze Ave. / 305-743-8088
Jeff's Bait & Tackle, Mm 54, 12650 Overseas Hwy. / 305-289-9991
Pancho Fuel Dock & Supplies, 1280 Oceanview Ave. / 305-743-2281
Sure Thing, 1250 Oceanview Ave. / 305-743-0344
The Tackle Box, 1901 Overseas Hwy. / 305-289-0540
World Class Angler, 1996 Overseas Hwy. / 305-743-6139
Faro Blanco Outfitters, 1996 Overseas Hwy. / 305-743-9018
Boaters World Discount Marine, 5001 Overseas Hwy. / 305-743-7707

BOAT RENTALS

All-Aqua-Adventures, 1996 Overseas Hwy. / 305-743-6628
Beach Front Water Sports, 900 Overseas Hwy. / 305-743-0905
Biggs Watersports, 4650 Overseas Hwy. / 305-743-8090
Blue Water Resort Motel, 2222 Overseas Hwy. / 305-743-4832
Bud Boats Inc., 2660 Overseas Hwy. / 305-743-5221
Coco Plum Marine, 66 Coco Plum Dr. / 305-743-3959
Conch Vacations With Boats, 9583 Overseas Hwy. / 305-743-8877
Hawk's Cay Water Sports, Duck Key Dr. / 305-7430145
Island Seafari, 11833 Overseas Hwy. / 305-289-2188
Marathon Boat Leasing, 901 43rd St. Gulf / 305-743-5716
R & R Watersports, Inc., 13201 Overseas Hwy. / 305-743-9385
Rhumb-Line Water Sports, Inc., 12648 Overseas Hwy. / 305-743-3700
Rick's Watercraft Rentals, 4590 Overseas Hwy. / 305-743-24507
Mile Marina, Mm 47.5, 1090 Overseas Hwy. , Bayside / 305-289-9849

MARINAS

Captain Hooks Marina, 11833 Overseas Hwy. / 305- 743-2444
Captain Pips Marina and Hideaway, 1410 Overseas Hwy., Mm 47.5 / 800-707-1692
Burdines Waterfront, 305-743-5317

AIRPORTS

Marathon Airport, 9400 Overseas Hwy. / 305-296-5439

HOSPITAL

Fisherman's Hospital, 3301 Overseas Hwy. / 305-743-5533

CAR RENTALS

Alamo Rent-A-Car, 800-327-9633 Airport / Locations / www.alamo.com
Dollar Rent-a-Car, (800 800-4000 / www.dollar.com
Avis, 800-452-1494 / www.avis.com

EMERGENCY INFORMATION

Coast Guard, 305-743-6388 or VHF 16
Seatow, 1-800-4-SEATOW / Marathon: 305-743-7556 / 24-hour dispatch

Marathon Marina Services

Marina	Phone	Slips	Tackle	Gas	Groceries	Boat Ramp	Restrooms	Restaurant	Repairs
Bonefish Marina	305-743-7015	0	No	No	No	No	No	No	No
Burdines	305-743-5317	10	Yes	Yes	Yes	No	Yes	Yes	No
Coco Plum Marina	305-743-7743	0	No	Yes	No	No	No	No	No
Fish N Fun	305-743-2275	0	Yes	Yes	Yes	Yes	Yes	No	Yes
Key Colony Beach Marina	305-289-1310	2	Yes	Yes	Yes	Yes	Yes	Yes	No
Marathon Marina	305-743-6575	40	Yes	Yes	No	No	Yes	Yes	Yes
Captain Hook's Marina	305-743-2444	0	Yes	Yes	Yes	No	Yes	No	No

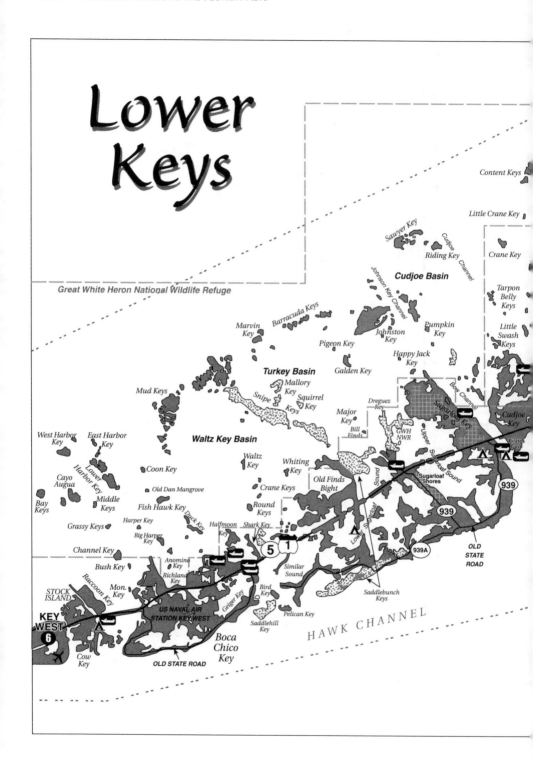

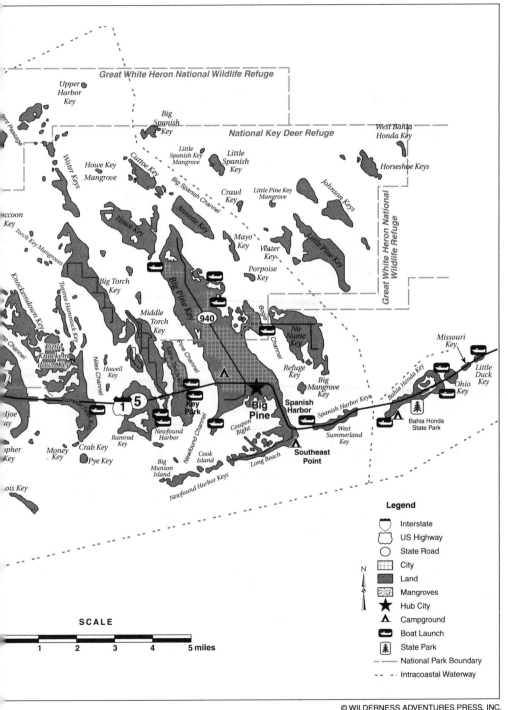

You now get to see a bit of what the rest of the Keys looked like years ago as you travel down. Much of the land along the highway in this region is undeveloped, though off in the distance you can see large residential areas here and there. What is considered the Lower Keys, the stretch between Bahia Honda and Stock Island, is a maze of narrow channels and relatively small basins.

The bridges are short in height and length with the exception of the Bahia Honda Bridge. The road is relatively peaceful and offers a better view of the surrounding "wilderness" than elsewhere in the Keys. Commercial development has been drastically limited for years, yet a good mix of eateries, tackle shops, and marinas cater to visitors. There is a slight exception to the tranquility; Big Pine feels a bit congested at times. It's not a horrible problem, but you will want to clear the island early in the day on weekends and holidays if you're traveling. The speed limits are low and road improvement is unlikely for environmental reasons. It's worth a delay as the island is the hub of shopping activity in the region and offers myriad fishing opportunities.

Sleeping arrangements are sometimes tough to find in the Lower Keys but worth searching for. The area requires some pre-planning if you want to stay here, and the limited rooms drastically reduce random boat traffic. It is a relatively short drive from other parts of the Keys, though. As of 2000, the legality of renting a room in a house or an entire house for a short-term stay anywhere in the Keys is determined on a neighborhood-by-neighborhood basis if you're visiting for less than a month. If you can find in-home accommodations off the highway here, there is a wonderfully remote feel unavailable in much of the Keys.

Navigation in the Lower Keys is a little tougher than anywhere else in the Keys. Secondary channels and cuts are narrow and edges are mostly rock hard. Much of the area is poorly marked in hopes of eliminating random boat traffic in more pristine areas. It works! You can sometimes find miles of shoreline all to yourself if you avoid the obvious attraction points.

Our favorite shallow water species seemingly enjoy the relative calm on the water, often moving slower and responding better to good presentations. There is more to the equation than limited boat traffic, though. For tailing species it likely has something to do with differences in the amount of forage on hard and soft bottom. Keys bonefish are seldom thought of as "goofy" yet fish cruising over hard bottom everywhere from Key Largo west seem easier to feed than fish digging in marl. They don't see as much food. Current is definitely a factor and the narrow passages in the Lower Keys focus a lot of water.

Tides in the Lower Keys are a bit complicated, but they provide lots of opportunity. You may stare across a gap between islands while sitting on a flat with a rising tide though the tide is falling on the flat along the face of the next island. Since the fish often follow the water seeking a comfortable depth, the variety of tidal situations within a relatively small area allows you to keep up. Tide charts available at area tackle shops and marinas typically list all the time variances you need to know to follow the water level the fish prefer each day.

The Lower Keys are a permit paradise. Permit prefer the often crunchy bottom, swift flow of water, and abundance of tangled edges to forage or rest in. Tarpon anglers are often amazed at the numbers of permit that filter by the boat along shallow migration routes.

A number of Lower Keys guides spend lots of time permit fishing and have a pretty good handle on the daily comings and goings of the fish. There are enough fish in the region to expect to see some fish on prime spots during their favored tidal stage most days. They follow rays with some regularity, too. Once upon a time they put up with cormorants following and robbing rays, and it is still worth a minute of your time to see what a cormorant is up to.

The Lower Keys—It's a maze! The Lower Keys offer a wealth of shallows and lots of places to hide from the wind, as the chart on the following pages shows.

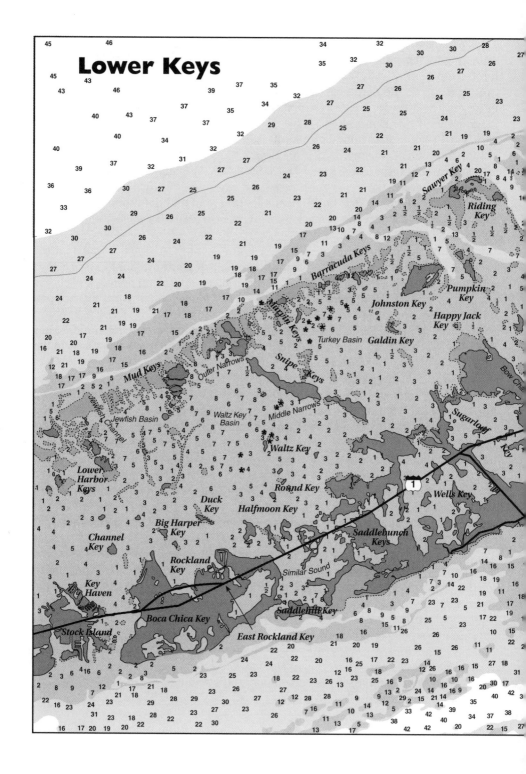

Lower Keys

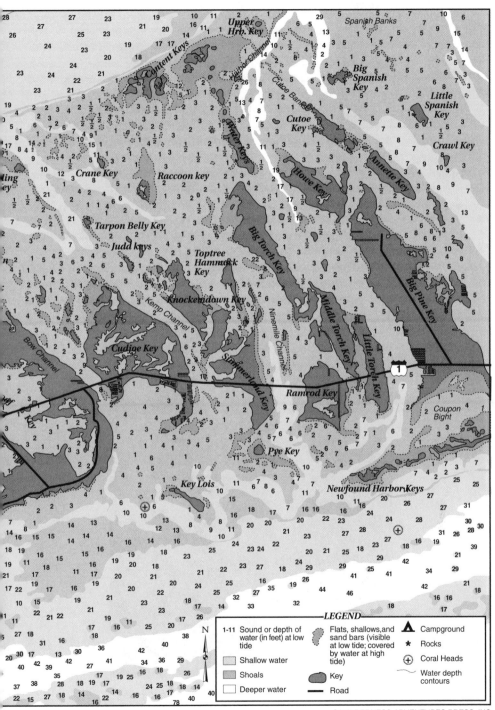

LEGEND

1-11	Sound or depth of water (in feet) at low tide	▲ Campground
	Shallow water	★ Rocks
	Shoals	Coral Heads
	Deeper water	Water depth contours
	Flats, shallows, and sand bars (visible at low tide; covered by water at high tide)	
	Key	
	Road	

N

Digging rays deserve a lot of attention in the Lower Keys. Bonefish follow them along with an occasional mutton snapper or barracuda. In the late '90s, and likely now, they also attracted jack crevalles capable of giving anglers fits on a 10-weight fly rod or a 12- to 15-pound spinning rig. On the Gulfside during winter and early spring, cobia frequently haunt rays and are an outstanding light tackle target.

Tarpon are friendly throughout the area. There are lots of them most years and the season is extended due to quiet water that encourages an abundance of smaller fish to spend much of the year here. It's somewhat easier for sight fishermen to find a big fish during the migration, and they eat with abandon. Late summer through fall, fishing for 10- to 30-pound fish is by the far the best in the Keys.

The Lower Keys are famous for hatches of palola worms, typically occurring during spring tides in late May or early June. No, I can't honestly explain what triggers the hatch, although reasonable weather seems to help, and they usually occur dur-

This kingfish is going home for dinner.

ing the afternoon and early evening. They happen during the Oceanside rising tide along some island faces, but many think the falling tide is better elsewhere. It's all a matter of luck in the end. Local tackle shops are a good source of rumors as hatches often attract enough fish that no one seems to mind an extra boat or two taking part in the fray.

Fish often disappear throughout much of the Keys around the hatches except where the tarpon expect the hatch. They seem to appear out of nowhere, and at times you could never guess so many tarpon existed or might be so greedy. The hatches also appear to have some impact on the migration as fish mostly head from Miami toward Key West until the hatches are over. Suddenly, after the hatches, they all turn around and make their way back to the coast and the turn doesn't seem to relate to the weather.

Flies for the hatch or around the hatch are pretty simple. Most folks like something mostly orange or orange and yellow. An olive-headed rust colored rabbit strip fly works pretty well. When I didn't know any better years ago, I did well with a pink fish hair streamer one might consider more appropriate for barracuda. I don't recommend it, having a lot more faith in the rust and olive, but I mention it so you feel some confidence in using something a bit off the wall if you're there during the miracle. Spin anglers can do well during a hatch with rubber worms, small jerk baits, or bait tails ranging from peach to pumpkinseed in color. We see hatches elsewhere in the Keys from time to time and when the fish are "wormy" they eat a worm-type fly better than others almost everywhere on the Oceanside.

The almost ever-present population of resident small tarpon will eat a black or white bucktail streamer most of the time. Some anglers get creative and blow up a bonefish pattern to size 1/0 for them. A favorite of the fish, if not all anglers, is something with grizzly, ginger, or cree feathers, somewhat representative of the segmented body of a shrimp or the kicker legs of a crab. The fish are easiest to find along mangrove edges fed by a rising tide. Spin folks find them easy pickings with a live shrimp, a small crab, or plastic bait tails and smallish swimming plugs. A silver spoon isn't bad, either.

In much of the Keys we expect tarpon to move toward shorelines and edges as the tide pushes at them and fall away when the tide shifts. In some parts of the Lower Keys they push toward the shallows on both tides. You may find them crawling along at bonefish depths with the tide screaming in their face. They show this trait throughout their Keys range but it is more pronounced here. Perhaps they are hiding from shark attacks on the Oceanside as the shallows shelve steeply into the depths.

During the heart of the migration you may find laid-up fish scattered anywhere on both sides of the islands. The area is justly famous for huge solitary fish hiding in random small corners. They tend to lay up more on rising tide edges and drop into the funnels of the bridge channels to feast when the tide falls. Keep in mind that you can find rising tide spots within minutes of falling tides spots.

If you're new to the sport and the area, you'll find it easier to begin your exploration on the Atlantic side. The fish eat just fine and navigation is greatly simplified. Shallows seemingly jump up out of nowhere so you have to pay attention to your chart and stay aware of where you are.

__Bahia Honda Key Area__—You won't find much soft bottom in front of Bahia Honda Key, but you will find a lot of tarpon. The bridge is one of the hottest live bait spots in the Keys. There's a good public ramp on Little Duck Key. Be careful idling out, though. For waders there is rare public access to the flats at Little Duck and Missouri Keys. You might throw at tarpon while wading here along with bonefish and permit.

Throughout the region, bonefish average a bit smaller than their Middle and Upper Keys counterparts. The size of schools doesn't rival those in Florida Bay, either, but there are enough fish to draw attention. The tides work a bit differently in the Lower Keys since the water is very deep on the edges. The water floods or ebbs across many backcountry flats almost like a wall and the fish come in waves. They don't hang around as they might where the tide comes and goes gradually. Instead, they often run across a flat with the water and follow the water to the next flat.

You'll find plenty of single fish and small groups working almost any time the water is moving if you poke around. Seasonal variances have them running from neighborhood to neighborhood, but when weather is consistent they settle into easily understood patterns. You can follow the waves of fish when you figure out their routine of following a wall of water, but a lot of folks chum to try to keep them around for a while. Screaming currents broadcast scent over a pretty good distance and enough fish hang out on the edges to keep things interesting.

Sushi, anyone?

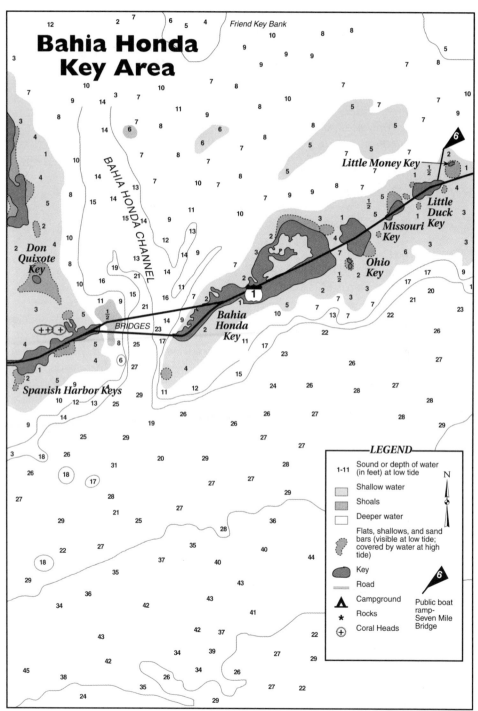

Bahia Honda Key Area

12 2 7 6 5 4 *Friend Key Bank*
                                        8   8
                                   10
3   9   9   5
                              9   9
                                9   8
   10   10   7   7   8   7
7   9   14   3   7   10   10   7   9
   8   6   8 11   8
3   14   6   9   8   8
4   14   7 8   6   7   5   7   7
1   7   8   6   8   7   5   *Little Money Key*   2
5   10   13 7   10   7   9   8 7 1/2
Don 4 15 14 14   9   11   1 1/2   *Little Duck Key* 3
Quixote 10   15 14 12 13   3 1 5
Key   8   13 14 10 9 14   *Missouri Key* 3
2   16 19 21 14 7   *Ohio Key* 17 17 9
10   15 11 21   16 2   5   21 20 1
11 9 1/2   14   7 10 13 22 23
BRIDGES 14 23   17 5 7 22 26
17 25   2 *Bahia Honda Key* 11 23 27
6 4 27   11 17 26 28
Spanish Harbor Keys 12 15 24 26 28 29
29 11 19 26 27 28 29
LEGEND

Cudjoe Key Area—This is one of the easier areas for many anglers to get in front of Lower Keys flats species. The darkest shaded areas represent marl flats attractive to bonefish and permit. Large numbers of big tarpon filter through the channels during the migration, and the nooks and crannies provide sanctuary for smaller clan members much of the year. The chart is not even reasonably accurate, missing some wonderfully submerged ridges routing tarpon as they push and some basins they rest in as the tides falter. Many boat teams run here from Islamorada during fly tarpon tournaments for the same reasons as those who can plan years ahead for a week of tarpon fishing. I landed my first Keys tarpon and bonefish here, and while I now live 70 miles up the road, I try to find an excuse to visit each year. You might think that distance minor, but not with the wealth of fishing in the Keys. I live two minutes from a boat ramp and about three minutes from easy early morning summer bonefish on a rising tide or nine minutes away from unbelievable fall bonefishing, along with some good permit and tarpon fishing. It takes a lot for me to justify spending an hour and a half on the road to go fishing! This area is classic.

The Lower Keys backcountry offers some of the best fishing for glamour species found anywhere in the world. This is where you'll find tarpon fishing nine month a year or so, unmolested bonefish following walls of water, and relatively calm permit.

When the water rises from the Gulf, while it is falling on the Oceanside, tarpon are shoved into the myriad small basins and their many corners. Smaller fish crawl up onto ledges leading to the mangroves and under the mangroves. It's possible to guard the right point here and catch a flats grand slam: a tarpon, bonefish, and permit during the same tide. All species come with the water and the swift flows encourage aggressive feeding.

As the new century begins we're seeing a few redfish moving into the backcountry. The fish are scattered and the fishing is a bit random but should get better over time. While often thought of as preferring soft bottom, they thrive over hard bottom with lots of current. Crabs are one of their favorite foods. As the population explodes elsewhere in the Keys, they'll likely become a focus of activity in the Lower Keys, too. For now, much of the action centers around the bottom of the tide for singles and very small schools, but some fish up to 40 pounds are haunting nearby wrecks in the fall and winter.

Another area bonus for sight fishermen is a late winter and spring cobia fishery. The fish push along Gulf edges as they escape chilly water to the north. They often run fairly regular routes like tarpon when they're really on the march, but you'll find some good fishing for singles and small groups by chasing rays and sometimes larger sharks. Cobia love following potential food sources. The quality of the run depends on garbage weather elsewhere. They'll eat almost anything when in the mood, although cuda baits, such as a long fish hair streamer on a fly rod or a tube lure for spin folks, are favored by many.

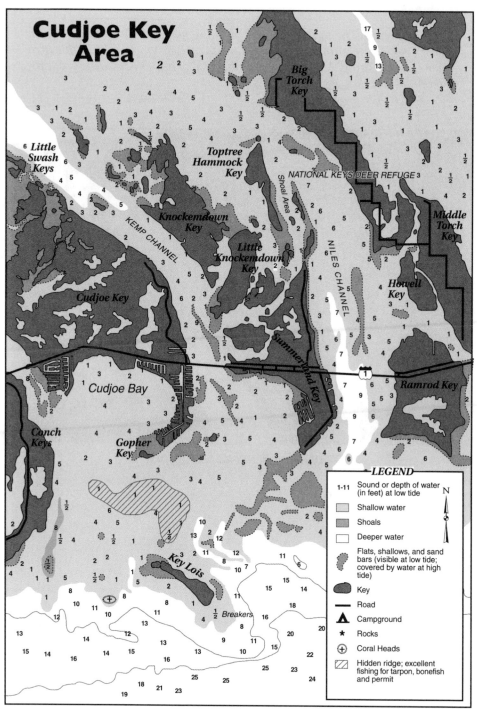

Cudjoe Key Area

Big Torch Key

Little Swash Keys

Toptree Hammock Key

NATIONAL KEYS DEER REFUGE

Knockemdown Key

KEMP CHANNEL

Little Knockemdown Key

Shoal Area

NILES CHANNEL

Middle Torch Key

Howell Key

Cudjoe Key

Summerland Key

Ramrod Key

Cudjoe Bay

Conch Keys

Gopher Key

Key Lois

Breakers

LEGEND

N

1-11	Sound or depth of water (in feet) at low tide
	Shallow water
	Shoals
	Deeper water
	Flats, shallows, and sand bars (visible at low tide; covered by water at high tide)
	Key
—	Road
▲	Campground
★	Rocks
⊕	Coral Heads
▨	Hidden ridge; excellent fishing for tarpon, bonefish and permit

© WILDERNESS ADVENTURES PRESS, INC.

Cudjoe Bay—*The terrain here forces politeness. This is another stealth chart. Look at the numbers. If you point straight at landmarks in this area you'll hit something! All those ridges mark travel routes or feeding grounds, though.*

With the right rod all fish are fun.

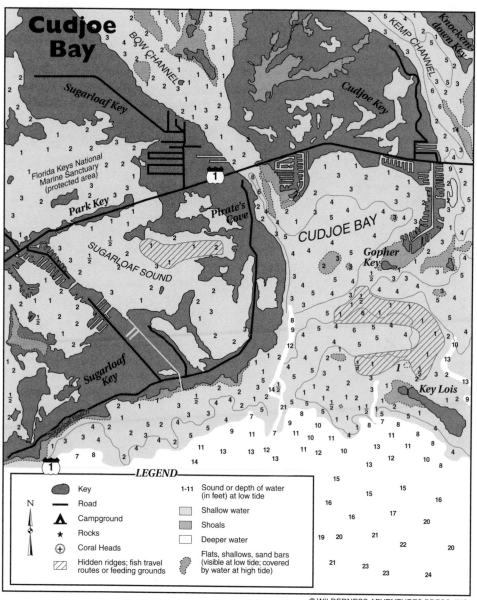

Cudjoe Bay

BQW CHANNEL

KEMP CHANNEL

Knockem down Key

Sugarloaf Key

Cudjoe Key

Florida Keys National
Marine Sanctuary
(protected area)

Park Key

Pirate's Cove

SUGARLOAF SOUND

CUDJOE BAY

Gopher Key

Sugarloaf Key

Key Lois

Sugarloaf Beach

LEGEND

Key		1-11	Sound or depth of water (in feet) at low tide
Road			Shallow water
Campground			Shoals
Rocks			Deeper water
Coral Heads			Flats, shallows, sand bars (visible at low tide; covered by water at high tide)
Hidden ridges; fish travel routes or feeding grounds			

N

© WILDERNESS ADVENTURES PRESS, INC.

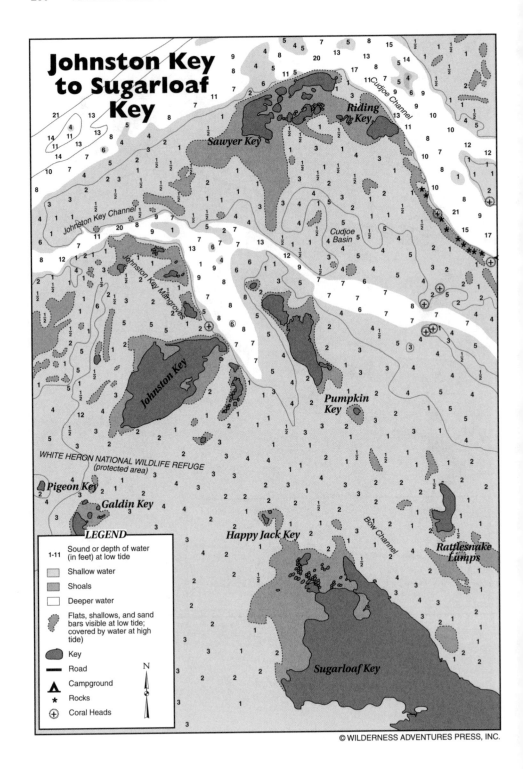

Johnston Key to Sugarloaf Key

LEGEND

1-11	Sound or depth of water (in feet) at low tide
	Shallow water
	Shoals
	Deeper water
	Flats, shallows, and sand bars visible at low tide; covered by water at high tide)
	Key
—	Road
▲	Campground
★	Rocks
⊕	Coral Heads

N

© WILDERNESS ADVENTURES PRESS, INC.

Johnston Key to Sugarloaf Key—*You'll find lots of bonefish on the marl flats along with permit popping up on the channel edges. The deep ditches hold tarpon in season during the worst of weather. It's a great grab-bag fishing area, too, since the water shelves so steeply into the Gulf. A bag of chum or a chum pot works wonders.*

Melanie Dahlberg with a nice little grouper.

Snipe Keys to Bay Keys—This might be an easier area for many anglers to learn quickly as the obstacles are fewer and choke points for fish a bit more obvious. All the little cuts facing the Gulf focus hard charging currents and the marl flats hold plenty of food. You'll find snappers in the ditches and our favorite glamour species on the flats.

This trout is too big for dinner and lived to spawn again.

Snipe Keys to Bay Keys

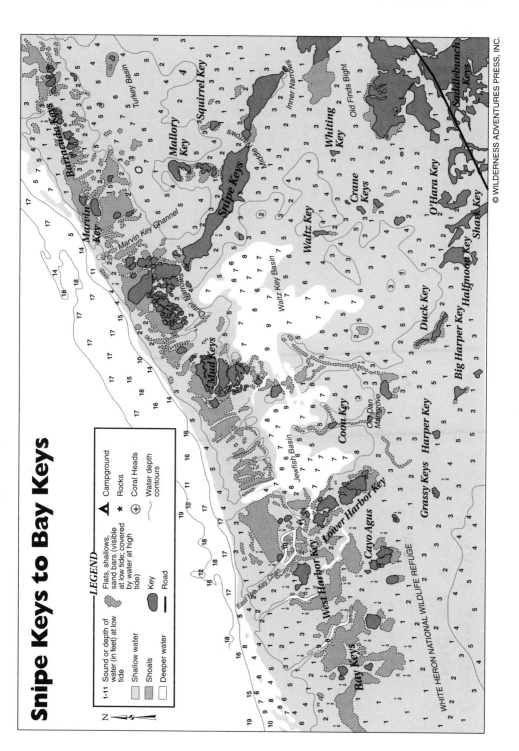

LEGEND

1-11 Sound or depth of water (in feet) at low tide

Flats, shallows, sand bars (visible at low tide; covered by water at high tide)

Shallow water

Shoals

Deeper water

▲ Campground

✳ Rocks

⊕ Coral Heads

Water depth contours

Key

Road

© WILDERNESS ADVENTURES PRESS, INC.

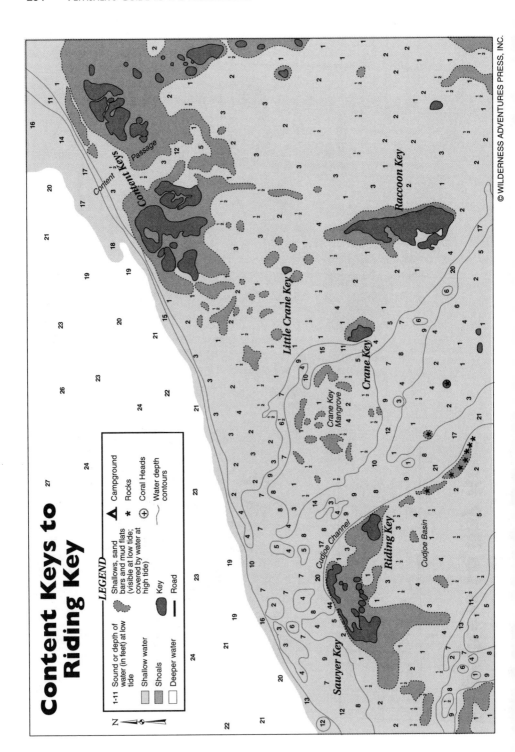

Content Keys to Riding Key, Gulfside—Many anglers talk about the bonefishing around the Contents in hushed tones. The quality of the fishing is not a secret, but the right time to greet the fish is often a mystery. It's sometimes only hot for select moments during a given tide. There are ditches here favored by tarpon that also funnel plenty of permit toward surrounding edges.

Many Lower Keys residents spend a lot of time on the reef or offshore. Days are even quieter here as the vast waters of the region swallow up lots of boats. Fishing is still much of what it was years ago in selected spots. The area is loaded with structure on the inner reef. We're not talking much about deep-water fishing as we move through the regions, however, fly and light tackle anglers will find many reasons to head toward the steep drop-offs and offshore.

This snook lived to see another day.

Lower Keys Hub City Information

Big Pine Key and Other Lower Keys

HOTELS AND MOTELS

Barnacle Bed & Breakfast, 1557 Long Beach Rd. / 305-872-3298
Big Pine Key Fishing Lodge, 33000 Overseas Hwy. / 305-872-2351
Big Pine Resort Motel, 30725 Overseas Hwy. / 305-872-9090
Caribbean Village, 1211 U.S. Hwy. 1, Big Coppitt / 305-296-9542
Dolphin Resort And Marina, Mm 28.5, Little Torch Key / 305-872-2685
Little Palm Island, 28500 Overseas Hwy., Little Torch Key / 305-872-2524
Looe Key Reef Resort, Mm 27.5 Oceanside / 305-872-2215
Old Wooden Bridge Fishing Camp, 1791 Bugle Dr. / 305-872-2241
Parmer's Resort, 565 Barry Avenue, Little Torch Key / 305-872-2157

VACATION RENTALS

Heavenly Days Vacation Rentals, 29643 Constitution Ave. / 305-872-0323
Mark's Rental, 467 Heck Ave. , Little Torch Key / 305-872-4688
Paradise Lodging, 31316 Ave. J / 305-872-9009
Sun and Serenity Corp, 17376 Jamaica Lane, Sugarloaf Key / 800-491-7715

RV RESORTS AND CAMPGROUNDS

Bahia Honda State Park, Mm 37, 36850 Overseas Hwy. / 305-872-2353
Sunshine Key Fun Resort, 38801 Overseas Hwy. / 305-872-2217
Big Pine Fishing Lodge, 33000 Overseas Hwy. / 305-872-2351
Sunshine Key Fun Resort, 38801 Overseas Hwy. / 305-872-2217
Seahorse RV Park, 201 County Road / 305-872-2443
Sugarloaf KOA, 251 County Road, Summerland Key / 305-745-3549
Germer's Mobile Auto Repair, 21091 1st Ave. East, Cudjoe Key / 305-745-2846
Breezy Pines RV Estates, Mm 30 Hwy. 1 / 305-872-9041
Castaway RV Park, Mm 30 Oceanside / 305-872-9710

RESTAURANTS

Annie's Sports Bar, 305-872-4341
Baltimore Oyster House, Mm 30.5 / 305-872-2314
Big Pine Coffee Shop, Mm 30 / 305-872-2790
Black Swan Mexican Pub, 1st St. / 305-872-2326
Bobalu Southern Cafe, Overseas Hwy., Big Coppitt Key / 305-296-1664
    Boondocks, Mm 27.5, Ramrod Key / 305-872-0022
Cedar Inn, Mm 31 / 305-872-4031
Co Co's Cantina, Mm 21.5, Cudjoe Key / 305-745-1564 / Spanish, American and
    Nicaraguan.
Coconuts Lounge, 305-872-3795
Coco's Kitchens, Big Pine Shopping Plaza / 305-872-4495
Dip N' Deli, Mm 31 / 305-872-3030
Dutchman's The, Mm 30.5 U.S. Hwy. 1 / 305-872-9277

Galley Grill, Mm 25, Summerland Key / 305-745-3446 / Homestyle cooking, reasonably priced, family atmosphere.
Hop Sing's Chinese Take Out, Mm 31 / 305-872-0895
Indian Mounds Racquet & Swim Club, Sugarloaf Key / 305-743-3276
Island Reef Restaurant, Mm 31.3 / 305-872-2170
Isle O'bones Restaurant, Key West / 305-296-1250 K D's Big Pine
KD's Steak/Seafood House, Mm 30.5 / 305-872-2314
Key Deer Bar And Grill, Mm 31 / 305-872-1014 / Pizza and pasta dishes
Light-House Restaurant The, Mm 31 / 305-872-2326
Mariner Resort, Mm 31 / 305-872-2222
Mark's Place Gourmet Deli, Mm 30 / 305-872-1230
Montes Restaurant & Fish Market, Summerland Key / 305-745-3731/ Eat in or take out / Fresh seafood sold daily
No Name Pub, Northwest Side of the Bogie Channel Bridge / The oldest bar in Big Pine / Pizza and a fine beer selection
Newfound Harbor, Little Palm Island / Access via boat / Renowned French restaurant / Reservations a must
Peg Leg's Restaurant At Mariner Resort / 305-872-2202
Pepe's Cafe, 806 Caroline St., Key West / 305-294-7192
Raimondo's Ristorante Italiano, 457 Drost Dr, Cudjoe Key / 305-745-9999
Key Deer Bar And Grill, Mm 31 / 305-872-1014 / Pizza and pasta dishes.

BAIT AND TACKLE
Big Pine Key Fishing Lodge, Inc. 33000 Overseas Hwy. / 305-872-2351
Chevron Island, Mm 25, Summerland Key / 305-744-9717
Dolphin Resort & Marina, Mm 28.5, Little Torch Key / 305-872-2685
Jigs Bait & Tackle, Gulfside # 30.3 /305-872-1040
Murray's Food Mart, 24550 Overseas Hwy. , Summerland Key / 305-745-3534
Ms Marguerite Bait Shack, 3194-320 Overseas Hwy. / 305-872-0650
Sea Boots Outfitters, Mm 30 Gulfside / 305-872-9005
Sugarloaf Marina, Sugarloaf Key / 305-745-3135

MARINAS
AAA All Marine, 77 Industrial Road, Big Pine Key / 305-872-1516
Cudjoe Gardens Marina, 477 Drost Dr, Cudjoe Key / 305-745-2357
Dolphin Marina Resort, 28530 Overseas Hwy., Little Torch Key / 305-872-2685
Final Effort Mobile Marine Repair, 1457 Sunset Road, Big Pine Key / 305-515-0259
Keys Sea Center, P.O. Box 430515, Big Pine Key / 305-872-2243
Peninsular Marine, 6000 Peninsula Ave. / 305-296-8110
Sugarloaf Marina, P.O. Box 14, Sugarloaf Shores / 305-745-3135

BOAT RENTALS

All Aboard Boat Rental, Mm 24.5, 1051 Caribbean Dr. E., Summerland Key / 305-745-8877

Big Pine Key Fishing Lodge, Inc., 33000 Overseas Hwy. / 305-872-2351

Chevron Island, Mm 25, Summerland Key / 305-744-9717

Cudjoe Boat Rentals, Mm 21, 477 Drost Dr., Cudjoe Key / 305-745-2357

Dolphin Resort & Marina, Mm 28.5, Little Torch Key / 305-872-2685

HOSPITAL

Big Pine Medical Complex, U.S. Highway 1 Mm 30 Oceanside / 305-872-5600

EMERGENCY INFORMATION

Coast Guard, 305-295-9700 or VHF 16

Seatow, 1-800-4-SEATOW (Florida Keys): 305-872-2752 / 24-hour dispatch

TowBoat/US, 800-391-4869 / 24-hour dispatch

There are a couple pairs of teeth in the mouth of a seatrout.

Lower Keys Marina Services

Marina	Phone	Slips	Tackle	Gas	Groceries	Boat Ramp	Restrooms	Restaurant	Repairs
Bahia Honda State Park	305-872-3201	28	No	No	No	Yes	Yes	No	No
Big Pine Key Fishing Lodge	305-872-2351	0	Yes	Yes	Yes	No	Yes	No	Yes
Boca Chica Naval Air Station Marina	305-293-3468	1	Yes	Yes	No	Yes	Yes	Yes	No
Cudjoe Gardens Marina	305-745-2357	5	Yes	Yes	No	Yes	Yes	No	Yes
Dolphin Resort and Marina	305-872-2685	2	Yes	Yes	No	Yes	Yes	No	No
Geiger Key RV Park & Marina	305-296-3553	0	Yes	Yes	No	Yes	No		
Keys Sea Center	305-872-2243	0	Yes	Yes	Yes	No	No	No	Yes
Little Palm Island	305-872-2524	14	No	No	No	No	Yes	Yes	
Looe Key Reef Resort	305-872-2215	0	No	Yes	No	No	Yes	Yes	No
Sugarloaf Marina	305-745-3135								

Key West

Legend

⬭	Interstate
⬯	US Highway
◯	State Road
⊞	City
▦	Land
▨	Mangroves
★	Hub City
▲	Campground
⬒	Boat Launch
⛃	State Park
- ⸺	National Park Boundar
- - -	Intracoastal Waterway

Key West National Wildlife Refuge

N

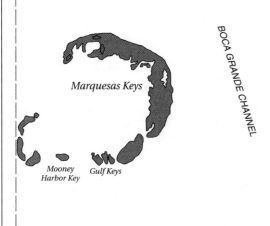

Marquesas Keys

BOCA GRANDE CHANNEL

Mooney Harbor Key

Gulf Keys

Boca Grande Key

Woman Key

ATLANTI

SCALE

0   1   2   3   4   5 miles

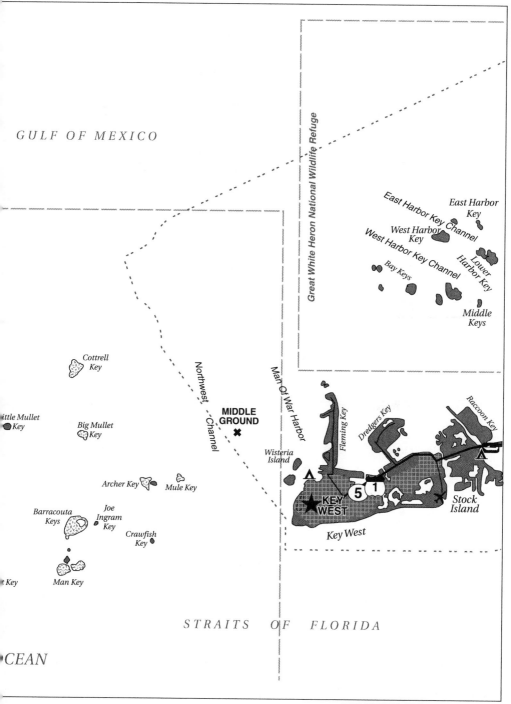

GULF OF MEXICO

Great White Heron National Wildlife Refuge

East Harbor Key Channel

East Harbor Key

West Harbor Key

West Harbor Key Channel

Lower Harbor Key

Bay Keys

Middle Keys

Cottrell Key

Little Mullet Key

Big Mullet Key

Northwest Channel

MIDDLE GROUND
✖

Man Of War Harbor

Wisteria Island

Fleming Key

Dredgers Key

Raccoon Key

Archer Key

Mule Key

Barracouta Keys

Joe Ingram Key

Crawfish Key

5 1

KEY WEST

Stock Island

Key West

Man Key

Key

STRAITS OF FLORIDA

CEAN

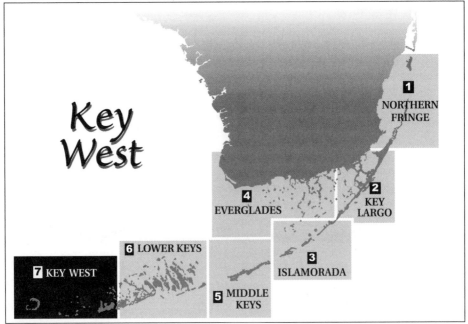

Key West

1 NORTHERN FRINGE

2 KEY LARGO

4 EVERGLADES

3 ISLAMORADA

6 LOWER KEYS

7 KEY WEST

5 MIDDLE KEYS

© WILDERNESS ADVENTURES PRESS, INC.

Key West is rich in history with century-old or older homes that laugh at hurricanes. When you finally get off the beaten path, the area provides a touch of what it felt like to make a living from the sea many years ago. Many people find it romantic or find romance in its legacy. Its waters are wondrous, and fortunately for us, many visitors ignore them.

The Keys are often nationally advertised as the Florida Keys and Key West. Key West is totally different in many ways from the rest of the Keys, and residents are proud of it. Key West is a city, home to 4,000 residents per square mile, and a tourist industry often focused on the city's land-based charms. The influx of visitors typically doubles or triples the local population on a daily basis.

Other areas of the Keys offer somewhat better all around flats fishing during prime time, but Key West is often less impacted by chilly temperatures during the winter and is the ultimate spot in the Keys for hot permit fishing much of the year. Tarpon show up sooner here than elsewhere, too, but they are often drawn to water depths less than attractive to fly anglers until they flood the flats when temperatures warm. The depth of the water in the immediate area is a bit of a barrier for those seeking a classic flats fishing experience, although the fish are greedy feeders, easily found at sight fishing depths by local experts.

Key West shines as an attraction for fly and light tackle anglers seeking a wide variety of inshore and offshore species. We're altering our course a bit. While you can easily find a fleet of typical flats skiffs operating in the neighborhood, many operators lean toward jack-of-all-trades boats as some do in the Middle Keys. There are plenty of flats fishing opportunities, but the area offers many other options for those in small boats. Either way, you are going to find plenty to like as many species of fish not often available to those in small craft are found in shallower and more sheltered nearby waters.

The waters of the Gulf and Atlantic join uniquely here. Much of the water between the Gulf and Atlantic surrounding the rest of the Keys is too shallow to encourage travel through the bridges by many species of migratory fish. The steeply shelving waters surrounding Key West often bring seasonal weather-related migrations far closer to shore. For instance, you'll find cobia at easy sight fishing depths, sails sometimes less than a mile from shore, and kingfish as shallow as 20 feet or so. A chum line in a deep trench may well attract mutton snappers or a variety of grouper weighing double digits along with some amberjacks big enough to wear you out.

Amberjacks are often Gulf Stream species elsewhere in the Keys unless you find smallish clan members on near shore wrecks in a hundred or more feet of water.

Dentist Buzz Defilice wanted to compare teeth with this barracuda.

You'll find fish capable of making you forget about tarpon on fly gear over wrecks in 20 feet of water around Key West at times, and they are year-round residents along the reef here.

The last vestiges of the Keys shrimping industry still ply the waters of Key West in the new millennium. While the industry's by-catch waste is controversial, there is little doubt chum lines fed with shrimp by-catch and fishing around shrimp boats is often red hot. It is part of the local recreational fishing tradition as a lot of Key West fishing focuses around chumming to raise fish from the depths, both inshore and off. It's possible to sit in a comfortably sheltered 20 feet of water and chum 100-foot depths. Local shallow wrecks harbor a wide variety of otherwise deep-water dwellers, varying with the season.

Those serious about bonefishing often make the short run into the Lower Keys, but you will also find a few gathering spots for fish if you head west. There are fish in the Marquesas and along some of the strip banks leading towards them. Fish average smallish here for some reason, but they are easy to feed as they are not widely targeted. There may be too much current for their favored foods, although all the current is an attraction for permit. Bonefish like a lot of current too—especially big bonefish—but they insist on favored forage.

You'll find permit almost everywhere the current shoves them against banks or feeds them chow over wrecks if you learn when and why they use spots. The top fly, of course, is a Del's Merkin, a mostly carpet yarn pattern with some rubber legs and serious lead eyes. The way the fly sinks is far more important than what it looks like. Artful crab look-alike patterns do more to satisfy the tyer's dreams than those of the fish. Good suggestive patterns providing the action the fish expect work best. The top artificial food for a permit is still a jig, or a fly that works like a jig, and it doesn't matter what it looks like if it attacks the bottom with enthusiasm. The Merkin is a perfect suggestive pattern.

Permit respond well to chum in deeper water. Those using spin or conventional tackle do fine baiting with a crab or a chunk of something from their chum and free drifting it in the current. Many fly pros tie a marabou pattern that resembles some chum chunk and drift it across the current like a nymph.

Key West—Much of the Key West Oceanside shoreline is actual beach so there's not a lot of flats fishing action for bottom feeders in the immediate shallows, but tarpon do filter along the steeper edges. There is a lot of deep water relatively close to shore. The stiff flow of water around the end of the island chain attracts a wide range of species that are often sought farther from land in other areas. For instance, the deep water around Middle Ground often holds some of the largest kingfish available in the Keys during the winter along with good numbers of cobia. You can also chum here for tarpon and there is no telling what you might catch while blind casting a streamer on the end of a sinking line.

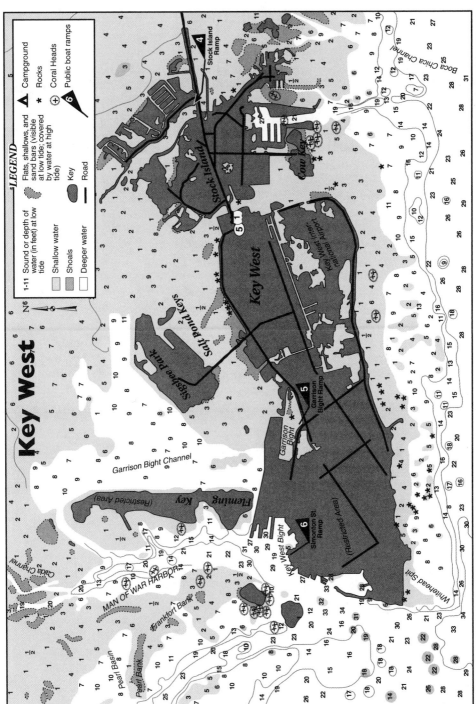

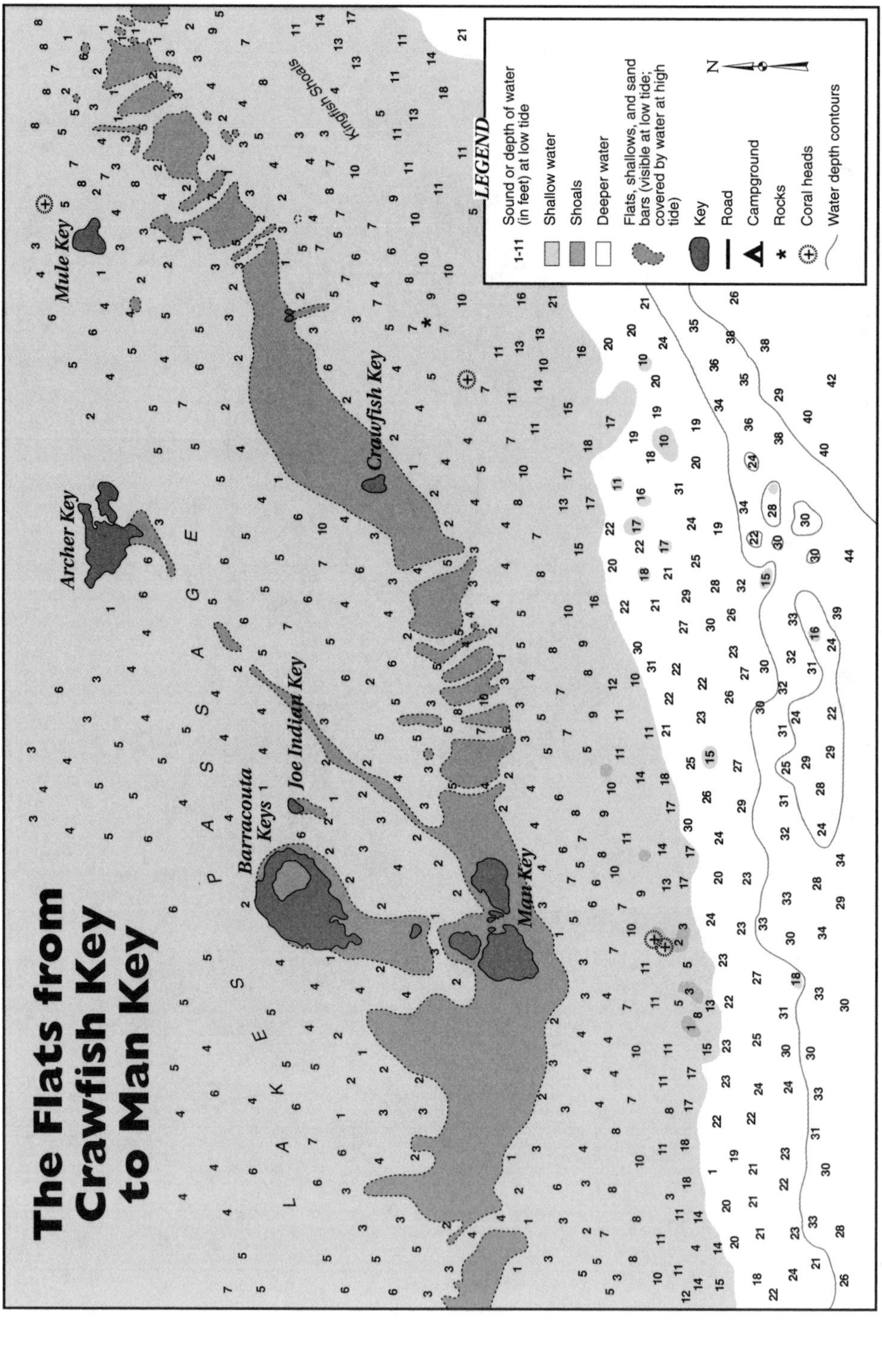

The Flats from Crawfish Key to Man Key

Archer Key

Mule Key

Kingfish Shoals

Crawfish Key

Joe Indian Key

Barracouta Keys

Man Key

P A S S A G E

L A K E S

LEGEND

Sound or depth of water (in feet) at low tide

1-11

Shallow water

Shoals

Deeper water

Flats, shallows, and sand bars (visible at low tide; covered by water at high tide)

Key

Road

Campground

Rocks

Coral heads

Water depth contours

N

© WILDERNESS ADVENTURES PRESS, INC.

The Flats from Crawfish Key to Man Key—This string of flats just west of Key West offers some bonefishing, great permit fishing, and routes some migrating tarpon during their season. Plenty of corners and cuts hide resting tarpon, too. It's also a great place to catch bait, easily found under diving birds. It's a favored haunt of barracudas just after the passage of a cold front.

Before we get too far I might caution you about gathering shrimp chum. You have to know where the shrimp boats are, something not easy to do without some sort of existing relationship with them. A trip to shrimping grounds is also an adventure for the uninitiated, and it might feel like quite a commitment if you don't understand the value of the chum. Throughout the Keys you will find that anglers well versed in the use of fresh dead chum or live chum spend lots of time gathering it. They might sacrifice a half-day in gathering it as the quality of the fishing usually far exceeds that of a whole day without it.

One must consider steeply shelving water when traveling and picking spots to fish. It doesn't take a lot of wind to kick up uncomfortable seas for easily poled boats. You'll want to learn travel routes to your favored spots on both sides of islands or flats. When you get there on windy days, though, you'll find much of the fishing is best where it is roughest–not in the ever-popular lee. On the string of flats between Crawfish and Boca Grande Keys, you'll often find tons of mudding rays in rough water whether it is raised by wind with the current or wind against the current. The rays are hounded by permit, some bonefish, and the occasional mutton snapper. In recent years they've also attracted a fresh influx of large jack crevalles. Most species will eat anything fished directly over the ray if it will fit in their mouth.

The author gets to fish once in awhile—here he is with a black drum.

The Marquesas— Perhaps the most fabled Keys shallow water fishing destination. They are not a routine everyday fishing destination. While seemingly large, fishing grounds do not provide room for many boats without hurting the fishing for every boat there. One should never take the trip across the Boca Grande Channel lightly in a boat small enough to be easily poled. Winds against the current raise very nasty seas here. A competent guide won't take you to the island on a day when you shouldn't go and will normally know if the area is too crowded to fish before trying the trip. You do owe it to yourself to see the fishing here at least once if you can do so.

Other things happen in the waters surrounding the Marquesas and in the Boca Grande Channel. The edges are rotten with barracuda, and big ones at that, during the winter. Permit filter all along the edges along with ray-following mutton snappers and cobia. The vast flow within the channel between the Gulf and Atlantic is quietly famous for some of the best sight fishing for sharks in the world.

It is home to all the fly-caught hammerhead shark world records and almost anyone can hook a 400- to 600-pound shark of one species or another on a fly here on any windy winter day. This large-shark fishing is one of a kind, although similar fishing for smaller sharks is available elsewhere in the Keys and along the southeast Florida coast.

Maybe the biggest surprise is the number of cobia, mutton snapper, and large jacks that follow the sharks along a scent trail. If they beat the shark to the fly, or whatever other food you offer, they are tough to land. The host shark often eats them before you can get them to the boat. I've only managed to do this here a couple of times, but it is some of the most exciting fishing I've seen. The only sharks we landed were small enough to properly fight on 12-weight fly gear. One was a 250-pound lemon. Once we also fought a likely class tippet world record hammerhead to a standstill before it got its back across the tippet. We hooked lots of 400- to 600-sharks on a fly when I did this, and it is rather routine action. At least it's routine for the area if not the anglers!

There is plenty of tarpon fishing around Key West. They are almost a year-round fixture in the deeper channels. When deep, the fish respond best to bait, but you can raise them some with a chum line. They flood the flats and shallow shelves pretty good when things warm up. You can blind cast flies on sinking lines for them much of the year if you insist. Casting a 12-weight fly rod all day without an obvious target can be boring and exhausting—until you get a bite.

In season, this is one of the best sight fishing destinations in the world and only a very short hop from the miles of shoreline along the Lower Keys. At times tarpon vanish into ditches, but if the weather is nice—and has been nice—they're cruising around. You should be on their pathways or searching for their bedrooms.

The water surrounding Key West is loaded with shallow water wrecks and natural structure rapidly falling into the depths. A wide variety of species are easily chummed within flyfishing reach and anything you can catch on a fly is easy prey for

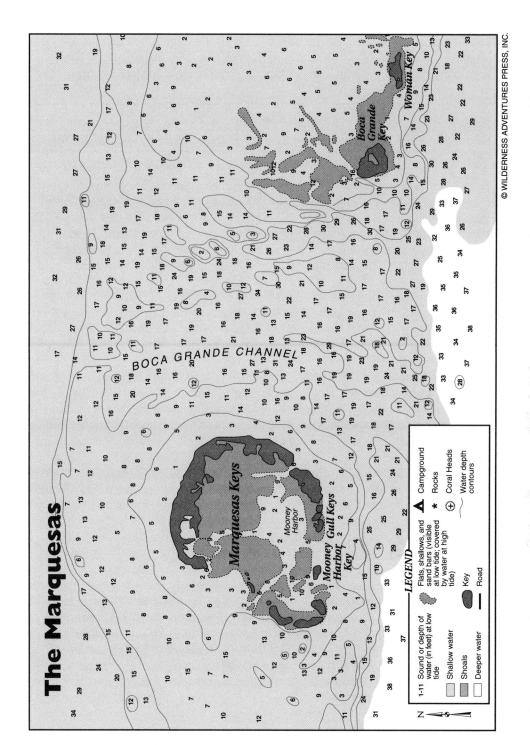

The Marquesas

BOCA GRANDE CHANNEL

Boca Grande Key

Woman Key

Marquesas Keys

Mooney Harbor

Mooney Harbor Key

Gull Keys

N

LEGEND

1-11 Sound or depth of water (in feet) at low tide

Flats, shallows, and sand bars (visible at low tide; covered by water at high tide)

Key

Road

Shallow water

Shoals

Deeper water

▲ Campground

✱ Rocks

⊕ Coral Heads

〜 Water depth contours

© WILDERNESS ADVENTURES PRESS, INC.

bait or lure anglers, too. I continually talk about the winter, but there is a marked migration of yellowtail snappers along the reef line in surprisingly shallow water then. They are joined by an ever-improving population of Spanish and cero mackerel.

All these species are easily fooled with a simple bucktail streamer or jig, and you'll find keeper-sized mutton snapper and grouper willing to rise for artificials high in the water, too. Plumbing unseen water with fish hair streamers, swimming minnows, or tube lures might turn up some giant barracudas.

I can't say fishing offshore is better around Key West than it is elsewhere in the Keys, but I have enjoyed some heated days here on area wrecks, mostly courtesy of live wells full of freshly caught living chum. The use of live chum is a real hallmark of the Keys fleet, and it makes fooling the toughest deep-water species a reasonable hope. The most willing species to crawl off a wreck are bonito and blackfin tuna. When hot in a livie chum line, both species jump all over flies. A 20-pound blackfin on a 12-weight fly rod is a real challenge. You owe it to yourself to book a pro for a day of this fishing.

It's surprisingly quiet on Key West waters considering the hustle and bustle on land. It's like this in much of the Keys if you stay away from known and easily found hot spots. In the water, things are often more crowded with a wider variety of fish very close at hand. Fishermen around Key West are well cared for with plenty of marinas and tackle shops.

Nearly 70 miles west of Key West lies a cluster of seven islands, composed of coral reefs and sand, called the Dry Tortugas. Along with the surrounding shoals and waters, they make up Dry Tortugas National Park. The area is known for its famous bird and marine life, and its legends of pirates and sunken gold. Ft. Jefferson, the largest of the 19th century American coastal forts built in the early 1800s, is a central feature. As the military value of Fort Jefferson waned, its pristine reefs, abundant sea life and impressive numbers of birds grew in value. In 1935, President Franklin Roosevelt set aside Fort Jefferson and the surrounding waters as a national monument. The area was redesignated as Dry Tortugas National Park in 1992 to protect both the historical and natural features.

The Dry Tortugas Ferry sails at 8:00 AM and departs from Land's End Marina. It returns at 5:30 PM. The phone number is 305-294-7009.

The Quicksands to the Dry Tortugas—The adventure continues for miles if you head west and northwest from the Marquesas, but it's beyond reach of traditional flats skiffs. A seaworthy center console (at a minimum) provides an opportunity to harass fish from the Marquesas to Rebecca Shoals. Many prefer a sportfisherman for overnight trips into the Tortugas area, and if you prefer to fish with conventional and spinning gear, party boats regularly spend the night .

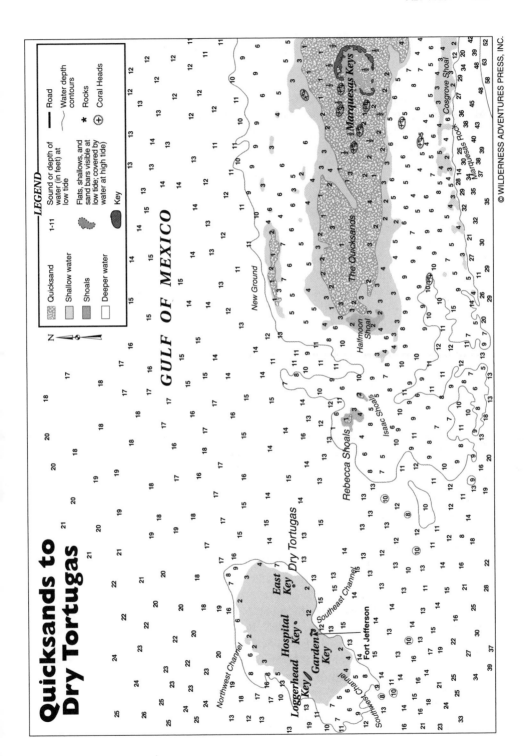

Quicksands to Dry Tortugas

GULF OF MEXICO

LEGEND

1-11	Sound or depth of water (in feet) at low tide
	Flats, shallows, and sand bars visible at low tide; covered by water at high tide
	Key
——	Road
～	Water depth contours
✳	Rocks
⊕	Coral Heads

Quicksand
Shallow water
Shoals
Deeper water

N

Marquesas Keys

The Quicksands

Halfmoon Shoal

New Ground

Cosgrove Shoal

Marquesas Rock

Rebecca Shoals

Isaac Shoals

Dry Tortugas

East Key

Hospital Key

Loggerhead Key

Garden Key

Fort Jefferson

Southeast Channel

Southwest Channel

Northwest Channel

© WILDERNESS ADVENTURES PRESS, INC.

Key West Hub City Information

HOTELS AND MOTELS

Actors, 1128 Margaret St. / 305-296-2210
Alexander Palms Court, 715 South St. / 305-296-6413
Angelina Guest House, 302 Angela St. / 305-294-4480
Atlantic Shores Resort, 510 South St. / 305-296-2491
Banana Bay Resort Of Key West, 2319 N. Roosevelt Blvd./ 305-296-2543
Banana Veranda, 1031 Eaton St. / 305-294-3333
Banyon Resort, 323 Whitehead St. / 305-296-7786
Best Western Hibiscus Motel, 1313 Simonton St. / 305-294-3763
Blue Lagoon Motel, 3101 N. Roosevelt Blvd. / 305-296-1043
Blue Marlin Motel, 1320 Simonton St. / 305-294-2585
Caribbean House, 226 Petronia St. / 305-296-1600
Case 325, 25 Duvall St. / 305-292-0011
Casa Alante Guest Cottages, 1435 S. Roosevelt Blvd. / 305-293-0702
Casa Key West, 811 Washington St. / 305-296-1141
Cayo Hueso Cottages, 505-515 United St. / 305-294-4819
Chelsea House, 707 Truman Ave. / 305-296-2211
Coconut Beach Resort, 1500 Alberta St. / 305-294-0057
Coconut Mallory Resort, 1445 S. Roosevelt Blvd. / 305-292-0017
Colony Exclusive Cottages, 714 Olivia St. / 305-294-6691
Comfort Inn, 3824 N. Roosevelt Blvd. / 305-294-3773
Conch House Heritage Inn, 625 Truman Ave. / 305-293-0020
Courtyard By Marriott, 3031 N. Roosevelt Blvd. / 305-296-6595
Courtyard, The, 910 Simonton St. / 305-296-1148
Cuban Club Suites, 422 Amelia St. / 305-296-0465
Curry Mansion Inn, 511 Caroline St. / 305-294-5349
Cypress House, 601 Caroline St. / 305-294-6969
Days Inn Of Key West, 3852 N Roosevelt Blvd. / 305-294-374
Dewey House, 1319 Duval St. / 305-296-5611
Douglas House, 419 Amelia St. / 305-294-5269
Duval Gardens And Spa, 1012 Duval St. / 305-292-3379
Duval House, 1319 Duval St. / 305-294-1666
Duval Inn, 511 Angela St. / 305-295-9531
Eaton Manor Guest House, 1024 Eaton St. / 305-294-9870
Econo Lodge Resort Of Key West, 3820 N. Roosevelt / 305-294-5511
Eaton Lodge – Historic Inn, 511 Eaton St. / 800-294-2170
Eden House, 1015 Fleming St. / 305-296-6868
El Patio Motel, 800 Washington St. / 305-296-6531
El Rancho Motel, 830 Truman Ave. / 305-294-8700
Equator Resort, 818 Fleming St. / 305-294-7775
Fleming Street Inn, 618 Fleming St. / 305-294-5181

Fairfield Inn By Marriott, 2400 N. Roosevelt Blvd. / 305-296-5700
Garden House, 329 Elizabeth St. / 305-296-5368
Gardens Hotel, 526 Angela St. / 305-294-2661
Gato E H Jr. Guest House, 1327 Duval St. / 305-294-0715
Halfred Motel, 512h Truman Dr. / 305-296-5415
Hampton Inn, 2801 N. Roosevelt Blvd. / 305-294-2917
Harborside Motel & Marina, 903 Eisenhower Dr. / 305-294-2780
Heartbreak Hotel, 716 Duval St. / 305-294-0220
Heron House, 512 Simonton St. / 305-294-9227
Hilton Key West, 245 Front St. / 305-294-4000
Holiday Inn Beachside, 3841 N. Roosevelt Blvd. / 305-294-2571
Holiday Inn, La Concha, 430 Duval St. / 305-296-2991
Hostelling International Key West, 718 South St. / 305-296-5719
Hyatt Beach House Resort, 5001 U.S. Hwy. 1 / 305-294-0059
Hyatt Key West- Resort & Marina, 601 Front St. / 305-296-9900
Hyatt's Sunset Harbor Resort, 200 Sunset Lane / 305-292-2001
Incentra Carriage House Inn, 729 Whitehead St. / 305-296-5565
Island City House Hotel, 411 William St. / 305-294-5702
Key Lime Inn, 728 Truman Ave. / 305-294-5229
Key Lodge, 1004 Duval St. / 305-296-9915
Key West Bed And Breakfast, 415 William St. / 305-296-7274
La Mer Hotel, 506 South St. / 305-296-5611
La Pensione Inn, 809 Truman Ave. / 305-292-9923
L'habitation Guest House, 408 Eaton St. / 305-293-9203
Lightbourn Inn, 907 Truman Ave. / 305-296-5152
Marquesa Hotel, 600 Fleming St.,305-292-1919
Marrero's Guest Mansion, 410 Fleming St. / 305-294-6977
Merlinn Inn, 811 Simonton St. / 305-296-3336
Nancy's William Street Guesthouse,329 William St. / 305-292-3334
Nassau House, 1016 Fleming St. / 800-296-8513
Newton Street Station Guest House, 1414 Newton St. / 305-294-4288
Oasis Guest House, 823 Fleming St. / 305-296-2131
Ocean Breeze Inn, 625 South St. / 305-296-2829
Ocean Key House Suite Resort, Zero Duval St. / 305-296-7701
Palms Hotel (The), 820 White St. / 305-294-3146
Papa's Hideaway, 309 Louisa St. / 305-294-7709
Paradise Inn (The), 819 Simonton St. / 305-293-8007
Pegasus International Hotel, 501 Southard St. / 305-294-9323
Pilot House Guest House, 414 Simonton St. / 305-648-3780
Quality Inn Resort, 3850 N. Roosevelt Blvd. / 305-294-6681
Rainbow Horse (The), 525 United St. / 305-292-1450
Ramada Inn, 3420 N. Roosevelt Blvd. / 305-294-5541
Red Rooster Inn, 709 Truman Ave. / 305-296-6558

Sheraton Key West Resort, 2001 S. Roosevelt Blvd. / 292-9800
Simonton Court-Historic Inn & Cottages, 320 Simonton St. / 305-294-6386
South Beach Oceanfront Motel, 508 Ocean St. / 305-296-5611
Southern Cross Motel, 326 Duval St. / 305-294-3200
Southernmost Motel In The USA, 1319 Duval St. / 305-296-6577
Southernmost Point Guest House, 1327 Duval St. / 305-294-0715
Spanish Gardens Motel, 1325 Simonton St. / 305-294-1051
Speakeasy Inn, 1117 Duval St. / 305-296-2680
Spindrift Tropical Hideaway, 1212 Simonton St. / 305-296-3432
Sunset Key Guest Cottages, 245 Front St. / 305-292-5300
Sunset Marina and Waterfront Residences, 5555 College Road / 305-296-7101
Tilton Hilton, 531 Angela St. / 305-294-8697
Travelodge Suites, 3444 N. Roosevelt Blvd. / 305-296-7593
Watson House, 525 Simonton St. / 305-294-6712
White Street Inn, 905 White St. / 305-295-9599
Grand Key Resort, 3990 S. Roosevelt Blvd. / 888-310-1540
Sara Cook Inc Rentals, 905 Truman Ave. / 365-294-8491
Nassau House, 1016 Fleming St. / 800-296-8513
The Fleming Street Inn, 618 Fleming St. / 305-294-5181
The Mermaid & the Alligator, 729 Truman Ave. / 305-294-1894
The Blue Parrot Inn, 916 Elizabeth St. / 800-231-Bird
La Mer Hotel & Dewey House, 504-506 S. St. / 800-354-4455
Best Western-Key Embassador Resort Inn, 3755 S. Roosevelt Blvd. / 305-296-3500
The Peak Resort, 1435 Simonton St. / 305-296-5000
Quality Inn, 3850 N Roosevelt Blvd, 800-533-5024
Casa Marina Resort, 1500 Reynolds St. / 305-296-3535
La Concha Hotel, 430 Fleming St. /

VACATION RENTALS
At Home In Key West, 3106 Flagler Ave. / 305-296-7975 / Condominium rentals
Key West By The Sea, 305-294-6069 / Condominiums on the beach
Truman Annex Vacation Rental, www.trumanannex.com / 305-292-1881
Schmitt Real Estate, 1201 White St. / 305-296-7727
Sara Cook, Inc, 905 Truman Ave. / 305-294-8491
Key West Realty, Inc., 1109 Duval St. / 305-294-3064/www.keywestrealty
M/R Preferred Properties, 526 Southard St. / 800-462- 5937/www.realkeywest.com

RV PARKS AND CAMPGROUNDS
Bluewater Key RV, 1-800-237-2266
Boyd's Key West Campground, 6401 Maloney Ave. / 305-294-1465
El Mar RV Resort, 6700 Maloney Ave. / 305-294-0857

RESTAURANTS

A and B Lobster House, 700 Front St. 305-294-2536 / Fresh lobster, waterfront views of Key West's historic seaport, strong wine list / Open 5:30 PM to 11PM / Boat docking and reservations recommended

Ambrosia, 1100 Pacher St. / 305-293-0304

Angler's Steak/Seafood House, 3618 N. Roosevelt / 305-294-4717

Antonia's, 615 Duval St.. / 305-294-6565 / 3 course Prix Fixe, regional Italian Cuisine / Open 7 days 6-11 PM, Parking

Appelrouth Grille, 416 Appelrouth Lane / 305-294-5662

Asia China Restaurant, 221 Duval St. / 305-292-0090

B's Restaurant, 1500 Bertha St. / 305-296-3140

Bagatelle, 115 Duval St. / 305-296-6609 / Local seafood and southern cooking

Baiamonte's Italian Restaurant, 1223 White St. / 305-296-2200

Banana Cafe, 1211 Duval St. / 305-294-7227 / French creperie restaurant with open air dining serving breakfast, lunch and dinner / Jazz on Thursday evenings

Benihana, S. Roosevelt Blvd. / 305-294-6400 / Cuisine cooked at your table

Big Dawg's Grog & Cantina, 613 Duval St. / 305-293-6909

Billie's Bar & Restaurant, 407 Front St. / 305-294-9292

Bleeker Street Bagelry, 2796 N. Roosevelt Blvd. / 305-293-0665

Blue Heaven, 729 Thomas St. / 305-296-8666

Bobalu Southern Cafe, Mm 10, Overseas Hwy., Big Coppitt Key / 305-296-1664

Café Alia, 601 Duval St. / 305-294-9566

Café Marquesa & Hotel, 600 Fleming St. / 305-292-1244 / Contemporary American cuisine / Fine dining / Grilled meats and seafood

Café Solé, 1029 Southard St. / 305-294-0230 / Upscale restaurant concentrating in Provence repasts / Fine dining

Camille's, 703 Duval St. / 305-296-4811 / "Inexpensive gourmet" / Serving breakfast, lunch and dinner / Usually a long wait, but worth every minute

Capt. Bob's Restaurant, 2200 N. Roosevelt Blvd. / 305-294-6433

Capt. Tony's Saloon, 428 Greene St. / Originally The Blind Pig, the original Sloppy Joe's, was a common haunt for Ernest Hemingway – a must stop for a brew or wine

Celebrities at Holiday Inn Laconcha, 430 Duval St. 305-296-2991

Chico's Cantina, 5230 Overseas Hwy., Stock Island / 305-296-4714

Compass Rose, 232 Margaret St. / 305-294-4394

Crab House, 2001 Roosevelt Blvd. / 305-294-1370

Crab Shack, 908 Caroline St. / 305-294-9658

Crabby Dick's, 712 Duval St. / 305-294-7229 / "The best seafood in Key West".

Diner Shores, 510 South St. / 305-294-9658

Don Pedro Restaurant, 11399 Overseas Hwy. / 305-743-5247

Duds & Suds Café, 829 Fleming St. / An antique gas station that is now a charming breakfast & lunch nook

Duffy's Steak & Lobster, 1007 Simonton St. / 305-296-4900

Duval Grille, 609 Duval St./305-292-2247 / Indoor & outdoor patio dining / Dinner daily from 6-11PM / Fresh local seafood, steaks & ribs, large beer & wine, elegant desserts

Dynasty Chinese Restaurant, 918 Duval St. / 305-294-2943

808 Duval Restaurant, 808 Duval St. / 305-293-0006

El Meson De Pepe, 1215 Duval St. / 305-296-6922 / Cuban conch cuisine

El Mocho Restaurant, 5708 Maloney Avenue / 305-296-7490

El Siboney, 900 Catherine St. / 305-296-4184

Europa Seakruz, Truman Annex / 305-296-Play

Faustos Food Palace, 522 Fleming St. / More than just a grocery store, prepared foods – a Key West classic

Fat Bull's Real Smoked Bar-B-Q, 305-295-0909

Finnegan's Wake, 320 Grinnell St. / 305-293-0222

Five Star Cafe, 1100 Packer St. / 305-296-0650

Five Brothers Grocery, Southard/Grinnell Streets / One of the last Key West corner groceries / A must-visit for a true Key West experience

Flagler's, Casa Marina, 1500 Reynolds St. / 305-296-3535

Flamingo Crossing, 1105 Duval St. / 305-296-6124

Gato Gordo Café, 404 Southard St. / 305-294-0888 / Tex-Mex and Key West's Largest Margarita!

Granny's Kitchen, 3412 Duck Avenue / 305-296-8870

Green Parrot Bar, Corner of Southard & Whitehead / 305-294-6133 / "Spine tingling cocktails" / An infamous Key West bar with pool tables / Open air

Gringo's Cantina, 509½ Duval St. / 305-294-9215

Half Shell Raw Bar, Lands End Village / 305-294-7496 / Authentic Key West fish house

Harbour Lights, 711 Eisenhower Dr. / 305-294-9343

Hard Rock Café, 313 Duval St./305-293-0230

Harpoon Harry's, 832 Caroline St. / 305-294-8744

Hemingway Cafe, Holiday Inn, 111 N. Roosevelt / 305-294-2571

Hog's Breath Saloon, 400 Front St. / 305-296-4222 / Raw bar restaurant and world famous T-shirts

Holiday Inn Beachside, 3841 N. Roosevelt Blvd. / 305-294-2571

Indigo Island Bistro, 724 Duval St. / 305-294-3663

Isle O'bones Restaurant, 305-296-1250

Jerome's, South Street Cafe, 910 South St. / 305-294-1055

Jerry's Oyster Bar & Grill, 1114 Duval St. / 305-294-7061

Joey Harrison's Bar & Grill, 627 Duval St. / 305-296-2115

Ose's Cantina, 800 White St. / 305-296-4366

Jupiter Crab Company, 2001 S. Roosevelt Blvd. / 305-293-9792

Kelly's Caribbean Bar & Grill, 301 Whitehead / 305-293-8484 / Owned by actress Kelly McGillis

Key West Bar & Grill, 1970 N. Roosevelt Blvd. / 305-294-1057
Key West Diner, 2814 N. Roosevelt Blvd. / 305-294-1968 / Classic diner with break-
fast, lunch and dinner / Salad Bar
Kyushu, 921 Truman Ave. / 305-294-2995
La Creperie, 124 Duval St. / 305-294-7677
La Lechonera, 3100 Flagler Ave. , Havana Plaza / 305292-3700
La Trattoria Venezia, 524 Duval St. / 305-296-1075 / Key West's favorite Italian
restaurant, cocktail bar, fine wines and Italian cuisine
Lighthouse Cafe, 917 Duval St. / 305-296-7837
Lj's Beachside Restaurant & Cafe, Higgs Beach / 305-296-4030
Loguns Lobster House, 1420 Simonton St. / 305-294-1500
Loony's Bar & Grill, 3101 N. Roosevelt Blvd. / 305-294-7419
Lorenzo's Italian Restaurant, 1900 Flagler Ave. / 305-296-0000
Lotsa Pasta, 609 Duval St. / 305-294-7874 / Italian and Seafood in Victorian home.
Louie's Backyard, 700 Waddell St. / 305-294-1061 / One of the best restaurants in
Key West with a great oceanside bar
Louie's Island Panty & Bakery, 3212 Flagler Ave. / 305-296-1820
Mangia Mangia, 900 Southard St. / 305-294-2469 / Pasta café with changing daily
selection, fine wine list
Mangoes, 700 Duval St. / 305-292-4606 / Indoor/outdoor tropical restaurant/bar
specializing in brick oven pizza
Margaritaville, 500 Duval St. / 305-292-1435 / Parrot-head haven for all Jimmy
Buffet fans serving American cuisine
Martha's, 3591 S. Roosevelt Blvd. / 305-294-3466 / Fresh seafood and steaks /
Piano music nightly
Martin's Cafe, Eden House, 1015 Fleming St. / 305-296-1183 / German food and
Seafood in a cozy atmosphere
Michael's, 532 Margaret St. / Famous for great steaks served inside or on outdoor
patio – fine dining
Mrs. Baker's Electric Kitchen, 830 Fleming St. / Hemingway and his pals' favorite
local for breakfast
Nicola Seafood, Hyatt Resort, 601 Front St. / 305-296-9900
Nick's Bar & Grill, Hyatt Resort, 601 Front St. / 305-296-9900
Ocean Club, The Reach Resort, 1435 Simonton St. / 305-296-5000
Ocean Key House, The, Zero Duval St. / 305-296-7701
Olive Oils Cafe, 708 Duval St. / 305-294-8994
Palm Grill, 1208 Simonton / 305-296-1744
Pancho & Lefty's S.W. Cafe, 632 Olivia St. / 305-294-8212
Papa's Banyan Tree Cafe, 217 Duval St. / 305-293-0555
Pavilion, Corner of Southard & Duval / Indian Spices and local delicacies
Pepe's Cafe, 806 Caroline St. / 305-294-7192 / Intimate dining known for their
Thanksgiving dinner every Thursday night
Perry's Of The Florida Keys, 3800 N. Roosevelt Blvd. / 305-294-8472

Pier House Restaurant, 1 Duval St. / 305-296-4600
P.T.'S Late Night, 920 Caroline St. / 305-296-4245
Riviera Coffee Shop, 3100 Flager St. / 305-293-9108
Rooftop Cafe, 310 Front St. / 305-204-2042
Rusty Anchor, 5th Avenue, Stock Island / 305-294-5369
Savannah Restaurant, 915 Duval St. / 305-296-6700
Schooner Wharf Bar, 202 William St. / 305-292-9520
Seven Fish, 632 Olivia St. / 305-296-2777
Shula's on the Beach, 1435 Simonton St. / 305-296-6144 / Oceanview steaks and
    seafood
Siam House, 829 Simonton St. / 305-292-0302
Silverado Steak House & Saloon, 1477 Overseas Hwy. / 305-743-5600
Sky Dragon, 2804 N. Roosevelt Blvd. / 305-293-0290
Sloppy Joe's Bar And Eatery, Corner Of Greene And Duval Streets / "A Key West
    Tradition", good food, fun & live entertainment
Smuggler's Cove, Mm 85.5, Islamorada / 305-664-5564
South Beach Seafood & Raw Bar, 1405 Duval St. / 305-292-2727 / Oceanside place
    to enjoy lobster and a gorgeous view
Square One, 1075 Duval St. / 305-296-4300 / American and fresh Local Seafood
    with a superb wine list / Piano nightly, reservations preferred
Sun Sun Pavilion, Marriott's Casa Marina / 305-296-3535
TGI Friday's, 2710 N. Roosevelt Blvd., Key West / 305-296-4093
Thai Garden, 921 Truman Ave. / 305-293-7885
Tootsie's Deli & Bar, 925 Duval St. / 305-292-1433
Top O'spray, Ramada Inn / 3420 N. Roosevelt Blvd. / 305-294-5541
Tortuga Bay Restaurant, 1990 N. Roosevelt Blvd. / 305-293-9941
Turtle Kraals & Half Shell Raw Bar, 512 Front St. at Land's End Village / 305-294-
    2640 / Southwestern fare and fresh seafood with open air dining on the water-
    front / A popular local landmark
Twisted Noodle, 628 Duval St. / 305-296-6670
Two Friends Patio Restaurant, 512 Front St. / 305-296-3124 / Casual Breakfast
    lunch and Dinner / Karaoke.
Ugly Rooster Cafe, The, 525 Duval St. / 305-292-3969
Vicky's Restaurant, 6406 Maloney Avenue, Stock Island / 305-294-9279
Viva Zapata, 903 Duval St. / 305-296-3138

FLY SHOPS/BAIT AND TACKLE
Saltwater Angler, 243 Front St. / 305-296-0700
Big Kahuna Bait & Tackle, 3580 Overseas Hwy. / 305-743-4500
Gamefish Gallery & Outfitters, 608 Greene St. / 305-294-7111
Garrison Bight Marina, Garrison Bight Causeway / 305-294-3093
Island Angler/Water's Edge Outfitters, #20 Whistling Duck Lanen/n305-295-9444
Key West Marine Hardware, Inc., 818 Caroline St. / 305-294-3519

Oceanside Marina, 5950 Peninsula Ave. / 305-294-4676
Waterfront Bait & Tackle, 241 Margaret St. / 305-292-1961
Boaters World Discount Marine, 105660 Overseas Hwy. / 305-295-9232
Key West Bait and Tackle, 241 Margaret St. / 305-292-1961
West Marine, 725 Caroline St. / 305-295-0999

BOAT RENTALS
Al Watersport, 2319 N. Roosevelt Blvd. / 305-296-7929
Club Nautico Of The Florida Keys, 245 Front St. / 305-294-2225
Florida Yacht Charters & Sales, Inc., 830 Eaton St. / 305-293-0800
Garrison Bight Marina, Garrison Bight Causeway / 305-294-3093
Key Cat Rental And Sales, 3101 N. Roosevelt Blvd. / 305-294-4515
Key West Boat Rentals, 617 Front St. / 305-294-2628
Key West Water Sports, Mariott's Casa Marina Inn / 305-294-2192
Land's End Boat Rentals, 201 William St. / 305-294-6447
Schooner Western Union, 202 William St. / 305-292-1766
Sea Horse Marina, 5001 5th Ave. , Stock Island / 305-292-9111
Sunset Watersports, 305-296-2554
Sunset Marina, 5555 College Rd, Stock Island / 305-296-7101

MARINAS
Conch Harbor, 951 Caroline Street / dockmaster@conchharbormarina.com / 305-294-2933
Garrison Bight Marina, 711 Eisenhower Dr. / 305-294-3093
Key West Municipal Marina, Mm 29.5 Overseas Hwy. / 305-292-8167
Keys Sea Center, Mm 29.5 Overseas Hwy. / 305-872-2243
Oceanside Marina, 5950 Peninsular Ave. / 305-294-4676
Peninsular Marine, 305-296-8110
Safe Harbor Marina, 6810 Front St., Stock Island / 305-294-9797
Sea Horse Marina, Stock Island / 305-745-9880
Sunset Marina and Waterfront Residences, 5555 College Road / 305-296-7101
Email: information@sunsetmarina-keywest.com

HOSPITALS
Old Town Medical Center, 520 Southard St. / 305-296-8593
Lower Keys Medical Ctr, 5900 College Rd. / 305-294-5531

FERRY'S
Dry Tortugas Ferry, Sails at 8 AM, Departs from Land's End Marina / 305-294-7009 / Two-hour trip one way. Returns at 5:30 PM
Sunny Days Catamaran, 305-292-6100

SEAPLANES
Key West Air Services, 305-292-5201
Seaplanes of Key West, 305-294-0709

AIRPORTS
Key West International, 3491 South Roosevelt Blvd. / 305-296-5439

CAR RENTALS

Dollar Rent A Car, 800-800-4000 / www.dollar.com
Avis Rent A Car, 800-452-1494 / www.avis.com
Hertz, www.hertz.com

EMERGENCY INFORMATION

Coast Guard, 305-295-9700 or VHF 16
Seatow, 1-800-4-SEATOW / Florida Keys, 305-295-9998 / 24 hour dispatch
TowBoat/US, 800-391-4869 / 24 hour dispatch

ADDITIONAL LOCAL INFORMATION

Fort Taylor State Historic Site and Public Beach, named for the country's 12th president, was built between 1845 and 1866. Once referred to as "Fort Forgotten," buried under tons of sand, the structure was rediscovered and excavated thanks to a grass-roots restoration effort. The centerpiece of an 87-acre state park, today the fort is a National Historic Landmark believed to hold the largest number of Civil War artifacts in the nation. It also is the site of the popular annual Civil War Days event in February.

The acreage surrounding the fort includes a shaded picnic area as well as the Key West's premiere 1,000-foot beach fronting on the Atlantic that features excellent offshore fishing.

Entrance is through Truman Annex on the west shores of Key West and there is a small fee. Call 305-292-6713.

Aquasport trouters—make sure those fish are legal.

Key West Marina Services

Marina	Phone	Slips	Tackle	Gas	Groceries	Boat Ramp	Restrooms	Restaurant	Repairs
Conch Harbor	305-294-2933	No	Yes	Yes	Yes	No	Yes	Yes	No
Garrison Bight Marina	305-294-3093	250	Yes	Yes	Yes	No	Showers	Yes	Yes
Key West Municipal Marina	305-292-8155	10	No	Yes	No	Yes	Yes	No	No
Keys Sea Center	305-872-2243	0	No	Yes	No	No	No	No	Yes
Oceanside Marina	305-294-4676	40	Yes	Yes	Yes	Yes	Yes	Yes	Yes
Peninsular Marine	305-296-8110	1	No	Yes	No	No	Yes	No	Yes
Safe Harbor Marina	305-294-9797	2	No	Yes	Yes	Yes	Yes	No	No
Sea Horse Marina	305-292-9880	5	Yes	Yes	Yes	Yes	No	No	No
Sunset Marina	305-296-7101	75	Yes	Yes	Yes	No	Yes	Yes	Yes

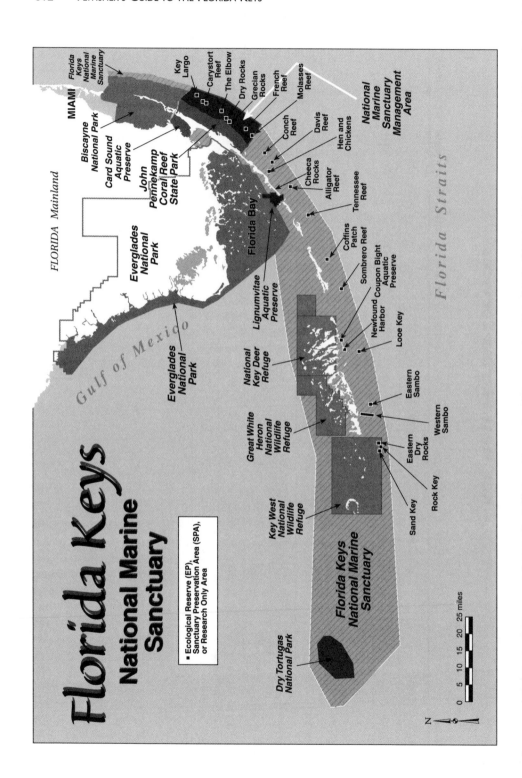

Florida Keys
National Marine Sanctuary

■ Ecological Reserve (EP),
Sanctuary Preservation Area (SPA),
or Research Only Area

FLORIDA Mainland

MIAMI

Florida
Keys
National
Marine
Sanctuary

Key
Largo

Carystort
Reef

The Elbow

Dry Rocks

Grecian
Rocks

French
Reef

Molasses
Reef

Conch
Reef

Davis
Reef

Hen and
Chickens

National
Marine
Sanctuary
Management
Area

Biscayne
National Park

Card Sound
Aquatic
Preserve

John
Pennekamp
Coral Reef
State Park

Everglades
National
Park

Florida Bay

Cheeca
Rocks

Alligator
Reef

Tennessee
Reef

Florida Straits

Everglades
National
Park

Gulf of Mexico

Lignumvitae
Aquatic
Preserve

Coffins
Patch

Sombrero Reef

Coupon Bight
Aquatic
Preserve

Looe Key

Newfound
Harbor

Florida Straits

National
Key Deer
Refuge

Great White
Heron
National
Wildlife
Refuge

Eastern
Sambo

Western
Sambo

Key West
National
Wildlife
Refuge

Eastern
Dry
Rocks

Sand Key

Rock Key

Florida Keys
National Marine
Sanctuary

Dry Tortugas
National Park

0   5   10   15   20   25 miles

N

The Sanctuary

Twenty-six hundred square miles of our water lies within the boundaries of the Florida Keys National Marine Sanctuary. The sanctuary provides many meaningful benefits for the environment without unduly inconveniencing anglers, except in a few circumstances. There are problems, of course, and the bureaucrats running the sanctuary still seemingly put closure above wise use.

I urge you to use caution within sanctuary boundaries. Keys residents are serious about treating our resources with respect. I will say, as this was written in 2000, enforcement of sanctuary rules is relatively even-handed if mistakes are innocent rather than blatant. Some regulations are confusing and easily violated. Pay attention to the rules and learn to navigate. Running aground and running your boat in closed areas are the most likely mistakes of visitors.

Sadly, catch and release fishing came under fire during the regulation forming process and some charter groups failed to defend what has long served as the cornerstone of our sport. We now have some areas closed to all fishing activity.

Currently, most closed zones are fortunately small. The support of no fishing zones as trade offs for the benefit of a few suggests that coastal anglers will have to fight for fishing access forever. Indeed, closure rather than responsible management has now become a battle cry for sanctuary supporters and the weak hands in the National Marine Fisheries Service. We are defending against closed fishing waters around the United States as a result of the actions of those participating in the regulation formation process of the Florida Keys National Marine Sanctuary.

Fortunately, a vote by Keys residents against the sanctuary in a referendum led to more responsible rules that make sense for all involved. There is no good argument for anchoring on living coral, and digging trenches across flats with motors is downright rude. A fight against poor rules in the sanctuary led us to a sanctuary we could live with that helps protect our surroundings.

The following Sanctuary rules may be viewed online at:

http://www.fknms.nos.noaa.gov/

These regulations apply throughout the entire area of the Sanctuary, including other protected areas and Sanctuary zones. The purpose of these regulations is to protect Sanctuary resources from both direct and indirect threats. These regulations focus on habitat protection, reducing threats to water quality, and minimizing human impact to delicate resources. The following activities are prohibited Sanctuary-wide:

- Removing, injuring, or possessing coral or live rock.
- Discharging or depositing trash or other pollutants.
- Dredging, drilling, prop dredging or otherwise altering the seabed, or placing or abandoning any structure on the seabed.
- Operating a vessel in such a manner as to strike or otherwise injure coral, seagrass, or other organisms attached to the seabed, or cause prop-scarring.

- Having a vessel anchored on living coral in water less than 40 feet deep when you can see the bottom. Anchoring on hard bottom is allowed.
- Operating a vessel at more than idle speed/no wake within 100 yards of residential shorelines, stationary vessels, and navigational aids marking reefs.
- Operating a vessel at more than idle speed/no wake within 100 feet of a "divers down" flag.
- Diving or snorkeling without a dive flag.
- Operating a vessel in such a manner that endangers life, limb, marine resources, or property.
- Releasing exotic species.
- Damaging or removing markers, mooring buoys, scientific equipment, boundary buoys, and trap buoys.
- Moving, removing, injuring, or possessing historical resources.
- Taking or possessing protected wildlife.
- Using or possessing explosives or electrical charges.
- Collecting marine life species — tropical fish, invertebrates, and plants — except allowed by law.
- Florida Marine Life Rule (46-42 F.A.C.). Sanctuary regulations have been established to complement this rule and apply throughout the Sanctuary.

These activities are prohibited in the Ecological Reserve and Sanctuary Preservation Areas:
- Discharging any matter except cooling water or engine exhaust.
- Fishing by any means - removing, harvesting, or possessing any marine life. Catch and release fishing by trolling will be allowed in Conch Reef, Alligator Reef, Sombrero Reef, and Sand Key SPAs only.
- Touching or standing on living or dead coral.
- Anchoring on living or dead coral, or any attached organism.

SPECIAL USE AREAS

There are four Special Use Areas designated within the Sanctuary as research only areas. These areas are closed to all activities. They are located in the vicinity of: Conch Reef, Tennessee Reef, Looe Key (Hawk Channel Patch Reef), and Eastern Sambo Reef.

Western Sambo Ecological Reserve (ER): In addition to Sanctuary-wide regulations, special regulations have been set in place in this area in order to protect resources. Spearfishing, shell collecting, tropical fish collecting, and other activities that result in the harvest of marine life by divers and snorkelers, and all fishing activities will be prohibited in this zone type. In addition, direct physical impact to corals in this area is restricted.

Sanctuary Preservation Areas (SPA): There are 18 small SPAs that protect popular shallow coral reefs. In addition to Sanctuary-wide regulations, special regulations have been set in place in these areas in order to protect resources. Activities that will be prohibited in the Sanctuary Preservation Areas include spear fishing, shell collecting, tropical fish collecting, fishing and other activities that result in the harvest of marine life by divers, snorkelers, and fishermen. In addition, direct physical impact to corals in these areas is restricted.

Wildlife Management Areas (WMA). There are 27 WMAs. The majority of these areas (20) fall under the jurisdiction of the U.S. Fish and Wildlife Service (USFWS) and Sanctuary regulations have been established to complement the existing USFWS management plan. Public access restrictions in these areas include idle speed only/no wake, no access buffer, no motor, and limited closures.

Existing Management Areas (EMA). Sanctuary regulations have been established to complement those in existing management areas, including Looe Key and Key Largo Management Areas as well as the Great White Heron and Key West National Wildlife Refuges, and all the state parks and aquatic preserves.

Special Use Areas. There are four areas designated: Conch Reef, Tennessee Reef, Looe Key (patch reef), and Eastern Sambo Reef. These are all designated as research-only areas. No person may enter without a valid permit. All closed or regulated areas are clearly marked by round yellow marker buoys.

Bonito are a great fly target.

DEFENSIVE FISHING

One group offered support for no fishing zones in an attempt to eliminate all high-speed boat traffic in the shallow waters. As boating and Jet Ski operation activity in the Keys exploded, the quality of easily accessed fishing deteriorated during the late '80s and early '90s.

Jet skis or water bikes became an easy and popular target for flats anglers. Their elimination from all sanctuary waters, or severe usage restrictions, was promised. It did not happen, although in 2000, the sanctuary is finally considering restrictive zoning for jet ski operators some seven years after the fact.

No one is forced to fish where jet ski operation is a problem. Over 1,500 square miles of water surrounding the Keys is totally off limits to them, including the waters of Everglades National Park and all of the Lower Keys refuges. You can reach a restricted use area within about 15 minutes from almost anywhere in the Keys.

I suggest you fish in areas where jet ski use is either restricted or uncommon. Even so, jet ski use and rude boat operation creates a problem. As more flats are rendered useless, our remaining fishery becomes increasingly crowded.

Try hard to pick ambush spots not easily reached by boats. I look for places where the current shoves fish hard against banks and pushes them far into corners that boats cannot easily reach without running aground. It works on many days.

ENVIRONMENTAL CONCERNS

During the early to mid 1990s the Keys became the subject of many nationally published articles focused on the very narrow view that its waters were dying. I don't want to downplay the impact of excessive human activity on the environment anywhere or suggest Keys waters remain unchanged. However, emotion colored the issue far beyond the scope of the problem and our ability to deal with it. Many folks quit visiting the Keys because of these exaggerated tales published all over the country.

In human terms, we did have an unsettling disaster in the Keys in the 1990s. Much of the water on the Gulf side of our little world shifted from gin clear to vegetable-laden green. Sea grasses died. Fish abandoned some flats. Many, myself included, conducted bitter campaigns directed against mainland farmers, sugar growers, and flood controls that altered historic freshwater flows into our estuary, Florida Bay.

Certainly, man always profoundly alters his surroundings without full awareness of the consequences, but nature outdoes man any time she has a chance. We've since learned that boom and busts cycles are normal in the Gulf and particularly within the shallow Gulf reaches surrounding the Keys. Core samples drilled from the bottom and carbon dated back 3,500 years show a pattern of drought and excessive rain established over centuries. The Keys and the south Florida peninsula suffered from a drought in the late 1980s. Sea grass populations died and shifted as they have

Danny Strub prepares an amberjack for release.

through eons as shallow water salinity levels change while rainfall patterns alternate, but we humans had never seen it and panicked.

Hurricane Andrew compounded the situation as it laid waste to 80,000 acres of mainland Everglades' vegetation. Silt and detritus-laden water slowly seeped into the Gulf and Florida Bay. Relatively light winds easily suspended both silt and detritus and many flats lacked meaningful populations of filtering sea grasses. The dirty water further compounded the problem, inhibiting photosynthesis, adding to sea grass weakness.

Dirty water is no fun for sight fishing anglers and fishing patterns did change. Some anglers did not change with the pattern and made a lot of noise. An untimely confluence of human events led to much of the sensationalism surrounding what was nature's normal adjustment to weather patterns.

The problem was a perfect banner ad for sanctuary support. Many people supported the sanctuary concept, willing to pay any cost, somehow believing that federal funding—that never came as this is written in 2000—would undo the works of nature they did not fully understand. Much of what you read about problems in the Keys resulted from attempts to gain support for the sanctuary.

It's over now as nature provided rain, and sea grasses more tolerant of existing salinity levels repopulated the flats. Florida successfully initiated an inshore net ban and the results are staggeringly good. Good management works. Today, the average seatrout caught during a single day of fishing is often larger than the biggest fish caught in Florida Bay before the ban. It took three or four redfish and a bonefish to win a late 1980s two-day Redbone tournament in Islamorada. Forty-plus fish catches were not enough in the late 1990s.

We set the tournament scoring record for the 30-odd-year-old Gold Cup Tarpon Tournament in 1998, after setting one the year before. The same happened with single day all-time bonefish tournament records in the spring, then again in the fall, of 1997.

In the early 1990s those seeking king mackerel couldn't keep one during the heart of the season, but they are plentiful now. After the elimination of fish traps in the Atlantic near shore waters in the mid '90s, yellowtail fishing is now described as the best ever by longtime charter boat operators.

The Keys still offer some of the world's best fishing for many species and the most convenient good fishing in the world for others. Our fishing is improving and should continue to do so under good custody. As suggested earlier, inshore fishing in the Keys is more compromised today by boating habits than fish numbers. We have plenty of fish, and thanks to the net ban we should continue to have excellent fishing for species that were considered rare here less than decade ago.

Doris Holmes shows off a redfish.

Shallow Water Ethics

Getting along with other anglers and the fish is a confusing problem in the Keys, particularly on the flats. It's easy to make mistakes despite the best of intentions. Many species respond poorly to engine noise and run in fear from impolite encounters with anglers. It doesn't take much to spoil fishing for other boats in the neighborhood. We also have to consider how rude boat handling impacts fishing over time, not just day to day.

Our first concern is the rights of anglers already on a spot, whether they're poling along or tied to their pole or on anchor while guarding an edge. Most of time the bow of the boat is pointed toward the fish. It's bad manners to get between another boat and their fish. Defining "their" fish takes a bit of judgment. Bonefish on a short edge probably belong to them, and you need to find another spot or get behind them. How far in front of someone you might politely fish depends on the territory. A mile may not be far enough where the fish run post haste for long distances without feeding much. In some spots, fish work in from the depths to feed only in very small pockets. A quarter mile gap might work there. If you're not sure, just move away. Finding bonefish spots is seldom a problem.

Folks might leave an understood tarpon spot open in front of them. They might prefer how the fish move across the tide on the second spot or decide to wait out a tide change. Before you stick your nose into a situation like this you need to know for sure where you are.

Ignoring the rights of others and disturbing the fish creates a different problem. Such errors compounded over time seriously altered travel and feeding patterns of spooky glamour species as the 1990s progressed, making some fishing a bit difficult. It's something we all need to think about.

Once, fishing mile-long edges alone was the norm during the 1980s and early 1990s. I remember the protocol once used for sharing such an edge. As an example, one of the best sight fishing tarpon edges in the Keys is a long point jutting off the bank separating the Gulf from Florida Bay. It was routine way back when for only one or two boats to fish this edge. The first boat on the scene often sat on the very point of the bank.

Fishing the point left a large expanse of undisturbed water for fish seeking a nap, and we didn't run boats where tarpon slept years ago. If you came along wanting to share the edge, you stopped and asked if the other boat wanted to move up the edge or if you could pole by. One boat or the other usually poled up the bank, leaving enough room so the second boat had "happy fish." Sometimes you might pole across the flat if you knew the folks on the point and knew their preferred travel pattern there. So many of us are fishing now, we can't keep track of everyone on the water or their preferences.

Today, if folks think there's room on the bank for them, they rudely either jump across the bank or run around the same point to a spot making them happy. Jumping a bank or crossing it involves running most boats far shallower than good judgment dictates. It also involves running over fish either traveling or resting on the near side. Running around the bank disturbs fish resting off the edge and those traveling. It's harmful to the bank and screws up travel and feeding habits of non-target species you might want to fish for some other time, like bonefish or redfish. Poling off and on spots is a sadly forgotten art.

After a couple of hours of this every day, around the dozen or so points of interest along the bank, there are few "happy" fish remaining. We have succeeded in driving the fish off the bank. Once, seeing a 500-fish school along this edge was not a surprise. Today, seeing 500 fish on a tide is cause for celebration. The fish are still there. They just track in six to eight feet of water and hide when possible, seldom rolling or throwing a wake. For big wads of laid-up fish you really have to search off the beaten path.

Some fish adapt much better than others to boat problems. Near civilization, on a channel edge, you might catch a bonefish tailing in a boat wake. In the backcountry, where bonefish deal with fewer boats, they often blow off a bank when a boat runs within 400 to 600 yards of them. Redfish everywhere may well put up with motor noise if you don't run directly over them. You can usually run to the edge of a mullet mud or even through it and still catch the predators in it.

No matter what you are doing, good manners demand the consideration of other anglers and the fish. There are lots of places to fish and if you're not sure how close is too close or where you belong, you should seek another spot. The fish are not the only attraction in the Keys. Some sense of solitude is a big part of the experience and finding fewer fish all your own often provides a better experience than fishing in a crowd. Tarpon runs are often crowded, but you should have little trouble finding space of your own for most other species.

Ladyfish are a riot on light tackle of any kind.

Skiffs: Smaller Is Better
For The Flats

Late fall in the Keys is often punctuated with warm, calm evenings. Owners of shallow watercraft pursue giant bonefish with vigor. In February visions of snook and redfish fill shallow water anglers' dreams as they await the May Oceanside migration of tarpon. How do you pick a boat that will float anywhere a bonefish or red can crawl, that will let you live-bait tarpon fish, and make comfortable journeys across open water? It's tough, but today's new 16-footers are as close to all-around boats as a flats angler can get.

There are a lot of compromises involved in choosing a skiff. Consideration must be made for the size of your normal fishing party, how much gear you are determined to carry, and the amount of time you actually spend sight fishing. If most of your fishing is jigging channels and live baiting bridges, shallow draft is not a consideration.

To complicate matters for those that do little else but pole into the shallowest possible water, today's angler must also face the issue of noise. It doesn't do a lot of good to be able to pole shallower than the fish if the boat slaps so much that it spooks them. Prime water is crowded these days, the fish recognize slap and pressure waves from hulls as danger.

There wasn't much progress in skiff design during the formative years. Shallow water angling was dominated by Hewes, Maverick, and Willy Roberts. A few diehards ran around in Challengers and Nova Scotia hulls, but they were tough for riding or storing gear. In 2000 more companies make boats for flats fishing than there were Keys guides in 1985 when the fishery became every man's dream.

The revolution started when Action Craft and Maverick started utilizing foam core construction, devised really dry storage, and provided a good riding craft that one might pole in reasonable conditions. The Flatsmaster line offered something new: While being a comfortable boat to be in, it could crawl up in skinny water almost as well as the little boats. It took Hewes several years to catch up.

The dominant sight fishing boat in the late '80s was the Dolphin Super Skiff, still considered by some as the ultimate tool for getting close to wary fish. The revolution really took hold, though, with the improvements in the 16-foot Hewes and the introduction of the Silver King. Both went shallow, offered good storage, and rode dry enough on most days. Since then, the Maverick Mirage has gained a lot of fans for its fishability while meeting most of the same criteria. The Mirage does not float well shallow, but it is deathly quiet along edges Mudding fish will feed under it in the depths.

Little boats have endearing qualities. They perform very well with 90-horsepower motors even when carrying three anglers. The dominant big 16s, the Hewes and the Silver King, will get as shallow as any bonefish. You can stake them out on nasty days for tarpon, they float like corks, and they have capable live wells for bait-fishing. The quiet 16s, the Super Skiff and Mirage help anyone catch fish at ridiculously close range.

Giant gunnels provide plenty of get-around space if someone gets busy in the middle of the boat. On windy days when you can barely stop an 18-footer for a shot, the 16s remain maneuverable with a bit of effort. The key to the success of the little boats is how well they fish. A great ride in an 18-footer means little if the boat can't be poled to fish when you get there.

Don't be fooled, though. There are tons of fish caught in bigger skiffs, and they sure make long rides more comfortable. Boats should be chosen for the type of fishing you do the majority of the time. If you try to compromise for a few days of use each year, you'll be miserable most of the time. Many 18-footers go plenty shallow and make non-poling days much more enjoyable. New lightweight construction has brought us 20-footers that serve well for occasional bonefish duty and offer versatility.

For the rest of us who absolutely have to sight fish every day, no matter what the conditions, the smallest possible boat will add immeasurably to success. The little Mirage, and similar boats, carry all the gear one can possibly hope to use, have a soft ride, and fish too well to be ignored.

Do stick with the dominant boats in the business. Someday you will have to sell your choice. Products dominate because they have the best balance of features, quality, and price. Any money you save today on a wannabe boat will be lost many times over in discomfort and resale value.

If at all possible, try to fish a few times in varying conditions in the boat you are most interested in. All boats work well when it's calm. Pay close attention to the noises the boat makes when sitting across a chop or pointed into it at bonefish depths. Wakes pushed forward from the bow will reach fish before your hook does.

Not so long ago we had to choose between good ride, enough dry storage, and the ability to go shallow along with easy poling. The newest offerings in small skiffs manage to provide a good balance of features, and some really help catch fish.

POLING

Poling a boat is a skill acquired over time. A push pole is a wonderful tool yet often seems to have a mind of its own. Poling feels somewhat clumsy when you begin the learning process, and there is an inclination to over-adjust. Unless you intend to turn the boat, your pole placement against the bottom should remain within the confines of the corners of your transom most of the time. If you fish with a guide you'll note their clothes are often frayed from their shorts pockets to the belly button region of their shirts. They are using their bodies as fulcrum points against the lever of the push pole to line up the boat.

Before you beat yourself up, realize that some hulls are not so easy to pole. Something bobbing like a cork with lots of freeboard is often pretty tough to hold into a stiff current or a bit of a breeze. A vessel with a relatively flat bottom near the transom is going to skid a bit while one maintaining some vee throughout its length is 'stickier." The hull with the skidding butt is usually easier to turn quickly but wanders some. Sticky hulls track well when you are comfortable with your path down an edge

A boat team prepares for a shot at a school of tarpon.

or across a lake corner. They do demand some athletic effort to turn for a shot, but they might sit longer in a good fishing position when you do line them up.

Poling requires a little bit of caution. The tendency is to really lean on the pole to move the boat. Much of the bottom in the fishiest spots is relatively firm, but you might lean a bit too far when the pole rests against a bottomless pit. Some hard bottoms offer no grip at all and the pole slides out from under you. In this situation most polers gingerly reach for the bottom using the point of the pole and some resort to steel spikes on the point end of the pole for a sound grip.

You can attack fish with too much enthusiasm. Some hulls are very quiet, but most are not. A pressure wave off the bow alarms fish, and few hull designs eliminate one. Once you have altered the pattern of the fish, they are unlikely to respond well to a cast. They may continue to feed, but if you turned them with the boat in some way, they are on the alert. You may never even get a fly or bait in the water with them before they flee.

Most flats species deal best with noise and pressure waves if you are in shallower water than they are. If they feel pinned against a flat, they show far less tolerance. Remember that most of these fish are constant targets of larger predators and even a 150-pound tarpon is not safe from sharks. Dragging bottom is a real problem, too, and you can get carried away trying to get shallow for most species except redfish.

Stopping the boat for a shot often demands a serious reach of the pole toward the bow while searching for some bottom to anchor the pole. Most of the time you need to shove the point in to begin a staking process. You have to watch the angle you use as you can stop the boat too quickly. Your angling buddy might slide off the front of the boat if you stop too fast, or you could end up with the boat hanging off the pole at a serious enough angle to break the pole or make it almost impossible to retrieve from the bottom without serious gymnastics and significant time delays.

I slid Keys guide Bruce Stagg off the front of the boat one day when I abruptly halted a boat charging along in a high wind as he cast to a permit. He made a great cast and the fish ate the fly, but he was in midair and could not set the hook. He was a good sport even though the day was far too chilly for a swim. A similar short stop did save me once, though, as I couldn't extract the pole as a school of bonefish ran by the boat in a bonefish tournament. Maverick and Hewes boat builder Scott Deal hooked a 200-point bonefish, giving us a 17-point win in a tournament on a going away cast. I might have blown the fish with excessive boat noise had I not been stuck. He didn't snag the fish, but it sucked the fly in so hard the leader ran through its gill cover and the hook was in its side.

Sticking a pole is a useful tactic. In the shallows we stake out more often than we anchor. Just plant the push pole like a tree in the bottom and tie the boat to it. Stick the pole into the bottom at a bit of an angle against the wind and current. The pole bends back toward the boat as the boat rides downwind or down current and the leverage of the bent pole against the bottom keeps it pinned.

In mostly firm bottom, you use the point to dig into the bottom. You might need to use the foot to find a firm grip in mud. Usually you tie the boat to the pole from a line tied to the poling platform. Obviously, with the foot in the air, the foot provides a nice stop for your line. Tying to the point end is not too difficult. You simply wrap the line around the pole and over the line several times and it cinches up like a nail knot. A clip on the end of your line lets you "tie up" without tying knots and you can clip the end of the line to an eyehook on board when you aren't using it.

If you're sitting on a migration run, you might want to use a line running from one side of your poling platform or the other. Some use lines attached to a cleat or eyehook on the gunwales to turn a boat even more across the current. Many carry a second and shorter stake out pole and tie down both ends of the boat to get a more exact angle in the wind along a migratory path.

A push pole is an essential tool for flats fishing and worth mastering. You should choose one proving a balance between strength and stalking capability. I'm pretty fond of Loomis composites as they are very quiet.

TROLLING MOTORS

Trolling motors certainly have some use in the shallow water Keys fishery. They are a bit controversial and are forbidden in some tournaments. I have never wanted one, but as I get older and as many areas become off limits to any use of gas motors, including just idling on and off an edge, I am increasingly tempted to mount just one.

They do have their uses in quiet situations. Poling in and out of areas closed to combustible motor use is time consuming and sometimes keeps us from checking out protected territory. On the other hand, electrics are easily abused in certain situations. Unfortunately, some folks use them to run at sighted fish in helter-skelter fashion, and they run over many unsighted fish on the way. Only you can decide if the expense, extra weight, and continual maintenance of trolling motors are worth the aggravation.

Resources

Florida Fish and Wildlife Conservation Commission
South Region (Includes Everglades National Park and the Keys)
8535 Northlake Blvd.
West Palm Beach, FL 33412
561-625-5122

***Florida Sportsman* Magazine**
Toll Free: 866-300-1745
Website: www.floridasportsman.com
(Magazine subscriptions and fishing charts)

International Gamefish Association
1890 Semoran Blvd.
Suite 237
Winter Park, FL 32792
407-672-2058
Website: www.igfa.org
(Information on world record gamefish)

MapTech
Toll Free: 888-839-5551
Website: www.maptech.com
Email: marinesales@maptech.com
(Great source for photocharts and charting software)

Waterproof Charts
320 Cross Street
Punta Gorda, FL 33950-9972
Toll Free: 800-423-9026
Website: www.waterproofcharts.com
(Great source for photocharts and charting software)

NOAA
National Oceanic and Atmospheric Administration
6501 Lafayette Drive
Riverdale, MD 20737
301-436-6990
Website: www.noaa.gov

DeLorme Maps
P.O. Box 298
Yarmouth, ME 04096
207-846-7000
(The best source for maps showing land and coastal features.)

Guides and Outfitters

Please note that these guides and outfitters are not endorsed by the author or Wilderness Adventures Press, Inc., nor does this list include EVERY guide and outfitter in this area - in addition fly shops and bait shops often run trips through their stores as well. This list is merely a reference tool for the purchaser of this book.

Additional listings: www.florida-fishing-guide.com; www.reelnative.com; www.flyfishingfloridakeys.com

Florida Guides Association — www.fishing-boating.com

Florida Sportsman magazine — www.floridasportsman.com

Northern Fringe

Capt. Adam Redford
P.O. Box 562723
Miami, FL 33256
Phone: 800-632-0394
Web: www.captadamredford.com/charters.htm
Miami, Ft. Lauderdale and Islamorada. Includes fishing on the shallow flats, back in mangrove country, some freshwater areas and in the channels around Miami and the Keys

Capt. Bart Blankenships
New Moon Fishing Charters
Phone: 954-764-3922
Web: www.newmoonfishing.com
Ft. Lauderdale/Miami in light tackle and sportfishing

Capt. Jerry Murphy
9631 NW 4th Street
Pembroke Pines, FL 33024
Phone: 954-432-0197
Flyfishing and light tackle

Capt. Mark Hlis
Phone: 954-632-2447
Biscayne Bay and Flamingo. Flats fishing for bonefish, permit, tarpon, snook and redfish

Capt. Tom Calandra
Capt. Marcia Calandra
Phone: 954-983-8135
Web: www.tmdusky.com
Light sport fishing

Capt. Jerry Balester
1394 SW 179 Terrace
Pembroke Pines, FL 33029
Phone: 954-433-9427
Web: www.capt-jerry.com
South Florida area offshore fishing

Capt. Dale Curmanskie
8540 SW 149th Terrace
Miami, FL 33158
Phone: 305-251-6692
Web: www.captdale.com
Flyfishing in South Biscayne Bay

Capt. Bob LeMay
Phone: 954-435-5666
Specializing in sight fishing - plug, spin and fly - Biscayne Bay and Everglades National Park

Capt. Joel Kalman
Phone: 305-361-5155
Specializing in Key Biscayne and Biscayne Bay area. Light tackle bonefish, tarpon and permit.

Capt. DJ Sutton Backcountry Charters
18721 SW 294 Terrace
Homestead, FL 33030
Phone: 305-248-6126
Fish Miami's Biscayne Bay and the Everglades

Capt. Larry Sydnor
3699 Davie Boulevard
Ft. Lauderdale, FL 33312
Phone: 954-581-9241
Flats and backcountry guide

Magic Fingers —
Capt. Mark Houghtaling
15920 SW 85 Avenue
Miami, FL 33157
Phone: 305-253-1151
Web: www.magicfin.com
Light tackle offshore

Capt. Frank Garisto
P.O. Box 490338
Key Biscayne, FL 33149
Phone: 305-361-5040

Ghost Hunter Charters—
Capt. Eric VanDemark
25775 SW 122 Court
Homestead, FL 33032
Phone: 305-258-9917
305-975-4499
Web: www.ghosthuntercharters.com
Flats fishing with light tackle and fly

Capt. George Mitchell
22301 SW 133 Ave.
Miami, FL 33170
Phone: 305-257-4665

"Flat Spot" Charters — Capt. Al Alesi
Phone: 305-891-5389
Biscayne Bay, Florida Bay and Flamingo

Dawn Patrol Fishing Charters —
Capt. Doug Lillard
Phone: 954-894-9865
Backcountry and flats fishing in Biscayne Bay, Flamingo and the Keys

Capt. Carl Ball
Phone: 954-565-2457
Web: www.awolfishingguide.com
Backcountry and flats flyfishing and light tackle in Ft. Lauderdale and Biscayne Bay area for tarpon, bonefish, permit and snook

Capt. Bouncer Smith
3741 NE 163rd St. Suite 291
N. Miami Beach, FL 33160
Phone: 305-945-5114
Web: www.captbouncer.com
Flyfishing and light tackle in Miami and the Bahamas

Low Places Guide Service —
Capt. Jorge Valverde
5040 SW 116th Ave.
Cooper City, FL 33330
Phone: 954-680-7844
Web: www.lowplacesguideservice.com
Flyfishing and sightfishing Biscayne Bay and Upper Keys

Key Largo

Aquatic Adventures — Capt. Ted Wilson
Phone: 305-664-9463
Flyfishing and light tackle in Upper Keys and Everglades specializing in bonefish and tarpon

Fish Tales — Captain Ron Allen
P.O. Box 1011
Islamorada, Florida 33036
Phone:305-664-0050
Web: www.fish-tales.net
Offshore and reef fishing

Tylon — Capt. Ty Cash
200 Pearl Ave.
Tavernier, FL 33070
Phone: 305-852-6924 (HOME)
Web: www.tylon.net
Keys flats and backcountry fishing in Islamorada and Key Largo

Bamboo Charters —
Capt. Matt Bellinger
Phone: 305-393-0909
Web: www.islamoradabackcountry.com
Light tackle and flyfishing

Capt. Ben Taylor (author of this book)
Tavernier, FL
Phone: 305-852-1775
Web: www.bentaylor.com
Flats, backcountry, and fly fishing the Florida Keys

Capt. Gary Ellis
P.O. Box 273
Islamorada, FL 33036
Phone: 305-664-2002
Web: www.redbone.org
Islamorada fishing

Capt. Joe Re
118 Pueblo St.
Tavernier, FL 33070
Phone: 305-852-8815
Flats fishing for bonefish, tarpon, redfish, permit, snook and seatrout

Florida Fishing Headquarters
84001 Overseas Highway
Islamorada, FL 33036
Phone: 888-tarpon4
Web: www.tarponheadquarters.com
Backcountry and flats fishing in Florida. Keys flyfishing, spin and live bait

Capt. Pete King
180 Harborview Drive
Tavernier, FL 33070
Phone: 305-852-4751
Flats fishing for bonefish, tarpon and redfish

Capt. Allen Finkelman
227 Treasure Harbor Rd.
Islamorada, FL 33036
Phone: 305-852-5233
Web: www.keysguide.com
Specializing in flyfishing throughout the Keys for bonefish, tarpon and redfish

Capt. Barry Hoffman
Tavernier, FL 33070
Phone: 305-852-6918
Web: www.flatsguide.com
Flats guide for flyfishing or light tackle

Capt. Bob Rodgers
P.O. Box 1510
Tavernier, FL 33070
Phone: 305-853-0933
Web: www.captbobrodgers.com
Flyfishing guide for tarpon, bonefish, permit and redfish

Capt. Len Roberts
P.O. Box 1479
Islamorada, FL 33036
Phone: 305-664-5420
Flyfishing and light tackle

Capt. Mike Brabham
P.O. Box 1134
Islamorada, FL 33036
Email: keysfishin@aol.com
Flyfishing and light tackle the backcountry flats and Florida Keys

Capt. Mario del Toro
P.O. Box 551
Islamorada, FL 33036
Phone: 305-664-9935
Web: www.captainmario.com
Flyfishing and light tackle in the Islamorada Flats and Everglades

EVERGLADES

Capt. Rick Killgore
Phone: 888-484-9107
www.fish-killgore.com
Light tackle and flyfishing

Capt. Mike Merritt
Phone: 877-795-3437
Web: www.everglades-angler.com
Fish the Everglades for snook, redfish, trout and tarpon

Blue Tail Charters — Mike Haines
Phone: 305-248-8859
Web: www.bluetailcharters.com
Fish the Everglades National Park for snook, redfish, trout and tarpon

Capt. Neil Baron
Flamingo, Florida
Phone: 305-270-8035
Web: www.fishfla.com
Light-tackle with live bait for snook, redfish, snapper, cobia, trout, black drum, grouper, tripletail and more in South Florida, Everglades National Park, Miami, Florida Bay, Flamingo

Capt. John Griffiths or Flamingo Lodge, Marina & Outpost Resort
Phone: 305-248-9470 or 941-695-3101
Web: www.captainjohngriffiths.com
Fishing is done at the world famous Flamingo Lodge, Marina and Outpost Resort in Everglades National Park

Capt. Steve Kantner
Phone: 954-761-3570
Web: www.landcaptain.com
walk-in/canoe in for flyfishing on South Florida's hidden backwaters

Captain Alan Perez
Phone: 305-253-0353
Web: www.nautic-al.com
Flats, light tackle and backcountry fishing—Everglades National Park, Flamingo, Chokoloskee, and 10,000 Islands

No Free Lunch Charters — Capt. Bruce Hitchcock
Phone: 561-362-4452
Web: www.backcountryfishing.net
Offering light tackle fishing for snook, tarpon, redfish, permit, cobia and trout in Everglades National Park

Thompson's Guide Service
P.O. Box 32
Copeland FL, 34137
Phone: 941-695-4102
Web: www.thompsonsguideservice.com
Light tackle fishing the saltwater flats, rivers, and backcountry bays of the Everglades and 10, 000 islands

Captain Quicks — Captain Lee Quick and Captain Larry Quick
905 Copeland Avenue (Under the Tower)
Everglades City, Florida 34139
Phone: 941-695-0006 or
1-888-657-0006
Web: www.florida-southwest.com/quick
Flyfishing and light tackle in the Everglades National Park and the 10,000 Islands

Captain Ned Small
Everglades City, Florida
Phone: 941-695-4993
Web: www.sightfish.com
Flyfishing and flats-style sightfishing on Florida's Mangrove Coast

Daffin Guide Service — Capt. Derrick Daffin
P.O. Box 310
Everglades City, FL 34139
Phone: 941-695-3513
Web: www.fishingguides.com/3093.htm
Fishing the Everglades National Park and 10,000 Islands

Capt. Eric Herstedt
Phone: 954-344-3641
Backcountry fishing in around Flamingo and Everglades National Park

Capt. Bob LeMay
Phone: 954-435-5666
Specializing in sight fishing - plug, spin and fly - Biscayne Bay and Everglades National Park

**Dawn Patrol Fishing Charters —
Capt. Doug Lillard**
Phone: 954-894-9865
*Backcountry and flats fishing in Biscayne
Bay, Flamingo and the Keys*

Aquatic Adventures — Capt. Ted Wilson
Phone: 305-664-9463
*Flyfishing and light tackle in Upper Keys
and Everglades specializing in bonefish
and tarpon*

Capt. Jon Holsenback
Phone: 877-550-8260
Web: www.evergladesfishing.com
*Flyfishing, light tackle and spin in the
Everglades National Park and Flamingo*

Middle Keys

**Capt. Pips Charters
@ Capt. Pips Marina and Hideaway**
1410 Overseas Highway
Marathon, FL 33050
Phone: 800-707-1692
*Offshore, reef, and bay fishing, tarpon
and night fishing and flats fishing*

**Two Conchs Charters —
Capt. Jack Carlson**
108 Saguaro Lane
Marathon, Florida Keys 33050
Phone: 305-743-6253
Web: www.twoconchs.com
*Spear fishing, bay wreck fishing, tarpon
fishing, offshore fishing, reef fishing, fly-
fishing*

Capt. Bill O'Bannon
P.O. Box 510016
Key Colony Beach, FL 33051
Phone: 305-289-0395
www.billfishcharters.com
Light tackle fishing in the Middle Keys

**Black Ghost Outfitting and Guide
Service at the Sombrero Reef Fishing
Lodge**
P.O. Box 501324
Marathon, FL 33050
Phone: 305-743-9666
Web: www.blackghost.net
*Flyfishing lodge, flats fishing: bonefish,
tarpon and permit and Everglades:
snook, redfish, speckled trout and tarpon*

**Little Native Sportfishing —
Capt. Ray Rhash**
110 Saguaro Lane
Marathon, FL 33050
Phone: 305-743-9191
Web: www.bonefishcentral.com
*Flyfishing, spin and light tackle from Key
Biscayne to Key West*

**Sweet Release Charters —
Capt. Rich Tudor**
P.O. Box 931
Long Key, FL 33001
Phone: 305-664-2859
Web: www.sweet-release.com
*Light tackle and flyfishing in Islamorada
and Florida Keys*

Capt. Jim Bourbon
Marathon, FL
Phone: 800-461-0527
Tarpon fishing

Lower Keys

Hooker Charters — Capt. Andy Bracket
149 Le Grand Lane
Cudjoe Key, FL 33042
Phone: 305-745-9478
Web: www.hookercharters.com
Flyfishing/light tackle in the Lower Keys

Back Country Guide Service
472 Sands Rd.
Big Pine Key, FL 33043
Phone: 352-666-6234

Elusive Endeavors
133 Sawyer Drive
Summerland Key, FL 33042
Phone: 305-745-2335
Flyfishing and light tackle in and around Key West

Seaboots Charters & Outfitters — Capt. Jim Sharpe
29975 Overseas Highway
Mm 30
Big Pine Key, FL
Phone: 800-238-1746
www.seaboots.com
Offshore and backcountry light tackle and flyfishing

Outcast Charters — Capt. Dave Wiley
27441 West Indies Dr.
Summerland Key Florida 33042
Phone: 305-872-4680
Web: www.keywestflats.com
Fly rod or spin in the Marquesas Keys, Key West, the Lower Keys and Marathon, both oceanside and back country. Target species include tarpon, permit, bonefish, barracuda, sharks, and cobia

Key West

Big Blue Flyfishing, Inc. — Capt. Tony Rowland
P.O. Box 701
Key West, FL 33041
Phone: 305-294-7447
Web: www.bigblueflyfishing.com
Flyfishing the flats from Key West to Marathon for permit, bonefish, tarpon

Andy Griffiths Charters
40 Key Haven Rd.
Key West, FL 33040
Phone: 305-296-2639
Web: www.fishandy.com

Capt. Dexter Simmons— Fly Fishing Paradise
P.O. Box 440145
Sugarloaf Shores
Key West, FL 33044
Fishing the flats of Key West, Lower Keys, Marquesas for tarpon, bonefish, barracuda, shark mutton, snapper, permit

Saltwater Angler — Jeffrey Cardenas
At the Key West Hilton Resort & Marina
243 Front Street
Key West, FL
Phone: 800-223-1629
Web: www.saltwaterangler.com
Flyfishing the flats, light tackle, and trolling offshore

Chaser Key West - Capt. Mike Wilbur
1075 Duval Street C-21
Key West, FL 33040
Phone: 305-296-7201
Web:www.chaserkeywest.com
Fishing, fly fishing in Key West and the lower Florida Keys flats for tarpon, permit, and bonefish.

FlyFishing Key West — Capt. Greg
PO Box 427
Key West, FL 33041
Phone: 305-293-8088
Web: www.flyfishingkeywest.com
Flyfishing and light tackle

Just for Today Flats Fishing Charters
PO Box 2496
Key West, FL 33045
Phone: 305-293-0520
Web: www.flatsfishingkeywest.com
Fly, spin and plug

Key West Flats Fishing — Capt. Larry Cohen
903 Eisenhower Dr.
Key West, FL 33040
Phone: 305-294-7670
Web: www.keywestflatsfishing.com
Fly or light tackle fishing

Miss Inclined Flats Fishing Charters — Lindsay Harper
70 Avenue E
Key West, FL 33040
Phone: 305-296-3673
web: www.flyfishkeywest.com
Fly, light tackle, spin or plug in the Lower Keys and Marquesas for tarpon, bonefish, permit, shark, and barracuda

Key West Fishing — Capt. Ralph Delph
Phone: 305-294-6072
Web: www.delphfishing.com
Fly or light tackle from Key West to the Dry Tortugas

Capt. Neil Bohannon
Key West, FL
leave from the Key West Bight Marina
Phone: 305-745-4634 or 305-294-4805
www.flatsfishingguide.com
Tarpon, bonefish, permit, shark, & barracuda

Back Country Guide Service—Captain Eric Bonar
Phone: 305-745-8545
Web: www.floridakeys.net/backcountry/
Lower Keys and Key West light tackle and fly fishing for tarpon, bonefish, permit, mutton snapper, barracuda and shark

The Electronic Angler

It's easy to plan a Florida Keys trip if you're wired to the World Wide Web. There's a wealth of sites dedicated to helping you find places to stay and things to do, along with plenty of help for anglers. You can find fishing reports, helpful hints, and plenty of weather information.

Don't beat yourself up with fishing reports. Use them wisely by checking what weather conditions were when the reporters fished. Over time they provide clues to what fish might do, although they might not relate perfectly to your trip. They do provide a good general idea of some fish activity.

A LIST OF SITES YOU MIGHT FIND HELPFUL:

http://www.fla-keys.com
The official site of the tourism council for the Florida Keys and Key West.

http://www.floridakeyslodging.com
Florida Keys Lodging–good all around facilities site

http://cyberangler.com/reports/fl/map.htm
Cyberangler–state-wide fishing reports including some good ones for the Keys, and plenty more.

http://www.floridasportsman.com
Florida Sportsman magazine–weekly and monthly fishing projections, links to regulations, weather, and an active fishing forum.

http://www.bentaylor.com
Flats, backcountry, and flyfishing the Florida Keys–Author Ben Taylor's site, learn more and send a fishing postcard.

FIND WIND AND TEMPERATURES ALONG WITH MARINE WEATHER FORECASTS:

http://www.nws.fsu.edu/B/buoy?station=MLRF1
Molasses Reef–Key Largo
http://www.nws.fsu.edu/B/buoy?station=LONF1
Long Key–Islamorada and Long Key
http://www.nws.fsu.edu/B/buoy?station=SMKF1
Sombrero Light–Middle Keys
http://www.nws.fsu.edu/B/buoy?station=SANF1
Sand Key Light–Lower Keys and Key West
http://www.intellicast.com
/LocalWeather/World/UnitedStates/Southeast/Florida/

FLORIDA WEATHER–CLICK TO YOUR DESTINATION.

http://tbone.biol.sc.edu/tide/sitesel.html
Predict tides for anywhere, including the Keys.
http://www.fknms.nos.noaa.gov/
Florida Keys National Marine Sanctuary–Keep up with changes.

Marine Symbols

The sea will attempt to kill you if you act foolishly in general, head out unprepared, drink lots of alcohol while boating, or fail to pay attention and think defensively. For instance, chart features don't always tell the whole story: an inlet that is flat at 7:00AM can be stacked with 10-foot rollers at 8:00AM; shoals (try running onto a rocky shoal at 20 knots some time); debris (flotsam and jetsam that can rip your lower unit off or go straight through the hull); sandbars (driving your boat up onto a sand bar at full throttle isn't funny). And then there are the squalls and water spouts with minds of their own (and they do have minds, I tell you). Those who ignore safety, common sense, and preparation at sea often pay with their lives.

Acquaint yourself with the symbols on the following pages and study your charts before a trip out onto the sea, or hire a seasoned professional guide.

Buoys and Beacons

1	·	Position of buoy	17	RB RB	Bifurcation buoy (RBHB)
2		Light buoy	18	RB RB	Junction buoy (RBHB)
3	BELL	Bell buoy	19	RB RB	Isolated danger buoy (RBHB)
3a	GONG	Gong buoy	20	RB G	Wreck buoy (RBHB or G)
4	WHIS	Whistle buoy	20a	RB G	Obstruction buoy (RBHB or G)
5	C	Can or Cylindrical buoy	21	Tel	Telegraph-cable buoy
6	N	Nun or Conical buoy	22		Mooring buoy (colors of mooring buoys never carried)
7	SP	Spherical buoy	22a		Mooring
8	S	Spar buoy	22b	Tel	Mooring buoy with telegraphic communications
†8a	P	Pillar or Spindle buoy	22c	T	Mooring buoy with telephonic communications
9		Buoy with topmark (ball) (see L-70)	23		Warping buoy
10		Barrel or Ton buoy	24	Y	Quarantine buoy
(La)		Color unknown	†24a		Practice area buoy
(Lb)	FLOAT	Float	25	Explos Anch	Explosive anchorage buoy
12	FLOAT	Lightfloat	25a	AERO	Aeronautical anchorage buoy
13		Outer or Landfall buoy	26	Deviation	Compass adjustment buoy
14	BW	Fairway buoy (BWVS)	27	BW	Fish trap (area) buoy (BWHB)
14a	BW	Mid-channel buoy (BWVS)	27a		Spoil ground buoy
†15	R "2" R "2"	Starboard-hand buoy (entering from seaward)	†28	W	Anchorage buoy (marks limits)
16	"1"	Port-hand buoy (entering from seaward)	†29	Priv maintd	Private aid to navigation (buoy) (maintained by private interests, use with caution)

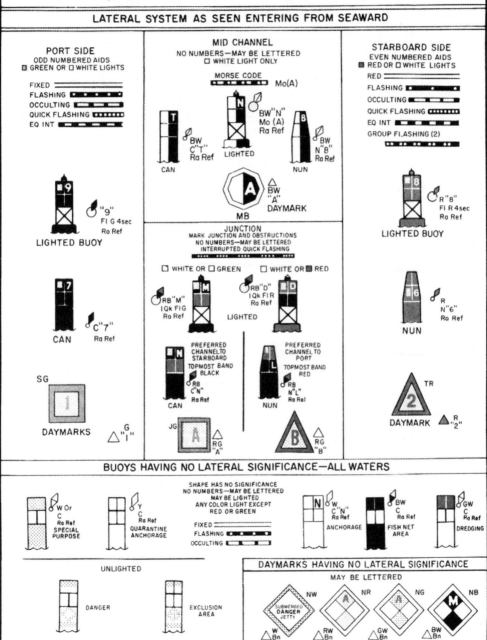

AIDS TO NAVIGATION ON NAVIGABLE WATERWAYS
except Western Rivers and Intracoastal Waterway

LATERAL SYSTEM AS SEEN ENTERING FROM SEAWARD

Dangers

1 Rock which does not cover (elevation above MHW)	11 Wreck showing any portion of hull or superstructure (above sounding datum)	27 Obstruction
		28 Wreck (See O-11 to 16)
Uncov 2 ft &Uncov 2 ft *(2) &(2)*	12 Wreck with only masts visible (above sounding datum)	29 Wreckage
2 Rock which covers and uncovers, with height in feet above chart (sounding) datum	13 Old symbols for wrecks	29a Wreck remains (dangerous only for anchoring)
	13a Wreck always partially submerged	30 Submerged piling (See H-9, L-59)
3 Rock awash at the level of chart (sounding) datum		
When rock of O-2 or O-3 is considered a danger to navigation	†14 Sunken wreck dangerous to surface navigation (less than 11 fathoms over wreck) (See O-6a)	30a Snags; Submerged stumps (See L-59)
†4 Sunken rock dangerous to surface navigation	15 Wreck over which depth is known	31 Lesser depth possible
		32 Uncov Dries
		33 Cov Covers (See O-2, 10)
5 Shoal sounding on isolated rock (replaces symbol)	†15a Wreck with depth cleared by wire drag	34 Uncov Uncovers (See O-2, 10)
†6 Sunken rock not dangerous to surface navigation (more than 11 fathoms over rock)	16 Sunken wreck, not dangerous to surface navigation	35 Reported (with date)
		Eagle Rk (rep 1958)
6a Sunken danger with depth cleared by wire drag (in feet or fathoms)	17 Foul ground	35 Reported (with name and date)
	18 Overfalls or Tide rips Symbol used only in small areas	36 Discol Discolored (See O-9)
7 Reef of unknown extent		37 Isolated danger
	19 Eddies Symbol used only in small areas	
8 Submarine volcano	20 Kelp, Seaweed Symbol used only in small areas	†38 Limiting danger line
	21 Bk Bank	39 Limit of rocky area
9 Discolored water	22 Shl Shoal	41 P A Position approximate
	23 Rf Reef	42 P D Position doubtful
	23a Ridge	43 E D Existence doubtful
	24 Le Ledge	44 P Pos Position
		45 D Doubtful
		†46 Unexamined
10 Coral reef, detached (uncovers at sounding datum)	25 Breakers (See A-12)	(Oa) Crib
		(Ob) Platform (lighted) HORN Offshore platform (unnamed)
Coral or Rocky reef, covered at sounding datum (See A-11d, 11g)	26 Sunken rock (depth unknown) When rock is considered a danger to navigation	(Oc) Hazel (lighted) HORN Offshore platform (named)

Light Symbols and Their Meanings

Symbol	Meaning	Description
F	Fixed	A continuous, steady light.
F Fl	Fixed and flashing	A fixed light at regular intervals by a flash of greater brilliance.
F GP Fl	Fixed and group flashing	A fixed light varied at regular intervals by groups of 2 or more flashes of greater brilliance.
Fl	Flashing	A single flash showing at regular intervals, the duration of light always less than the duration of darkness.
Gp Fl	Group flashing	Groups of 2 or more flashes showing at regular intervals.
Qk Fl	Quick flashing	Shows not less than 60 flashes per minute.
I Qk Fl	Interrupted quick flashing	Shows quick flashes for about 5 seconds followed by a dark period of about 5 seconds.
E Int	Equal interval	Duration of light equal to that of darkness.
Occ	Occulting	A light totally eclipsed at regular intervals, the duration of light always equal to or greater than the duration of darkness.
Gp Occ	Group occulting	A light with a group of 2 or more eclipses at regular intervals.

Chart Sources

Maptech sells NOAA charts (including the new photo charts) and software.

Maptech
1 Riverside Drive
Andover, MA 01810-1122
888-839-5551
Website: www.maptech.com
E-mail: marinesales@maptech.com

Also check out:
Seastore
Website: www.seastore.com

Navigation
Website: www.safenav.com

Black drum

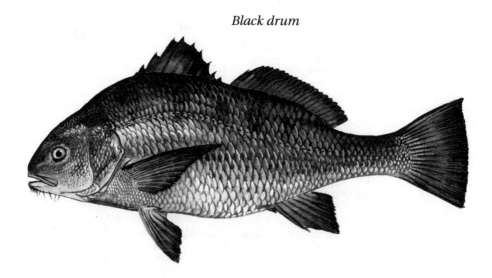

About the Artist

Duane Raver, Gamefish illustrations. A native of Iowa, Duane was educated in central Iowa schools and received a degree in Fisheries Management from Iowa State University in 1949. He was employed as a fishery biologist with the North Carolina Wildlife Resources Commission in 1950. In 1960, Duane transferred to the Education Division of the Wildlife Commission and was on the staff of *Wildlife in North Carolina* magazine. He was Managing Editor of the magazine until 1970, when he was appointed Editor.

Wildlife artwork has always been a major activity in his life, and Duane completed over 200 cover paintings for *Wildlife in North Carolina* during his 30 years with the Wildlife Commission. He retired in 1979 to do wildlife artwork full time.

Duane works primarily in acrylic and opaque watercolor. He does only wildlife subjects with emphasis on fish and gamebirds. He welcomes inquiries and visits at his home studio at 910 Washington Street, Cary, NC 27511. Duane can be reached at 919-467-9277.

Index

WILDERNESS ADVENTURES GUIDE SERIES

If you would like to order additional copies of this book or our other Wilderness Adventures Press guidebooks, please fill out the order form below or call **1-800-925-3339** or *fax 800-390-7558.* Visit our website for a listing of over 2000 sporting books—the largest online: **www.wildadv.com** *Mail To:*

Wilderness Adventures Press, Inc., 45 Buckskin Road • Belgrade, MT 59714

☐ **Please send me your quarterly catalog on hunting and fishing books.**

Ship to:
Name _____

Address _____

City _____ State _____ Zip _____

Home Phone_____ Work Phone_____

Payment: ☐ Check   ☐ Visa   ☐ Mastercard   ☐ Discover   ☐ American Express

Card Number _____ Expiration Date_____

Signature_____

Qty	Title of Book	Price	Total
	Saltwater Angler's Guide to Southern California	$26.95	
	Saltwater Angler's Guide to the Southeast	$26.95	
	Flyfisher's Guide to the Florida Keys	$26.95	
	Flyfisher's Guide to Colorado	$26.95	
	Flyfisher's Guide to Idaho	$26.95	
	Flyfisher's Guide to Michigan	$26.95	
	Flyfisher's Guide to Montana	$26.95	
	Flyfisher's Guide to Northern California	$26.95	
	Flyfisher's Guide to Northern New England	$26.95	
	Flyfisher's Guide to Oregon	$26.95	
	Flyfisher's Guide to Pennsylvania	$26.95	
	Flyfisher's Guide to Washington	$26.95	
	Flyfisher's Guide to Minnesota	$26.95	
	Flyfisher's Guide to Utah	$26.95	
	Flyfisher's Guide to Texas	$26.95	
	Total Order + shipping & handling		

Shipping and handling: $4.99 for first book,
$3.00 per additional book, up to $13.99 maximum